MODERN
CHINESE
WRITERS

Studies on Modern China

MODERN CHINESE WRITERS

SELF-PORTRAYALS

HELMUT MARTIN
and
JEFFREY KINKLEY
Editors

BA JIN   ZHANG AILING

BAI XIANYONG   WANG MENG

CHEN RONG   JIN YONG

ZHANG XINXIN   CHEN RUOXI

LI ANG   LIU BINYAN

AND THIRTY-THREE OTHERS

An East Gate Book

M. E. Sharpe, Inc.
ARMONK, NEW YORK
LONDON, ENGLAND

The present volume is the result of a one-year appointment, 1987–88,
of Dr. Helmut Martin as Research Linguist in the
Contemporary Chinese Language Project, Center for Chinese Studies,
University of California, Berkeley.

Copyright © 1992 by M. E. Sharpe, Inc.
80 Business Park Drive, Armonk, New York 10504

Available in the United Kingdom and Europe from M. E. Sharpe, Publishers,
3 Henrietta Street, London WC2E 8LU.

Library of Congress Cataloging-in-Publication Data

Modern Chinese writers : self-portrayals /
edited by Helmut Martin and Jeffrey Kinkley.
p. cm.
Includes bibliographical references.
ISBN 0-87332-816-7 (cloth)
ISBN 0-87332-817-5 (paper)
1. Authors, Chinese—20th century—Biography.
2. Chinese essays—Translations into English.
I. Martin, Helmut, 1940– .
II. Kinkley, Jeffrey C., 1948– .
PL2277.M65   1992
895.109′0052—dc20
91-31578
CIP

Printed in the United States of America
The paper used in this publication meets the minimum
requirements of American National Standard for
Information Sciences—Permanence of Paper for
Printed Library Materials, ANSI Z 39.48-1984.

HA   10   9   8   7   6   5   4   3   2   1

Contents

III. CHINESE LITERATURE FROM TAIWAN

MODERNISTS AND SEMI-ÉMIGRÉS

THE NATIVE REALISTS: BLACK HUMOR AND OTHER EXPERIMENTS

IDEOLOGISTS

ALIENATION, WITHDRAWAL, AND DISSENT

Preface

Helmut Martin

AT THE END of the campaign against "spiritual pollution" in the spring of 1984, I had the opportunity to work at Tongji and Fudan universities in Shanghai, as an exchange scholar from the Ruhr University in Bochum. The authors I met there, and the collections of autobiographical essays (*chuangzuotan*) that Chinese friends brought to my attention, helped me to understand the hopes, fears, and everyday problems of China's writers. I returned to Germany with a collection of these essays (see the Source Bibliography), determined to use them as a very personal introduction to contemporary Chinese literature. In 1985, I published a preliminary selection in German, with the cooperation of K. H. Pohl, in the Munich literary magazine *akzente*.

During a sabbatical year, 1987–88, I had the privilege of undertaking further work in the field at the Modern Chinese Language Project of the Center for Chinese Studies, University of California at Berkeley. There I read through dozens of additional collections of essays for the present selection.

Which writers were selected? A list of one hundred was compiled, in collaboration with colleagues from the Chinese Academy of Social Sciences in Peking, for a Chinese-German project of the Deutsche Forschungsgemeinschaft (German Research Society). Mounting political pressure in 1986–87 necessitated abandonment of that project. Later, China published a preliminary Chinese version of the project, including 107 PRC writers but omitting Bei Dao, Cong Weixi, Liu Binyan, Wang Ruowang, Wu Zuguang, and others: [Xu] Jiemin, *Dangdai Zhongguo zuojia bairen zhuan* ([Auto]biographies of one hundred contemporary Chinese writers) (Beijing: Qiushi chubanshe, 1989). For the present anthology, controversial names were restored, Taiwan writers were added (and one from Hong Kong), and then the list was reduced to a more manageable nucleus of forty-four. My selection naturally favors "serious" authors, with Jin Yong representing popular authors and their strained relations with the "serious" ones—and an often overlooked link between the tastes of readers on Taiwan and the Chinese mainland. Permission was solicited from all living authors to print their work in this book, and it was obtained from all who answered, including Bei Dao, who was represented by the transcript of an interview I had conducted with him in Chinese, translated by Beata Grant. Bei Dao, however, had second thoughts about making it public. In the end, I felt obliged, with utmost reluctance, to leave Bei Dao unrepresented, as no new text could be found that did him as much justice. Hence the final tally of forty-four pieces by forty-three authors (including a second, postmassacre selection by Zhang Xinxin).

In the early stages of selecting texts for this anthology, I benefited from the advice of many friends in the San Francisco Bay area: Dr. Chiang Yung-chen, the writers Nora Chen (Chen Shaocong), Chen Ruoxi, Dongdong (Liang Dong), Dr. Chuang Yin of Stanford University, and Orville Schell. I profited from the suggestions of the comparatist Zhao Yiheng from Peking, now at SOAS, London; the human rights activist and prominent dissident Xu Bangtai; Beata Grant, who was then at the University of California, Berkeley; and Ellen Yeung, then of Stanford University. Many distinguished Sinological colleagues put aside their other projects to translate essays for this book, for which the editors are profoundly grateful.

Following consultations at the 1986 international conference on contemporary Chinese literature at Jinshan, Shanghai, Jeffrey Kinkley joined the project. He became a full co-editor of the book; he corrected, revised, and, when necessary, rewrote the draft translations, after consulting the original Chinese texts. He also finalized the reference material, using my manuscript as a basis. I drafted the introductions to the individual essays, which he then edited. Apart from the individually signed overview and introductory essays, we share responsibility for the accuracy of editorial fact and opinion in this book.

We advise the reader that we abridged some pieces for reasons of space, relevance, and consistency, and we devised the chapter titles. The original title of each essay, in Chinese and English, and the source appear at the end of the essay. Every effort has been made to preserve accuracy, but we have discovered abridgments and errors even in the Chinese originals, particularly the research collections; for example, Cong Weixi's piece in this volume is typically annotated as having been written in July 1983, although it had already been published some months before.

We give special thanks to Karen Finney-Kellerhoff for her patient and skillful assistance with draft manuscripts in Germany, and to Anita O'Brien, our copy editor. We are above all most grateful to Christa Gescher, then a graduate student and assistant in Bochum doing research on Liu Binyan, whose enthusiasm for the project, superintendence of trans-Atlantic communications, and conscientious guardianship over editorial integrity when English texts went into German computers made her a true collaborator of the editors on both sides of the Atlantic.

The professional photographer Barbara Zabka of Witten, Germany, spent much time and energy preparing photographs and other materials for publication.

In China, Feng Jicai and Ding Cong provided caricatures for the volume. The following authors provided photographs of themselves: Ba Jin, Bai Xianyong, Chen Ruoxi, Jia Pingwa, Shen Congwen, Song Zelai, Wang Anyi, Wang Ruowang, Wang Zengqi, Wang Zhenhe, and Wu Jinfa. I took the photographs of Acheng, Chen Yingzhen, Dai Houying, Huang Chunming, Huang Fan, Li Ang, and Wang Tuo. The following authors were photographed by my wife, Tienchi Martin-Liao: Han Shaogong (in Paris), Liu Xinwu, and Zhang Xinxin (in Paris). For Jin Yong, the photo is by *Cheng Ming* (Hong Kong); Liu Binyan, *Die Zeit* (Hamburg); Qideng Sheng, *Unitas* (Taibei); Wang Meng, photo by Eike Zschacke, Bonn; Wang Wenxing, *Unitas*. The photographs of Ding Ling, Lao She, Lin Shuangbu, Lu Xun, Mao Dun, Yu Dafu, and Zhang Ailing were taken from their books. Zhang Ailing drew her own stylized self-portrait.

In addition to the Center for Chinese Studies at the University of California, Berkeley, and St. John's University, New York City, we are grateful to the Hoover Library, Stanford; the C. V. Starr East Asian Library of Columbia University; the Gest Oriental Library of Princeton University; and the library of Rutgers University, for access and reference assistance.

The German-language counterpart of the present volume has been published by Helmut Martin and Stefan Hase-Bergen as *Bittere Träume, Selbstdarstellungen chinesischer Schriftsteller* (Bonn: Bouvier, 1991); the essays were translated directly from Chinese into German.

This volume is dedicated to my revered teachers, the writer Tai Jingnong and the scholar Zheng Qian, who passed away recently. They taught me to understand the cultural atmosphere of Republican China and the spirit of Chinese literature in general.

Overview

Chinese Writers on Writing

Jeffrey Kinkley

This is a book of personal reflections on literature and life by China's leading modern writers. The subject is how Chinese society and its creative writing have supported, competed, and fought with each other for the past forty years and more, on both sides of the Taiwan Strait. Most of the selections were meant for Chinese eyes; they reveal political treachery and social cowardice with a directness that is by turns hair-raising and humorous. But many of the authors' concerns are universal. One sees their apprehensions about breaking into print, their resentment of the power of editors, their fear of getting into a rut, and of failing to serve "the needs" of readers. Writers are also buffeted by raw commercial pressures, and not just in Hong Kong and Taiwan, but, more recently, even in the People's Republic (hereafter, PRC). In 1987, an author from inland Hunan Province was already proclaiming literature to be dead in Guangzhou, the metropolis nearest Hong Kong, because so many of its writers had switched to the lucrative new careers available in advertising.

The essays in this book were selected by Helmut Martin of Germany for publication in Chinese as well as in German and English, for never before has this particular selection of Chinese authors from all over the world been brought together, even in their native language. The Chinese title for the book came to mind more easily than the English title: *Chuangzuotan*, or "writing about writing." Another translation of the term, Professor Martin's favorite, is "casual remarks on the creative process." He adds that ideally, *chuangzuotan* is

> a short autobiographical essay genre, embracing as many facets as in the European series *Writers at Work* (*The Paris Review* interviews). The author tells us how his or her literary career started, what important stages he or she went through in life as a writer, why and how a particular work came to be

written, and perhaps why it was well received by the public. Some *chuangzuotan* are close to an explanatory essay, or present themselves as *suibi*—"casual notes" in the traditional Chinese sense. Interviews with writers and speeches by authors may also occasionally be categorized as *chuangzuotan*, as long as they touch on similar questions. The genre of autobiographical essay has always been closely linked with China's literary journals; PRC editors try to satisfy the interest of their readers by giving background information about the authors. The earliest *chuangzuotan* collection I have come across dates from the 1930s. Its compilation and presentation mark it as a transplantation of a Soviet prototype, introduced to China by leftist intellectuals. It seems, however, that the "political" origin of such collections has altogether faded into oblivion—both for contemporary editors of the genre and for the general reading public in China. In fact, the genre does not enjoy equal popularity on Taiwan. Much sifting was needed to find comparable texts by Taiwan's writers.

I find it significant simply that "writing about writing" is taken so seriously as a genre in China—that it is itself a kind of *writing*. In a way, this fact highlights the contradictions in Chinese thinking about writing. Despite the elite status and unique sense of "mission" that the Chinese writer enjoys, as is only too apparent in the essays below, China has for some decades encouraged everyone to write. It has published volume after volume about how to do it, and, just as important, "how to be an author." Even some of the essays in this book appear to address the old-fashioned 1930s' topic, or latter-day old-fashioned socialist topic, of "how I came to embark on the path of literature." Today, however, Chinese literature is much more than just a path. Although still an elevated and restricted-access highway, with booths dispensing rather than collecting tokens by the mile, it is broad enough to accommodate foreign-engineered sports cars, heavy pulp-guzzling domestic models, and quaint peasant bicycles; some right-of-way has to be provided for slow vehicles pushed from behind, too. Whether or not the road must lead somewhere, whether there is a race going on, and why there is travel in the first place—if not to please the spectators in the stands—is still up for debate.

Yet, as the Chinese authors refer over and over again to their social responsibility, it becomes apparent that writing about writing must also be an instrument by which they celebrate and rationalize their intellectual and moral superiority. By stressing writing as an act—a process best entered into after one is cognizant of the higher nature of creativity—writing about writing even maintains a continuity with the old Chinese literati ethic. The latter held that good writing was infused with a special spirit—a higher spirit, but an "amateur," moral insight, not a professional technique. In writing as well as painting (Wang Zengqi still links the two in his essay below, and favors "the old school" in his literary models), traditional art aims at allowing the reader or viewer to reexperience the act of creativity. The Chinese literary work has never been a static icon. It partakes of the forces that go into its making and appreciation, which are themselves differentiated reenactments of a universal elevating experience.

Thus, despite the official Chinese fixation on the doctrine of realism, Zhang Jie and Wang Meng declare literature to be in an ideal realm, above life. Literature is written for the masses, of course—to deny this is still heresy in the PRC—but the essays below hint at the fact that literature is above all a performance for fellow literati, and for students (see Dai Houying's piece), the literati of the future. China's new society has its deviants—its Zhong Achengs and Han Shaogongs, and in Taiwan, its Wang Wenxings and Qideng Shengs—as the old society had its monks and literati who painted with their fingernails or their toes. But they have always been, in the final analysis, *writers*. They continue, for one thing, to look down on the popular. The presence of entertainment values in one's work is cause for self-examination or self-justification, as the essays of Jin Yong and Zhang Xinxin indicate. Still, it is clear from the testimony of Gao Xiaosheng, Gu Hua, and Shen Congwen that old-fashioned novels considered "merely entertaining" (until scholars took them up as objects of research) had a major influence on the development of China's serious authors of today.

The essays in this volume, however, were selected not for their generic characteristics, but because they break old Chinese molds, or at least hold them up to the light for our scrutiny. Lu Wenfu, for instance, thinks and obliquely states the unthinkable—that literary standards under Mao were so low that many middle-aged writers today might well ask whether or not they are really writers at all. Several selections, from both the PRC (see the essays by Wu Zuguang and Chen Rong) and the Taiwan-oriented community (Chen Ruoxi), detail case histories of censorship; as we read Wu Zuguang inveighing against the people who wield the scissors, we get to see from the italics which parts of that very speech had to be excised before it could be printed. Two young women writers (Zhang Xinxin from the PRC and Li Ang from Taiwan) "interview themselves," the better to satirize pearls-from-a-great-author idolatry from the ground up. Chen Rong comes right out and complains about being constantly asked to write "occasional" essays—a problem that already bothered Ding Ling in her 1933 essay included here. Other pieces seem revealing at subconscious, even collective subconscious, levels. When ex-"rightist" Cong Weixi bends over backward to make it clear that his literary dissonance is not dissent, his piece turns into self-parody. Similarly, Song Zelai of Taiwan inadvertently reveals the paranoia that built up in Taiwan simply because the island (with its overseas extensions) was once so small and self-contained that every writer knew what every other writer—in Taiwan's world—was thinking. Meanwhile, proud male personalities as different as the PRC writer Wang Meng and Taiwan's Wu Jinfa feel no compunction about referring to literature as a female—as a "lover"—although, to be sure, the female writer Li Ang refers to her writing as a *male* "lover."

These are personal essays for the most part. Individual authors tell what was unique about their upbringing and education, their economic hardships and political setbacks, and the ways in which their traditional Chinese families supported or stymied them, if they were not rent asunder by the pressures of harboring a controversial writer. The authors speak of their fictional characters as if they had lived; indeed, Ba Jin and Liu Xinwu "love" certain personalities they have created. Yet Chinese writers from both sides of the Taiwan Strait see the heavy hand of abstract "society" defining not only their career and their historic mission, but even their personal make-up. Surprisingly, it is the Taiwan writers (Chen Yingzhen, Huang Fan) who are full of talk about social-class determinants, while writers on the revolutionary mainland, particularly young folk like Zhong Acheng and Han Shaogong, tend to emphasize the onus of ancient tradition. Some authors, however, do see writing as mostly an inner struggle with the self—Wang Anyi, Dai Houying, and Zhang Jie, for example, who all happen to be women.

Certainly it has been hazardous to be a writer of critical sensibility in the PRC, and even in Taiwan. The authors in this anthology were generally selected in accordance with their international reputation, not because they are dissidents (Mao Dun and Wang Meng served as ministers of culture in the PRC government, and some of the Taiwan writers have been denounced by "nativists" as establishmentarian). Even so, it is interesting to note how many of our twenty-six mainland authors who lived under the PRC government were personally vilified during a national campaign *besides* the pandemic persecutions of the Cultural Revolution and post-1989 massacre eras. That is, they were silenced either years before the Cultural Revolution, or years after it was over and proclaimed a mistake. (Liu Binyan represents those who were persecuted both before and after.) My conservative count is seventeen, not including Jia Pingwa (although a magazine he edited was closed down in the 1987 campaign), or young authors whom semi-official critics took swipes at for their modernism, negative views, and other faults but could not blacklist. Some who were spared, like Mao Dun, Ba Jin, and Lao She, were virtual institutions of the New China; others, like Feng Jicai, missed their "opportunity" to be persecuted prior to the Cultural Revolution because they had not yet seriously begun a writing career.

Of the eight Republican-era authors, three were hunted (one imprisoned) by the ancien régime of the Nationalists (Kuomintang or KMT); all but Zhang Ailing, who spent her young adult years in Hong Kong and Japanese-occupied or isolated Shanghai, were harassed to some degree. Among the five "lucky" ones, Yu Dafu was killed by the Japanese, Lao She was driven to his death in the Cultural Revolution, and Zhang Ailing fled to Hong Kong and the United States. Did the three who were "unlucky" under the KMT then prosper under communism? One had already died in 1936 (Lu Xun), one went to prison again (Ding Ling), and one became minister of culture (Mao Dun). Of course, the Cultural Revolution and its aftermath brought sorrow and suffering to all twenty-six of the surviving mainland contributors, including Wang Zengqi. For details about 1966–76, see the texts below, notably Feng Jicai's. And to see how bad it was for authors who were allowed to be active "under the Gang of Four" to adjust to the new anti-Gang dictatorship, the main text is Chen Rong's.

Meanwhile, two of the thirteen writers resident or formerly resident in Taiwan were imprisoned (Chen Yingzhen and Wang Tuo). They do not provide details in their testimonials, for that might have sent them back to jail. All this is not to speak of the massive smear campaigns by conservative social forces aimed at writers such as Li Ang, or the KMT-orchestrated attacks on Huang Chunming, Wang Zhenhe, and their Taiwan "nativist" associates. Then again, as one may judge from Song Zelai's essay in this volume, "nativists" could give as well they got, making life unpleasant for "modernists" such as Wang Wenxing and Bai Xianyong.

The benign "responsibilities" of the author as public figure are, again, the stuff of which statistics are made. Chen Rong and Liu Binyan allude to the weight of mail (often more serious than mere fan mail) that writers receive and feel obligated to answer. Liu goes on to speak of how authors have been and ought even more, in the future, to be consulted on affairs of state. Bai Hua, thinking precisely of authors such as Liu, celebrates literature as the masses' "most illustrious tribunal, with writers as their supreme impartial judges." This reminds us once more that in China's traditional culture, the man of letters aspired to serve in the government as a magistrate. In a more purely literary vein, Lin Shuangbu still wants to put himself in proper sequence among the ancients by selecting a worthy, classically flavored pen name.

Breaking into print can be more than a rite of passage and the opening of a channel of communication with the public, as Huang Chunming of Taiwan describes it to be (his feelings must be familiar to any writer in a capitalist country); in the PRC, publication is an initiation into a moral elite that is carefully managed by the people's government, its publishing houses, its writers' association, and its censors. Even to freethinkers like Wang Ruowang, appearing in print has the psychological impact of salvation, particularly when it signals the end of a period when one has been banned. Hence, going through the censorship process is not simply dangerous, but a potential source of self-esteem, and assurance, for having "passed."

Do the authors have any time left for art, then? By international standards, the discussions of art in these pages are austere and even vague. What sticks in the mind are the authors' moving accounts of social phenomena they have witnessed and, in many cases, tried to influence through direct political action. The veteran writers whose careers are centered in the pre-Communist era are no exception: Ba Jin tells of his struggle against the feudal family; Lao She confesses a passionate, to our ears shocking, sympathy for the obscurantist Boxer Uprising, because of the international punitive expedition that followed; Mao Dun outlines a brief Marxist political economy of Shanghai; and Shen Congwen and Yu Dafu, the supposed aesthetes of their generation, dabble in outright sociology.

The strengths and weaknesses of these essays are a window on those of modern Chinese literature itself. "Realism" was the favored literary doctrine of the day, so most of these essays, too, can be given a first reading as if they "spoke for themselves"—about war, revolution, betrayal, and commitment. But the individual and the self were also important discoveries of the age. A second reading will reveal much about the writers and their personal bearings. A few of the essays are deliberately satirical, even self-mocking. One or two others are vehicles for a direct enlightenment: the author's views may make you fume.

Retrospective Introduction
Enforced Silence or Émigré Uncertainties: Options for Chinese Writers after a Decade of Experiments and Growth

Helmut Martin

> We are poor, we are behind the times, we have been made stupid, and we
> spend our days quite miserably. But we have an ideal, which is freedom and
> democracy. We have only this one thing of which we can be proud: Freedom!
> At the moment, it is difficult for the government to give us prosperity; it
> cannot possibly provide us with riches. But the government can give the
> masses of the people one thing to win their hearts. It can give us the right to
> democracy! It can give us freedom!
> —Chen Mingyuan, Peking University professor,
> addressing a campus crowd, April 23, 1989

The "Chinese Solution" and the Crisis of Perception

Any crisis or turning point in China's general policy, like the events of June 4,
1989, has always tended to become a crisis of Western perception. Thus, for
example, after the massacre, foreign investment in China declined,[1] and the
number of Western students studying things Chinese dwindled. Sinologists accused members of their own ranks of having drawn an egregiously unrealistic
and overly enthusiastic picture of China during the past decade, instead of soberly describing a gradual process of opening since 1976–79.[2]

Evaluating such a turning point in perception—triggered by the Tiananmen
events—one must reconsider the origins of the democracy movement, reviewing,
as far as possible, the so-called decade of reforms. We wonder why such a
breakdown of trust, hope, vision, and legitimacy on the part of the Chinese
government was possible in the first place. It remains hard to believe that the
savage attempt by the Rumanian government to suppress its own people

during the last days of Ceaucescu, or the threat by the East German Communist party to use brute force just prior to the demise of Honecker, could suddenly be called a "Chinese solution." After a decade of bold "Chinese reforms" that had gained sympathy from the whole world and were much admired in Eastern Europe and the Soviet Union, such a volte-face in perception should have become an alarming sign for the Chinese leadership as it weighed its options for the future.

The Tiananmen incident in 1989 radically changed many things. Contemporary Chinese literature, the achievement of a stormy decade, abruptly ended in a state of quandary. The "first decade," from 1979 to 1989, suddenly had to be seen as a self-contained period shortly destined to become history.

Obviously, the 1989 movement had deep roots. There had long been discontent and anxiety among the population. Some intellectuals had cautiously begun to criticize the slowdown in the pace of reform and major political blunders of the recent past. Some of them had formulated concrete solutions for a new sociopolitical order. Philosophers, political scientists, historians, sociologists, natural scientists, futurologists, and outright dissidents had joined in the discussion further characterized below.

Chinese writers played a leading role in this unfolding debate, especially during the first half of the 1980s. Since 1949, they have been a highly sensitive group and consequently suffered more severely than other groups in Chinese society whenever the party chose to stifle criticism, even though their words were uttered only on a symbolic platform and through literary works—novels, reportage, lyrics, plays, films, and television productions.[3]

We have, therefore, to look into the situation of the literary avant-garde especially during the critical months after the Tiananmen crackdown, which led to a period of Brezhnev-like stagnation—economically, politically, and in the literary field. The need for such a study seemed especially urgent because the regime in many ways tried to cover up the rough treatment it was meting out to intellectuals. As usual, the treatment of writers remained symptomatic for the treatment of all Chinese intellectuals.

A host of PRC writers presented in this volume through their self-portrayals became actors in the drama of 1989 and its aftermath. Enforced silence, or the uncertainties of an émigré existence—such have been the options for many of them after a decade of experiments and encouraging literary growth. The sketch below of China's literary and intellectual scene during 1989–90 has thus unintentionally become a kind of epitaph for the decade of the 1980s.

Purges in the Cultural Sector, 1989–90

Following June 1989, comprehensive purges began in China, aimed at eliminating the influence of "troublemakers," the activists behind the democratic movement. Observers had few illusions as to the extent of the purge among the intellectuals, in the party, and among the cadres in general. The line that the government under Li Peng took after the overt brutality of the first few weeks was aptly characterized by Chinese commentators as "soft on the outside, hard on the inside" (*waisong neijin*).

In the field of literature, this meant that those writers who had been leading critical spirits and, in addition, exposed themselves during the movement were refused permission to travel abroad to congresses and meetings. The books of many of them were blacklisted and disappeared from the shelves of bookshops. A large-scale reshuffle of jobs was initiated in the culture bureaucracy, from the national and local organizations of the Chinese Writers' Association to the boards of publishing houses and editorial staffs of the existing four-hundred-odd literary journals. Old Maoist hard-liners who had been standing on the sidelines for years moved into leading positions, such as the mediocre writer He Jingzhi, who was appointed acting minister of culture at the beginning of September 1989.[4] The writer Liu Xinwu, born in 1942 and a representative of the lost generation of the Cultural Revolution, had been editor-in-chief of *Renmin wenxue* (People's literature) but was ousted in 1990 and replaced by a notorious old writer in the army, Liu Baiyu. Born in 1916, Liu had implemented, among other things, the 1981 campaign against Bai Hua and his film script *Unrequited Love*, which protested the party's treatment of intellectuals.[5]

A Campaign That Did Not Get Off the Ground

For those writers who remained, silenced, in the People's Republic, these developments meant numerous losses of privileges and an indirect ban on writing. At the very least, the writers no longer had the opportunity to publish controversial works. They were pressured into withdrawing from the public scene, and their positions were gradually taken over by people prepared to toe the party line. Although greatly reduced in number during the last few years, the aging radicals who chose to return to the limelight did so with vindictiveness, for they had been practically ignored, even scorned, as yesterday's men, excluded from the privileges of foreign travel and the perquisites that flowed from having their works translated into foreign languages. Waiting to be given a free hand in 1990 by the political leaders, they planned a persecution of the former "stars of the literary stage" with great severity. The purge in the Ministry of Culture and its subordinate organizations, the editorial boards of journals, and sundry associations implicated 2,800 cadres, or about 15 percent of this group within China's culture bureaucracy.

Serious ideological problems arose after the massacre. In late 1989, no one seemed quite sure how to redefine the heritage of the last decade. Theoreticians had used emphatic language describing a "New Era" (*xin shiqi*) from 1979 to 1989, during which Chinese literature "reached out to the world" (*zou xiang shijie*).[6] Those radical bureaucrats surrounding He Jingzhi were no doubt prepared not only to take a hard line against all reformist literati, but also to denounce the "excesses of intellectual pollution" through Western influence following the opening up of China. This, however, would have meant a denial of many important achievements of the New Era.

A wave of passive resistance by writers demonstrated the ineffectuality of official pressure to make them comment positively on the events at Tiananmen Square and engage in self-criticism, as Bai Hua had been forced to do in 1981. In 1989, the same Bai Hua had actively participated in the democracy movement. He, together with a few other writers, set the tone for the new mood of defiance among Chinese writers and artists. He gave a courageous interview to a Japanese journalist in Shanghai in late March 1990, in which he condemned the use of force at Tiananmen and declared that although he was continuing to write, he was not willing to publish anything at the moment, as he suspected an imminent literary purge.[7]

The bureaucrats who were planning a campaign of criticism and intensified purges in the cultural field were thus faced with an unsurmountable problem: if contemporary literature were condemned outright, an important element of Deng Xiaoping's reform policies would automatically be invalidated.

Until 1990, the political leadership had apparently not had time to deal with such "secondary" matters, and until the necessary decisions were made, the culture bureaucrats were powerless to move. Since the entire political leadership, including the military, had been going through one of its most severe crises since 1949, with the threat of further eruptions of violence,[8] it appeared that the last word on the literature of the reform period had yet to be heard. For the writers themselves, however, a quite different issue was in the forefront, one that distracted them from the superficialities of political repression. After the disaster of the Cultural Revolution and the subsequent decade when the Communist party rejected its own tradition, the intelligentsia were left empty-handed where culture was concerned. The 1980s' Literature of the New Era, in a way, had been an attempt to set up a new sense of "self"; it had contributed to establishing a new cultural identity. Seen from this angle, the convulsions of the June massacre in 1989 had driven China's intellectuals yet again into a situation of hopelessness and alienation. China's contemporary literature had once more been pushed into the role of outsider on the world literary stage, into the role of the gagged and silenced observer.

The Purge of Prominent Figures

Hardly any news about the fate of prominent Chinese intellectuals initially reached the outside world after June 1989. Rumors circulated with no means of checking their authenticity. During the first months after the massacre, dozens of Chinese intellectuals were preoccupied in foreign exile, looking for suitable employment and not easily available for comment.

Among the prominent figures directly affected by the purges was Minister of Culture Wang Meng, who was forced by the events to step down. Hou Dejian, a singer from Taiwan who had settled in Peking and played an active role at Tiananmen Square, was arrested, as were the poet Ye Wenfu, who was hated by the military, and Dai Qing, special correspondent for the *Guangming Daily* newspaper, who had left the party in protest. She fell victim to the purges in spite of being closely related to the clan of Marshal Ye Jianying.[9] Hou and Dai eventually regained their freedom, the singer being expelled to Taiwan and Dai eagerly publishing a compromise statement about her involvement in the 1989 movement and her time in prison.

Many other authors were also accused as agitators or ringleaders in the democracy movement and either imprisoned or placed under house arrest, among them the prolific novelist and reportage author Ke Yunlu;[10] the regime critics Wang Ruowang, who tells us about his personal tragedy in this volume, and Ren Wanding;[11] Liu Xiaobo, the *enfant terrible* among China's critics (released in 1991); Wang Luxiang, who with Su Xiaokang co-authored the critical television series "River Elegy" that attracted millions of viewers in 1988; the writer Zheng Yi; the publisher, director, and legal specialist Yu Haocheng; the activist and Chinese Academy of Social Sciences historian Bao Zunxin; and the liberal journalist Qin Benli, whose Shanghai weekly, the *World Economic Herald*, had consistently exceeded the limits set by the Communist party.[12] Nobody in the Chinese or Western media was in any doubt that Su Xiaokang had also been arrested immediately after the massacre. He had, however, managed to go underground; a hundred fearful days later, he succeeded in reaching Paris, having escaped via Hong Kong. It would probably not have been possible for him to reach the crown colony had he not had the active support of the people and the tolerant sympathy of local security forces at the border in Guangdong Province. This was even more true for the surprising escape from the PRC of the radical student leader Chai Ling and her activist husband Feng Congde, as late as April 1990.[13]

I have mentioned here only a few of the writers and intellectuals who are well known in the West. The list of those arrested or effectively isolated is much longer, and it was obvious that even the reports published by Amnesty International, Asia Watch, and the Hong Kong Alliance in Support of the Patriotic Democratic Movement in China listed only a fraction of the arrests that took place.[14]

A Literary Journal Is Brought into Line

The party also took measures to undermine the influence of radical intellectuals. The party's banned lists, which were increasingly circulated only internally, included the political scientist Yan Jiaqi and Bao Zunxin, and prominent mention was given to the astrophysicist Fang Lizhi ("traitor to his country"), the novelist Zhang Xianliang (after Acheng the foremost PRC writer known on Taiwan), Su Xiaokang, and the popular journalist Liu Binyan.

One example of the insidious purge was the "redesigning" of the journal *Wenxue pinglun* (Literary criticism), which used to be the liberal flagship of literary studies under the literary theorist Liu Zaifu, director of the Institute of Literature of the Chinese Academy of Social Sciences in Peking, and He Xilai, his deputy. Both were hated by the "Maoist" culture bureaucrats. In the August 1989 edition, Liu and He were still listed as editors, but by the October issue, there was only a *collective* mention of the Institute of Litera-ture, as had been the case during the prereform days. The issue of the journal to celebrate the fortieth anniversary of the founding of the PRC included an article on basic principles by Zhang Jiong, a notorious hard-liner from the institute, in which he revived Mao Zedong's *Yan'an Talks* as a guideline for China's new literature. Zhang even managed to see some positive things in a Cultural Revolution speech about literature and art made by Mao's wife, Jiang Qing (a speech revised and approved by Mao). Zhang polemicized against He Xilai, without naming names, praised the "glorious" tradition of China's intolerably tedious propaganda literature about model soldiers like Lei Feng (which had been an object of mockery in recent years), and stooped to revive old attacks against the tragic figure Hu Feng, a writer and critic who during the 1980s had been very hesitantly rehabilitated by the authorities and whose ideal of a modicum of freedom in the literary field had been destroyed by Mao Zedong personally in 1954–55. Zhang Jiong dissociated himself rather cautiously from the literature of the 1980s, summarily criticizing the "pornography" and violence that had, he alleged, been evidence of the ex-tremes to which its "bourgeois liberalization" had been allowed to go.[15]

The relatively moderate tone of this major attack strikes a paradoxical note. Anticipating yet another general political change of direction, Zhang Jiong and others maneuvering like him might later claim they had merely tried to protect the literary community by voicing comparatively mild criticism that had been extracted under pressure. Apparently the times demanded that even extreme opportunists like Zhang exercise considerable caution.

The Rise of Chinese Emigration

About a quarter of China's hundred-odd best-known intellectuals and writers were forced into exile in the West as a result of the events of June 1989. They fled from China either because they were more or less entangled in the democ-racy movement or because they belonged to the group of avant-garde authors most likely to be persecuted. Others had no option but to prolong their stay in the West rather than return to a China that was bound and gagged. Thus, they found themselves in a situation similar to that of the Czech intellectuals who happened to be abroad during the Soviet invasion of 1968.

Chinese literary scholars who ended up in exile in the United States during the latter half of 1989 included Liu Zaifu, the critic Li Tuo, Zhong Acheng, Liu

Binyan, Zhang Xinxin, Zhang Jie, Lao Gui (reportage writer and author of a best-selling novel about the young people of the Cultural Revolution), and the poet [Huang] Beiling, who was active among China's young "underground" poets.[16] The controversial writer Dai Houying took part in the protests in Shanghai, went underground after the massacre, and then escaped to safety in the United States, where her daughter was living. Kong Jiesheng escaped from Guangzhou and established himself in the United States, where after March 1990 he became editor-in-chief of a short-lived new literary journal, *Guangchang* (Square, after Tiananmen Square), in collaboration with the Taiwanese writer Chen Ruoxi. The poets Yang Lian and Gu Cheng stayed in New Zealand, and the adventure-writer Ma Jian withdrew to Hong Kong for some time. The reportage author Zu Wei and the poet Jiang He fled abroad,[17] and the dramatist, painter, and critic Gao Xingjian settled in permanent exile in Paris.[18] So did the powerful sculptor and poet Ma Desheng, who had already sought exile some years earlier.[19] China's famous younger poet Bei Dao prolonged a visit to West Germany and then took up a teaching post at a Danish university. In 1990, he revived the journal *Jintian* (Today), which had been part of the Peking Spring in 1979, until the magazine was suppressed.

Leading writers and intellectuals were now forced to accept the idea of an emigrant existence. *Liuwang zuojia*, "émigré writer," was the new status with which authors such as Zhang Xinxin tried publicly to come to terms—writing for Taiwan newspapers from the United States.[20] A glance at the Soviet Union and Eastern Europe showed them the dimensions of their new situation and the demands that might be made on them.

Had there not been three different areas of Soviet literature since the 1960s: the exile literature of emigrants and those expelled, which was circulated in small editions; the typewritten copies of underground literature distributed in secret; and the official, toothless domestic literature? It was only through Gorbachev's policy of glasnost that these three literary realities coalesced and became one again. Émigré and underground literature had always claimed to be the real mainstream. Now they were able to take up the position they deserved in the USSR, thanks to the delayed official acceptance.[21]

According to some intellectuals, China's writers in exile were obligated to continue to write, even though they were isolated from China and living under difficult conditions. The question remained whether those who managed to escape would be able to carry on the promising literary beginnings of the decade 1979–89. It had become impossible to continue with a number of projects, such as Zhang Xinxin's collection of historical reports on the early post-1949 period, because she was now cut off from China. Some authors soon gave up their self-imposed exile. Zhang Jie, for example, declared from the United States that as a writer she had no choice but to return.[22] Dai Houying and others likewise left America and returned to the mainland.

One could compile yet another list of politically influential figures who went into exile, such as Zhao Ziyang's former adviser Ruan Ming, or Chen Yizi, who provided readers in the West with valuable information about the real situation inside China during the pre-Tiananmen years. The society China Initiative (Zhongguo Xueshe) at Princeton, organized under the guidance of the historian Yu Yingshi, became a harbor for many of the most prominent émigrés, including Fang Lizhi.

Political Emigration

Another aspect of life in exile was the attempt to create a united democratic movement incorporating all the forces abroad. Various groupings had been formed in France, Germany, England, the United States, Canada, Australia, Japan, and other countries, most of which discussed quite different programs. Should a party be set up? Should the aim be merely to overthrow the Li Peng government and then, once again, introduce reforms through the Communist party, or should a radical new start be made, aimed at overthrowing the Communist system?

Such were the political dimensions of the early period of exile after 1989. Some intellectuals argued that an umbrella organization was necessary to unite all these different forces. Otherwise, efforts might remain ineffectual for two reasons: lack of coordination among the various groupings would not permit a consistent strategy, and developments within China could well silence even those writers in exile. The Interforum conference held during April 1990 in East Berlin on "Eastern Europe and China in Transition" was an attempt to establish such unity and solidarity among democratic political groups and parties in Eastern Europe and the USSR. Eventually, however, the democratic movement, under increasingly heavy pressure, ran out of funds, and in 1991 many members became inactive.

New, Defiant Publications Abroad

Since 1989, many intellectuals who were forced to leave China have attempted to establish some kind of platform from which to spread their ideas to China, or at least to other Chinese abroad, in the hope that all this also might eventually influence the Chinese mainland. Many endeavors, however, folded within a year.

The poet Xu Gang, a former senior editor of the *Guangming Daily*, planned unsuccessfully to set up a publishing house in exile in Paris for the democratic opposition.[23] The writer Ma Jian published a short-lived magazine in September 1989 in Hong Kong, *Da qushi* (The trend of developments), with the intention of providing a forum for the younger generation of Chinese intellectuals abroad.[24]

It was Ma Jian's reportage on Tibet that had earlier nearly cost the writer Liu Xinwu his job as editor of *People's Literature*. The journalist Cao Changqing, together with friends from newly founded opposition organizations, headed for some time a newspaper in Los Angeles, the *Xinwen ziyou daobao* (Press freedom herald), which appeared three times a month.[25] Cao had earlier been forced by official pressure to close down the comparatively liberal newspaper *Zhongguo qingnianbao* (Chinese youth) in the special economic zone of Shenzhen near Hong Kong. The journal *Nahan* (Outcry) was founded in England as a bimonthly. Kong Jiesheng edited *Guangchang* in San Francisco.

In terms of numbers, the center of Chinese emigration was, of course, the United States, followed by Taiwan and Hong Kong. Paris became for some time the official center for the newly established Federation for a Democratic China (Zhongguo Minzhu Zhenxian, or Minzhen for short), because the French authorities quickly and readily provided Chinese refugees with passports, accommodation, and employment. Within months, the federation had built a network of national and regional organizations from Paris. The end of the year was marked by attempts to set up the federation's own monthly periodical for exiled intellectuals. The first issue of *Minzhu Zhongguo* (Democratic China) appeared in April 1990 for international distribution.[26] Su Xiaokang and Yan Jiaqi were leading figures on the board of the periodical, along with such familiar names as the former political adviser Yuan Zhimin. The objective of the journal was to provide further documentation of the democracy movement and its suppression, as well as to develop and discuss strategies for China's future democratization.[27] Despite a remarkably high theoretical level it had to close down during 1991—again, apparently because of a lack of funds. Jin Guantao's *Ershiyi shiji* (Twenty-first century), reissued in Hong Kong and edited from a more general scholarly perspective, took over as the leading intellectual journal during 1990–91. Thus, in a way the exile publications continued the modernization and reform debate, which I will shortly outline below.

The Origins of the Movement: Chinese Intellectuals on the Crisis in Their Society

Within China, there had been increasing debates about reform, about the deficiencies of the system, and, to a certain extent, about negative impulses from tradition.[28] Since the early 1980s, these statements had become more and more exasperated, but because they were scattered in newspapers and journals, they were not adequately taken into account. Many "books" by these intellectuals, which were published since 1989 in Hong Kong and on Taiwan, are in fact merely collections by later editors acting on behalf of these controversial and now suppressed authors. Better-known examples were astrophysicist Fang Lizhi's single-volume editions (and a more comprehensive four-volume Singapore edition),[29] Liu Xiaobo's writings, Bao Zunxin's and Gan Yang's essays, and other texts.[30]

Destructive Tradition and "Cultural Self-criticism"

First, there were those who traced the recent disasters to Chinese tradition. China's crisis and its "immense backwardness," emanating from traditional ways of life, were the subject of the television series "River Elegy"[31] and, to a certain extent, Liu Xiaobo's and Li Zehou's writings, as well as books by lesser-known authors such as the sociologists He Bochuan and Wang Yubo.[32] Bo Yang, widely read in the PRC as translator of the Song dynasty history *Zizhi tongjian* (Comprehensive mirror for aid in government), was perhaps the most articulate representative of this painful Chinese self-criticism.[33] One of the acts doomed to ridicule—like the erection of a worker-peasant-soldier monument in Tiananmen Square as a substitute for the students' Goddess of Democracy—was the official decision to order production of an anti-"Elegy" film, resurrecting the glories of China's great tradition.[34] A senior hard-liner, General Wang Zhen, appeared convinced that such measures would suffice to repair the damage done by the mischievous intellectuals who had dared to expose the "ugly Chinese."

The label "cultural self-criticism" may be given to writings about the role of the intellectual in Chinese society by Liu Xiaobo, Fang Lizhi, and others. Intellectuals were unmasked as servile tools of the government, neither willing nor able to play the role of an independent force in Chinese society. The lack of adequate formal education had never prepared young Chinese intellectuals for such a critical role, the authors argued. Jin Guantao, in his comparisons of China to ancient Rome and medieval Europe, had tried, from a very different angle, to warn his compatriots against further indulging in isolationist Sinocentric perspectives.[35]

Reportage Authors as Journalists and Historians

Second, reportage literature, a symbolic substitute for the true investigative journalism of a free press, was able to comment on the sociopolitical situation of the authors' own society. In their reportage pieces, writers have acted as "historians," evaluating the history of the ruling party and PRC society in general.

By bringing to light cases of corruption with his literary journalism, Liu Binyan had hoped that the ruling elite would eventually find the moral strength to regenerate itself from within the system.[36] The events of June 4 showed that such thinking was much too "idealistic"—they instead demonstrated why the student generation turned for guidance to intellectuals more radical than Liu. This also explains more drastic statements by Liu since 1989, at a time when his evolutionary concepts, for many younger intellectuals, had become questionable or even obsolete.[37]

As acknowledged by Liu Binyan himself, Su Xiaokang and Dai Qing to some extent took over Liu's techniques, wielding the instrument of reportage in an even more forceful way. Zhang Xinxin, with her *Beijingren* (Chinese lives), and Feng Jicai, with his thwarted attempt to cover the Cultural Revolution through one hundred socioliterary personal case studies, worked along similar lines.[38] Liu's revelatory reportage literature has been emulated by Ke Yunlu and many other writers, all of whom have tried to develop their own individual styles.[39]

Dai Qing emphasized the role of the intellectuals behind the reforms.[40] She endeavored to reverse wrong verdicts and rehabilitate the innocent—in short, to rewrite party history. And she was instrumental, like the writer Xu Gang, in bringing ecological themes to the broad public, the best-known examples being the great Heilongjiang forest fire of 1987 and the protest against the Yangzi Gorges Project.[41] Her attacks on Chinese puritanism and the degeneration of personal relations between the sexes during long years of social pressure are a theme common to Dai and Su Xiaokang. Dai Qing has documented the conflicts of sexually emancipated Chinese women with the "law,"[42] and Su, the social problems emanating from the pressures to forgo divorce even when couples were hopelessly mismatched.[43] I have already mentioned his depiction of the harmful effects of tradition in "River Elegy," which led to a nationwide 1988 debate even he had not expected. His efforts to rewrite the history of the party, the 1959 Lushan conference,[44] and Mao's ultra-leftist policies in the Great Leap Forward and Cultural Revolution resemble Solzhenitsyn's efforts, in *The Gulag Archipelago*, to describe the aberrations of Stalinism and Russia's concentration camps.

Futurologists and Social Scientists

Some scholars set a new trend in the use of the social sciences to diagnose China's illnesses. The "futurologist" professor He Bochuan[45] from Guangzhou and others attempted to enumerate the basic problems: China is confronted with excessive population growth, educational backwardness (including illiteracy), grave economic problems in industry and agriculture, a badly functioning cadre bureaucracy, and a diffident intelligentsia. He defined the huge ecological threat to the country and unmasked the myth that emphasis on electronics might lead the country out of its difficulties. Scholars such as He have called for the development of a true "Chinese Sinology," a science of China pioneered by Chinese intellectuals instead of foreign-based scholars. Other attempts, such as Wen Yuankai's *Restructuring the Chinese National Character*, have sought to establish a new value system, a rather theoretical exercise, since how to implement value changes in contemporary society is an unresolved problem.[46] Political scientists such as Yan Jiaqi have proposed, through comparative analysis, the introduction of Western political concepts.[47]

These are some of the characteristics of the pre-1989 debate as it has become visible through the process of editing and reprinting initiated in Hong Kong and on Taiwan by the scattered émigré community and continued in journals abroad.

Many current research projects by international Sinologists focus on these Chinese-language materials and will, eventually, create a much more precise picture of China's complex debate during the 1980s. What, meanwhile, can one infer about the perspectives for China's intellectuals in general and writers specifically?

China's Intellectuals and the Future of the New Literature

The organizations of official party watchdogs within the cultural bureaucracy, including the Federation of Literature and Art Circles (Wenlian) and Chinese Writers' Association (Zuoxie), were reconstituted during 1989 and 1990. In the process, the association assumed the role that critics have accused it of playing for years: as an organization for the prevention of creative literature. In November 1989, Liu Binyan was relieved (in absentia) of his position as deputy chairman of the Writers' Association, and Su Xiaokang, of his post as member of the board (*lishi*). Publishers were forced to close down. The reversal of newly acknowledged values took place rapidly. The young literature from the decade of reform, which Peking's politicians had frequently cited as evidence of China's cultural and social prosperity, was now partly depicted as a devilish tool of harmful Western influence. Both writers and readers had been tricked by modernism, psychoanalysis, existentialism, and other contemptible movements. In the aftermath, books disappeared yet again from the shelves of shops and libraries.

The repercussions after June 1989 prove that China had not yet really advanced beyond the stage of mere *preconditions* for creative freedom. Any literary historian of the period must still concentrate largely on the struggle between the writers' demands for autonomy and the constraints imposed on them by the prevailing cultural policy—instead of exclusively following literary developments. On the threshold of the achievement of creative freedom, the fight against its suppression has again become the main subject of Chinese authors, independent critics, and literary scholars. A new cycle in China's ceaseless struggle for these preconditions has now begun.

Let us ignore the present for the moment, and wonder what might happen if there were another liberalization in the future, as no doubt there will be. It may be considerably more difficult for new Chinese art, be it literature, painting, or film making, to rearouse the interest the West felt in the 1980s, and to persuade an international public that yet another "new" Chinese art might be emerging. The notion of another social and intellectual renaissance is neither convincing nor attractive. The thought of a period in the near future when we might yet again be faced with new exposure novels—this time about the postmassacre period—fills this observer with dread; seven-tenths of the literature from the 1980s was devoted to the subject of the Cultural Revolution and its long-term effects.

Life in exile, however, is a reality not only for the artists. A high percentage of the Chinese students and scientists who were being trained and educated in the West chose to stay rather than return to their country. It becomes obvious here, finally, that the crisis into which China's intelligentsia has fallen is merely one aspect of the profound dilemma of the nation as a whole. Whether China will see the next turnaround in two, five, or ten years, is anybody's guess, however. It remains to be seen whether the political activists and intellectuals among Chinese abroad will remain influential in exile, and how the debate will end between those who argue for reform of the Communist party and those who aim at overthrowing the regime.

A Preliminary Evaluation of the Past Decade

It would seem that previous Western evaluations of the past decade, including its literature and literary policy, were insufficiently critical. The development of literature since 1979 was increasingly obstructed by notions from the Mao era about literature being a kind of propaganda, faithful and useful to the government. We certainly noticed these ominous signs, but we failed, or refused, to anticipate that the authorities might reverse course in such a violent way. Many dark clouds in the Chinese skies had been explained away as minor inconveniences—unavoidable in times of such drastic social change.

Today it is clear that the decade was overshadowed by conflict over basic freedoms of artistic expression. Many writers, it is true, were induced to make compromises, hoping for a happier time; but in 1989, they found themselves thrown right back to the beginning, in a situation in which only a political solution could effect a new start. At the very moment when many writers decided to make their voices heard without compromise, literary and artistic development were violently interrupted. The West, with all its translations and studies of contemporary Chinese literature, was left with little more than preliminary documents of an interrupted process of new Chinese literary creation.

And yet, in the middle of the 1980s, there were increasing signs of a problematic change in the function of contemporary literature in Chinese society. It had driven literature into the confines of a specialist public and made many writers nervous, for they saw themselves as public figures with a suddenly dwindling audience. Critics such as Liu Binyan pointed out that the focus of the debate in support of the reform movement in China would shift from contemporary literature to the social and natural sciences if younger writers were to continue their arcane literary games rather than face up to their social responsibility. Finally, the young literature of the 1980s was threatened not only by political pressure, but also by a tendency among more cautious writers to withdraw into "pure" art. The young literature was also ill-prepared to withstand the flood of cheap entertainment fiction that replaced the earlier predilection of Chinese readers for "Literature of the Wounded" and other exposé writing from the beginning of the reform decade.

On the Reception of Contemporary Chinese Literature Abroad

Considering the process of reception, a breakthrough in recognition for China's literature was achieved on Taiwan much later than in the West and its Chinese communities. The most prominent authors from the PRC have been reprinted on Taiwan only since 1987–88. The political climate on Taiwan at that time suddenly accorded greater freedom of publication to writings from the mainland, and the first individual studies giving more generous evaluations of PRC literature were also published on the island at that time.[48] Interest soon faded again, however, in a Taiwanese society that had become accustomed to all kinds of sensations and novelties. A degree of weariness developed, due to the artistic immaturity of many of the PRC works, a general aversion toward things Chinese after June 1989, and, above all, a suspicion that PRC realities did not deserve the specific attention of Taiwanese society. All these features led to considerable reservations following Taiwan's initial mania for mainland literature (*dalu wenxue re*).

In the West, in both Europe and the United States, and to a lesser extent in Japan, the 1980s had begun with great enthusiasm, as audiences in those areas were able to listen to Chinese voices in literature again for the first time in many years. Chinese authors were frequently invited abroad. They represented the PRC as cultural ambassadors in semi-official delegations, and many of their works became known to a wider public through translations—though questions about the quality of the literature were raised.

There have already been first attempts to characterize this reception process, through bibliographical surveys of Western publications discussing and translating contemporary Chinese literature.[49] Even now, such surveys convey a colorful picture of the whole stormy development. Chinese works of the 1980s gained a Western audience much faster than had the Chinese literature of the Republican period, in the 1920s and 1930s. The attacks by official literary critics in the PRC at the end of the 1980s, maintaining that the process of reception in the West had been deplorably one-sided or had even been carried out with sinister intentions, can thus be put aside, as criticism formulated from a very narrow perspective. The new avant-garde of Chinese writers, which had meanwhile established itself and been introduced fairly objectively by individual translations in the West, was, anyway, never to earn approval from these critics close to the government. Indeed, the works became targets after 1989.

Preconditions for a Literary Revival

We are still too close to the events of June 1989 to know what may follow. While social change is taking place at a breathtaking pace in East and Southeast Asia, particularly in cities such as Hong Kong, Taibei, Singapore, Tokyo, and

Seoul, China is once more in danger of isolation. Yet again, it is displaying its tragic capacity to neutralize or crush its own rich potential through internecine strife. The forced return to outdated Maoist positions having little support in the PRC will be achieved only after a considerable period of futile reorganization. Even after renewal of reform confirms the hopelessness of the radical Maoist policy of China's reestablished gerontocracy, the country will need at least another five years before reaching a starting point similar to that of the early 1980s.

Such simple calculations show that the forces behind the June massacre have thrown China back by at least a decade. The future will probably bring first a reshuffle of personnel and persecutors and finally, replacements by reform-conscious cadres and intellectuals. Thus, there seems little hope of a dazzling start into a new era of reform before the end of the century.

Certainly the words quoted at the beginning of this introduction, from Chen Mingyuan of Peking University, will continue to reflect the aspirations and hopes of China's urban population. Until there is greater freedom of thought in China, writers within the country and overseas, international translators and scholars, and potential readers at home and abroad have all been thrown into a phase of reflection and reorientation. The dark aspects in this volume of self-portrayals by PRC writers, of biographies originally presented as a kind of introduction to the newly flourishing Chinese literary scene, may now get more serious attention than the writers and editors of this volume initially had intended.

Notes

During research visits to Hong Kong and Taibei from August to September 1989, and again in January 1990, I collected sources in Chinese on the democracy movement and June 4 massacre, as well as selected materials concerning social criticism by Chinese intellectuals between 1985 and 1989. Earlier versions of this essay appeared in a series of six articles in *Neue Zürcher Zeitung* (September 1989) and in the literary journal *die horen*, Hannover, 155 and 156 (1989).

1. Ernst Hagemann, "Öffnung mit Zugluft: Getrübte Aussichten in der Aussenwirtschaft," in *Nachdenken über China*, ed. Ulrich Menzel (Frankfurt, 1990), pp. 105–25.

2. When German and Japanese Sinologists met at a November 27–29, 1989, Berlin symposium on the current situation in China ("Das nachmaoistische China aus japanischer und deutscher Sicht"), one paper expressed this idea: Jürgen Domes and Marie-Luise Näth, "Die Innenpolitik: Ergebnisse." Cp. Jürgen Domes and Luise Näth, *China im Aufbruch: Analyse und Dokumente der demokratischen Bewegung in Peking 1989* (Zürich, 1990).

3. See Merle Goldman, *Literary Dissent in Communist China* (Cambridge, MA, 1967); Howard Goldblatt, ed., *Chinese Literature for the 1980s: The Fourth Congress of Writers and Artists* (Armonk, NY, 1982); and Yue Daiyun, *Intellectuals in Chinese Fiction* (Berkeley, 1988).

4. He Jingzhi (b. 1924) was already semiretired. On He, see the Hong Kong journal *Chaoliu* (Trends) 30 (August 15, 1990), and *Jiushi niandai* (The nineties) (April 1990): 23–25.

5. On Liu Baiyu and the Bai Hua affair, see Anna Dolež alová, "Two Waves of Criticism of the Film Script Bitter Love and of the Writer Bai Hua in 1981," *Asian and African Studies* (1983): 27–54.

6. On the 2,800 cadres, see *Dangdai*, April 14, 1990, pp. 4–5. On the "New Era," see *Xin shiqi wenyixue lunzheng ziliao* (Materials on literary debates during the new period) (Shanghai, 1988), 2 vols.; *Xin shiqi wenxue liu nian* (Six years of literature from the New Era) (Beijing, 1985); He Xilai, *Xin shiqi wenxue sichao lun* (On literary trends of the new period) (Huaiyang, 1985); and Zhang Jiong, *Xin shiqi wenxue lungang* (Critical articles on the literature of the new period) (Fuzhou, 1986).

7. On Bai Hua's self-criticism, see Anna Dolež alová, "Two Waves of Criticism." More recent essays by Bai Hua are in *Bai Hua liuxue de xin* (The heart of Bai Hua— bleeding) (Hong Kong, 1989). Bai Hua's courageous postmassacre interview is in *Yomiuri shimbun*, March 22, 1990.

8. Liu Binyan has warned of further eruptions of violence. According to a report by the journalist Zeng Huiyan, Liu said at a New York conference on "China's Future as Seen from Taiwan," February 21, 1990: "Blood will be spilled and in some places blood will form a river," in *Baixing* 212 (March 16, 1990).

9. For details about personnel changes in the culture bureaucracy and in the field of literature, see the article by Bi Hua in *Jiushi niandai* (April 1990), p. 61, and the report following, pp. 70–72. See also the sources in note 6 on the reshuffle at the Ministry of Culture. There were reports about an imminent campaign against Wang Meng, and attacks against Yan Jiaqi, Liu Binyan, Su Xiaokang, Jin Guantao, Liu Zaifu, and others abroad. The next targets were said to include Li Zehou.

Dai Qing comments on her relation to the Ye clan in her collection of essays, *Zhuisui mogui zhuazhu shangdi* (Changsha, 1988). Reports on Dai Qing in prison are in *Zhengming* (January 1990) and in *Mingbao yuekan* (January 1990).

10. Ke Yunlu wrote, among other works, the novels *Ye yu zhou* (One night and one day) (Beijing, 1986) and *Shuai yu rong* (Decline and glory) (Beijing, 1988). On Ke Yunlu, see also Helmut Martin, "The Drama *Tragic Song of Our Time* (*Shidai di beige*): Functions of Literature in the Eighties and Sociopolitical Limitations," in *Drama in the People's Republic of China*, ed. Constantine Tung and Colin Mackerras (Albany, NY, 1987), and Jeffrey C. Kinkley, "Problems and Prospects for Literature in Mainland China," *Issues and Studies* 22, 1 (January 1986): 114–16.

11. Wang had been expelled from the party in 1987 and gained further status by the publication of his speeches and writings in Hong Kong and Taiwan, while Ren had been imprisoned for several years following the Peking Spring of 1979. On Ren, see *Tiananmen 1989* (Taibei, 1990), pp. 219–20. On Wang, *Wang Ruowang xuanji* (Selected writings) (Hong Kong, 1987) and *Tiandi you zhengqi* (There is still justice) (Hong Kong, 1989), a text that was smuggled out of China. Bo Yang has initiated publication of another collection of essays: Wang Ruowang, *Di erci jiehun* (Second marriage) (Taibei, 1990). It contains short stories written between 1940 and 1985, including Wang's well-known piece, *Ji'e sanbuqu*, translated by Kyna Rubin with Ira Kasoff as *Hunger Trilogy* (Armonk, NY, 1991). Bo Yang carried the manuscript to Taiwan on his trip back from the mainland; see his *Jiayuan* (Return home) (Taibei, 1989). A German translation, by Jürgen Ritter, is forthcoming. In China, some referred to China's outspoken critics of the 1980s as "Liu in the North and Wang in the South" (*nan Wang bei Liu*).

12. See Zheng Yi, *Laojing* (Old well) (Taibei, 1988); for Bao's collection of articles on Confucianism today, see Bao Zunxin, *Pipan yu qimeng* (Criticism and enlightenment) (Taibei, 1989). Shi Shuqing, *Wentan fansi yu qianzhan* (Writers rethinking the situation and future prospects) (Hong Kong, 1989), features interviews with Dai Houying, Feng Jicai, Zheng Yi, Zhang Xianliang, and Wang Zengqi.

Longnian de beizhuang—"Heshang" : Zhengming yu huiyi ("River Elegy"—tragedy of the year of the dragon: debate and recollections) (Hong Kong, 1989) details the impact of that work. Rudolf Wagner's interpretation of the "conflict between the yellow and blue cultures" was printed in the *Frankfurter Allgemeine Zeitung*, November 7, 1989.

Qin Benli's dismissal by Jiang Zemin on April 25, 1989, helped stoke the democracy movement. Tony Saich, ed., *The Chinese People's Movement* (Armonk, NY, 1990), pp. 149–55. Qing died April 15, 1991.

13. On China's public security forces, see *Zhongguo zhi chun* (January 1990) and *Dangdai*, January 6, February 17, and March 2, 1990. *Dangdai*, February 3, 1990, relates PRC activities in Hong Kong and Shenzhen. *Dangdai*, April 7, 1990, tells of Chai Ling's escape.

14. Asia Watch, *Punishment Season: Human Rights in China after Martial Law* (New York, February 7, 1990). The Hong Kong Alliance in Support of the Democratic Movement in China published their own figures. In Chinese, see the Hong Kong journal *Shiyue pinglun* (October review), 1/2, 147 (1990): 10–14, which carries a December 30, 1989, declaration by forty-eight groups under the alliance Zhilian Xianggang Shimin Zhiyuan Aiguo Minzhu Yundong Lianhe Hui, calling for the immediate release of 465 people. The Asia Watch list includes 592 names. Both lists include Bao Tong, Bao Zunxin, Cao Siyuan, Dai Qing, Ke Yunlu, Li Honglin, Liu Xiaobo, Ren Wanding, Wang Dan, Wang Luxiang, Wang Ruowang, Wang Xizhe, Wei Jingsheng, Wen Yuankai, Wu Qiang, Ye Wenfu, Yu Haocheng, and Zheng Yi.

15. See the Peking journal *Wenxue pinglun*, issues from August and October 1989. On He Xilai and Zhang Jiong, see note 6.

16. On Acheng, see Shi Shuqing, *Wentan fansi*, and my interview with the writer in this volume. On Liu, see, for instance, Liu Zaifu, *Wenxue de fansi* (Coming to terms with the past in the literary field) (Beijing, 1986), and *Xingge zuhelun* (On the integral character of literature) (Shanghai, 1986). On Dai Houying, see Shi Shuqing, *Wentan fansi*, and Carolyn S. Pruyn, *Humanism in Modern Chinese Literature: The Case of Dai Houying* (Bochum, 1988). Lao Gui wrote *Xuese huanghun* (Blood-red sunset) (Beijing: Yantai, 1987), praised in the West in Liu Binyan, "Stark Truth vs. 'False Realism': The Book that Stunned Beijing," *New York Times Book Review*, November 6, 1988, pp. 3, 36.

17. Yang Lian, *Pilgerfahrt, Gedichte aus China* (Innsbruck, 1988); see also the poetry by Gu Cheng in German translation, in Peter Hoffmann, ed., Gu Cheng, *Quecksilber und andere Gedichte* (Bochum, 1990).

18. The journal *Guangchang* was a quarterly, published in West Lafayette, Indiana, in two thousand copies. Gao Xingjian, *Die Busstation* (Bochum, 1988); Monica Basting, *Yeren—Tradition und Avantgarde in Gao Xingjian's Theaterstück "Die Wilden" (1985)* (Bochum, 1988). On Zu Wei's activities during June 1989, see *Chaoliu* 30 (August 15, 1989); on his writings, see *Dangdai*, April 14, 1989, p. 19.

On Ma Jian, see his collection *Nila goushi: Ma Jian xiaoshuo ji* (Prose by Ma Jian) (Hong Kong, 1989) and his novel *Yuanbei* (Pillar of hate) (Hong Kong, 1989).

19. An excellent review of the activities of Ma Desheng and other artists in the group Xingxing (Stars) is Wang Keping, "Xingxing wangshi" (Xingxing in retrospect), *Jiushi niandai* (January 1989).

20. Zhang Xinxin has written articles for *Zhongguo shibao* (China times, Taibei) from the United States; for more on the situation in exile, see articles by the poet [Huang] Beiling, in *Baixing* 213 (April 1, 1990): 44–45, and the novelist Lao Gui, on pp. 42–43.

21. On Soviet literature, see Wolfgang Kasack, *Die russische Literatur 1945–1982* (München, 1983) and *Russische Literatur des 20: Jahrhunderts in deutscher Sprache* (München, 1985).

22. Zhang Xinxin eventually published the materials as a novel. In an interview with

Le Monde, Paris, October 6, 1990, Zhang Jie explained why she intended to return to China.

23. The writer and poet Xu Gang, born in Shanghai in 1945 and sometime editor of the literary section of the *People's Daily*, became known for his reportage on China's ecological crisis, "Chenlun de guotu" (Our sinking land), *Renmin wenxue* (June 1985). Cp. Xu Gang, *Chenlun de guotu* (Hong Kong, 1990).

24. Ma succeeded in publishing only two issues of the journal *Da qushi*, in October and November 1989.

25. Cao Changqing left the emigrant newspaper after nine months and went to Columbia University in New York to study. His report on his work during this period is "Fengfeng yuyu jiuge yue" (Nine months of turbulent activities), *Baixing* 212 (March 16, 1990): 62–64. See also his series about his first visit to Taiwan, *Baixing* 211 and 212 (1990).

26. First issue: *Minzhu Zhongguo* 1 (April 1990). The journal was printed by the *Lianhebao* (United daily) in Taibei and distributed internationally from Paris. The editor-in-chief was Su Xiaokang.

27. The debate among the collaborators was apparently about whether the journal should be published independently rather than as an organ representing the federation. The editors had first decided for the politically more neutral title *Liming* (Daybreak).

28. There was much criticism of the federation's activities, such as the journalist Lu Keng's letter (to Hu Juren) in *Baixing* 212 (March 16, 1990). On this debate, see Helmut Martin, *China's Democracy Movement 1989: A Selected Bibliography of Chinese Source Materials* (Köln, 1990), section 2, "Chinese Intellectuals on Their Own Society," preamble to the notes.

29. *Fang Lizhi zixuanji* (Singapore, 1988), 4 vols., is probably based on Fang's own selection. The CCP Central Control Commission printed a pamphlet against Fang called *Fang Lizhi de zhen mianmu* (The true face of Fang Lizhi) (Beijing, 1989). For a selection of Fang's speeches in German, see Helmut Martin, ed., *Fang Lizhi, China im Umbruch*, introduction by Erwin Wickert (Berlin, 1989).

30. *United Daily*, ed., *Tiananmen 1989* (Taipei, 1989); Liu Xiaobo, *Xuanze de pipan* (Selected criticism) (Taibei, 1989); Liu Xiaobo, *Beiju, haixiu, ziyou* (Tragedy, disgrace, and liberty) (Taibei, 1989); Bao Zunxin, *Pipan yu qimeng* (Criticism and enlightenment) (Taibei, 1989); see also Gan Yang, *Women zai chuangzao chuantong* (We are creating our tradition) (Taibei, 1989).

31. On "Heshang," see note 12.

32. He Bochuan, *Shan'aoshang de Zhongguo: wenti, kunjing, tongku de xuanze* (China surrounded by mountains: problems, difficulties, and bitter choices) (Guiyang, 1989); He Bochuan, *Zhongguo de weiji* (The crisis of China) (Taibei, 1989); Wang Yubo, *Da fanlong—xiao fanlong* (Big cage—small cage) (Beijing, 1989); Li Zehou, *Zhongguo xiandai sixiang shilun* (A survey of modern Chinese intellectual history) (Beijing, 1987).

33. Sun Guodong, *Ping Bo Yang* (A criticism of Bo Yang) (Hong Kong, 1989).

34. Xinhua News Agency, October 16 and 19, 1989, in *Summary of World Broadcasts* (BBC), October 18, 1989; *China aktuell* (October 1989): 761–66.

35. Jin Guantao, ed., *Xifang shehui jiegou de yanbian* (The evolution of Western social structure) (Hong Kong, 1987); Jin Guantao and Liu Qingfeng, *Wenti yu fangfa ji* (A volume on problems and methodology) (Shanghai, 1986); *Jin Guantao, Liu Qingfeng ji: fansi—tansuo—chuangzao* (A collection by Jin and Liu: Reevaluation, search, and creation) (Harbin, 1988).

36. *Liu Binyan yanlunji* (Speeches and articles by Liu Binyan) (Hong Kong, 1988), 2 vols., and *Liu Binyan zizhuan* (Liu Binyan's autobiography) (Taibei, 1989). An exhaustive bibliography on Liu in Chinese and in Western languages is in Carolin Blank and

Christa Gescher, *Gesellschaftskritik in der Volksrepublik China: Der Journalist und Schriftsteller Liu Binyan* (Bochum, 1991).

37. Liu's opinions about the role of the Communist party and the need for freedom of the press became much more radical in debates on China's future. See note 8.

38. Zhang Xinxin and Sang Ye, *Chinese Lives: An Oral History of Contemporary China*, ed. W. J. F. Jenner and Delia Davin (New York, 1987). Feng Jicai, *Yibaige ren de shinian* (One hundred persons during the ten years) (Hong Kong, 1987), vol. 1; a second volume was not allowed to be published; see Helmut Martin, "What If History Has Merely Played a Trick on Us? Feng Jicai's Writings, 1979–1984," in *Reform and Revolution in Twentieth Century China*, ed. Shaw Yuming (Taipei, 1987), pp. 277–90.

39. On Ke Yunlu, see note 10.

40. Dai Qing, *Xuezhe dawenlu* (A record of interviews with scholars) (Nanchang, 1988).

41. Dai Qing, *Hongse jingbao* (Red Alarm: Reportage from the conflagration in the Daxing'an forests) (Hong Kong, 1987); see also Harrison E. Salisbury, *The Great Black Dragon Fire: A Chinese Inferno* (Boston, 1989); and Dai Qing, *Changjiang sanxia gongcheng yingfou xingjian* (Should the Yangzi Gorge Engineering Project flourish or not?) (Hong Kong, 1989). Taiwan has reached a much higher ecological sophistication. See the excellent survey by Chen Yuling on Taiwanese literature and ecological protest in the journal *Taiwan wenxue guancha zazhi* 1 (1990): 32–43.

42. Dai Qing et al., *Xingkaifang nüzi* (Sexually emancipated women) (Hong Kong, 1988).

43. Su Xiaokang, *Yinyang daliebian* (The great rift between the sexes) (Taibei, 1988).

44. Su Xiaokang's collection of reportage, *Ziyou beiwanglu* (A memoir of freedom) (Hong Kong, 1989); Su Xiaokang et al., *Wutuobang ji* (Memorial of a utopia, record of the Lushan conference) (Hong Kong, 1989).

45. On He Bochuan, see note 32.

46. Wen Yuankai, *Zhongguo guominxing gaizao* (Restructuring the Chinese national character) (Hong Kong, 1988).

47. Yan Jiaqi, *Shounao lun* (On state leadership) (Hong Kong, 1989); *Quanli yu zhenli* (Power and truth) (Beijing, 1987); and *Wo de sixiang zizhuan* (My intellectual biography) (Hong Kong, 1988). On Yan's utopias, see Helmut Martin, "The Future of China, Taiwan, and Hong Kong: Perspectives Explored by Contemporary Writers," in *Ideology and Politics in Twentieth Century China*, ed. King-yuh Chang (Taipei, 1988), pp. 174–95.

48. Cai Yuanhuang, *Haixia liang'an xiaoshuo de fengmao* (The status of fiction on both sides of the Taiwan Strait) (Taibei, 1989), and Chen Xingyuan, *Cong Taiwan kan dalu dangdai wenxue* (Contemporary mainland literature as seen from Taiwan) (Taibei, 1989). See also the literary journals *Wenxun, Lianhe wenxue*, and *Xindi* (New land literature, commenced April 1990) from Taiwan.

49. Compare my bibliographical survey in Helmut Martin and Christiane Hammer, eds., *Die Auflösung der Abteilung für Haarspalterei: Texte moderner chinesischer Autoren von den Reformen bis zum Exil* (Hamburg, 1991), pp. 313–19.

Contributors

Marty Backstrom has a Ph.D. degree in East Asian languages from the University of California, Berkeley, and is doing research on fellowship at the University of Alberta.

Charles Belbin is a poet and free-lance translator living in San Francisco.

Kim Besio is an instructor in Chinese at the University of Minnesota.

Catherine Pease Campbell is an assistant professor of Chinese at Middlebury College, Middlebury, Vermont.

Rey Chow is an associate professor of comparative literature at the University of Minnesota.

Ding Naifei teaches in the foreign languages department of Tsing Hua University, Taiwan.

Michael S. Duke is a professor of Chinese literature at the University of British Columbia.

Fung Mei-cheong has an M.A. degree in East Asian languages and history from the University of Wisconsin, Madison.

Howard Goldblatt is a noted translator of Chinese fiction and a professor of Chinese at the University of Colorado, Boulder.

Beata Grant is an assistant professor of Chinese language and literature at Washington University, St. Louis.

Linda Greenhouse Wang is a Ph.D. candidate in East Asian languages at the University of California, Berkeley.

Juliette Gregory is a program coordinator at the Association for International Educators, Washington, D. C.

Edward Gunn is a professor of Chinese literature at Cornell University.

Theodore Huters is a professor of East Asian languages and literature at the University of California, Irvine.

W. J. F. Jenner is a noted translator of Chinese fiction and a professor of Chinese at the Australian National University.

Frances LaFleur is curator of the Chinese collection, C. V. Starr East Asian Library, Columbia University.

Linette Lee is taking her Master's degree in East Asian languages at the University of California, Berkeley.

Pu-mei Leng is a researcher in the field of Chinese literature living in the Washington, D. C. area.

Peter Li is an associate professor of Chinese at Rutgers University.

Patricia Da-yi Pang is a faculty associate at Arizona State University.

Carolyn S. Pruyn is the student affairs officer for the Group in Asian Studies, University of California, Berkeley.

Deborah Rudolph is a Ph.D. candidate in East Asian languages at the University of California, Berkeley.

Patricia Sieber is a Ph.D. candidate in East Asian languages at the University of California, Berkeley.

Raymond N. Tang is head of the Chinese division of the East Asian Library, University of California, Berkeley.

Tang Yiming is an associate professor of Chinese literature at Wenhua University, Yangmingshan, Taiwan.

Marsha Wagner, formerly director of the C. V. Starr East Asian Library, is ombuds officer, Columbia University.

David Wakefield is a Ph.D. candidate in history at the University of California, Los Angeles.

Tien Rita Wang is a translator of poetry and an instructor in the City College of San Francisco.

Natasha Wild is a departmental secretary at the department of East Asian languages of the University of California, Berkeley, and teaches Chinese extension courses at the university.

Philip Williams is an assistant professor of Chinese at the University of Vermont.

Sau-ling C. Wong is an associate professor of Asian-American studies at the University of California, Berkeley.

Yang Xianyi and **Gladys Yang** are noted translators of ancient and modern

Chinese fiction and drama, semiretired from the Foreign Languages Press, Peking.

Ellen Lai-shan Yeung is a noted translator of Chinese fiction and an instructor in the San Francisco Community College district.

Yu Fanqin is a professional translator at the Foreign Languages Press, Peking.

Ming-bao Yue is a Ph.D. candidate in Asian languages and comparative literature at Stanford University.

Zha Jianying is a program officer at the Center for Psycho-Social Studies, Chicago, Illinois.

Zhang Yingjin is a Ph.D. candidate and teaching fellow in comparative literature at Stanford University.

Anthology Editors

Helmut Martin, b. 1940, a professor of Chinese language and literature at the Ruhr University in Bochum, Germany, was Carl Schurz Memorial Professor at the University of Wisconsin, 1985, and research linguist at the University of California, Berkeley, 1987–88. He is editor of the series "Chinathemen" of Brockmeyer, Bochum, and of the "neue chinesische bibliothek," published by Diederichs, Cologne, 1985–87, which produced individual volumes devoted to the works of Wang Meng, Feng Jicai, Ba Jin, Qian Zhongshu, Bai Xianyong, Zhang Xinxin, and Li Ang. Since 1990, he has been director of the European Project on China's Modernization, funded by the Volkswagen Foundation. His publications include *Li Li-weng über das Theater* (Heidelberg, 1966); *Chinakunde in der Sowjetunion* (Research on China in the Soviet Union) (Hamburg, 1972); *Index to the Ho Collection of Twenty-eight* Shih-hua (*He shi lidai shihua suoyin*) (Taibei, 1973); *Chinesisch-Deutscher Wortschatz, Politik und Wirtschaft der VR China* (Chinese-German glossary of political and economic terms) (Berlin, 1977, 1987); *Mao Zedong Texte* (German-Chinese bilingual edition of the *wansui* texts), 7 vols. (München, 1979–82); *Cult and Canon: The Origins and Development of State Maoism* (Armonk, NY, 1982); *Chinesische Sprachplanung* (Chinese language planning) (Bochum, 1982); and *Cologne-Workshop 1984 on Contemporary Chinese Literature* (Köln, 1986). He has edited *Deng Xiaoping: Die Reform der Revolution* (selected speeches of Deng Xiaoping) (Berlin, 1988); *Fang Lizhi, China im Umbruch* (selected speeches of Fang Lizhi) (Berlin, 1989); Liu E, *Die Reisen des Lao Can* (The travels of Lao Can) (Frankfurt, 1989); Bei Dao, *Gezeiten* (Waves) (Frankfurt, 1990); and *Origins and Consequences of China's Democracy Movement 1989* (Köln, 1990). Christa Gescher has edited *Literature, Language and Politics: Helmut Martin, Writings on China, 1965- 1990: Selected Bibliography* (Bochum, 1991).

Jeffrey Kinkley, b. 1948, is an associate professor of history at St. John's University, New York, and assistant editor, China and Inner Asia, of *The Journal of Asian Studies*. Author of *The Odyssey of Shen Congwen* (Stanford, 1987), published in a Chinese translation by Fu Jiaqin (Beijing, 1990), he edited *After Mao: Chinese Literature and Society, 1978-81* (Cambridge, MA, 1985, 1990), *Surviving the Storm: A Memoir*, the autobiography of Chen Xuezhao (Armonk, NY, 1990), and the Chinese section of the special China issue of *Fiction* 8, 2-3 (1987). His translations include *Traveller Without a Map*, the autobiography of Hsiao Ch'ien [Xiao Qian] (London, 1990) and fiction by Fang Ji, Li Rui, Lu Wenfu, Shen Congwen, Zhang Xinxin, Zhao Shuli, and Zheng Wanlong. His recent research has been about Chinese crime and detective novels, Taiwanese kitsch, and the fiction of Chen Yingzhen, Gu Hua, Han Shaogong, He Liwei, Wang Zengqi, Wang Zhenhe, Zhang Xianliang, and Zhang Xinxin.

MODERN CHINESE WRITERS

I

Literature from the People's Republic

THIS section of the anthology features writers from the People's Republic of China notable for their activity since 1978–80.

The first group of selections deals with "Historical Blunders." In it, the writers look back on the devastating impact of the Cultural Revolution and other mass campaigns of the Mao era, typically to contemplate the effect on their own writing.

The second group of selections, entitled "Further Victims of Politics in the 1980s," concerns conflicts between China's intellectuals and political authorities *since* the beginning of Deng Xiaoping's reform policies in 1978.

The third heading is "Patterns of the New Literature." This section addresses a variety of conditions experienced by contemporary writers, some very personal, some part and parcel of the social changes since the 1950s.

The fourth section addresses literary "Schools and Tendencies" in China during the 1980s. One group of writers provides "Accounts of Rural Realities"—realities possibly of greater importance than the more noticeable developments in China's great cities.

"Rising in Protest: A New Generation," represents younger writers who oppose the old literary conventions. Their gesture of protest against what they perceive to be China's social decline is part of their own self-definition and also a measure of their inner self-confidence.

Many consider women writers to be China's most active and successful writers, and to have a unique self-consciousness. Essays by female authors are to be found in the other sections, too, but "Against Complacency: Women Writers" features selections by two women writers whose art has shown unusual range and excellence.

"Documentary Literature" (*baogao wenxue*) has come to the fore largely due to China's dearth of press freedoms and its politicized and unpredictable legal system. Indirect social criticism featuring specific instances of misjudged cases is a widely successful genre in the PRC.

In China, the phrase "coming to terms with the past" typically means reckoning with the Cultural Revolution. Sometimes it includes a reexamination of all the mass campaigns of the Mao era, but contemporary writers must also reconsider the place of traditional history and culture. The historical search for social and ethnic "Roots" (*xungen*) is an attempt to redefine the past and, not least of all, the contemporary role of the Chinese intellectual in light of the past.

In "Combining Past and Present," Wang Zengqi seems one of the few PRC authors to have retained a strong, conscious relationship with China's cultural heritage.

Wang Ruowang

WANG RUOWANG (b. 1918) has passed his adult life, indeed part of his pre-adult life, as a dissident. As a teenager he spent three years in a Nationalist jail for criticizing Chiang Kai-shek. Though already a twenty-year Communist party member at the time of the Antirightist movement, he was expelled in 1957 after having criticized that party's abuse of power in its turn. Four more years of prison during the Cultural Revolution left Wang undaunted; in the post-Mao years, when he was reinstated into the party, his productivity in essay and fictive genres redoubled. His works were banned in January 1987, however, when he was expelled from the party again, at the same time as Liu Binyan and Fang Lizhi. Unlike them, Wang Ruowang was not allowed to travel abroad, perhaps because he allowed his new writings to be smuggled out of the PRC for publication in Hong Kong. He supported the marchers for democracy in Shanghai in 1989 and openly called for the resignation of Premier Li Peng after the massacre. His uneasy days under house arrest in the summer of 1989 naturally eventuated in a third imprisonment, on September 8. Perhaps because of his advanced age, or because he made sufficient perfunctory confessions so as to be able to get on with one last master work, his memoirs, Wang Ruowang was released on October 29, 1990, much to the surprise and relief of the international community.

Even when they did not lead to imprisonment, the Communist party's mass campaigns molded careers and personalities in tragic ways. The text below expresses the grief felt by Wang Ruowang at the sorry fate and ultimate death of his first wife, much as another famous essay, by Ba Jin, mourns for his wife, who suffered and died in the later and more notorious Cultural Revolution.[1] Wang reminds us that the Cultural Revolution was not wholly unprecedented. One also might call the essay a tragic "modern love story" that has much in common with

---

[1]Ba Jin, "In Loving Memory of Xiao San," in his *Random Thoughts*, trans. Geremie Barmé (Hong Kong, 1984), pp. 21–42.

the wonderful literary pieces on the relationship between Li Qingzhao and her husband in Song times, or the unlucky Shen Fu and his wife during the late Qing, told in his *Fusheng liuji* (Six records of a floating life, 1809). In the end there can only be silence, the effects of the mass movements and the inner urges of an intellectual to express herself having resulted in a personality crushed, a once sensitive mind driven to insanity.

The Enigmatic Laughter of Insanity
A Modern Love Story

Wang Ruowang

August 1981

I MUST speak of a short story that had terrible repercussions, "The History of One Big Pot" (*Yikou da guo de lishi*). The story first appeared in the July 1962 number of *Literary Monthly* (*Wenyi yuebao*). Though it was by no means a remarkable piece of work, its publication was responsible for the devastation of my home and, ultimately, the loss of a human life. It is steeped in my tears and blood, charged with bitter suffering and indignation. The story itself reflects the period of the Great Leap Forward. What the story went through, from the time it was written until it was suppressed, reflects the era's blundering policies on literature and the arts. Now, finally, I have an opportunity to tell readers of the bitterness that has massed inside of me these past twenty years—an opportunity, too, to offer some compensation to Comrade Li Ming, who lost her life on account of this story. If it is true that souls reside in heaven after death, then I beg to offer this collection [of stories] in tribute to the soul of my dear Li Ming in heaven.

The first to open fire on me when I was caught up in that sudden storm of 1957 were the secretary of the municipal party committee [Ke Qingshi], who was known as the "Boss of Shanghai," and his two right-hand men, Zhang Chunqiao and Yao Wenyuan. My wife, Comrade Li Ming, hadn't the least understanding of this sharply expanded political movement and its ruthless struggle; her thoughts and sentiments from beginning to end were always with me, and for this she suffered through cruel struggle sessions, one after another, in her own unit. She had been director of an industrial corporation and secretary of its party committee, as well as alternate member of the municipal party committee. When all of these public appointments were revoked, she simply let them drop. At last, a self-styled representative of the organization came and passed down to her an order in the form of an ultimatum.

"Do you want to be a party member, or do you want Wang Ruowang? It's your decision."

Crying, Li Ming replied, "With so many children, I can't give up Wang Ruowang!"

The fellow left in an angry huff.

From then on, she began to behave oddly, her spirit and her faith in shambles. (Later, as it turned out, she wasn't expelled from the party.) Sometimes she would hold me fast and cry out loud; sometimes she would rebuke me—"Why did you have to oppose the party?"—and slap me or kick me or butt me with her head. At the time I received her blows with all docility; it never occurred to me to defend myself against her. I knew that she was only directing her inner resentment toward me. Perhaps it lessened her pain. If only I could have, I would willingly have walked through fire or water. I blamed myself and my writing for having brought on this terrible calamity, for having hurt her and driven her to the margins of schizophrenia. But I had to keep myself in check. I simply had to maintain my own sanity so that I could tend to her, comfort her, and requite her for her suffering on my behalf.

The entire household was shrouded in a gloomy and disconsolate atmosphere during those years. When I was sent down to the countryside to do manual labor, neither the political pressure nor the social discrimination—I was hardly treated as a human being—wounded my will or my spirit. To tell the truth, none of those pressures could awe me into submission any more, for my nerves were numb and my senses dulled. The one thing I cared about was my poor, unbalanced Comrade Li Ming. "How is she now? Is she cooperating and taking her medicine when she should? I wonder if she's smashing things in the house now that I'm not there. I wonder, might she—during a mental lapse—jump out a window?"

As I pictured this tragic and all-too-possible outcome, I broke into a cold sweat and my breathing became strained. Unable to stop myself, I took off down the road west. After running a few steps, I immediately grew tired. My legs were stiff and sore, I was panting and out of breath. Only then did I pause to think that the tragedies that had just passed before me were only figments of my imagination, palpitations of the heart that I could reveal to no one. I knocked myself on the forehead and lectured to myself: "Steady, Wang Ruowang. Don't let yourself slip into schizophrenia, whatever you do. You've got to keep going, for Li Ming and for the children. You cannot lose your mind." Aware once again that I was there to do "penal labor under the surveillance of the masses" and that taking absence without leave could only call up a new series of persecutions, I slowly walked back, dragging my weary feet.

The days went on like this, filled with misery, until, in 1960, my hat of "rightist element" was removed and I was allowed to return to Shanghai to work for the Shanghai branch of the Writers' Association. Actually, the removal of my hat did not substantially improve my treatment. My party membership was not reinstated and my lost wages were not restored; before the tag "rightist" they simply added one more word, "uncapped," and that was that. However, I used any favorable situation to fullest advantage. Stretching the good points and steering around the bad, I described for Comrade Li Ming, in rather exaggerated terms, how my political standing had improved, how much the party organization valued me, and so on, to cure her psychological wounds and restore her reason. A mental illness demands a mental cure. Li Ming believed every word I said, and her illness slowly abated. She was even able to return to work. She was assigned to a medical instruments factory not far from our home.

Having passed through this traumatic experience, the love that had always existed between us was lifted onto a still higher plane. In our spare hours, we read the *Romance of the Western Chamber* together out loud. I taught her to play chess and to appreciate Tang verse. Locomotives under full steam could never have pulled us apart. We grew still closer, inseparable.

In the past we had both held quite demanding jobs, so we had never experienced the conjugal happiness of being at leisure to enjoy our infatuation with art. It no longer mattered that one of us had lost his reputation. We had time enough now to make our dormitory quarters over into a secure and happy retreat, to ignore fully the political biases of the outside world, its senseless punishments, its mean, even fatal, abuses. Only once did I ever again provoke her to tears. It was when I carelessly recalled that she had slapped me while not in her right mind. Hearing my painful recollection, she turned ashen white and had to see the spot where she had struck me. "I'd never slapped you before. Did it hurt? Can you forgive me?" As she spoke, she bent over me and broke into tears. At the time I couldn't say a word. I knew only that my nose was twitching and my eyes were brimming with tears. I resolved never again to speak when distracted. "Don't look back": I soon learned through experience just how well put this phrase was.

In 1962, a spring breeze blew in from Guangzhou: at the Guangzhou Conference that year, Premier Zhou Enlai and Comrade Chen Yi delivered their speeches on the Three Nots and formulated a policy relaxing restrictions on art and literature, a policy that was an inspiration to all. Comrade Ye Yiqun told me the good news and encouraged me to take up my pen again and write. At first I was apathetic, even disheartened, about writing, having been involved in the labor movement for more than ten years. In the past I'd only done a bit of after-hours scribbling, never dreaming of the head-over-heels tumble my writing would kick off or the ensuing loss of party membership. I had sworn that from then on I would continue going to the factory and mixing with workers, that I would never again involve myself in such a dangerous avocation.

But I was also subject to various personal considerations. To get my articles published in the periodical press would be the greatest consolation for my Li Ming, medicine to close her gaping wounds. It would also enable me to let those friends who were so concerned about me know that Wang Ruowang was back on his feet again. By Chinese custom, for a writer to get published is equivalent to taking out an advertisement announcing that he is no longer an enemy of the people. It was on impulse, then, that I wrote "The History of One Big Pot." Working from my own impressions of the period of the Great Leap Forward and using the mildest and most subtly suggestive terms I could muster, I criticized the great iron-and-steel-smelting drive that called for peasants to smash the pots they used to cook their rice. The pot in the story was not smashed; on the contrary, the pot met with a glorious end. Heaven alone knows how sorely I taxed my heart and mind on this.

Comrade Li Ming looked over my rough draft without finding any fault in it. She simply kept asking me, "Are they really going to print it?"

"They will," I said.

"Smashing cooking pots for steel-smelting—it was madness, madder even than I ever was. Thank heaven you managed to write about it in such a round-about way." Li Ming's valuation of my short story was no more than this, but for me these simple remarks were the highest reward.

The story finally came out. My pride and happiness at reappearing in print far, far exceeded the joy I experienced when I first broke into print as a young man. They swept away every trace of the sorrowful, gray atmosphere that had come to cover our household, and seemed almost to be ushering in days of honor and glory. Our perceptive children all congratulated their papa on his new life. Laughter and happiness returned, all retrieved by "The History of One Big Pot." I myself was thrown into a dizzying headspin by my "victory." The pressure that had been weighing down on my heart lifted like a mist. Unaffected and artless as a child, I began humming "The Sky Over the Liberated Areas Is Bright."

One day in October 1962, a little over two months after the story's publication, I went home after work to await Li Ming so that we could have dinner together. It was just about seven o'clock and the sky had already darkened when she staggered through the door. The minute she saw me, tears welled up in her eyes. In a voice drained of all hope, she uttered, "It's all over," and threw herself on the sofa. She stiffened all over and began to cry like a child. Her face was alarmingly pale and her eyes were lifeless, just as in 1958. I was so worried I didn't know what to do. Softly I plied her with questions: "What is it? Are you sick again? Shall I take you to the hospital?"

Wresting her hand from mine, she said, "No, don't, don't pay any attention to me."

I had the children help their mother to bed and get her to lie down. Our eldest daughter automatically went to pour out water to take with medicine, but her mother waved her away, saying, "Don't pay any attention to me." Then she pulled the covers over her head and wept beneath the blankets.

I still didn't know what new calamity had descended on our home. The bright sky hadn't stayed long. Now black clouds spread thickly overhead again. China was beset by disaster; China's intelligentsia were beset by disaster; and Wang Ruowang and Li Ming were beset by disaster!

As it turned out, a citywide meeting of cadres had convened that afternoon at the Shanghai Exhibition Hall. The report of the secretary of the municipal party committee, the Boss of Shanghai, spoke exclusively of the spirit of the Tenth Plenum of the Eighth National People's Congress and its determination not to forget class struggle. Comrade Li Ming had attended this meeting and heard the secretary speak the following words:

"Shanghai's rightists are wriggling, getting ready to make their move. Wang Ruowang, for instance, who has just had his rightist hat removed, cocked his tail the moment he sensed a little disturbance. Recently he has written "The History of One Big Pot," a public attack on the Three Red Flags. Find a copy and look through it; you'll see for yourselves just how poisonous and how ingenious his attack is. Another piece of his that was printed in *Wenhuibao*, "In Praise of Little Electric Meters" (*Xiao huobiao zan*),[2] attacks socialist collectivization. When the proletariat unbends, the bourgeoisie strikes. Just imagine what would break out if we were to relax our class struggle."

For Li Ming, this was a crack of thunder on a clear day, a dagger thrust deep into her heart. The Boss of Shanghai was a big wheel who had made a career of attacking others; he had built his reputation on it. I had written my story with such restraint and given it such a bright ending. But in the airtight and wholly uniform ideological sphere of the times, keen noses still picked up the scent of barbs beneath the story's smooth surface. It was audacious enough to provoke heaven, perverse and treacherous heresy, a challenge to the Highest Authority, who was so sacred and inviolable. The Boss of Shanghai was known for two famous pronouncements: "Our faith in Chairman Mao must be no less than superstition," and "Our obedience to Chairman Mao must be blind." That short story of mine had touched a nerve in him. He had seized upon the new trend in class struggle and was effecting his denunciation on a grand scale, with drums sounding and flags unfurled. When he dropped a name at such a citywide meeting of cadres, it was tantamount to passing a death sentence on the one who bore it.

A roar had arisen in Li Ming's ears. A million gold stars filled her eyes, and

---

[2]A five-hundred-character essay published in *Wenhuibao* (Encounter daily, Shanghai), July 7, 1962, opposing the communal principle of letting everyone "eat from one big pot." Wang points out that households conserve electricity best when each household has its own meter.

they became a million eyes. Everyone at the conference, it seemed, recognized her. They stared at her, aware that Wang Ruowang's wife was at that very moment sitting in a corner of that great auditorium. A suffocating pressure bore down on her and blocked her breath. She left the meeting quietly and alone. Her spirit could not stand up to this sort of mortification, such a sudden attack. As if running from floodwaters rushing downstream, she left that damnable place, bringing away with her dread, perplexity, and resentment.

Li Ming quit the conference hall with labored steps, one hand on the wall for support. Already she was having trouble distinguishing one direction from another. As she crossed the street, she felt as if everyone recognized her. Her soul had fled her, she was stripped of her wits; she could only think of hiding from the eyes of everyone else on earth. Only this abject, pitiful wish got her home, as she hugged the wall and spent the last of her strength. By that time she was already displaying symptoms of schizophrenia.

She muttered deliriously—fitfully—between sobs: "Dear Wang, the snake's come out of his hole again. . . .You'd better prepare yourself, they won't let you off lightly this time. . . .

My heart was crushed and my blood coursed within it. My last remnants of love and warmth were destroyed by "One Big Pot." I had seen a strong, steadfast woman struggle to pull herself up out of misery, only to be violently and mercilessly beaten down again by a big stick.

My original purpose in getting into print had been to heal her broken heart and mind. Never did I dream that my story would be the blast that would finally destroy us: our home, the props of Li Ming's mental health, the pitiful hopes so recently arisen.

It was I who had harmed her, I who had incurred our ruin. It was I who had stubbornly made a show of my "antiparty ideology," thereby giving the Boss of Shanghai a handle by which to grab hold of me. I had been careful not to give him one; still, with a tiger's watchful eye he had found one. I bitterly regretted the rightist hat just removed from me. Why couldn't I have written something prudent, something circumspect, something that wouldn't have provided them with that handle? Why did I have to bare the scabs that had festered under the layers of poultices and plasters? Was I impatient with life? Was I bent on ruination, like a moth attracted to flame?

Earlier I had been able to stretch the good points and steer around the bad, concocting a fine set of circumstances to comfort Li Ming. Now I had no capital left to work with. She had heard the municipal committee secretary name me in public and knew the details better than I. She had experienced that terrifying feeling of suffocation herself. If only she'd been absent from that meeting and I had attended, everything might be all right now, I said to myself. Yet, if I had really been there to face that onslaught head-on from the start, suffering that storm of hailstones and ice—I'm afraid I wouldn't have been able to bear it either. But to let her bear the full force of the attack was just too cruel. I had become utterly helpless; I could do nothing but rally my wretchedness and despair to receive this calamity from heaven. My sole source of comfort was Li Ming's delirious raving, spoken in the midst of tears and weeping. The children couldn't understand it, but I got every word. Nor did they sound like the words of a woman out of her mind: she spoke with incisiveness, her intellect still lucid. She remained concerned about my fate! Even now, whenever I recall her voice crying "It's all over" as she walked through the door—it resounds in my ears with the regularity of a recording—it is the voice of helpless indignation, of someone wrestling with the madness of persecution, a voice that welcomes death.

Her schizophrenia took a much different form this time than it had in 1958 and 1959. This time around, she laughed without provocation or reason, and slept very little, even after taking sleeping tablets. She looked really horrid and pathetic during her mysterious fits of laughter. Once in a while she would have lucid moments. When I saw her combing her hair while reciting lines of Tang poetry, I decided she had recovered. It was as if shafts of sunlight were shining through the windows of our home again. Wild with delight, I hugged her, hot tears in my eyes. I took her to the movies, sang her favorite songs and Peking opera arias to her. I myself seemed transported to the time when we were first in love. I was just as young, just as energetic—I seemed to have forgotten all suffering and all distress.

If even a flash of joy and light appears in a life that has long been sunk in irremediable darkness, we feel we are gazing on the clouds and rainbows of a fine morning. We savor this joy to our heart's content; from it we glean a joy of living, and love, more precious and more honored than ever before.

When her mind was clear, she never spoke a word of reproach to me. As for that frightful "One Big Pot," she never brought it up again. With care and with caution she avoided touching my sensitive wounds.

Only once, when she was critically ill, did she earnestly warn me: "Listen to me just this once, for our children's sake: don't write anything ever again."

Because of complications arising from her psychosis, she grew as thin as a piece of kindling, nothing but bone. This strong body that during the war years could shoulder baskets on a pole, cross mountains, and ford streams, lived only to its forty-fifth year. In August 1964, still harboring feelings of injustice, she left us.

Li Ming, gone from me forever! Your life was sacrificed for the sake of my scribbling. A hundred deaths could never atone for this, the regret of my winter years. Now I've taken up my pen again, unable in this small instance to comply with your final exhortation. I can comfort you with the news that I have been rinsed clean of the filth and muck heaped on my head throughout those horrid years; not a trace remains. The frenzy of those bouts of mental illness is already past history. And the children, though they have suffered unendurable repercussions of all kinds, have grown up with sound and healthy bodies. I have taken up my pen again for the children's sake, that they might create an ideal world for coming generations, a land of contentment where one's spirit may be at peace. Perhaps this pen can still do a little good.

Comrade Li Ming was a female worker at Shanghai's Nanyang Cigarette Factory. She entered the factory at seven years of age. At eleven, she lost both her parents and took on the burden of supporting all four members of her family: her younger brother and sister, her maternal grandmother, and herself. At sixteen, she joined the revolution. She also joined the left-wing drama movement organized by comrades Cui Wei, Chen Huangmei, and Yao Shixiao, and she went on to become one of the workers' best loved performers. After the August Thirteenth Incident of 1937,[3] she left her home to go to Yan'an. She studied at the Central Party School and at China Women's College. In 1940 we married. In 1943, at the first meeting of the model workers conference held in the Shaanxi-Gansu-Ningxia border region, she was promoted to "labor hero"; and at the frontier region party representative assembly, she had the honor to be designated a "model worker." After Japan's surrender, she went to Shandong, where she served as deputy head of personnel for the Bohai District administrative office. When Ji'nan was liberated, she served as chief of personnel for the Ji'nan railway administration. After Shanghai was liberated, she served as chairman for the food workers' labor union and as party committee secretary for the electrical machinery company under the Bureau of Machines and Electricity, among other positions. . . .

Because "The History of One Big Pot" won me a reputation in 1962 as one who "repeatedly received instruction but would not change," I didn't publish a single word for the next seventeen years. Finally, in August 1979, I went to Zhuzhou to join my [second] wife, who had waited a full ten years for me. There I put aside a month of my new life of hard-earned quiet to write the *Hunger Trilogy* (*Ji'e sanbuqu*). Not long after it appeared, a publication up north ran a review article that only granted one sentence to this novella: "Some of his fiction depicts the eating of insects and toads, which, it must be pointed out, is a naturalistic tendency." . . .

This explains why, then, I have held back so much in "portraying the truth," although such restraint on the part of writers appears to aid neither the revolutionary cause nor the growth and advancement of art and literature. It only goes to show the importance of a writer remaining true to life in his works, and how easy it is to talk of writers and editors having to remain faithful to reality.

But I have wandered too far from the point; let me break off here.

"Qianyan" (Preface), August 1981, in Wang Ruowang, *Yanbuzhu de guangmang* (Unsuppressible streaks of light) (Beijing, 1983), pp. 1–15.

—Translated by Deborah Rudolph

---

[3]The beginning of the Japanese attack on Shanghai, and therefore of the 1937 Sino-Japanese War in the South.

Feng Jicai

"THE GREAT FENG," as the two-meter-tall one-time athlete Feng Jicai (b. 1942, in Tianjin) has been called by his friends, is known for the brilliant caricatures he draws; perhaps his writing, too, has benefited from years of experience copying traditional paintings. Feng is also interested in creating an independent literary criticism in China, and he proved well-versed in Western music and art during interviews in Germany in 1986.

Of particular impact was Feng Jicai's short novel *A!* (Oh!, 1980). While depicting scholars' secret intrigues and mutual ruination in a Chinese historical institute of the post-1957 era, it weaves a symbolic tale of the inner destruction of scholarship, describing bureaucratic society under communism so powerfully that the Soviet Sinologist Boris Riftin's translation of it went far to reawaken his country's interest in current Chinese literature.

Feng Jicai's essay below expresses a sense that he has a duty to break the Chinese wall of silence around the Cultural Revolution: in deference to his friends who died, and as a warning for later generations. He has, like the responsible writers who emerged from the Soviet Gulag, decided to act as *historian*—for, as *Oh!* indicates, professional historians can neither resist the trends of politics nor pursue their professional duties.

A Written Testimonial
About the Cultural Revolution

Feng Jicai

January 20, 1981, in Tianjin

THE EARLIEST footprints I left on the path of literature were a disorderly hodge-podge—some deep, others shallow, some pointing forward, others retreating backward—as if impressed with intense unwillingness, constraint, and hesitancy. How did this all come about?

Before the wild disorders of 1966 arrived, my world resembled the ocean on the eve of a storm. Not the slightest premonition or ill omen made its presence felt; in an expanse of extraordinary tranquility, warm sunlight caressed the softly and rhythmically undulating waves of my life. I was only a bit over twenty at the time and I had a passion for art. I was the most tractable captive Chopin, Tchaikovsky, or Beethoven had ever taken. Alone in my room, I loudly recited Bo Juyi's "Song of Everlasting Sorrow," Li Bo's "Hard Roads to Sichuan," or Pushkin's "Ode to the Sea." Finally, in a spirit of splendid self-sacrifice, I decided to dissolve every moment of the rest of my life in the artist's palette. Boats amidst rain, birds atop branches, flowers thrust up from the soil, indistinct but vibrant faces in the twilight—all these things held me securely in front of my easel. I couldn't imagine ever leaving it.

However, like a huge and inescapable hammer arcing downward from Heaven, the sudden calamity of 1966 smashed my world into smithereens. Overnight, the fate of tens of millions drastically changed. Families in the tens of millions acted out weird tragedies never before seen even in books. Facial expressions, postures, and gestures that had once caught my eye now lost all significance for me; what appeared before me now was one naked heart after another, each washed red by a tumultuous political tide. These hearts were hidden without a trace in the most inaccessible reaches of the body. Some were more beautiful than precious stones, others were uglier than demons. The world would never again see such a vast gulf between one person and another, a gulf between human hearts.

Reality forced me into unrelenting alertness, cautiousness, and evasive behavior: a necessary condition for existence amidst the social entanglements threatening me on all sides like a forest of sword blades. From that time forward, those dappled landscapes, bird songs, and flowery fragrances of days gone by dissipated like a winsome dream.

There is a place on the banks of the Hai River in Tianjin called Gua Jia Temple. Now and then during summertime, someone would get careless while swimming there and drown; the corpse would be hauled onto the riverbank for the family of the deceased to claim. But during the Cultural Revolution, it seemed that no day passed without somebody committing suicide in that river; the corpse would be fished out with an iron hook bound to the end of a long pole, then hung up in a row with others as a warning to the public. The two long mats hung up to cover the corpses' heads soon grew insufficient. Bystanders could hardly bear to look at the faces protruding from underneath. Some of the cadavers were old; others were young; some were women who had taken with them an infant strapped to their waist. As I stared in horror at these people who had so cruelly done away with themselves, I realized that their hearts must have held hidden anguish and suffering that they could not overcome. Then there was the toppled chair used as a platform by a man who had hanged himself. The many footprints left by the deceased as they paced in indecision made me shudder.

At such times, I often found myself constructing life stories for those hapless souls. Of course, it is possible that my imaginings bore no relation to their real lives. Still, the things I heard about and witnessed in daily life at that time created a multitude of impressions, and they crowded in upon the stories I was constructing. Once a story had begun to take shape in my mind and had turned over and over in my thoughts, I would experience an intense desire to express it.

At first, I told these stories only to close relatives and good friends. To keep out of harm's way, I transplanted the stories' characters, locales, and social milieux to various foreign settings, as if they were really old foreign novels or movie scripts. A number of close relatives and good friends listened to my stories. Since the nation's cultural activity was a virtual nullity at the time, they were more than happy to be my audience. I, however, told stories to vent my desire for expression and as a distraction from pent-up feelings. Little did I know that these recitations were my works of the future, in embryonic form.

One evening, as a cold wind blew outdoors, an old friend whom I hadn't seen for years suddenly hurried up to my house. Before I could open my mouth he had launched into a long and unbroken tale of his strange misfortunes. I listened to him with tears in my eyes, unaware that the cigarette between my fingers had long since gone out.

While my friend narrated his misfortunes in a spate of nervous anxiety, I began to fear that he might go off half-cocked and do something awful after he got home. When he'd finished his tale, he suddenly asked me in a voice that trembled with excitement, "Tell me, will future generations know about the kind of life we've had? The kind of things we've been through? If things just keep going on this way without change, in another few decades all of us alive now will be dead; won't future generations have to rely on authors who make up stories about us out of thin air? Tell me, is there anybody nowadays who's writing these things down? If you did, you'd be taking your life in your hands, wouldn't you? Still, it would be of value to future generations."

What an age that was!

We both grew silent. Our unextinguished cigarette butts in the ashtray sent out thread-like wisps of smoke that curled around the dim lamp. It was as if that story of his had started each of us on his own long train of thought. That was the day I first thought of writing down my stories.

I locked myself in my room and started writing on the sly. If anyone knocked on the door, I would immediately put down my pen and hide anything I'd written. Had someone discovered even a line or two of it, not only would I have been a goner, my family would have been wiped out as well; one couldn't bear even to imagine such things.

Whenever a new rectification campaign got underway, I would hide my writings under bricks in the courtyard, or stuff them between cracks in the floorboards; I might even paste a pile of them together and glue them to the backside of a propaganda poster, waiting for the day when I could soak the whole mass in warm water and peel the sheets off page by page.

Nonetheless, a person who hides things never feels that any place is safe. Once I rolled up a manuscript of mine and stuffed it into one of the bars of my bicycle frame. During workdays this bike was at my workplace, which went into an uproar one day because of a directive that we search each other for "leads on enemy spies." I kept thinking that somebody would pounce on the bike and pull my manuscript out of the frame. Anxiety wracked me the entire day. On returning home, I stealthily took it out and burned it to ashes. This at once calmed me, but with that came a feeling of dejection and amazement over what I had done.

Later, whenever an uncontrollable impulse to write welled up within me, the ink would hardly be dry before I'd tear my writing into shreds and flush them down the toilet. In winter, I wrote next to the stove; when I'd finished a manuscript, I'd softly read it through, at least until I got an emotional response out of myself, and usually a few more times after that. Yet in the end I'd have no choice but to toss it regretfully into the stove. When the dancing flames had reduced those pages onto which I'd poured my thoughts to thin layers of ash, my heart itself felt pierced by the scorching flames.

Along that far-reaching road that ended no one knew where, everyone proceeded with hesitation and vigilance. But such thoughts were of little comfort. My writing had been futile, a waste of energy! What was the use of writing something you couldn't publish, show to anybody else, even keep for yourself? What a foolish endeavor. What silly impetuosity. What unrealizable yearnings. Yet what pained me most were times like these, when I suddenly turned cold and rational, negating the value of my own actions.

I needed to look within myself to find energy enough to restore my sense of wholeness. Thereupon I discovered that I did have a conscience, that I loved my country and its people, and that I had been quietly doing my small part on behalf of my country's future. Moreover, I had the conscience of an artist; I hadn't written for profit or pursued fads that went against my personal convictions. I adored literature and would allow no low, selfish cravings to sully it.

I no longer destroyed each page that I had written. I made a resolution to follow my own bent, no matter what might lie ahead, or how far off the "bright future"; no matter how burdensome and lonely my literary path or how great the obstacles and hidden misfortunes before me. I still have the poem I wrote to myself on the occasion of this resolution. It is entitled "A Path":

> Each person must tread his own path, must not meddle with others;
> here is the kind of path I've chosen:
> a path sometimes of joy, sometimes of suffering;
> a path bristling with thorns, and riddled with gullies;
> a path that's unbounded where it's wide, and scary where it's narrow;
> a path arduous to climb, and dangerous to slip down from;
> a path without end, nor any home to return to;
> a path without signposts, nor any place to ask directions;
> a path that sometimes breaks off, growing nearly invisible.
>
> Yet I am resolved to travel this path,
> for it is a true path.

When I think back on it now, these were indeed my first steps along the path of literature.

While in southern Yunnan the year before last, I was entranced by my first encounter with the grandeur of nature in the tropics. It was a deeply moving experience to see the giant thatched-roof dwellings of the Hani people, the bamboo lodges of the Dai people, the gorgeous short skirts of the Miao women, all amid stands of palm, plantain, and bamboo, with kapok wafting down like snowflakes, amid the shadows of blue mountains. Before I knew it, my old desire to paint had reawakened. As soon as I returned home to Tianjin, I retrieved the painting supplies I had put aside for so long and simply stayed indoors and painted for several days. Some of my friends must have suspected that I was about to return to my old profession. No, I merely felt possessed for a while. Fictional characters submerged deep in my consciousness began to well up, torturing me day and night. I put away my painting materials, wiped my desk clean, and brought out a new stack of writing paper.

Yes, it seems I left my treasured calling of painting and switched to literature at the prompting of fate. And not just my own fate, but the collective fate of my people, my nation, and my era. I still cannot explain this word "fate," yet I have strongly felt its presence.

"Mingyun de qushi" (At the prompting of fate), Tianjin, January 20, 1981, in *Wenxue zhi lu* (The path of literature) (Changsha, 1983), pp. 82–87.

—Translated by Philip Williams

Cong Weixi

CONG WEIXI was one of the first to write about life in prisons and concentration camps during China's ultra-leftist period under Mao Zedong, in "Daqiang xia de hong yulan" (Blood-stained magnolias under the towering walls, December 1978). It was a daring piece in those days, and Cong Weixi has come under pressure again since the June 1989 massacre; he had to resign as editor of the Zuojia Chubanshe (Writers' Press) in Peking. His writing has limitations, however; this text was selected to show how far a fearful and obedient writer such as Cong Weixi or Liu Shaotang is able to estrange himself from modern concepts and ideals of the writing profession, by listening to his political "masters' voice." Cong Weixi is proud *not* to be compared with Solzhenitsyn, who also knit together the multifarious life stories of those who disappeared in his country's Gulag, but to more dissident effect. In the mid-1980s, Cong continued to write about prison camp life, as in *Feng lei yan* (The eye that cries in the wind, 1986). Some of his works make camp life seem a redeeming, almost romantic, experience. Cong Weixi's account below thus may be read as a kind of antitext, showing the limitations of a generation that became weak and timid under the pressures of a lifetime. It also explains why the youngest generation of writers must be considered the most promising group.

I Am Not Solzhenitsyn

From an Eyewitness of the Labor Camps

Cong Weixi

1983, in Peking

DEAR Yan Huo,

In March 1982 I was in a hurry both times as I passed through Hong Kong on my way to and from Australia. My failure to reply to your questions about my creative writing really was due to the pressure of time, as I'm sure you understand. Shortly after my return home, I received another letter from you with questions for me in several areas. Frankly, I feel very frightened, like a primary school student facing an examination. My intellectual capacity often pushes my grades into the negative numbers. Though I have written several articles about my creative writing in recent years, most of them are but fragments; I haven't reflected upon my writing career in a systematic way. . . .

I've been employed at all sorts of work, both inside the reform-through-labor "Towering Walls" [as we call our outdoor "Big Houses"], and out. I've mined iron and coal; operated bleaching machines at a chemical plant; done lathe work and mill work; baked bricks in a kiln; driven horse carts; worked in the rice fields; and tended a garden. The work scenes in my stories such as "Blood-Stained Magnolias under the Towering Walls" are more of a self-portrait than a description of others. Severe tests of my stamina and conviction followed one after another; the excess of pressure, spiritual as well as physical, nearly crushed us. The greatest burden was knowing that my wife was in a labor camp, too. Only my old mother and my newborn son were left at home. . . .

During the Cultural Revolution, the tides of extreme leftism pushed my wife and me up into Shanxi Province. Only then did we begin to live under the same roof again. Beside our pillow we always placed a book by the revolutionary martyr Fang Zhiming—*Beloved China*. You could say this was the spiritual sustenance and spiritual armament that spurred us on. My story "The Umbrella" is basically about our life "then." Besides *Beloved China*, the books that followed me from one "post" to another were Sun Li's *Lotus Lake*, M. A. Sholokhov's *Virgin Soil Upturned*, volume 2, Gogol's *Taras Bulba*, and the works of Belinsky. They were the favorite books of my youth. Under the heavy yoke of my new life, however, my literary interests changed. I spent more time with Jack London's *The Call of the Wild* and Hugo's *Les Misérables*. I liked the solemnity and depth of those two novels very much, particularly the driving and sweeping tragic forces in Hugo. If my novellas published after the downfall of the "Gang of Four," such as "Blood-Stained Magnolias under the Towering Walls," "Muddy," "Forgotten Footprints on the Beach," and "White Sails Afar," evidence an abrupt change in my style, this is first of all owing to my miserable life, and second to the influence of Hugo. While reading about Jean Valjean and Fantine, I would burst into tears and then jump up in indignation.

During those many hard years of my life, I kept some uplifting aphorisms deep in my heart.

A great Russian critic once said: "Hardship is the best university." I wrote this down. Balzac said: "Hardship is a teacher." This, too, I wrote down. Thackeray had a character in *Vanity Fair* voice a philosophy of life for trying times: "Life is like a mirror: you weep and it weeps with you: you laugh and it laughs back at you." I used these words to encourage myself to be strong instead of dispirited, above all not to consent to my own degeneration.

Perhaps because so many forces were driving me forward even during reform-through-labor—at the very lowest level of society—I still experienced vague creative impulses. This was only "playing sweet music under a castor-oil tree," or seeking pleasure amid bitterness, yet it provided me with one of my few spiritual comforts. In 1963 I was a citizen again, excused from the rest of my sentence and with my "rightist hat" taken off, because of good conduct. I submitted a story, "Caifeng Takes Up the Challenge," to the journal *Chinese Women*, and I was told by the editorial office that it was well written and would be run; but not long after, the editors wrote me a long letter. Reading between the lines, I could see that they sympathized with me but were gently telling me that for various reasons the story would not be printed. From this episode I learned that I was not yet a true citizen, but a "citizen" under the dictatorship [of the people]. After that, though creative ideas often flashed through my mind, I stored and froze them—I kept my pen still. Up until 1975, when the movement to counter the "rightist trend of reversing correct verdicts" was at its peak, I felt virtually suffocated as a victim of the extreme left. On a reform-through-labor farm by the Yellow River, I spent seven nights writing a somewhat autobiographical novella, "White Sails Afar" (published in *Harvest*, 1982). The direct stimulus for that work was a very good reform-through-labor brigade leader whom I met there. That got me to thinking of another character who was incredibly "leftist," brigade leader Luo. The story took place in "the great western wasteland," as your letter indicates. One day, they were looking for "dirty" books. I opened my suitcase and handed Luo a collection of my old stories, *Dawn*, and *Mother*, by Gorky. I wasn't surprised that he confiscated my writings, but I couldn't stand to see him take away *Mother*.

I said, "This is by Gorky."

He replied, "Gorky, Whoreky, take it away!"

I said, "Lenin himself praised this book."

He said, "A good foreign book hasn't been written. They're all banned."

I said, "*The Communist Manifesto* was written by foreigners."

He yelled at me, "You rightists are too much!"

So it happened that power won out over truth, and knowledge was swallowed up by ignorance. I still vividly remember this "scene." As the man and a long string of his antics came back to me, I took up my pen. I put the amusing dialogue above directly into my story, without changing a word.

This example suffices to show that my twenty years of life at the bottom of the heap gave me some experiences denied to most writers. After 1957, I sank to "the ocean floor" like a bull forced under water when it refuses to drink. But collecting pearls and coral at "the bottom" benefited me much more than gathering kelp while floating on the surface, or collecting shells on the beach. The tuition was high, though—twenty years of the prime of my life. On my return to writing, my teacher Sun Li encouraged me in a letter: "In all these years, you've lost something but gained something else; from the literary point of view, you gained more than you lost." He was right. I'm a rich man when it comes to life experience.

In his article "We Need Novelettes," Comrade Kong Luosun praised "Blood-Stained Magnolias under the Towering Walls" as pushing the novella forward to the front line of our era, just as Liu Xinwu's "The Homeroom Teacher" had done for the short story (see *October*, 1981). I took this as encouragement for my generation, from its elders. But what I find especially comforting is that my "Blood-Stained Magnolias" was published right before the meeting of the Third Plenum of the Eleventh Central Committee of the Chinese Communist party. It was the first story of prisoners' lives, but it was also in line with the new spirit of the Third Plenum; besides, it offered a vivid picture of a dark period in New China's history.

I'm stupid; I believe in life rather than in "inspiration." My other novellas that have had a strong impact, such as "Muddy," "Forgotten Footprints on the Beach," and "White Sails Afar," were drawn not from fictive flashes of "inspiration" in a meditative moment, but from my solid experience of life. Artistic creation is not of course mechanical photography; it needs artistic processing. Yet the characters in these novellas are based on real life. Some of them even have prototypes.

I put my life during the hard years into fiction so as to be able to "reflect" on history and express my loves and hatreds, so that the historical tragedy of that time may never be repeated. I insist that my works be true to historical reality, without either prettifying or distorting life. In my view, when a writer's subjectivity overbalances objective truth, his work is likely to go to one of two extremes: a literature of lies that creates myths like the ones about five-thousand-kilogram-per-mu harvests during the "Great Leap Forward," or a distortion of the true nature of life that paints everything in the history of New China black. Both of these tendencies contradict literary realism, so I shun them.

During my last visit to Australia, a foreign Sinologist had a conversation with me about my fiction writing:

"I've read several of your tragic stories," he said.

"What do you think of them?" I asked.

"I've been to China. Your writings reflect historical reality to a certain degree, but they are not quite like the novels of life in prison by Solzhenitsyn.

"I'm glad of that."

"Why?" he asked, rather puzzled.

"Frankly speaking, I think Solzhenitsyn's subjectivism overbalances the objective truth. He was so full of anger that he didn't create any morally good characters. The domestic and foreign policies carried out by the Soviet ruling clique fly in the face of historical development, but you can't say that there isn't a good man in any corner of the Soviet social structure. Would you call that real life?

"Which of his books are you referring to?" he asked.

"*Cancer Ward*, for instance," I said. "Only the doctor is a good man. All the rest are stupid, unfeeling, cold-blooded animals. Would you call that objective truth? Or the hysteria of Solzhenitsyn's anger?"

"But how did you come to write about the life of reform-through-labor?" he asked.

I answered him very clearly: "In handling this tragic subject, I closely associated my personal sufferings with the fate of my motherland. So the victims in my stories, like Gao Shui in 'Muddy,' Lu Buqing in 'Footprints,' Ge Ling in 'Blood-Stained Magnolias,' and my own image in 'White Sails,' are all patriots. In writing about my past experiences, I didn't omit the evil characters, nor did I forget the good cadres. Those good comrades helped me and consoled me when I was miserable. They gave me spiritual light."

He asked, half-doubtingly, "Can you support this with some real examples?"

I only told the Sinologist one story: When I first went to the reform-through-labor camp, a cadre took away my Parker pen. Later, as our brigade was shifted from one place to another, I completely forgot about that pen. Quite coincidentally, I later happened to mention it while chatting with another cadre. Shortly afterward, the Parker pen was retrieved. The cadre enclosed a long letter, the end of which moved me very much. "Have faith in history," he said. "Some day you will take up this pen again. Real gold can survive melting. . . ." I told the

Sinologist that stories of this kind were not rare in the reform-through-labor apparatus. A leader who was in charge of reforming the "rightists" ended up becoming friends with many of them. Not long after my return to Peking, I paid him a special visit to express my gratitude for his spiritual support during my most difficult years. Sitting together over tea like brothers, we chatted about the past.

The Sinologist was moved.

I said, "Imagine writing about my bitter life in the past without including these characters. Would that be true to life? Some Western critics evaluate Chinese literary works only in terms of politics, not as literature, as if only dark portraits of life can be true. This of course is due to their politics. So, when Solzhenitsyn was awarded the Nobel Prize, I'd call it more of a political prize than a literary prize."

The Sinologist smiled. He agreed with my conclusion.

Yan Huo, that's the principle of "being true to life" I follow in my writing. I write about both the sunlight and the darkness of life. It's common knowledge that every era is full of struggles between light and darkness. The historic battles of the Ten-Year Calamity just past were but the moments of peak eruption during those struggles.

You will easily see that my present literary pursuit differs greatly from my past pursuit of the poetic and the picturesque. I believe that to limit a writer to offering people entertainment and aesthetic experience is to set a low standard for his social role. Only when a writer is fully imbued with the historic events of his day and pushes the tides of life forward can his standards be called high. . . .

"Wenxue de meng—Da Yan Huo" (The dream of literature—In answer to Yan Huo), Beijing, 1983, in *Huacheng* 21 (April 1983): 160–67.

—Translated by Zhang Yingjin

Dai Houying

DAI HOUYING (b. 1938, in Anhui) is famous for her novels *Shiren zhi si* (The death of a poet, 1982) and *Ren a, ren!* (Oh, humankind!, 1981, also translated under the title *Stones of the Wall*), the former a realistic novel, the latter an ostensibly modernist, but still rather sentimental, venture. She was unfairly attacked during the official 1983–84 campaign against "spiritual pollution," yet she has continued writing an epic trilogy of historical fiction set in her native corner of China, *Liulei de Huai He* (Tears of the Huai River, 1988–89).

The text that follows is the postscript to *Oh, Humankind!*, a novel that describes the fate of intellectuals from the 1950s until the late 1970s. Regrettably, both the English and German translations of the novel have omitted this afterword. It documents the writer's awakening and remorse after a stormy leftist career, harshly criticizing the "class struggle" exercises that misled an entire generation. The author feels she was duped during her youth, and that she eventually became a victim of the late Cultural Revolution. The reader may judge whether her plea for more "humanism" within the existing system, a concept she attacked as a student, is fully convincing—or as convincing as her claim to be a modernist writer.

On Behalf of Humanism
The Confession of a Former Leftist

Dai Houying

August 1980, in Guangzhou

TWENTY years ago, I graduated early from Shanghai's East China Normal University and stepped into the stormy and disaster-ridden literary arena. Ignorance and blind obedience gave me confidence and strength. I thought I already had a good grasp of the basic principles of Marxism-Leninism and a correct understanding of society and humanity. I stood on the rostrum and loudly read out the speech I had prepared according to my leaders' desires, criticizing the humanism that my teachers had advocated. I said, "I love my teachers, but I love truth more!"[1] The applause that then filled the hall was intoxicating; I felt proud to have become such a "warrior."

Now, on this day twenty years later, I have just finished writing a novel. In this novel I want to advocate precisely those things that I criticized in the past; I want to pour out nothing other than the "human essence" that I formerly tried so hard to suppress and remold. For me, this is a fact filled with irony.

A philosopher could explain my transformation in a single phrase—I've gone through a "negation of negation."[2] But I am not a philosopher, just an ordinary person with normal sensory organs. So what I perceived was the fate of my country and its people, my loved ones and myself. What a bloody, tearful, heartbreaking fate. And what I also saw was the tortuous course followed by a whole generation of intellectuals. That bitter, seemingly endless course!

I was once a sincere and naïve adolescent, with a head full of nothing but love for the party and the New China, and a desire to study diligently and serve the

---

[1]Modified quotation from Aristotle, *Nichomachean Ethics*, book 1, chap. 6.
[2]A phrase from Hegel that is cited in Mao Zedong's "On Contradiction."

people. My feelings for the party and socialism were totally genuine, because the liberation of my country opened up a road for me that former generations of my family had never traveled—I became the first woman to study, and the first person to receive a complete higher education. How the bright vistas of socialism and communism attracted and aroused my youthful heart. I firmly believed that our cause was righteous, our future bright, our path smooth. Without a care, selfless, and fearless, my heart overflowed with warmth and comradely affection.

In 1957 a new sinew vibrated in my heart: "class struggle." And then in 1966 another: "two-line struggle."

I strove to comprehend and "stretch tight the sinews of class struggle." I became a "little bombardier" in "mass criticism sessions," a "revolutionary rebel" for the "red commanders." I devoutly believed that in the world of men, class struggle was all. Year after year, month after month, day after day—never could we forget class struggle.

But I was after all a human being, and my senses were not numb; therefore I could feel the bumps in the road, I could see the traces of blood on people's bodies, the tear stains on their faces. And these people included me and my loved ones. Still I didn't dare, didn't want, to doubt the ultraleft line, yet I began to feel the stirrings of conscience, to hear the moaning of my soul. Often in the depths of my heart I asked myself: is our struggle going too far? Have we wronged any good people unjustly? Is there really a need to incite this incessant, relentless "class struggle" and "two-line struggle" on our Chinese soil?

As the struggle to expose the Gang of Four intensified, I found out many things I hadn't known and could never even have imagined. Suddenly in the midst of all this, I felt my faith shaking, as the pillars of my spiritual life began to collapse. I could not see anything clearly. Often, all alone, I would fall into a daze, a stupor, or cry and scream hysterically. How I wanted to seize hold of those gods I had worshiped and those people who made such an effort to fill my heart with idols. I would demand to know: Did all of this really happen? Then why did you say otherwise, at the time? Was it deliberate deception or was it a "process of cognition"?[3]

For a time, my soul remained in darkness.

It was the discussions about "practice as the sole criterion for testing truth" that led me from darkness into the light. It became clear to me that each of us, whether man, ghost, or god, was being tightly gripped by the huge hand of history and made to face up to the test of practice. All of us had to hand over our own book of deeds, offer up our souls, and stretch out our hands under the full light of day to see if we were tainted with blood or with dust. I am as insignificant as a blade of grass, but we are all equal before history. I, too, have to settle accounts, bring my soul to trial, cleanse my own two hands. Render to God the things that are God's, render to the devil the things that are the devil's. And

[3]A phrase from Mao Zedong.

what's mine, bravely hoist onto my shoulders, or even engrave upon my face.

From that moment, I began to reflect, to bind up those wounds that still oozed blood, even as I began dissecting my own soul. I perused my own history page by page, examined the footsteps I had trodden one by one.

And in the end, I recognized that all along I had been playing a tragic role in what had seemed to be a comedy: I had thought myself free when totally deprived of freedom of thought; showed off my spiritual shackles as if they were a beautiful necklace; and lived half my life without knowing or finding myself. I departed from that script and discovered myself. So all this time I was really a woman of flesh and blood who could love and hate, have feelings and desires, and think for herself. I ought to appreciate my own worth and not allow myself to be belittled, or abandon myself to being "an obedient tool." A single word in capital letters quickly appeared before my eyes: "HUMANKIND"! A song long ago forgotten and cast aside arose in my throat: human nature, human feelings, humanism.

I was like one just awakened from a bad dream. Although still wet with cold sweat, and not recovered from my fright, at least I was awake. And I wanted to proclaim my awakening to my fellow man, so I set about writing fiction. The year before last [1978], I wrote a novel called *The Death of a Poet* (*Shiren zhi si*), and this year I have written *Oh, Humankind!* (*Ren a, ren!*). The common theme of these works is "humanity." I have written of human blood and tears, of bitter groans from wronged souls, of sparks from the heart that burst forth in the darkness. Passionately I shouted, "Come back, oh soul,"[4] and with limitless joy I recorded human nature's return to life.

I have never read all of Marx's or Engels's works, still less have I made a special study of Marxism-Leninism, but from the few volumes that I have read, I believe that Marxism and humanism are one and the same. Even if I can't find a theoretical basis in any of the classic works, I do not want to suppress the voice in my heart. If it deserves to be criticized, then let it be criticized. It is after all my own thoughts and feelings. Even more, it is the expression of myself, freely offered. I have only myself to blame, so I shall take my punishment without complaint.

Whenever things reach one extreme, they are bound to reverse course. These days I am not a bit afraid of being associated with "self-expression." I am not afraid that people will ferret a "self" out of my works, still less am I afraid to take responsibility for this "self." Is it not because one wants to express something unique from one's experience that one picks up a pen to write? I am afraid that trying to cut off or draw a clear line between artistic creation and self-expression is only a delusion, or due to ignorance of [the nature of] art. The whole crux of the matter is the relationship between the self the author wants to present

---

[4]Quotation from the *Summons of the Soul* in the ancient poetry anthology *Chu ci* (Songs of the South), attributed to Qu Yuan.

and her people and her era. I believe that in life and in combat, an author should strive to forget herself and blend with the masses in a common cause. She should breathe with the people and share their fate. All her emotions and her judgments should be intimately linked with theirs. In this way, the "self" that she wants to express will be the manifestation of a concrete, individualized "self" of the masses. When she creates, however, an author must on no account forget herself. She should probe herself to the greatest extent possible, and express her own special impressions and opinions. She must sing with her own voice, and speak in her own language. An author standing before the people is like an infant appearing before its mother just after birth, completely naked and unashamed to bear traces of blood and fluid from the womb; it opens its big mouth and screams, not worrying how miserable its wrinkly little face looks. There is nothing to be ashamed about; joy and sorrow, beauty and ugliness have always been inseparable, brought into being with life itself.

Engaging in theoretical work on art for many years before taking up the pen, and now again engaging in the teaching of artistic theory, can be compared to "becoming a nun late in life" and "practicing the monastic life without undergoing tonsure"—inevitably, it's hard to "give up the worldly life" completely. When I'm in the midst of creation, I often can't help thinking of artistic theory. When I was writing *Oh, Humankind!*, I was particularly conscious of getting into theoretical questions as I went.

As I look at the great artists of the past and present, both Chinese and foreign, it seems to me that they are almost always great thinkers, too, even great philosophers. Isn't it a lack of penetrating thought and deep insight into life that produces stereotypes and generalizations? I am a teacher of artistic theory, so I can't help but come into contact with a great number of theoretical works in literature, philosophy, and even political economy. When I am creating, I can't just lay down a law that makes these concepts and logic temporarily recede into the background, giving their place over to some nebulous sort of "imagistic thinking." So I adopt this attitude: I allow thoughts and logic full play, to help me know and analyze life and even structure the content of my work. Usually, when some small experience occurs in my life, it is only after reflection that I come to feel it worthy of expression. I can't by any means enter into the creative process immediately. Only when I have a relatively clear understanding of a great many phenomena—that is, when I have a theme—can I begin writing. Not only does thought not hinder the movement of my imagination and feelings, it gives them impetus. I am a person who gets excited very easily, even more so in the midst of creative writing. However, I've never lost the sobriety of my reason. I always analyze and reflect upon what I have written. At times I even interrupt my work to read a little theory. I believe that the more thoroughly I understand what I'm writing, the more powerfully intense my emotion will be.

I certainly do not deny that artistic creation is made up of extremely complex mental phenomena. Our research and inquiries into them are woefully inadequate—on, for example, the function of imagination in constructing artistic forms; the laws governing imagination and its nurture; and the way inspiration takes shape, as well as its importance and function in art. In the ferment of artistic creation, what is the interplay of the author's subjective intention and the objective facts of life? What about the mutual interaction of the author's intellect and feelings? How do the author's life experience, level of cultural attainment, and unique personality traits become an individual style? And so on and so forth. There should be a branch of study set up to do research on these issues, called "mental phenomenology of art," or "psychology of art."

It is quite understandable that realism was put on a pedestal after the downfall of the "Gang of Four," to bring art back to life and pursue artistic truth. But I keep wondering if realism is the only method for arriving at artistic truth. This question cannot be answered categorically.

If imitation of life were the only true artistic understanding, then no doubt realism's method of "describing life by using life's original form" would be the best, and realistic art would be the truest art. Artistic truth is not an imitation of real life, however, but a true reflection that an author can get from real life. Strictly speaking, the highest duty of artistic creation is not to reproduce reality authentically, but to express truthfully and imagistically the author's or artist's knowledge, attitude, and feeling toward reality. The highest reality that art seeks is not simply true-to-life description, but a more accurate and vivid expression of a true understanding of life. It may seem that I am deliberately playing a game with concepts, but really I am not; I want to emphasize the importance of the author's subjective world in artistic creation, and of mobilizing all his or her artistic methods to manifest that world.

The realistic method, using the original appearance of life to reflect life, is of course one method an author can use to express his or her knowledge and attitude toward life. But certainly it is not the only method, or even necessarily the best. Some of an author's thoughts and emotions can be concretely expressed in a realistic way, but some cannot. Why did the author of *Journey to the West*, Wu Cheng'en, want to create fantastic ghosts and goblins like Sun Wukong? Why did Cao Xueqin want to write about a Realm of the Great Void beyond the real world in *The Dream of the Red Chamber*? Both did so to express more fully their own subjective world view. In the West, after the intellectual tide of realism subsided, modernist art arose. The rubric of modernism includes many different schools, holding very disparate views, but the most important or basic tendency shared by all is to adopt an abstract, fantastic method to counter realism. In the past, we Chinese categorically rejected modernist art; now we are beginning to analyze it scientifically, but as soon as anyone mentions drawing lessons from it, there are still comrades who endlessly shake their heads and say, "Why should we study bourgeois art?" I must reluctantly point out that comrades holding this opinion are forgetting that we have been studying bourgeois artistic methods all along, except that we only studied them in their ancestral and antiquated forms. I don't wish to analyze here the "factors of time and class" in the birth and rise of modernism. All I want to say is that serious modern artists are seeking artistic truth, too, and they correctly perceive that the methods of realism are hampering their pursuit of it. Only because of this do they launch artistic innovations. They strive for complete expression of their own subjective perceptions and knowledge of the truth of the world, while the realistic method advocates "objectivity" and self-concealment by the author. Realism carried to extremes becomes objectivism or naturalism. Obsessive and detailed objectivity engulfs or suppresses the author's subjective vision, and naturally an author opposes this. Therefore, speaking simply from the standpoint of art, the rise of modernism has its inevitability; it is both a denial of realism by modernist authors and also realistic art's negation of itself.

Today, the situation we are facing is this: now that we have passed through the Ten-Year Calamity, the ranks of authors and the spiritual state in which they find themselves are greatly changed. We have entered an age of deep reflection, an age of transformation. Everyone is thinking things over, each has his or her own unique experiences and feelings. And each has her own demands and fantasies that she is impatient to tell others. Can the increasing prevalence of a lyrical and philosophical flavor in the works of these past few years be wholly accidental? Obviously, some comrades already feel that realism's traditional methods are inadequate to express their thoughts and feelings, and thus inadequate to express our age. They have begun artistic exploration and innovation, and what's more, they have produced concrete achievements. But there are still a great many young comrades who find it hard to publish their works, although *their* artistic explorations may well be considered even more successful. Will they become a new Chinese modernist school? It is my view that barring unforeseen storms, such an outcome is very likely. I enthusiastically hail the early formation of a new school. I want to be one of the infinitesimal drops of water that converges with the stream that is now still so small.

When I was writing *The Death of a Poet*, I adhered fairly rigorously to the methods of realism. One friend politely said, "Your methods are classical." I understood. His meaning was that my methods were old-fashioned. So while writing this novel, I consciously sought to make a few breakthroughs. I'll never again strive for a consistent and deliberate plot, or concrete and detailed descriptions. And I will never again rack my brains to work out a history for each character in order to reveal all the factors that have contributed to his or her nature. Every method I adopt will press toward my own goal: to express my understanding and ideals for "humankind." For this reason, I will concentrate all my energy on portrayal of my characters' souls. I will let each of my characters stand up and open his or her own heart, exposing the infinitely complex world harbored there. I have absorbed some "stream of consciousness" techniques of expression, like writing of a character's perceptions, fantasies, associations, and dream world. I believe this more closely approaches true human psychology.

However, I am certainly not a worshiper of the irrational. I strive to find the logic still inherent in psychological behavior that seems to cross over into abnormality. I have also absorbed some abstract techniques of expression, because these techniques can express certain thoughts and feelings more accurately and economically. I have written of the dreams of several of my characters. These dreams all have symbolic significance. The content they manifest is perhaps not all that profound; however, if I were to adopt another method of expression, I would have to waste more effort and ink.

I do not know what measure of success I have achieved in my explorations. But I hope my young friends will like my works. To speak truthfully, what I write is for them. I dearly love them and strive to understand their thoughts and feelings and artistic tastes. Perhaps I've misunderstood, but I have no regrets. I will continue to take young people as my friends and as my teachers. Of course, I also hope that I can give them a little help. And I hope that there will come a day when I can write a work in which they themselves are the protagonists.

"Houji" (Postscript), Guangzhou, August 1980, in Dai Houying, *Ren a, ren!* (Oh, humankind! *or* Stones of the Wall) (Guangzhou, 1980), pp. 351–58.

—Translated by Frances LaFleur

Wu Zuguang

The playwright WU ZUGUANG (b. 1917) might not have figured in this section of the anthology had he not been pressed by the authorities into leaving the Communist party in early 1987, following the December 1986 student protest movement. The essay below was read at the September 1986 meeting of the Board of Directors of the Chinese Writers' Association. It was enthusiastically received, for courageously addressing more general problems than those usually considered in Chinese works of drama and fiction. Ironically, only a censored version was printed, in the *Yangcheng Evening News* of Guangzhou, on November 11, 1986. A thousand characters felt to be too "acrimonious" were deleted. Here, the piece is restored to its original form (apart from our own abridgments of blocks of text, for reasons of space), with the "acrimonious" words back in their original places, and printed in italics, as per the Hong Kong reprint.

Against Those Who Wield the Scissors
A Plea for an End to Censorship

Wu Zuguang

September 30, 1986, in the morning

A RECENT headline read: "USSR Abolishes Drama Censorship System."

I wonder if our own drama world noticed this item? My reaction was rather strong.

Half a century ago, in 1937, the War of Resistance Against Japan broke out, and I entered the world of drama by writing my first spoken drama [*huaju*; differentiated from Chinese opera]. Prior to that, spoken drama had not played much of a role in our people's lives. *There was only one professional school for spoken drama in the whole country and only one professional drama troupe.* But because this type of drama can best reflect current life and express and communicate people's thoughts and emotions, it immediately became the most powerful inspiration and propaganda weapon in the glorious War of Resistance, which was waged by our whole nation.

The Initial Strengthening of the Censorship System in the 1940s

During the eight-year War of Resistance, spoken drama developed to an unprecedented extent. That was the most glorious period in the history of the genre. During the first two or three years of the war, there was not much interference by government drama censors; but as we entered the 1940s, the rotten Nationalist party [Kuomintang or KMT] began to feel that the popular masses, under the influence of the Communist party, were increasingly opposed to their reactionary government and looking forward to the democratic revolution with ever greater fervor. Extremely sensitive to and frightened by this trend, the Nationalists inaugurated and gradually strengthened a censorship system in literature and the arts, especially in the area of the drama. The so-called Central Book and Periodical Inspection Committee under the control of the Nationalists' Central Propaganda Ministry played the role of executioner. The speed of censorship increased rapidly, but their standards and methods were extremely simple: all negative characters in a play (those that were repudiated or satirized) were regarded as referring to the Nationalist party, while all positive characters (those whose roles were affirmed or praised) were just as certainly tagged as Communists. All this only confirmed that this extremely corrupt Nationalist party had already lost any semblance of confidence in itself and placed itself in the position of an accused criminal destined for certain destruction. Furthermore, all of this made everyone feel that the regime was on its last legs.

In 1949, after three years of the War of Liberation, the Jiang [Chiang Kaishek] dynasty was finally banished from the Chinese mainland and escaped to Taiwan in disarray. New China was about to be born. *I had been forced to go to Hong Kong, because during two years of directing two of my own anti-Nationalist dramas in Shanghai, I had encountered great harassment from drama censors. I was extremely heartened by the imminent collapse of the Jiang regime. My first reaction was that this execrable reactionary drama censorship system was also coming to an end.* So it was with elation that I published an article in Hong Kong's *Wenhuibao* entitled "An Obituary for the Censorship System." I was working at the time as a director in the Hong Kong Yonghua Film Company. On the day my article appeared (January 24), I bumped into the company manager, my boss Li Zuyong, *and he told me he had already read my article.* He said, "Of course, nothing could be better than abolishing the censorship system. But," he asked me with a sly smile, "do you think New China won't censor plays and films? Perhaps things won't necessarily work out that way." *He shook his head as he spoke.*

At the time, I didn't share his doubts *and even laughed to myself about this rich capitalist's obstinate point of view.* But many years later I painfully admit that I was the one who was wrong.

A Censorship System Retakes the Stage in New China

In our socialist New China, a policy of strict control over literature and the arts was put into effect right from the founding of the country. Furthermore, differences in literary and artistic theory and opinion would quite often have a political nature imputed to them *and be raised to the level of opposition to socialism, and counterrevolution....*

Flagrant Interference Indicates a Loss of Self-Confidence

In the last analysis, why do we have all these levels of control over literature and the arts, all this "flagrant interference"? There can only be one answer: because of a psychology of fear—fear of the masses, and disbelief in the masses—*that indicates a loss of self-confidence*. Because they have many very obvious deficiencies and no intention of reforming themselves, preferring instead to hold on to their outmoded ways, they are most fearful of exposure. They begin suspecting everyone and everything and drive themselves into a state of nervous exhaustion by checking to see that everyone is toeing the line. *From any reasonable point of view, this can only be the desperate expression of a last-ditch struggle on the part of a regime on the verge of destruction. It is not at all remarkable that the Nationalist party of the 1940s did so many ugly things on that account. What pains one is that we have actually inherited the shameful traditions of that rotten and moribund regime in our own literature and art and perpetuated them for so long. This is really unimaginable and laughably absurd.*

At the Fourth National Congress of Writers and Artists in 1979, Comrade Deng Xiaoping said, "Writers have the freedom to write what they want in the way they want; we should not flagrantly interfere." *Upon hearing that, everyone present was so moved that they applauded for minutes without stopping. They clapped until their hands ached. Despite all that, interference in creativity did not cease at all.* Again, at the Fourth Congress of the Chinese Writers' Association in 1984, Comrade Hu Qili, representing the Party Central, offered a guarantee of "freedom to create." In a very short time, however, creativity was throttled once again. For the past several years now, incidents of flagrant interference in fiction, drama, film, and even poetry have repeatedly occurred *and made us laughingstocks both inside and outside our country. The most excruciatingly embarrassing thing for me personally is to hear foreign friends ridicule us. It leaves me with no place to hide my head in shame.*

Even though the times have changed and the party's policy of openness cannot be shaken, the stubborn power of the extreme left cannot be taken lightly. The amount of outside influence the arts suffer from naturally varies with the genre. Fiction and poetry, for example, get by much better because one must first carefully read them, word by word, and the hatchetmen are unwilling to work so hard. In general, the fine arts can get by all right, too, and music is so deep and mysterious that it can survive well above the fray. Drama and film, however, are most unfortunate in being easily understood and therefore having no place to hide. *All those frantic leaders at various levels are very good at putting themselves out checking up on others, just like Ah Q with his fear that someone might say "light bulb."* [1] *They're even taken in by people who ruin others by wreaking petty vengeance, making up false accusations and rumors, playing up to higher-ups, and filing secret reports on people. The many sordid little farces that have been played out in the field of film and drama these past few years are obvious to everyone and needn't be mentioned here.*

---

[1]The eponymic antihero of Lu Xun's "The True Story of Ah Q" avoided words evoking the "shiny" baldness with which ringworm had left him.

In the past, more than a few actors have complained to me about the following situation. After the entire troupe has painstakingly expended untold labor and material resources, and not a little time, finally to produce a play, they call in the leaders for an inspection. After the leaders watch the play, they remain silent and emotionless for a long time, quite obviously unable to make a decisive critique. Neither repudiating nor condoning the play, they nod their heads and shake them, too. Finally they get up and walk out without saying a word. Thus, all of the troupe's human and material resources are completely wasted and a play is wiped out before it even hits the stage. Why do things like this repeatedly occur? It's simply the result of the leadership's psychology of fear. They're afraid to take responsibility. Furthermore, because their own cultural level is very limited, they cannot tell for certain whether the play presents any [political] problems or not. But if by any chance it should, they couldn't stand the flak; best not to stage it at all.

The situation with regard to films is even more serious. How many finished but unreleasable films are now piled up in our film warehouses? Isn't the memory still fresh in our minds of a case in which one film was refused public showing, though everyone was mobilized to criticize it, causing a furor all over the world?

Similar cases involving book, newspaper, and journal editors could be mentioned. *I began to publish essays and plays in newspapers and journals in the 1930s, under the old society when the Nationalists were in power. Although, as I recall, my works were shallow and immature, none of them was ever altered or expurgated by an editor. After the entire country was liberated and the new society began, they at first continued the practice of not altering or expurgating our works; but at some point along the line, I don't recall just when, our editors gradually began to expurgate and change our works like elementary and middle school teachers correcting their students' compositions. And the more they altered our works, the stranger they became. Many celebrated writers were unhappy and even protested.* Why did things turn out this way? It was due to the exact same frame of mind as mentioned above in relation to drama and film censors: the editors had to take responsibility for the bad consequences of any work they published. *Just like the various levels of leadership in drama and film—directors, bureau heads, and even ministry heads—they have had to take "political responsibility." This psychology of terror among various levels of leadership was created entirely by the censorship system. It is an occupational disease, a form of nervous exhaustion, and it has become the main factor stifling creative freedom.*

Freedom to Create Is Protected by Law in Western Countries

I cannot help mentioning Western capitalist countries. They do not have a censorship system for film or drama, much less for literature. *They simply lack that sort of censorial institution.* This shows that Western bourgeois politicians, even when they become rulers of their country, do not dare to restrict criticism. Nor can they misuse their power to stifle public opinion, much less interfere with the creativity of artists. *All of this makes one feel that their tolerance and self-confidence must be far greater than ours. If I had made such a comparison a few years ago, someone would surely have become infuriated: Why are you comparing our country with capitalist countries—even with the Nationalists and the Soviet Union? But I would have to ask in return: If not with them, then with whom? And if we cannot be compared favorably with them, what sort of socialist country are we?*

Actually, the reason for the situation in the capitalist countries is quite simple. It is only because freedom to create is protected there by law. Everyone has the right. "Flagrant interference," on the other hand, violates the law.

A careful observer will have noticed that in recent years a new situation has arisen here that never existed in the past: some newly completed plays have been stifled before they were even released for the stage. When such things took place in the past, during the rule of the ultraleft, the newspapers would mount a full-scale attack for them at the outset, with a barrage of articles in which the authors, directors, and even actors would be criticized and punished. Today the method of handling such cases has completely changed. They now employ strange, covert methods in which nothing is done openly. No reasons are given, no one takes responsibility, and everyone remains anonymous. If any inquiries are made, they simply stonewall it, equivocate, or say something utterly insincere. It's little wonder, then, that the saying, "secret assassination has taken the place of public execution and the government has gone underground," which was current in literary and art circles not long ago, has already been transmitted far beyond our borders.

This is, of course, an extremely anomalous phenomenon, but it is actually a good thing. It shows that those who interfere know that they are in the wrong and that their actions are shameful. They can no longer do as they please, and with such swagger, regardless of the injustice of their cause. Now they have to hide behind the scenes to carry out their dirty tricks.

The Constitution of the People's Republic of China long ago included clauses guaranteeing freedom of speech, publication, literary and artistic creation, and other cultural activities. Interference with these freedoms is obviously a violation of the constitution. From the point of view of the law, the drama censorship system that is so diametrically opposed to the freedom to create has always been in violation of the constitution.

In China, ruled by a feudal system and feudal consciousness for several thousand years, the will of the officials has always overpowered everything else. This kind of feudal consciousness has seriously harmed socialist New China. If at the founding of the nation we had emphasized democracy and the legal system as we do today, those repeated and extremely destructive political movements, which ultimately led to the vast and incomparably disastrous tragedy of the Cultural Revolution, with its ten years of complete lawlessness, simply could not have taken place. Today China's leaders actually sit down together and listen respectfully to legal experts who teach courses on the legal system. I know from personal experience just how serious and necessary this is and what a tremendous influence will come from it.

Only the Law Should Restrain Literary and Artistic Creativity

Do we mean to say that there are no restraints on literary and artistic creativity? Of course there are: those of the law, and only the law. Aside from that, all creativity is free, and so, too, criticism and countercriticism. If we go back to the way things were so often done in the past—that is, if a censorship system manipulated by an extremely small minority bears down on the necks of writers and those pitiful souls have to carry on their creative activities bound hand and foot, always worrying whether they will make it past the censors—how can any good works be produced in the future?

China is now in the midst of vigorous development, and our most urgent tasks are sweeping away long-accumulated abuses and actively moving forward. For a long time in the past, we heard too much praise and indulged in too much self-eulogy. Today, however, it is more necessary to listen to a few contrary opinions and accept a little criticism. Besides, not very many of our plays and films are really critical anyway. . . .

In fact, a moment of dispassionate thought makes it all come clear: if one day the drama censorship system really were abolished, the first to be liberated would not be the writers and actors, but the various layers of leadership above the troupe. If they once laid down the burden of that bizarre and anomalous system, how relaxed and contented they would become! How often have I seen the embarrassed looks of innocent leaders as they finished watching a play, not knowing whether to be for or against it. In my heart I protested the injustice done to them. Of course, leaders who enjoy censoring others and feel bitter about any loss of power are a different case, *and perhaps they aren't in the minority, either.* Editors are innocently embroiled in the same way. We ought to reinstate the old tradition that the writer takes responsibility for his own writings and the dramatist takes responsibility for his own plays; that's the only reasonable and humane solution. Therefore, besides creative freedom, we should guarantee editorial freedom. The latter must not be overlooked. . . .

"Li dang quxiao 'xiju shencha zhidu' " (The "drama censorship system" should be abolished), speech of September 30, 1986, from a reprint that restores the censored portions in *Dongxiang* (Trends, Hong Kong) 34 (January 1987): 58–61.

—Translated by Michael S. Duke

Bai Hua

BAI HUA (pseud. of Chen Youhua, b. 1930, in Henan) was a noted poet before 1981, but it was in that year that he became a national scapegoat—and cause célèbre among intellectuals willing to speak their minds—because his film script *Kulian* (Unrequited love, lit. "Bitter love") became the leading "negative example" in a national campaign against "bourgeois liberalization." Some thought this earned him somewhat "undeserved" fame, as a victim. But in his creative writing since, Bai Hua has shown great talent and versatility; his essays and public statements reveal a man of honest convictions and courageous determination to fight for the democratization of Chinese society. The essay below was prepared for an international conference on contemporary Chinese literature that was initiated by Wang Meng and organized by the Chinese Writers' Association in Jinshan, Shanghai, in November 1986. Little did the participants know at the time that this was to be one last liberal gesture from the authorities before cold winds of repression blew again, following student protests the next month.

China's Contemporary Literature
Reaching Out to the World and to the Future

Bai Hua

November 1986, in Jinshan, Shanghai

IT IS widely known that contemporary Chinese literature has gone through a very difficult and painful phase, and yet also surpassed itself. Like the Yangzi River as it bursts through the Kui Gate, it carries with it a long history, heavy vicissitudes of the human world, the sun and the moon, stars and planets, green hills and sparkling waters. Of course, it also carries turbid mud and silt. Right now it is flowing out to the world and to the future, along a course that daily becomes broader and freer.

The pulse beats in time with the heart. The history of Chinese literature tells us that when the philosophy of literature becomes a part of the contemplation of national destiny, the literature will be magnificent. From the *Shijing* (Book of odes), *Chu ci* (Songs of the South), poetry of the Tang and Song, Yuan songs (*qu*), fiction of the Ming and Qing, up to the great Lu Xun—all these are our people's ardent laments, sad sighs, angry resistance, and biting satire about their own destiny. No other nation emphasizes literature as the Chinese nation does. Commoners, emperors, generals, ministers—through the ages almost all of them have used literature to express their feelings directly. Therefore, we possess an illustrious literary legacy, from Qu Yuan's *Encountering Sorrow* to Lu Xun's *Outcry*, that is the finest essence of our literature.

For several thousand years, the achievements of literature and the misfortunes of literature have always been twin brothers.[1] Historically, all important events have been intensely reflected in Chinese literature; all great literary works are witnesses to history, the conscience of their era, the crystallization of its thought,

---

[1]Bai Hua himself has a twin brother.

the encyclopedia of its styles and customs. Therefore, we can experience ancient worldly affairs and human feelings directly from the *Book of Odes*, and we call the poetry of Du Fu history. Although readers with a hundred different interests can get a hundred completely different impressions from *The Dream of the Red Chamber*, everyone can perceive the author's form and spirit and the unique historical environment and atmosphere in which he lived. This very precious tradition has lived on. We can see from the works of Lu Xun his own native home and the native home of the Chinese people. From the works of Mao Dun, we can perceive his midnight and the midnight of the Chinese people. We can observe from the works of Ba Jin his family and the family of the Chinese people.[2]

Unfortunately, this tradition was interrupted for a considerable period. We were forced, in our observations, our thought, and our writing, to do our utmost to avoid, and to criticize in others, the firsthand experience that most aroused our writer's heart and body; our conscience; all real knowledge of, and clear insight into, history, culture, society, and human nature. Certain of China's authorities on theory have for years endeavored, on the basis of subjective indulgence and political efficacy, to lay down a model of creativity for artists and writers that transcends life and the rules of artistic development but corresponds with current standards of politics, morality, and ethics. Ultimately, during the Ten-Year Calamity that started in 1966, this effort reached its peak in a few so-called dramatic works perfected by the Jiang Qings, who called them "models." The essence of literature was completely lost. These few "models" certainly will become immortal works, just as the Jiang Qings hoped: they will be the worst models in the history of human civilization. A thousand years from now, people will wonder why in the 1960s there were people who made such a stupid attempt, and why it occurred in a civilized country with an ancient history.

For years, Chinese writers have been like tall deciduous trees, carefully and cautiously gazing at the sky and observing changes in the wind and clouds, but finally still living and dying once a year, losing their yellow leaves—or their red leaves. Many were crushed by the weight of the snow. We can compile a long list of well-known names, such as the world-renowned Lao She, Fu Lei, a translator who was superior and upright, and many others. Beginning in the 1950s, a virtual majority of all writers with individuality were stripped of their right to create and their rights as citizens. A group of writers who survived but had long since lost their youth formed the nucleus for the recovery of Chinese literature in the 1970s. Since all contemporary Chinese writers have traveled a long and rough road, they have universally evoked deep concern and sympathy from the masses. Please allow me here to recite a short poem, "Reply to Readers." It relates my experience of this.

---

[2]Mao Dun comments on his novel *Midnight* and Ba Jin on his novel *Family* in their respective articles in this anthology.

Reply to Readers

How can you know,
your gifts far exceed my desire.
If you allow me to weep for love and gratitude,
a river of tears will appear at our feet;
but I have not shed a single drop,
because what you need is not my cowardice.
I am a bird that easily forgets disasters,
as soon as the arrow has flown by, I begin to sing again;
I sing so cheerfully, it seems the world
exists only to hear my song.
I fly down onto the hand of each one of you,
"jumping for joy," as it says in the proverb.
If the arrow flies by again, which is quite possible,
I hope it will not accidentally injure your hands.

In the last ten years, contemporary Chinese literature has received an unprecedentedly enthusiastic and widespread welcome. Numerous writers have become trustworthy spiritual friends of the masses. Many of the latter have poured out their hardships and grievances to the writers, going so far as to consider literature their most illustrious tribunal, and writers their supreme impartial judges. This is another kind of value attached to literature. Obviously, writers cannot completely fulfill the concrete expectations of these anonymous people as they would like, but this trust and attention give impetus to literature. It makes Chinese writers even more clearly understand their own existence, the reason for it, and what they ought to be doing. At the same time, it balances the emphasis coming from the other side [i.e., the state].

For many years, Chinese writers were like Chinese women before the May Fourth movement, who walked on feet forcibly bound into three-inch "golden lotuses." There were two purposes: it helped preserve women's chastity, and the malformations it created appeared beautiful. Later, amid jeers and fines levied by people whose souls had already turned to stone, they gradually began loosening their bound feet. But in their hearts they were still afraid. Once unbound, the feet do not feel like their own. They are unused to them and reluctant to part with the fine slippers they have themselves embroidered so painstakingly and meticulously. Only a few young girls, such as Zhang Xinxin, Wang Anyi, and Tie Ning, who never had their feet bound, run and jump naturally, as they wish. I believe that no authority is great enough to force us to bind our feet again. That goes for both the "reformed feet faction"[3] of my generation, who once submitted to

---

[3]A pun on a Chinese political term that dates back at least to the 1928: "reorganization-ist faction" (*gaizu pai*), i.e., those favoring a governmental shake-up.

binding and now are unbound, and the justifiably proud young women with never-bound feet—unless we are punished the way King Hui of Wei punished Sun Bin, by having our feet cut completely off.[4]

In the future, our stride may lengthen somewhat. But how will we walk? And where? These are questions worth pondering. Recently there have been many works called exploratory (*tansuo*). They are somewhat imitative and derivative in form. We should recognize that although form has a power of its own, the purpose of exploring it is not novelty for novelty's sake, but to accomplish our historic mission. What the world wants most from contemporary Chinese literature are incisive literary recreations of contemporary China: China's progress, China's struggles, China's blood and tears, China's poverty and weakness, China's illusions, China's hopes, China's living and dying. In that regard, we are well set. We all grew from [China's] branches; the branches are connected with the trunk, and below the trunk are the roots, which we can always rely on to transport nourishment and moisture to us. When did we ever lose our roots?[5] Even if you want to free yourself of your roots, it's very hard to do. Certainly some people tried. In the end, they failed. Half a century ago, Mr. Lu Xun was a very active advocate of learning from the experience of foreigners, but the literary characters he created were all true descendants of the Yellow Emperor and the Yan Emperor. And he never concealed our people's ignoble sloth or his own profound grief. Therefore, he has shaken men's souls for generation after generation.

At present there are, to be sure, writers who do not dare honestly to confront human life; who shirk social responsibility; who seek to "soar in the sky and surpass others"; who attenuate the social meaning of life; who shrink back after learning the difficulties; or who retire into their own labyrinths once their cart has been upset. Others, with excellent driving skills, negotiate even the narrow Liulichang street market without a collision. Still others gain dispensation from everyone by smiling in all directions. I am for the blooming of a "Hundred Flowers," even under these conditions, but the kinds of literary waffling, retreats, and betrayals that bring peace to literary people gain praise, while writers who fulfill their duty to history and society gain only censure, as if the calamity in literature were their doing.

National disasters cannot be caused by just a few people. During the Cultural Revolution, even many writers who had rested their pens since the 1940s could not escape difficulty. I believe we should first blame the life that has been ground out of our bodies: "Why are you so imperfect? Why so hard and tough? And why so full of intricate and complex contradictions?" Writers of course

---

[4]Amputation of feet as a punishment for criminals was practiced during the Warring States period (403–222 B.C.), when King Hui reigned.

[5]This is counterpoint to the views of young Chinese authors of the "Finding Our Roots" group. See the essay in this volume by Han Shaogong.

need intelligence, but even more, they need courage and wisdom. Otherwise, they cannot penetrate the superficialities of life and see into its deepest core. Nor can they free themselves of deep-rooted prejudices formed over many years, and transcend conventional norms to observe the boundless variety of this universe that is so laden with contradictions. We cannot let our Chinese contemporary literature, which is already revived and possessed of powerful thought, become weak and commonplace because of staleness of sensibility and laxity in skills. Of course, writers may adapt as they wish, but we Chinese living in a period of upheaval will not accept inferior products. Writers can satisfy themselves while pleasing us, too. But the Chinese people—as a whole and as individuals—must all withstand a severe test of history. There is no other choice. Thus, I feel extremely honored to be an ordinary Chinese, and an ordinary writer among them.

To end, allow me to recite another short poem, as epilogue.

Even Sighing Has Its Echo

I never intended to be a winner,
only one who loves and is loved;
I am not, and do not intend to become, anyone's mortal enemy,
for I seize nothing, I only give.
If I have finally become a strong person in other people's eyes,
it is a misunderstanding, deep as the sea!
I only stand, always together with the silent masses,
involuntarily humming a few lines of song.
Sometimes I will heave a long sigh,
I had not realized that even a sigh echoes like a storm!
I cannot restrain the moaning that draws off my pain,
loved, and loving, I sing joyfully, like a mountain swallow;[6]
the most painful thing is,
you must put your own hands to your throat to strangle the song.

"Zou xiang shijie he weilai de Zhongguo dangdai wenxue" (Contemporary Chinese literature: Reaching out to the world and to the future), essay written for the International Conference on Contemporary Chinese Literature, Jinshan, Shanghai, November 1986, reprinted in *Dongxiang* (Trends, Hong Kong) (January 1981): 34–35.

—Translated by Tang Yiming and Marsha L. Wagner

---

[6]A forest-dwelling swallow noted for quasi-human qualities; said to be very smart, and capable of being trained to tell fortunes.

Liu Xinwu

LIU XINWU (b. 1942, in Chengdu; a longtime resident of Peking) wrote a short story called "Banzhuren" (The homeroom teacher, also translated as "The class counselor," or "Form master"), published in November 1977, that was retrospectively canonized as having initiated China's "Literature of the Wounded"—the first wave of post-Mao literature to begin openly to criticize China's social and political shortcomings. He has composed many detailed works of social manners since, including a novel about the common people of Peking called *Zhonggulou* (The drum and bell towers, 1985).

Liu Xinwu fell victim to the repressive winds that blew in 1987, when Deng Xiaoping tried again to discipline China's intellectuals. As editor of *People's Literature*, he came under heavy pressure and nearly lost his post for having let his journal print a story by Ma Jian describing Tibetan sexual customs deemed indecent by conservative culture bureaucrats, and allegedly the Tibetans themselves. Besides fiction, Liu has written controversial and critical essays on social problems. Deciding against exile in June 1989, he became a major target of government repression. The essay below manifests his characteristic spirit of simple and moralistic patriotism.

Reflections in the Hot Springs at Hakone

China, Our Impoverished, Trouble-Ridden Motherland

Liu Xinwu

August 16, 1981

THIS past April, I toured Japan for two weeks as the guest of the magazine *Bungei shunju* (Springs and autumns of the literary arts). Following a whirlwind visit to Tokyo, Kyoto, Nara, Osaka, and Kobe, the other two Chinese writers and I were taken by our hosts to the hot springs resort at Hakone for a day's relaxation. I opened the French windows of my room in the Scandinavian-style mountain inn where we were staying and stood on the balcony, which looked out over the rippling blue waters of Lake Ashi. The lakeshore was surrounded by rolling green hills covered with clumps of peonies—red, purple, pink, white. Gabled roofs of gothic European buildings and the flying eaves of Shinto shrines peeked through the stands of trees, while out on the lake, cinnabar-colored pleasure boats made their slow way back and forth; though the boats were the old-fashioned, multimasted type, they were outfitted with all the modern conveniences.

After eating a meal of roasted Bordeaux snails and bathing in the hot springs, I took a bottle of liquor and some ice cubes out of the refrigerator in my room and mixed myself a whiskey. I had only taken one swallow when my mind was suddenly flooded with so many thoughts that I was overwhelmed and couldn't calm down, no matter how I tried. Our hosts had set aside this night for us to catch up on our sleep after an exhausting schedule, before starting the second phase of our visit. But for me, it was the most restless, sleepless night of all.

The first switch on the nightstand next to my bed produced the soothing sounds of bird calls, the second classical music, the third contemporary music. I was in no mood for any of that. My thoughts went back to a hospitalization of many years back, when my mother had brought me some peaches, which she washed and placed on a small table beside my bed. I ate two of them, but left the third, and largest, uneaten. Then, when I was released from the hospital, I forgot to take that last peach home with me. It was already starting to turn bad. Since the parents of the boy in the bed next to mine didn't have money to spend on peaches, I had offered him mine. But he wouldn't accept it, even though the look in his eyes revealed how tempted he was. Why hadn't I been more forceful? I wonder if he ate that big peach after I left. Since it was already turning bad, might it have brought him more problems—what would happen to him then?

I hadn't thought about this incident for many, many years, and now the memory of that boy and the nearly spoiled peach came flooding back to me in this strange place hundreds of miles from my native land, so vivid it seemed like yesterday. Yes, a peach, lots of peaches—it was last year: a child standing in the middle of an open market near my home was crying bitterly as his father beat him. The boy, it seemed, had knocked over a large basketful of juicy, hard-to-come-by peaches that his father had brought to the market to sell, ruining most of them by breaking the skins or soiling them in the mud. Onlookers managed to get the father to stop beating his son, but the child cried louder than ever, since he felt worse over the loss of the peaches than his father; possibly he had spent more time and effort tending the fruit than his enraged elder. Would the family's peach trees manage to produce such a bumper crop the following year? Certainly the sun would have to rise and set many times before they'd know. More thoughts of the market came to me then.

The peasant wore a hopeful expression, giving him a carefree yet cautious look, and I could see the wheels spinning in his head. I bought a pound of cucumbers, tender vegetables covered with prickly thorns. When I gave the fellow several ten-cent bills, one slipped through his fingers and was whisked away by one of Peking's frequent little whirlwinds. He instinctively abandoned his stall and took out after the filthy, dog-eared bill. I yelled at him to watch out for the truck that was barreling down the street toward him, telling him to forget it, that I'd give him another bill. But either he didn't hear me or he was oblivious to all sounds, for he darted across the busy street in his pursuit of the errant bill. He returned forlornly to the stall, where I offered him another ten cents, but he just rubbed his thick, sweaty chest with his large hand and shook his head. I stuffed the bill into his hand and walked off. Just then something grabbed hold of my shopping basket. I turned around. It was him; he was putting a cucumber into my shopping basket. There in Hakone, Japan, in my comfortable and tastefully furnished room, those were the thoughts that accompanied me. I felt like crying, not because I was sad or melancholic, but because my soul was stirring.

The accumulation of garbage floating in a silted-up stream a hundred meters or so from the market stank terribly on hot days. A middle-aged, freckle-faced woman was standing beside the stream, deep in thought, tears suddenly filling her eyes. She was a stranger to me, and I to her, yet a fleeting exchange of glances was all we needed to gain a profound understanding of one another. China, this most impoverished, trouble-ridden motherland of ours, what must your sons and daughters do to make you as rich and as lovely as you should be?

The first batch of saplings had just been planted around our newly developed residential area. Whenever Uncle Wu, who lived in one of the basement rooms, had time on his hands, he took a stool outside and sat in front of his building to keep watch over the saplings. On one occasion a mischievous youngster came over and shook one of the anemic little trees, sparking the old man to get to his feet and shout, "Don't do that, don't shake it so lively!"—stressing the word "lively." The youngster shook it even harder. "What's wrong with shaking it so it's *lively*?" The youngster scampered out of reach as the old man took a few steps toward him, then walked over to lovingly stroke and minister to the young tree. With the arrival of spring, delicate green buds appeared on the trees—tiny, transparent, anemic, bashful. Uncle Wu went through the building, upstairs and down, urging the tenants to tell their children not to injure the trees. From beside Lake Ashi in far-off Japan I felt as though I could hear his footsteps and his labored breathing as he climbed the apartment stairs.

On the day we were leaving Japan to return to China, some minor complications arose at Haneda Airport, raising the possibility that we would have to return to Tokyo and postpone our departure until the following day. Our Japanese friends immediately began making plans to entertain us for another day, including a unique performance and some Jewish cuisine. But the three of us were so eager to return home that I said, candidly, "My heart is tied to my homeland by a string that will only allow me to wander for two weeks. Every day that string has been pulled more and more tightly, and today it's so taut that it hurts me. The thought of returning to Tokyo is more than I can bear. I beg you to do whatever is necessary to resolve the problem so we can return to Peking today." The problem was taken care of, and when I stepped into the airplane cabin I felt as though I had been relieved of a heavy burden.

Dear readers, I'm telling you all this so you can better understand me and can appreciate the three novellas I'm placing before you in this collection.

When I accepted the invitation of *Bungei shunju* magazine to visit Japan, I told them, "I am an ardent patriot." I meant what I said. I truly love every inch of my homeland and every person who lives in our great country. To me, "the people" is anything but an abstraction, for I live in their midst. Naturally, I love the heroic model citizens and the progressives, but I also love the ordinary workers, peasants, urbanites, and intellectuals. Does that mean that I love their weaknesses and shortcomings, too? Of course not. But I've learned how to discover and reveal the golden qualities of their hearts, and I earnestly hope that, like me, you will learn to love those who labor, even though they have their shortcomings. This love should embody a respect for and a hearty approval of their merits, as well as an understanding of their circumstances and a willingness to help them remove the stains from their souls. Beyond that, we must draw strength from their virtues and rigorously cleanse our own souls with what we learn from them.

I revere realism; literary realism is a wonderful medium for understanding and has great potential for social transformation. Among the many functions of realism, I am particularly fond of its ability to mold the spirit. As far as I am concerned, the material and spiritual worlds are not only equally important, but mutually complementary. I cannot imagine the realization of widespread spiritual cultivation without the concomitant construction of socialist material cultivation. Nor is it reasonable for us to abandon our exposure of and struggle against such uncivilized spiritual phenomena as vulgar philistinism just because the level of socialist material cultivation is low. And we must steadfastly praise and encourage the minority of people whose material cultivation has not reached an acceptable standard but whose spiritual cultivation has managed to reach laudable heights. A single novella can do no more than emphasize the expression and propagation of one aspect of all this. I earnestly hope that my readers will reflect on the three novellas in this collection and will gain some understanding of the efforts I have put into examining spiritual cultivation from a number of different angles.

I revere the spirit of humanism. The goal of revolutionary humanism is the ultimate expunging of oppressive systems in order to resolve the problem of alienation among the people. I love such characters of my own creation as Shi Yihai, into whom I have poured my understanding of revolutionary humanism. I deeply understand and sympathize with characters like Gang Hua, and I hope that all struggles against deviant behavior will, to the greatest extent possible, be based upon a desire to come to the aid of comrades who have taken the wrong road. To my way of thinking, this is one aspect of revolutionary humanism. I have striven to depict the sparks emanating from the soul even of characters like Hou Yong.[1] I honestly believe that the vast majority of people in the world are capable of goodness. I have given up all hope only for a tiny minority of disgraceful people who have abandoned their conscience and destroyed their own humanity. It is they whom I despise. But I am incapable of creating that type of image.

I am an advocate of literary experimentation. I have been criticized for including an excess of commentary in my short stories. In the three novellas that follow I have done my best to suppress this tendency, to the point that even one more deletion would have been unbearable. I have striven harder and harder to conceal my personal viewpoint and curb my tendentiousness by allowing the situations and character depictions to develop naturally. And yet there are still some critics

---

[1] Shi Yihai is a character in "Ruyi" (As you wish); Gang Hua appears in "Litijiaochaqiao" (Overpass); Hou Yong, in "Da yan mao" (Big-eyed cat).

who equate my fictional characters with me personally. This has caused me to ponder this question: Has it come to the point where unless at least one of the characters in a novella directly and openly represents the philosophy of the author, the work is a failure?

Still a long way from being mature, I am moving ahead like an explorer. I yearn for serious, well-intentioned criticism; at the same time, as I become conscious of my own shortcomings and mistakes, not only will I be willing to undergo self-criticism, but my progress will be reflected in my subsequent works.

Step by earnest step I will make my way down the long road ahead.

"[Ruyi] houji" (Afterword [to As you wish]), August 16, 1981, in Liu Xinwu yanjiu zhuanji (Special collection of research on Liu Xinwu), ed. Zhu Jiaxin, Huang Chang-chang, and Zhu Yuying (Guiyang, 1988), pp. 88–92.

—Translated by Howard Goldblatt

Wang Meng

WANG MENG (b. 1934, in Peking) is perhaps contemporary China's best-known literary author, a writer with a penchant for bold formal experimentation but more conservative plots and artistic messages. A story he wrote as a young man, "The Young Newcomer in the Organization Department" (1956), made him, like Liu Binyan, a primary target in the subsequent Antirightist campaign. He was exiled for twenty years in the border province of Xinjiang.

Rehabilitated in 1979, Wang Meng helped many young talents publish their first works. In 1986, he was appointed minister of culture, a bold move by the reformist faction in the government around Hu Yaobang. Wang Meng's creativity did not end when he took office. Like the writer-officials Malraux and Fuentes, he kept on writing and experimenting, though his detractors would have preferred that he remain aloof from politics in principle. His novel *Huodong bian renxing* (Interchangeable-parts man, 1987) belongs to the new Chinese aesthetics of ugliness, being the fictional biography of a wavering and "superfluous" Westernized intellectual before the war, ending in his utterly desperate demise under the post-1949 Communist regime. It is based on autobiographical reminiscences and episodes from the life of Wang Meng's father. Wang Meng resigned as minister of culture in 1989, his honor intact; he had refused to criticize the students and workers who protested for democracy at Tiananmen, and so was forced out.

In this piece, the author reflects about his inner development, from propagandist nourished on Soviet proletarian novels to a writer of much more complex and contemporary literature. Wang Meng's deliberations might be seen as belonging to the tradition of the genre of "autobiographical prefaces and postscripts" (*xu*) that Chinese readers have enjoyed since the time of the Grand Historian Sima Qian in the first century B.C.

Banished to Xinjiang
Or, About Bestial Hatred of Literature

Wang Meng

1980

ONE EVENING late in the fall of 1953, in a small, new two-story building near Beixinqiao [Peking], I, a nineteen-year-old Communist Youth League cadre, harbored a fervent secret desire. I closed the door of the tiny sunless room that served me as both office and sleeping quarters, and by lamplight began writing one line after another on a pad of unruled white paper. Beside me files, unfinished reports and summaries, had accumulated in stacks; if someone were to knock at the door, I was ready to grab a report manuscript and put it on top of my writing pad, making it look like I was spending all night on materials connected with my job. Worried about failure and ridicule as I began my writing career, I suffered from the notion that my abilities were inferior to my ambitions.

Nevertheless, as I sat at my desk and took up my pen, I realized that I was engaged in something that would influence the course of my entire life. I sensed a kind of sacredness, a solemnity, and was deeply conscious of my efforts to record this beautiful though swiftly passing existence—to give shape to burning and elusive passions. I felt sincerely that, though I might capture only the tiniest fraction of the rich variety of real life, it was still a crystallization of ardent emotions, a lustrous glow from life, an imprint of youth; and that it was more enduring and comprehensible to people at large than the events of life themselves. What I wrote was a message from the heart that would not change with time or weaken with distance.

And then I came to see that a writer was the happiest of people, able to understand others and be understood by them; to speak from the heart with thousands upon thousands of friends; never alone, always together with the multitudes, building an entirely new, wonderfully happy, decent and abundant life.

Just outside the courtyard of the Communist Youth League District Committee where I was working was a Xinhua Bookstore outlet, where I often went to inhale the fragrance of printers' ink. I would stroll up and down through the forest of books, lingering by their side, heedless of time. I hoped one day that my own book—my own heart—would be displayed there.

Such was the state I was in when I wrote *Long Live Youth*. It was finally published, not back when I wrote it, but when my own child was already older than I had been at the time. Twenty-six years elapsed between writing and publication, over a quarter-century. When it appeared, in 1979, I was less excited than I might have been before, having become acquainted with the responsibilities and risks that writing involves, and the cost: painstaking effort, tears, years of youth—sometimes one's blood, one's very life.

Because literature seeks light, yearns for truth, and thirsts after development and progress, and also because literature is the study of people, it puts people at its core, demands that they become true human beings, and requires that their relationships become true human relationships—communist relationships, in which one treats all elders and all children as one would one's own.[1] Therefore, literature must do battle with exploitative systems. It must fight darkness, ignorance, all reactionary and conservative forces and ideologies, all hypocrisy, all lies. All the dark and reactionary forces will then see literature as their nemesis. When I was in middle school, I already knew of writers who had been executed by firing squad: Rou Shi, Yin Fu, Hu Yepin. During the Ten-Year Calamity [the Cultural Revolution], I was astounded again and again at how violent, instinctive, even bestial was the dread and hatred evoked in Jiang Qing by the mere mention of writers.

My first literature teacher was my mother's sister. She came to visit me at my home in 1967, which was then in Ili, Xinjiang. A few days later, she died there, of a cerebral hemorrhage. I still remember how she took my first essay, written when I was seven and in the second grade, and added an exhortation at the end. As I remember, it was an "essay" on the spring wind, and she completed it with this: "Oh wind, may you drive away the darkness from this earth!" Never questioning whether these words could have come from the mouth of a child, my teacher in her excitement had thickly underscored them in red.

Indeed, literature should become a refreshing breeze, dispelling darkness; a spring wind reawakening the hundred flowers, and summoning the swallows and larks. It was precisely in order to dispel darkness that when I was young I joined the people's revolutionary struggle against Chiang Kai-shek and the Kuomintang, which at the time was led by party organizations still underground. I became, as a youth, a warrior for this party. In the student movement, literature

---

[1] A reference to the *Mencius*, I.1.VII.12, about King Hui of Liang.

was the clarion call for revolution. Not just the works of Lu Xun, Ba Jin, and Ding Ling, but also *How the Steel Was Tempered, Iron Flood, Cement, The Ballad of Li Youcai, The White-haired Girl, The Heroes of Lüliang, The Story of an Iron Bucket,* and *My Two Hosts* were circulated among students in the Kuomintang-controlled areas. I have always felt that works like *How the Steel Was Tempered* nurtured a generation, or several generations, of revolutionaries in the Soviet Union, China, and the world at large.

I have always believed literature and revolution to be inherently unified in purpose and inseparable. They have a common aim: to defeat the old order utterly, and let the brilliant red sun shine over the whole earth.[2] Literature is the pulse of revolution, its beacon, its conscience; revolution is literature's guide, its soul, its source. *How the Steel Was Tempered* could nurture a generation of revolutionaries primarily because Ostrovsky and his book were nurtured by the raging fires of the revolution, by its ideals, and its practice.

Therefore, when people mounted a full-scale attack on literature in the name of revolution, spouting splendid-sounding and specious rhetoric, and in the end even used that name to rape and destroy it, I felt the pain of my conscience being torn asunder, my body and soul split apart. My very being was divided: to be loyal to the revolution meant betraying literature, to love and create literature meant becoming a shameful traitor to the revolutionary camp.

Nearly every political movement since Liberation had begun by bringing literature under the knife. Now, at last, it was time for my head to be put on the block.

So I "voluntarily" strove to deny literature, to reject it. It began with the denial of my own self. "How insignificant you and your writings are! How contemptible!" I tried hard to believe those pronouncements at the criticism sessions, shouted out so loudly and so righteously. I did indeed discover the insignificance of literature: it lacked the power even to match voices raised in criticism. I hoped further to discover its contemptibility; having done so, I could lie down peacefully on the bed they were showing me: the garbage heap of history. If, after the literature I had loved was destroyed, a burgeoning "new epoch" of literature was born, ornamented with all the flourishes of revolutionary rhetoric; and if, after I had thrown myself onto the garbage heap, China indeed became purer, better, and happier, how could I not be content to lie there in meek docility?

And so with all my heart I took up the cry, "Let the mountains move aside! I am coming!" I earnestly tried to understand grand catchphrases like "towering hero," "soaring among the clouds," and "able to conquer nature." Laugh at me if you will—I saw through it only late in the game and, far from resisting, actually worked hard to grasp the Three Prominences and "lofty perfection," even though

[2]This phraseology echoes "The Internationale."

subconsciously I loathed such trash and often cried my pillow wet during the night.

At this time literature, which to me had been sacred, eternal, solemn, and majestic, really did become insignificant and weak, subject to being bullied and trampled on. It had become mere phrase-mongering by mediocre talents, self-deceiving and dishonest nonsense, a slave to authority, a tuft of hair on some big shot's hide. Alas, literature. Farewell!

Not surprisingly, literature did sink beneath contempt. It became sheafs of lies for cheating and numbing the people, a narcotic wrapped by brigands in human-hamburger dumplings to trap innocent wayfarers,[3] the executioner's mask, a pile of rumors and slander, a bag of sinister tricks.

Not only in literature, but in life, there was much bluster and bombast, many truly petty and contemptible people and events. Facing all these things, I reached the end of my rope. Lacking understanding, to say nothing of strength and courage, I just dragged on, waiting. Two decades after 1957, the year I was accused of being insignificant and contemptible, I had seriously come to feel that I was indeed despicable.

At the same time, however, I came to know true greatness and dignity. On the lowest rungs of society and in the remotest places, I shared joy and suffering with the people, breathed the same air with them, and saw from their standpoint the conjuring tricks, the shifting winds, the knavery of those years. I saw who was right and who was wrong, the winners and the losers, clear as a blazing fire.[4]

Those setbacks and failures tempered and enriched us. And then came October 1976, and the inevitable event people had so long awaited [the fall of the Gang of Four]. History is at once utterly ruthless and utterly compassionate. We achieved a second liberation, for it is a law of history that people will liberate themselves. If it does not work the first time, they will try again.

Thwarting chaos and restoring order was a kind of resurrection. The party gave me back my pen, and I was reconfirmed as an honorable party member with important responsibilities. Revolution and literature were one again, as were my soul and the core of my being; in other words, I came back to life in the world of letters. Alive again, I faced an arduous task: to find myself. In the vast ocean of life, of time and space, of literature and art, I had to find my position, my fulcrum, my own subjects, themes, form, and style.

For no matter how much I welcomed this second round of youth, no matter how I wanted to begin again at twenty-three and retrace my old footsteps, I was

---

[3]The reference is to a chapter of the classic novel *Water Margin*, in which notorious bandit innkeepers drug those who stop by, so as to convert them into refreshments for further unsuspecting travelers.

[4]After Wang's 1956 story, "The Young Newcomer in the Organization Department," was criticized in 1957, Wang was exiled to Xinjiang. *Long Live Youth*, already printed, was banned.

already in my forties. Thinking back on youth is wonderfully tantalizing, but we can never become children again. Rereading my story "The Young Newcomer in the Organization Department" and my essay "The New Year" still chokes me up, evoking both a teary smile and a firm and abiding hope. And yet, I also feel somehow numb, as if I were worlds away.

When I was twenty, life and literature seemed to me like a good and innocent young girl. She was, so to speak, my first love, and my works were love poems offered to her. Such poetry may be moving, but it is after all quite inadequate. Now, though, life and literature have become for me a dignified, capable, and benevolent mother. The lines on her brow tell how she stood firm in the storm, was reborn from a raging fire, from persecution by a whore and a witch [Jiang Qing]; her ample, warm bosom is nevertheless still pure and soft, overflowing with the milk of life, and a broad, far-reaching love.

However many well-meaning readers ask me to retain the style of the "organization department's young newcomer," that is both impossible and unnecessary. Twenty years have passed since I was expelled from the "organization department," and I am no longer young. I have gained more than I lost, however. I have gained a wide world in which to accomplish great things; I have braved the storm and faced the world; and I have accumulated twenty years of vital experience and tutelage. My starting point now is this ancient land that spans eight thousand li and thirty stormy years.[5] That is why my stories "Bolshevik Salute," "The Butterfly," "Eye of Night," and "Voices of Spring" all cover a far broader span of time and space. Those who study the "technique of fiction" might shake their heads, but never do I cease to think of, cry, and laugh over those eight thousand li and thirty years. That is the fulcrum of my stories.

I remain unswervingly and passionately loyal to youth, love, my faith in life, and the principles and ideals of the revolution. To say that my style has completely changed is not really true. I have become more of a realist, however. I've seen the hardships of life; I've seen that all good things must ripen and mature, temper and perfect themselves, and pass one test after another. In my romantic and transparent "Kite Streamers," for instance, there is still in the love songs a note of sobriety and remoteness. My songs are no longer simple serenades of youth. To praise this vast, ocean-like mother, so vigorous despite all she has been through, I need a symphony of all the instruments.

The writer of forty-six is, to be sure, far more complex than the writer of twenty-one. While I have displayed bitter sarcasm, freezing irony, and burning satire in the face of all the negative things, I now can see also how true it is that "the real is the rational."[6] I have learned to value "fair play," forgiveness, tolerance, and patience, as well as stability and unity. Behind my acid sarcasm is

---

[5]Note in the original text: Eight thousand li is the distance from Peking to Xinjiang.

[6]A reference to the Hegelian tenet that "The real is the rational and the rational is the real."

tenderness; understanding lies behind my cold irony and burning satire; and beneath my bitter hatred I still have hope, replete with zealous enthusiasm. I have also come to know that people must have ideals, but that ideals, after all, cannot be realized all at once; I know, too, that using fiction to delve into life is ultimately easier than getting one's hands dirty working to change life.[7] Therefore, when I write, I pay more heed to inspiring my readers and giving them encouragement and comfort than to using fiction to expose contradictions or push solutions to political problems.

As for hatred, mine has limits. Keeping a tight rein on hatred is, I think, essential to maintaining and developing stability and unity. But I am by no means indifferent or apathetic, nor am I just out to save my own skin. The weapons I have found useful are satire and humor. In the preface to "Anecdotes of Section Chief Maimaiti," I argue that humor is a vital element of life. The section chief's "humor," though, contains a streak of "Ah Q-ism," painful yet eliciting sympathy. Absurd laughter is a form of protest against an absurd life.

One friend has made it plain that he doesn't care for this laughter of mine. He thinks I use it to gloss over contradictions and prettify myself. Do I? My readers can decide for themselves. But I genuinely feel that we have cried too much already, that we need to laugh and have the right to. I would even say that laughter might well be a more sophisticated, more complex form of expression than tears. There are animals that can cry (as lambs bleat under the butcher's knife), but only people can laugh. Therefore, even in my most ordered, serious, and emotionally expressive writing, there is never a shortage of things to laugh at. At the same time, I seek the solemn component present in such literary forms as caricature or farce.

The increased complexity of experience, thought, emotion, and life itself all demand more complex forms of expression. In my writing I am experimenting with multiple narrative threads in what could be termed a radiating structure, rather than adhering rigidly to one main thread. I have attempted to use a kind of "psychological portrayal" that transcends the barriers of time and space to fully reveal the "eight thousand li" and "thirty years" mentioned above, and the connections and contrasts among the many things that filled them. All along I have searched up and down through contexts classical and modern, Chinese and foreign, for my creative identity. I cannot deny having drawn lessons from others, not just from foreign literature, but from the poetry of Li Shangyin and Li He,[8] and the xiangsheng comic dialogues of Hou Baolin and Ma Ji. Still, the forms I strive for always arise from the soil underfoot, from our own lives. As our lives have become more complex, and the tempo has accelerated, my writing, with its radiating threads and quickened stride, has followed suit. Have I found my

---

[7]The first alternative, "delving into life," is Liu Binyan's advocacy. See his essay in this anthology.

[8]Li Shangyin and Li He were famous poets but had unsuccessful official careers.

identity? Have I succeeded? Perhaps I am still groping in the dark, still in the experimental phase. Maybe what I really want to write is still before me. And maybe I will never find what I am seeking. . . .

"Wo zai xunzhao shenme" (What am I looking for?), in *Wenxue zhi lu* (The path of literature) (Changsha, 1983), pp. 1–10.

—Translated by Catherine Pease Campbell

Chen Rong

CHEN RONG (b. 1936, in Hankou, of Sichuanese parentage, whence her name in dialect, Shen Rong), gained notoriety early in the post-Mao era for her 1980 novella, "Ren dao zhongnian" (At middle age). It became a celebrated lament for China's hard-pressed professional people of that generation, particularly women.

The essay that follows is a most ironic description of a writer's experiences struggling for publication and political survival during two "opposite" political climates: in the later stages of the ultraleftist period prior to Mao's death in 1976, and in the early and uneasy reformist era at the turn of the 1980s, when the leftists had been overthrown. This essay may be something of a face-saving gesture by Chen Rong, but her impossible slalom may be taken as a concrete commentary on the more general judgments and warnings delivered by Wu Zuguang in his essay on censorship. All intellectuals who have lived under two regimes—as under the Nazis and the early postwar governments, in the German case—will appreciate and sympathize with Chen Rong's fate.

Novels Strangled in the Cradle
My Senseless Literary Battles

Chen Rong

December 4, 1983

I

THERE'S nothing I want to say or write about myself. For years I refused on principle to be interviewed, to be filmed, to appear on magazine covers, or to discuss how I write. This often makes me feel guilty, but I have no choice. I have no skeletons in my closet, I am no more modest than anyone else, and I have no secrets of how I write that cannot be divulged. It is just that the most important thing for a novelist, as I see it, is to write her works. But now that the editors of *Research Materials on Contemporary Chinese Literature* are bringing out a volume on me, I have to retreat from this position. When I think of all the written and unwritten nonsense about me, perhaps, too, I can take this opportunity to describe my life and writing for the record. At the very least it will clear up some misconceptions.

All the same, I never want to write anything like this again.

II

Ancestral home: Wushan, Sichuan. Born in Hankou, Hubei. Grew up beside the Jialing River and at the foot of the Great Wall, wandered to the ends of the earth, was a worker, went to university. Translated, taught, was reformed, "reformed" others. Now a professional writer and author.

If you want a brief life, that's it.

III

I have never been to Wushan, but when very young I was told that our ancestral home was in the mountains of Wushan and that my grandfather had a lot of land. He must have been a landlord.

My father graduated from China University and was president of the higher court and the supreme court in Kuomintang-ruled Beiping [Peking], Chongqing, Neijiang, and elsewhere.

My mother was from Baoding in Hebei. She graduated from the Hebei Women's Normal Senior Middle School before a brief term as a teacher.

I was born on October 3, 1936, into a China that was in travail. Before I was one, the war with Japan broke out and we had to flee to Sichuan.

When Chongqing was liberated at the end of 1949, I was in the second year of junior middle school at the Second Girls' Middle School. My father sent me and my sister to stay with a relation in Chengdu, the rich owner of a knitwear factory. I was both a guest and a special kind of apprentice. During that year I learned how to knit socks by machine, but it bored me.

Returning to Chongqing a year later, I took the tests to join an army cultural troupe. They accepted me, as did the Southwestern Workers Publishing House when I took the exams for them. It was an easy choice: I preferred books to dancing. But the publishing house was not in a position to publish: it only sold books. In 1952, we were taken over by the Xinhua Bookstore and I was transferred to the *Southwestern Workers Daily*. I was the lowest of the low in the editorial offices, logging in readers' letters, delivering manuscripts, and taking down and copying out news reports. I studied Russian, painting, and senior middle school subjects in my spare time. In 1954, I passed the exams for the Peking Russian Training School (now the Peking Foreign Studies University), and upon graduating in 1957, I joined the Central Broadcasting Bureau as a Russian translator and music editor, first in the Iranian section and then in the section broadcasting to the Soviet Union. I often fainted in the office. In 1962, I lost my job there and became a Russian teacher.

IV

Because I kept fainting, nobody would give me a teaching job. It was the most painful chapter of my life.

In despair, I took to writing. Not because I had any literary talent, but only because I could not go to work and had to have something to do. Literature then had to "serve the workers, peasants, and soldiers," and I chose the peasants, among whom I had lived a long time in my childhood. In the autumn of 1963, I sent my two children to stay with relatives in Shanghai. I took leave of my husband and went by myself to a brigade in Evergreen Commune, Fenyang County, Shanxi. The countryside was recovering then [from the catastrophic consequences of the Great Leap Forward], and the peasants were cheerful, having pigs, sheep, and chickens in their yards. I worked from dawn to dusk with my hosts. In my spare time, I painted pictures for the peasants and taught them reading and writing. I was so happy to be among them after having been more or less on the scrap heap in the city that I did not write a word. But their voices and smiles were etched in my heart and have kept reappearing in my fiction ever since.

When the Four Clean-ups campaign began the next winter, I, as a state cadre who knew quite a lot about the village [and who ran it], was urged to join the work team that came in from outside. Rather than betray my friends, I left.

Back in Peking, I wrote a couple of immature plays on rural themes, as a result of which Comrade Li Zhihua allowed me to sit in on his classes at the Central Academy of Drama. My third play, *Jiao Yulu in Lankao*,[1] was sent to the Peking People's Art Theater, but then the "Cultural Revolution" came along. When theater later revived, it looked as though the play was going to be performed, but nothing came of it.

These three failures destroyed my confidence in myself as a playwright and taught me that a script had to get past a whole series of barriers: the script office, the director, the theater leadership, and higher leadership. Only a ruthless fighter could cope. I gave up the struggle.

But I did not give up writing. My language was not hopeless, my characters were fairly credible, and I could convey something of the atmosphere of life. Why allow my characters to be hanged on the stage of dramaturgy? Why not put them into fiction?

But this was after the "Cultural Revolution."

V

During the "Cultural Revolution," I stayed on the sidelines, not because I was against it from the beginning, but because I belonged to no unit in which to "make revolution." Later I was sent to the countryside again, to be "reeducated by the poor and lower-middle peasants." This time it was in Tongxian, not far from Peking, but now I was doing it officially and on full pay instead of unofficially and on sick pay. I enjoyed working with the peasants and goofing off with them too, getting around stupid orders from on high, and sitting cross-legged with the women and girls, stitching soles for cloth shoes and listening to them talk.

Somehow or other we "stinking intellectuals undergoing reeducation" were turned one night into members of "Mao Zedong Thought propaganda teams" going into a lot of villages to carry out "education in the party's basic line." The result was to open my eyes wider to rural life and give me the greatest freedom of maneuver. I got to know cadres from the county level on down, as well as landlords, rich peasants, counterrevolutionaries, bad elements, and other people I would have kept clear of before in order to avoid suspicion.

---

[1] A play about Jiao Yulu (1922–1964), a county party secretary in the last fifteen months of his life. He became a model of selflessness and of how to apply Maoist policies to overcome rural poverty.

It was then that I started writing my ill-fated novel, *Evergreen* (*Wan nian qing*). Had I known the trouble it was going to provoke, I never would have put pen to paper.

VI

Evergreen, set in 1962, was about how a production brigade in North China resisted the policy of giving responsibility for production [from the commune organization] back to the family.

The story was not something I concocted myself. Such things happened in many Chinese villages. Jiao Yulu had publicized a village called Hancun that had remained determinedly collective, and his support for the poor and lower-middle peasants of Hancun in sticking to the collective road and overcoming natural disaster through collective strength had been the main theme of my unperformed play, *Jiao Yulu in Lankao*. When I turned it into a novel, I took the resistance of a village's poor and lower-middle peasants to contracting production back to households as the main story line, weaving in some of the more successful characters and scenes from a number of unperformed plays of mine to make a novel of it. All my "life capital" at the time went into it. Perhaps that was why it was fairly easy to write, even though it was my first novel. When I came back to Peking in November 1973 and was posted to the Number Five Middle School as a Russian teacher, one of my greatest achievements was that I was carrying the manuscript of this novel.

But when I finished the manuscript, I had no confidence in it. My first reader was Comrade Li Xifan. He wrote me an approving letter that gave me the confidence to submit it to a publishing house.

As it happened, Comrade Wang Yi, a former deputy chief editor at the *People's Daily* who had been "overthrown" and was then at home, offered to show it to his friend Comrade Yan Wenjing, who had just been given back his job at the People's Literature Publishing House. Yan Wenjing did not give my manuscript any special attention just because Wang Yi had given it to him; he passed it on to an editor, Xu Xianqing, to look over and comment on. I mention this in order to clear Yan Wenjing of the unfair trouble he later got into on account of the novel.

Xu Xianqing is a responsible and experienced editor. He read the manuscript and was in favor of it. The leaders of the People's Literature Publishing House at the time, including comrades Wang Zhiyuan, Wei Junyi, and Tu An, all read the novel. They unanimously agreed to include it in their publishing schedule, made suggestions for its revision, and applied to my employers for writing leave for me. I revised the manuscript very quickly and delivered it to the publishers.

My excitement while I waited for it to be sent to the printers, and then for the proofs to arrive, is indescribable. The labors of ten whole years were about to bear fruit.

But just then the movement to "repudiate Lin Biao and Confucius" began. Disaster struck me again.

A few rebels who had been placed in the publishing house put up a lot of handwritten posters attacking Yan Wenjing, Wang Zhiyuan, Wei Junyi, and other veteran comrades just back at their jobs, for " 'overcoming their desires and restoring the Rites,' in imitation of Confucius" [as Lin Biao was supposed to have done]. One of the heavy shells fired at them was that they were preparing to publish *Evergreen* and in so doing "revive extinct states, continue broken family lines, and raise up survivors of fallen dynasties" [another charge against Lin Biao]. Their grounds for saying this were that the publishing house was going to publish a novel by the daughter of a Kuomintang judge who, according to evidence they had cooked up, was responsible for taking seven lives.

Thus it was that my novel was strangled in its cradle by the movement to repudiate Lin Biao and Confucius.

VII

The great majority of the comrades in the publishing house felt that I had been given a hard time, but they were powerless to do anything about it.

I called on all the leaders of the publishing house to complain of the injustice. Although my father had been a judge under the Kuomintang, he had been guilty of no killings. The conclusion reached on his career during the reform of the legal system was that his were "ordinary historical problems." I had told the publishers all this when I first had dealings with them and kept nothing back. Only after the leadership had reckoned that according to party policy this was no problem had they put *Evergreen* into the publishing schedule. Why the change now? These senior comrades urged me to "trust the masses and trust the party." I knew that they were sympathetic, but there was nothing they could do about it. My only ray of hope, albeit a very faint one, came from their decision to keep the manuscript in their office.

Soon that hope, too, was extinguished. The campaign against Lin Biao and Confucius produced a drive against "going by the back door" that was aimed at veteran comrades. The rebels seized on my novel again, saying that instead of having been delivered by the post office through the front door, it had been brought in through the "back door" by Comrade Yan Wenjing. Under this pressure, Comrade Wang Zhiyuan, the editor mainly handling my novel, left town on business, and Yan Wenjing had to return the novel to me in an unmarked brown envelope.

For me this was a fatal blow, not just because of the ten years' wasted effort, but also because it meant that I had lost the right to be published. And writing was life itself to me. I felt that I could not go on living.

Spare-time writing calls for a great deal of hard work and also arouses resentment. To some people, you are "reaching above yourself" and "getting wild ideas," or at the very least guilty of "individualism" and "wanting fame and fortune." Like many other spare-time writers wanting to avoid mockery, I kept my writing secret until the People's Literature Publishing House asked my unit to give me writing leave. But what was in store for me now that publication of the book had been stopped on the eve of its going to the printers?

How could I accept such an attack?

There was nothing else I could do but write a letter to the person in the Central Committee who then controlled literature and art [presumably Jiang Qing], because nobody else was going to stick their neck out on a policy issue until she made her position clear. Let me add that the letter was posted by registered mail from the Beixinqiao post office in Peking, the one nearest my home.

Ten days later, two comrades from the Office of the Central Committee came to see me. Our talk was in the party branch office of Number Five Middle School. The two comrades found out from me about my family and asked what unit my father had belonged to and where his dossier was now kept. They also asked me to send the manuscript of the novel to the section of the Office of the Central Committee that handled correspondence and visits from the public. I remember very clearly their saying to me shortly before they left, "You must have confidence in the party's policy toward intellectuals." My reply was very short: "Would I have dared write that letter if I didn't?"

After about another forty days, a comrade from the northern fiction section of the People's Literature Publishing House came to tell me that the Office of the Central Committee had sent the manuscript of the novel back to the publishers with a directive along these lines: The novel is well founded; there are no problems about the author herself; and the publishing house should help with the revision and publish it. I was also told that the person in the Central Committee then in charge of literature and art had marked the directive with a circle, though I never saw it.[2]

The return of *Evergreen* to the publishing docket was but a small blow to the rebels in the publishing house, yet it let the veteran comrades who had "restored the Rites in imitation of Confucius" off the hook; they no longer had to be accused of "reviving extinct states, continuing broken family lines, and raising up survivors of fallen dynasties." Other novels that had been dropped from the publishing list for similar reasons also benefited from the amnesty. The unfortunate thing was that after the smashing of the "Gang of Four," some authors and certain comrades in publishing houses were to be in trouble again, over the publication of these novels.

For me, it was a great happiness that *Evergreen* smashed through enormous

---

[2]A circle in the margin of an official document means that a bureaucrat has read it, but it does not necessarily imply agreement.

barriers and was finally published. Never did I imagine at the time that this book was later going to cause me many more years of torture.

VIII

When I went back to the publishing house to discuss further revisions to *Evergreen*, I was particularly careful not to do or say anything out of line that could give the rebels an excuse to launch another attack. I was even more worried that the people at the top would go back on their word. The comrades in the publishing house were also very careful not to show how pleased they were to be editing again, and between us we worked to ensure an uneventful publication.

When *Evergreen* came out in September 1975, my school, the education bureau, and the district party committee showed my writing the greatest concern and support. I was given writing leave, and some of the comrades in the district treated the book's publication as one of their achievements. They asked me to talk about my experience in writing it. I "modestly" refused. Thanks to their help, however, my writing leave was extended, and early in 1976 I arrived in the Lüliang Mountains of Shanxi.

All I wanted was to get away from the chaos of Peking and all that sincere and insincere adulation, and back to the peaceful countryside and the peasants who had given me so much of the milk of life. I met many old friends again. Some had risen from grass-roots cadres to become leading county party officials. This gave me the chance to meet many county party secretaries, go with them to meetings, on village visits, and on an inspection trip to Dazhai. I got a rough idea of their innermost troubles and of the skill with which they used any opening to defend the people's interests. It was on the basis of this period of my life that I wrote my second novel, *Light and Darkness (Guangming yu heian)*, and my long story, "Song of Praise." Of course, I also met many peasants driving their carts along the snow-filled valleys of the Lüliang Mountains. It was here that my long story "White Snow" was set. I loved this remote and peaceful place where I could forget all troubles.

But the Lüliang Mountains were still part of the world. The poems and blood of Tiananmen Square that shook the whole country [the Tiananmen incident or April 5 movement of 1976] disturbed these distant mountain valleys, too. I returned to Peking to experience the alarm of the Tangshan earthquake, after which I accepted the invitation of a sister of mine who was teaching in Hefei, Anhui, to go there with my two children to avoid further quakes. As an "author from Peking," I was given special treatment. I got to know many local cadres whose records went back to the days of the New Fourth Army, as well as a lot of "rocket cadres" [those who shot up suddenly] and vindictive party secretaries. To a writer who had made describing life and the age her function, stories of the rise of the rebel faction and their struggles with veteran cadres were well worth hearing.

After the "Gang of Four" fell, I wrote *Light and Darkness*. The original plan had been for it to be a nine-volume novel about the struggles between the various forces in a county party committee during the 1975 campaign to Learn from Dazhai. Included were veteran cadres of all kinds, as well as "revolutionary leading cadres" who had started their careers as rebels. I shut myself away and wrote night and day, hoping that with this new novel I would be able to greet the springtime for art and literature that followed the fall of the "Gang of Four." I never expected that the circumstances of the publication of *Evergreen* would be dragged up again.

IX

It started with an investigation of that letter and the channel by which it had been sent. As my husband worked for the *People's Daily*, he was suspected of having passed it to Lu Ying, who then controlled the paper. This was wrong; just at that time the "Gang of Four" had started a struggle to "repudiate the 'evil influence and force' represented by Hu Jiwei and Wang Ruoshui" in the *People's Daily*. My husband had the misfortune to be regarded as part of the "evil influence." I could not help sharing his misfortune; the last thing I would have done would be to try to cash in on his position. I don't know by what kind of sixth or any other sense I had been so careful, but I had actually kept the receipt for the registered letter. I now respectfully handed it in, "supplied" the names of the two comrades from the Office of the Central Committee, and asked the organization to investigate.

Next I was asked to make a written confession about my time in Anhui, when I had got to know those "rocket cadres" and "vindictive party secretaries." (I must point out that they said they were not asking me for a confession, but that it was in my own best interests to get everything sorted out.) Luckily I had kept a diary at the time of whom I had seen and when and where, as well as what we had talked about. I was able to make a very full written statement that ran to over ten thousand words. I later learned from friends in Anhui that investigators had twice followed the route I took, making detailed inquiries. Presumably they found no conspiracies, for they did not come to see me again. I do not know whether my statement and the report on the investigation in Anhui were destroyed or are on file somewhere. If, some years from now, anyone is still interested in me and my works, they may even be able to find these precious documents.

It was also said that as its characters included a party branch secretary called Jiang Chunwang and a production brigade head called Deng Wanju, *Evergreen* was promoting Jiang Qing and attacking Comrade Deng Xiaoping. I didn't know whether to laugh or to cry. It was a novel about a village, and like so many other

Chinese villages it was dominated by two or three big clans. My village had the Jiangs and the Dengs. There were good and bad characters in both of them. How could anyone make such a wild connection? Fortunately, Jiang Chunwang was a man, and Deng Wanju was not a capitalist roader. Otherwise, I would never have been able to clear myself.

In the end, my innocence was proved, which was fine. But I was also notified that my writing leave had been canceled, and that if I was not back at work by a given date my pay would be stopped. In response to my plea for help, Li Jingfeng, the head of the publishing house's northern fiction department, and Meng Xinlu, the editor who handled my books, went to explain and to apologize for not having gone through the correct procedures to arrange for the extension of my writing leave. (Nobody had actually said that such procedures were necessary, and everyone had been saying they supported me going off to write more novels.) All efforts failed, and in April 1977 my monthly salary of fifty-six yuan was stopped.

Despite the hardship of having no salary, I finished *Light and Darkness*, the first volume of which came out in July 1978. I went on to write "Eternal Spring" and "At Middle Age." When asked whether any of my own feelings about life had gone into "At Middle Age," I used to reply with diplomatic evasions, but let me now say it: Of course they did. For a long time I ate cold sesame buns, drank plain hot water, and sat writing at my three-drawer desk.

I will never forget the attempts many comrades made to have the injustice to me reversed. Sometimes I had to borrow money. I could never understand why there should be such a fuss just because some cadres had helped a writer to explore life more deeply and carry on her writing.

A talk by the leading comrade in the propaganda department of the Central Committee of the Communist party published early in 1979 included the remark that the propaganda department was the writer's logistical support and general staff. This made so deep an impression on me that I decided to write to the chief of this general staff. A few years back, *Evergreen* had been published because of "Central Committee" intervention. Only the Central Committee could now decide whether I had been wrong to write that letter about getting *Evergreen* published and whether it was right to stop my pay.

The leading comrade in the Central Committee's propaganda department issued two directives because of this letter, and other comrades from the department visited a lot of official yamens on my account. The problem, however, was only solved a year later, when my novella "At Middle Age" had created quite a stir. Many part-time and professional authors in Peking spoke up for me at practically every meeting. The Peking Writers' Association enthusiastically supported spare-time writers who wrote letters on my behalf. I also had the sympathy of the propaganda department of the Peking municipal party committee. In the end, the Peking municipality paid my back salary and transferred me to the municipal writers' association as a professional writer attached to it. By now it was September 1980.

X

Comment on my works is best left to readers and critics, but I would like to say a few words about *Evergreen* and *Light and Darkness.*

Neither of them will be republished, for the obvious reason that their political viewpoints are wrong and do not fit current policy. *Evergreen* is about resistance to contracting out production to individual households, the very policy that is now being practiced; and *Light and Darkness* is a story set in the movement to Learn from Dazhai, something no longer spoken about.

As to what to do with these two novels, it is very simple for libraries: take them off the shelves and treat them as if they had never been published. For the author it is not so simple. I cannot deny having written my first two books. I cannot rewrite history.

So why were these politically wrong books written? I cannot accept the view that it was because their author was cut off from real life and following politics too closely. As life and politics are inseparable in our society, literature that reflects life cannot be cut off from politics. In real life, contracting out to households was opposed by the Central Committee, by the party committees at all levels below it, and by the mass of the peasantry who were mobilized to do so. Moreover, a lot of people opposed it, in all sincerity. This opposition lasted from 1962 until after the fall of the "Gang of Four." It continued to the very eve of the Third Plenum of the Eleventh Central Committee.

When in 1974 I was writing about Chinese villages as they were in 1962, I could of course only describe how the party and the peasants resisted contracting out. I could not describe support for contracting out that did not then exist. Similarly, in 1975 there was a real-life campaign to Learn from Dazhai, and many veteran comrades actually used this campaign to struggle against the rebels who "only grasped revolution and did not look after production." The veterans hoped thereby to bring about stability, solidarity, and economic development. A novel about the life of a party committee in 1975 could describe tricks that the committee played during the campaign to Learn from Dazhai, but not criticism that never happened at the time.

In my view, literary works that reflect life have to reflect the distorted life that was warped by so many years of "leftist" politics in China. The reason for the appearance of such works does not lie in their authors: they are a unique phenomenon in the literary history of China. In a few years' time, someone may make a special study of it.

XI

Looking back on the course my writing has taken is exhausting. I am very tired.

This is nothing to get pleased or excited about. Writing is tiring, but so what?

Nobody asked you to take it up. What I cannot take is having to wage such long, hard struggles to win the right to create and to avoid slander. It has been ten years of endless small battles and two big ones. I have had to carry a shield in one hand, to protect me from potshots and arrows in the back, while using my other hand to hold my pen. It has been very tiring indeed.

I can hardly believe now that I could have had the courage and energy then to cope with such relentless struggles. I don't think I have the courage and energy for a third big battle. Next time I will give in without a fight.

Life is short and I do not have much time left. As long as my pen is not knocked out of my hand and I can carry on writing, I cannot bear to waste my time fighting senseless literary legal battles.

"Bing fei youqude zishu" (A thoroughly boring account of myself), December 4, 1983, in *Chen Rong yanjiu zhuanji* (Special collection of research on Chen Rong) (Guiyang, 1984), pp. 20–39.

—Translated by W. J. F. Jenner

Lu Wenfu

Lu Wenfu (b. 1928, in Jiangsu) is best known for his short stories, many of which draw inspiration from the picturesque city of Suzhou—the "Venice of the East"—which he has called home ever since the war. Lu Wenfu was sent down for "reeducation" numerous times, as during the Antirightist movement and the Cultural Revolution, so he has had two careers as a writer: the first in the 1950s and 1960s, and the second in the Deng Xiaoping reform era. Notable among his works in the latter period is the short novel *Meishijia* (The Gourmet, 1982), a wistful history of the destruction of China's culinary arts since 1949 that has many symbolic overtones.

In the excerpt below, Lu Wenfu addresses his own group, China's middle-aged writers. Many of them have complained about having had to waste so many years during China's political turmoil, while the younger generation in many cases had a luckier start and enjoyed infinitely better working conditions. Warning against bitterness and envy, Lu Wenfu soberly evaluates both the social clout and the artistic limits of writers at his stage of life. He acknowledges that they are ignorant of world literature and even of China's own major traditions. He is in fact conscious that the vicissitudes of his times have deprived middle-aged writers of the chance to equal the best of Chinese authors, such as Lu Xun, who were active during the pre-1949 years. Authors with such handicaps should not now try, in his opinion, for a tour de force that will paint a picture of a whole epoch (as the social realism in which his generation was tutored might tempt them to try to do). We find here also the conviction that the younger generation will create the more lasting works: thoughtful counterpoint to Ba Jin's more optimistic statements in his *Memoirs*, which rank the literature of the 1980s above Chinese works of the Republican era, in the 1920s and 1930s.

Spokesman for a Victimized Generation
Can There Be Progress after "Midlife"?

Lu Wenfu

April 1981

NONE of us [at this meeting] is particularly young any more; although our age may not be too pleasing to some of us, when it comes to creative writing, certain things about being older should make us happy. Life is the wellspring of creative work. Being older and more experienced, we have a lot more material to write about. Although our storehouse of memories is still far from full, there's a bit more in it now than when we were young. In our youth, we would finish one piece without knowing what we might write next. Now, lots of people and events are whirling around in our minds. Some have been there for quite a few years.

Writing is like making a cigarette: it must be a blend of fresh tobacco, old tobacco, leaves from Yunnan, from Xuchang, and some from other places. If you roll cigarettes from leaves grown on one tiny plot of land and they don't turn out well, then you've got "high-quality cigarettes made in the commune factory." The packaging may be nice, but the taste won't be very mellow. Many comrades here have been through the Sino-Japanese War, the War of Liberation, the Three Great Transformations [collectivization of agriculture, handicrafts, and industry and commerce], the Antirightist campaign, the Great Leap Forward, the Three Years of Adjustment, the Cultural Revolution, the fall of the Gang of Four—a complete history of modern China is stored in our minds. You can't say our lives have been impoverished. In this regard, China's writers appear heaven-blessed. We have no need to go out searching for strange and novel things. There's plenty to write about in our present-day lives and struggles. Times of peace and tranquility may give rise to economic prosperity, but literature usually emerges from periods of chaos, great transformations, and massive unrest. Literature is about human beings and their fates; when society is in great flux, human beings also experience all kinds of change and uncertainty. The power of the old is strong and the struggles of the new are ardent; people's quests are sincere, their emotions zealous; happiness and despair, gratitude and resentment, success and failure—these things that move the human heart must find a place in good works of literature. Just as distress regenerates a nation, so too is literature revived by hardship. "Literary talents have ill-starred lives." This saying doesn't just go for individuals, it should be broadened to include the destiny of a nation, of a people. Even when a nation and its people are engaged in bitter struggle, there will be a few people whose lot is not so bad who can continue writing good literary works that move people's hearts—this has been true in the history of literature both East and West. Poverty, backwardness, hardship, chaos: these are not necessarily obstacles to literature. Material wealth is not the same as spiritual wealth. In fact, blind pursuit of the material inevitably creates a spiritual vacuum. The spiritual and the material fulfill and complement each other; they spur each other forward and hold each other back. We work in the realm of the spirit. A good literary work must have that bit of "spirit," and the stronger it is, the more long-lasting significance the work will possess. If we look at our personal storehouse from this angle, can we not say that as the years mount, we not only fill it up, we fill it with good material: tobacco of the highest quality?

Those of us past middle age often lack confidence in our writing. This is a common enemy. In our youth, strong as an ox, we'd have made a mad dash without further ado. Often we'd fall down, and yet still be able to write something good, even something we couldn't surpass later. As we got older, we tended to become cautious and indecisive, having "great aims but petty deeds," so that even if we wrote something, we lacked the courage to bring it out into the open. Thus, in our case, it's still very important to encourage a little self-confidence. However, it must not be blind confidence. We must also awaken to our shortcomings.

There are those who would have us struggle to become great writers like Lu Xun and Mao Dun. Although this is a worthwhile aspiration and a well-intentioned encouragement, there are in fact some problems with that. Perhaps this hope can be realized in the next generation. This is my own personal opinion and may not represent everyone. I feel that those we call great writers become so not simply from writing a few good pieces; they are the embodiment of the cultural aspirations of an entire generation. If culture is compared to a mountain, they are the ones who stand on its peak. That peak is very narrow and sharp, but it is supported by a base several tens or several hundreds of miles wide. Without a base, there can be no peak; if the base is narrow, the mountain will not be very high, like a stunted stalk of bamboo.

Think how learned Lu Xun and Mao Dun were. They could write about China and foreign countries, the past and the present, astronomy and geography; they could create and they could translate; write a story or a research essay; and their every brushstroke was fine calligraphy! Of all of us gathered here, there is not a single person of our generation whose cultural base is as extensive as theirs was.

We cannot lay the entire blame on our own laziness and lack of ambition. From the time we could understand what was going on around us, we had to deal with the Sino-Japanese War, the subsequent chaos and recurring struggle that affected our lives, and finally, the Ten-Year Calamity [the Cultural Revolution]. At the time when our memories were at their best, we had neither the opportunity nor the conditions to learn more. In truth, we embarked on the road of creative writing mostly by chance, without adequate preparation; it was stop and go, as we fought and ran. Having simply lived stirring lives, read a few books, and scraped together a few literary skills, we became writers without giving it much thought.

Creative writing, especially the novel, betrays how cultured a writer is. One can't hide it. Sometimes we think we've described a person or an event color-fully and vividly, but when we read it, it seems to lack a little something—the breadth and profundity, the far-reaching vision, of a great writer. I think that Cao Xueqin would never have been able to write *The Dream of the Red Chamber* if it had been merely a question of knowing a little about the art of writing and being familiar with a few characters like Bao Yu and Lin Daiyu. A novel like *The Dream of the Red Chamber* is like an exhibit of traditional Chinese culture.

Of course, we may still be able to read a few books and learn a few things in the days to come, but there is a limit to our time, our energy, and the conditions we work in. When Lu Xun and Mao Dun ascended to the peak of that mountain, they were almost the same age as we are now. Great minds may mature late in life, but not accidentally or suddenly. This adage, "great minds may mature late in life" itself means to say that the making of a great mind requires thorough preparation. It can't be accomplished overnight.

Besides our weak foundation, there are still many restrictions and inhibitions implicit in our literary ideas, methods, and writing habits. We're still governed by lots of once-fashionable viewpoints that we don't completely understand or that were never correct to begin with. We all consider our own thinking to be very liberated, but that's not necessarily so. There is a difference between liber-ated thinking, subjective caprice, and wild impulse. I believe that there are two main things to liberated thinking: first, timely recognition of truth as it is demon-strated in practice; and second, firmly holding on to scientific predictions based on actual experience.

If there's anything to be learned from my analysis, maybe it's that if we want to improve our writing, we must start with what we have. We don't want to lose faith, but neither do we want to indulge in fantasy. We don't want to be indeci-sive or reluctant to move forward—time waits for no man! Neither do we want to produce a trilogy or try to encapsulate an entire era at the drop of a hat. We'd best spend a little time in our storehouses, examining what we've accumulated there, and weighing its significance anew. We must use the vision of the present to evaluate the past, and the perspective of history to examine our life today.

Once we see things correctly, and clearly, we can adopt the technique of "the rat eating dumplings" and "skip over to the filling." We ought not just to nibble at the skin, but we shouldn't desert the dumpling to go search for a dish of braised beef, either.

We mustn't be overly concerned with our own reputation; it doesn't matter if we can't produce a masterpiece, so long as we contribute a little something, if only sketch material, even a notebook—our successors can pull it all together. Our generation must be willing to serve as a ladder. The *Water Margin* gave rise to *The Golden Lotus*, and *The Golden Lotus* inspired *The Dream of the Red Chamber*. Cao Xueqin himself climbed to the top on a human ladder. It's not at all a question of stepping on other people's shoulders to get ahead oneself: culture is cumulative in its development. I don't mean to advocate less ambition, but rather to leave a little room for improvement, so that we can have a firm footing and get to work immediately. Since many things are in our favor, once our generation has taken this path, it may produce some peaks—a few major works and major authors—so long as we don't take them to be great works for all the ages.

Literature abhors empty talk and grandiose ambitions most of all. Literature is concrete, concrete, and again concrete, all the way down to the most minor details. Whenever you find the filling, you must go quickly and gnaw on it. Empty ideas, sweet fragrances, and wonderful delicacies won't do.

In those first few years after the Ten-Year Calamity, many of us were extremely excited. Sometimes we almost felt like pinching ourselves to see whether we were dreaming. Such a mood of exhilaration could not last forever. In our writing we often heated up till we got the chills, iced up till we got a fever, alternated hot and cold together, or progressed at a constant temperature. Add to all this the bringing order out of chaos, the setting of policy on a correct footing, the many things that had to be rethought, the many concrete matters that had to be attended to. In our writing we'd eaten more of the wrapper than the filling, but that was understandable and unavoidable. Now, though, it's time for the filling.

We had the ingredients for some tasty dishes. We prepared them as best we could and with good intentions, for those who might partake. But we couldn't ignore the question of method or skill. We couldn't just stir-fry some eggs and chopped chives together and claim it was anything more than eggs and chopped chives, generous in quantity but lacking in quality, enough to turn people's stomachs at that.

So now a lot of us are thinking about literary methods and skills. We must consider these questions because for a number of years we have not thought enough about them—we have, whether consciously, unconsciously, or purposely, been obstructed by policies like the Three Prominences and stereotyping.

I believe that this "literary method" is inseparable from a writer's manner of

thinking, personal conduct, and treatment of others; it's also linked with temperament, upbringing, hobbies, and habits. You can't force a serious and meticulous
person of practical habits to get the knack of romantic writing. Nor can you force
a bold and gregarious person with a lust for life to write tear-jerkingly sentimental descriptions. You can only "go your own way," playing to your strengths and
avoiding your weaknesses. You can't be always lamenting that the grass seems
greener on the other side.

A literary technique that is used quite successfully by one person may result
in disaster for another. The four-character phrase *biao xin li yi*—to start something new in order to be different—is quoted by some with approval, by others
not. The actual results clearly are both good and bad.

If one understands which parts of one's life are original or novel and which
are ordinary, then gives voice to the original, that's good. But if one abandons
one's own bearings and goes out in search of something novel, one may end up
with something affected and artificial, mere formalism.

I'd like to say one thing about writing technique, something I heard comrade
Mao Dun say when I was young: "Technique comes primarily from life." These
words have been circling around in my head for many years now, but only
recently have I come to some understanding of them. It really is true. The most
important technique of writing is the ability to take those things in your life that
have most moved you, the significant things that have left you with the deepest
impression and the clearest images, and bring them together organically. You
must understand when to hold tight and not let go, giving full play to your
emotions; and when to be content with a faint suggestion. "Marvelous mastery"
and "superhuman writing" are not simply a matter of technique. It's more often a
question of some inner light in your life demanding that you let it shine. As long
as you don't close the door to it, it will find a way to come in by itself. I've
seldom seen somebody first learn technique and then create. Most people who
write are "forced into it by life itself."

"Ren guo zhongnian hua tigao" (One's words improve with middle age), April 1981,
in Lu Wenfu, *Xiaoshuo menwai tan* (A layman talks about fiction) (Guangzhou, 1982),
pp. 89–98.

—Translated by Beata Grant

Zhang Xianliang

ANOTHER rehabilitated ex-rightist, Zhang Xianliang (b. 1936, in Nanjing) has depicted the humiliating experience of this group of outcasts in autobiographical fiction, much of it set in the barren Ningxia prison camps that became so familiar to him from the inside. Still drawing on the Sino-Marxist framework of the past, his longer fiction is of uneven quality, but he has dared to probe the subject of how sexual behavior was repressed and made aberrant by extraordinarily puritanical policies during the Mao era. Chinese readers appreciate his fiction for its overt and symbolic eroticism. His most famous novels written in this vein are *Nanren de yiban shi nüren* (Half of man is woman, 1985) and the more experimental *Xiguan siwang* (Getting used to dying, 1989). In the essay that follows, Zhang had the courage to point out general shortcomings in contemporary Chinese literature. His essay was prepared as a lecture for an American audience during his visit to the United States in 1985.

After Twenty Years of Silence We Lick Our Wounds

Our Battle for a Place in World Literature

Zhang Xianliang

May 20, 1985, in the United States

AFTER a dozen years and more of strict isolation, the doors of China were recently thrown wide open. The present policy of opening up to the outside and putting life into the domestic economy has brought China into the world economic system. It has also strengthened China's intellectual and cultural contacts with the rest of the world.

These of course include literature and art. China's progress in the last few years has changed the coordinates by which we Chinese measure our position and changed our scale of values. We no longer measure our achievements only by those of other Chinese, or of other parts of China. We want to be measured by universal standards. It was in this spirit that our highly respected Ba Jin expressed a noble aspiration on behalf of all Chinese writers at the recent Fourth Congress of the Chinese Writers' Association: "Chinese literature must take its place in the front rank of world literature."

Since the excitement and inspiration of the congress, writers have had time to think deeply on this proposition and come up with different views on propositions like Ba Jin's.

Some writers hold that in the last few years, the Literature of the New Era has already produced much outstanding work that can be placed without a blush in the front rank of world literature. The only reason why this work has not received its due recognition abroad is because of ingrained prejudices on the part of foreign critics and the linguistic barrier. Other writers believe that the uniqueness of China's social system, of the beliefs and ideals held by Chinese writers, and of the country's cultural traditions and aesthetic psychology, puts China's literature in a class of its own. Hence China cannot compete with other countries in literature on the basis of some universal standard in the way that is possible in science, technology, and athletics. According to this view, Chinese writers can only make their contribution to international exchanges by faithfully portraying the life and the values of the Chinese people and China's historical progress and evolution.

The great majority of writers, especially the younger and middle-aged writers now most active on the Chinese literary scene, agree to some extent with the first of the aforementioned opinions. We should not be spineless or belittle ourselves. We can take pride in the fact that in the last few years we have produced some writing that will stand comparison with the best of the contemporary world; we only regret that our foreign friends do not yet know about it. At the same time, we also believe that in literature, as in science, there are no national frontiers. "World literature" is a concept raised by Goethe long ago, and China should be a part of it. Italian, English, French, Scandinavian, American, and Russian/Soviet literature all have long been and are today recognized as standing in the front rank of world literature. They all have been and still are pathfinders and models. We have our own Chinese version of socialism, and we Chinese writers have our own philosophical beliefs and social ideals, while the Chinese people have their own cultural traditions and aesthetic psychology. But if we accept that the uniqueness of a literary work depends not on the profundity of its concepts but on its construction, and that the work consists not of what it describes but of the work itself, then it can be subject to shared and universal criteria. These criteria are the artistry and the emotional impact of the work itself.

On the other hand, we also recognize that, by these universal criteria, there really are some things wrong with contemporary Chinese literature taken as a whole and all by itself (averaging out the outstanding works with the run-of-the-mill ones, which can of course only be done intuitively).

Where then do we fall short?

Every single contemporary Chinese writer has lived a rich and unique life. During nearly twenty years of silence we all buried ourselves deep in thought, and each of us acquired our own original understanding of society and life. It was a case of a disaster turning out to have some good side effects. After all that high-pressure and high-temperature treatment, every Chinese writer's head has become an inexhaustible mine of raw material for writing.

But during that same period of nearly twenty years of isolation, Chinese writers almost completely lost their opportunity for artistic development. Under the high-pressure and high-temperature treatment we were cut off from the literature and art not only of the rest of the world but of China's past. The few connections that remained we were forced to repudiate.

In their universities, research institutes, and studies, or in their travels around the world, today's active and productive writers in the West have been educated in literary tradition, experienced what is special about many different kinds of culture and art, and had their eyes opened. They have sharpened their aesthetic sensibilities in preparation for new artistic explorations and breakthroughs. But today's active and productive Chinese writers have had to endure cold and hunger, biting winds, and drenching storms in the course of exile. We were in remote villages, completely cut off from culture and art, tilling the land, pasturing horses, and feeding pigs with the most primitive methods. Or we were behind bars, licking our wounds like dogs. All that the fortunate ones could do was write literature to order. Far from improving their artistry, it so restricted them that they lost all their individuality as writers.

The writers active in China today are talented and intelligent. Despite the big gap in our artistic experience, we only needed this change in the situation, bringing us creative freedom, to produce immediately works of a certain quality and make Chinese literature and art flourish as they never have before.

But that big gap in their artistic experience has caused the great majority of Chinese writers to lose out on their artistic formation. Art is art, after all, and literature is primarily the art of language. The great majority of contemporary Chinese literary works neglect a most important law of artistry in the use of language: economy. Thus, our language lacks ambiguity, subtle nuances, and multiple meanings. It is short on understatement and humor. Because we try to write everything that is on our mind, we often fail to set readers off on associated lines of thought of their own. This makes it hard for readers to bring their own creativity into play when they enjoy a piece of writing.

Because of this lack of linguistic artistry, we writers often express our ideas and the main themes of our works very directly and explicitly. We make too little use of detailed metaphorical and symbolic descriptions, or of images— real or unreal, precise or undefined—to create profound imaginary worlds in which there are "images beyond the images and thoughts behind the thoughts," worlds that readers must fill out and bring to life with their own imagination, experience, and aesthetic sensitivity. This gives them an ineffable artistic pleasure they can feel.

Most contemporary Chinese writers have a very well-developed aesthetic sense. They have a subtle capacity for sympathy and are imbued with the spirit of humanism. This is why they can write their unique stories and sketches of local customs, creating all kinds of typical characters that attract and move many millions of Chinese readers. But one often regrets that the stories and sketches based on these characters are not still better written and even more moving. A good piece of fiction is a three-dimensional world. The characters and the plot should be multicolored, polyphonic, many-layered, multifaceted. If writers are to create such works, it is not enough for them to have experienced life, felt stormy emotions and strong feelings. Novelists also need to know something of poetry, music, painting, aesthetics, history, and philosophy. They need the widest possible general knowledge. It is in precisely these areas that China's middle-aged and young writers, who have wasted ten to twenty years of their life, are now having to catch up on their education. Few of us can yet claim to have reached maturity.

That is why we commonly find in most contemporary Chinese fiction an inability to coordinate multiple artistic factors in the work's structure. Description and narrative tend to be thin and hackneyed, and three-dimensional space is presented to readers as a flat surface.

Here I have been dealing mainly with the shortcomings of our contemporary literature, and fiction in particular. What we call our "Literature of the New Era" is only seven years old, and China's contemporary writers are still growing up. This is why we do not mind talking about our shortcomings.

The year 1985 has been important in the history of Chinese literature. For one thing, at the Fourth Congress of the Chinese Writers' Association, the Communist party reaffirmed that its guarantee of creative freedom for writers was a firm and unshakable one. Another factor is that we writers active today are summing up what we have learned from our last seven years of writing. There is hardly a single writer who is satisfied with what he or she has achieved so far. We all want to outdo ourselves artistically and write things that are original. It starts with us.

Refinement, imagination, and quiet appeal to the emotions have always been special national emphases in China's aesthetic tradition. So, too, has the demand that writers reflect the multicolored, polyphonic, many-layered, and multifaceted nature of the external world in their spiritual world, which makes their writing natural. China's contemporary writers, who have long used the methods of realism and romanticism, can today derive more artistic techniques from Western modernism. We are simultaneously turning back to tradition and stretching our arms out to the world. By extending ourselves in these two directions, we increase our mental range. Given solid artistic and philosophical training within this vast area, Chinese literature, the literature of one-quarter of the human race, is bound to take its place in the front ranks of world literature.

"Zhongguo dangdai zuojia zai yishu shang de zhuiqiu" (The artistic quest of China's authors today), a May 20, 1985, speech delivered in Chinese in the United States, originally published in English in *Chinese Literature* (Spring 1986): 152–56. Chinese manuscript from the conference volume of the International Conference on Contemporary Chinese Literature, Jinshan, Shanghai, November 1986.

—Translated by W. J. F. Jenner

Gao Xiaosheng

GAO XIAOSHENG (b. 1928, in Jiangsu), like Gu Hua and Jia Pingwa, whose essays follow, concentrates on rural China and the plight of the peasantry. Gao is a representative of that middle generation whose literary expectations and limitations Lu Wenfu assesses in his essay above. At the same time, Gao Xiaosheng belongs to the fraternity of ex-rightists; the experiences of Liu Binyan, Wang Meng, and Lu Wenfu, are Gao's as well.

Literature on rural themes is as much a part of contemporary Chinese consciousness as the "village prose" by Ovečkin, Belov, Šukšin, and Rasputin is a part of Soviet consciousness. But Gao Xiaosheng's famous peasant characters, Li Shunda of "Li Shunda zaowu" (Li Shunda builds a house, 1979) and Chen Huansheng, who since 1980 has appeared in many stories, are more materialistic, more interested in reform, and more optimistically analytical. Gao Xiaosheng's stories lack the Russian nostalgia for disappearing forms of traditional rural life.

The author's sketch below reveals the "conventional" background of a writer of his generation—a childhood of poverty, with Soviet "socialist" and nineteenth-century Western fiction as the major literary leavening. Gao Xiaosheng evokes a somewhat glorified picture of the 1950s, which had come to appear pacific in light of the upheavals that shortly ensued.

Thrusts of Violent Creativity

"I Returned with My Hands Empty and Shame on My Face"

Gao Xiaosheng

1980

I

As A CAREFREE lad, I did not realize until late in my childhood that my family was very poor. My father, a language teacher, often had no work and was bad at farming. Meanwhile, my mother bore brothers and sisters one after another. The family's financial straits became so bad that we couldn't pretend otherwise. Since my grandfather kept a Chinese medicine shop in a small neighboring town, my mother sent me to Grandfather's so that I could go to school there. Thus the family burden was lessened as well.

There was at that time a bookstore in my grandfather's town that loaned out comic books. I soon became infatuated with them. Every day when I went to school, I clung to my grandfather as if we were twisted candy, until he gave me two copper coins. After school, I'd head straight for the bookstore, make my seat on the door-sill (which was the last place to get dark at night), and read my rented comics until it was pitch black. Several years passed this way, my mind always occupied with stories of every kind. I used to tell them to my friends when I went home during the summer and winter holidays. Sometimes when I forgot part of a story, I would cleverly fill in with details from other ones. My pals, who had no way of knowing the truth, praised me as a wonderful story-teller. I was elated. I felt I had a talent for telling stories and that it might not be so bad to compose them when I grew up.

Soon the Sino-Japanese War broke out. Since my grandfather's town was occupied and we were frequently disturbed by the "devils" [Japanese], I left for my family's home, which was more peaceful at that time. The village had no school in those days, so my father founded his own private one. There I had my first brush with classical Chinese. I can still remember the first essay my father taught me—of all things, it was "The Fighting Cricket" from Pu Songling's *Strange Tales from a Chinese Studio*. I was captivated by Pu Songling, and his book became my childhood favorite. My family had an excellent edition that explained every difficult phrase of the text. That book was practically the key to my mastery of classical Chinese.

I'd read a lot of fiction by the time I graduated from junior middle school—works of all kinds, from famous novels like *The Dream of the Red Chamber* and *Water Margin* to popular works like *The Life of Ji Gong (Ji Gong quanzhuan)* and *Four Men of Talent (Si caizi)*. I can't tell how they influenced me, but my taste for literature was already developing. Looking back on it now, it seems to me that there are good chapters in many works of traditional fiction, such as "The Mansion of the Jia Family" in the *Popular History of the Tang Dynasty (Shuo Tang)* and the chapter "Winning Out on the Military Drill Ground" in *The Life of Yue Fei (Shuo Yue quanzhuan)*. The styles of those works were so vivid that my works today still show their influence. I also conscientiously took it upon myself to study the *Historical Chronicles Made Simple (Gangjian yizhilu)*. I read it as fiction; I was influenced by the succinctness of its language.

With this preparation, I did well in language subjects when I went to school. The teacher's praise accompanied the return of all my compositions. It gradually became my conviction that I was going to be a literary man when I grew up.

Unexpectedly, my mother became seriously ill. She died, for we had no money for doctors. On her deathbed, she called me to her side and said, "Son, we are poor. Nobody will support your schooling after I die. Don't complain. Farm the land as you are told; if somebody takes you on to teach you a trade, go learn it."

II

A period of difficulties ensued. With the whole agricultural economy collapsing, my family was already unable to feed and clothe itself. My father joined the Kuomintang and went into the mountains near Yixing to fight the Japanese. Some of his friends were teaching in the local middle school then. Taking advantage of this opportunity, I got into the school informally. I had no money for tuition or board; I didn't even have any clothes to speak of. I lived off the charity of my classmates. I couldn't concentrate on my schoolwork and seldom thought of my future. My dream of being a man of letters was now becoming more and more remote. In all, I dropped out of school three times before I finished senior middle school. After the war, my father worked as a minor KMT functionary, but we were still financially hard up. Despite everything, I graduated from senior middle school. I wanted to sit for college entrance examinations in literature, but my father was opposed; he insisted that I try out in technical subjects, since a graduate from a literature department would go hungry for want of a job. But I knew I had little chance of success in the technical subjects, for my English wasn't good enough. During the period of occupation, I was so narrow-minded that I couldn't bring myself to learn foreign languages. It was cultural aggression and education for slavery, I thought. I took classes in Japanese for three years, without even learning the alphabet. I resisted learning English, too. I'm afraid that Daudet's famous story "The Last Class" confirmed my prejudice. In the end, I went into the department of economics. It was in fact a Hobson's choice, and in any case I only cared about my future livelihood. That's why I never took my college studies seriously. Literature, still my favorite subject, was constantly in my dreams. As the saying goes, "I stood in Cao Cao's camp, but my loyalty was still with the Han." Hence, I didn't study either subject very well. And to pay for college, I had to teach every night in a primary school. I had little energy left for classwork. What shall I do? I asked myself. Like many young people at that time, I felt weighed down and longed for emancipation.

III

What happy days came next. I joined the revolution and was assigned to work in literature.

So bright was the sky, so flat the earth, so aromatic the air, that my heart filled with optimism. I understood the reason for the revolution and came to love the Communist party. I saw what path to take, and I determined to begin my journey.

I will never forget the bright, beautiful sun that shone over the first half of the 1950s. Everything was so joyous and lucid. Every comrade seemed to wear a wreath of flowers on his head, and a halo over it, for every one of them was intelligent and good.

I made the best of my time studying. Within a few years I had read many works, such as those that had been awarded Stalin Literary Prizes, and books by Gorky, Chekhov, and Balzac. Few works in Chinese translation escaped me. I also dipped into the works of Tolstoy, Maupassant, Dreiser, Martin Andersen Nexø, Hugo, Mérimée, Kobayashi Takiji, and so forth. I was intent on filling in the gaps in my knowledge of foreign and socialist literature.

I also read many works of Chinese revolutionary literature written after Mao's "Talks at the Yan'an Forum on Literature and Art." They included Ding Ling's *The Sun Shines over the Sanggan River*, Zhou Libo's *The Hurricane*, Zhao Shuli's short stories, Ouyang Shan's *Uncle Gao*, Liu Qing's *Walls of Brass and Iron*, and Du Pengcheng's *In Defense of Yan'an*. These masterpieces improved my thinking and artistic senses. They impressed me particularly since I had grown up in the countryside and was familiar with life there. It was under the direct influence of these works that I began to write fiction reflecting village life.

I tried to spare every minute for my studies. I was absorbed in my books late into the night. If it took four hours to watch a play but only two hours to read the script, I would read it instead of going to see it. . . .

At that time I learned to write in all sorts of genres, including poetry, *chantefable*, short stories, opera, and screenplays. My short story, "Breaking Off the Engagement," and the libretto of my full-scale Wuxi opera, "Taking a New Road" (co-authored with Ye Zhicheng), were the ones best received by my readers. While these works generally followed the tradition of realism, they reflected life under socialism sanguinely and pointed in clear directions. They reflected my simple thinking at the time, and my utter devotion to the Communist party and to socialism.

But people progress. As my knowledge of politics and understanding of society gradually deepened, I came to realize that socialism was still in its infancy in our society. Although I believed it to be the best political system in the modern world, having unlimited potential, vestiges of the old society remained and we lacked experience in how to establish socialism. Hence, our lives bore witness to all sorts of problems that urgently called for solution. To solve them, we would have to go conscientiously in search of the answers. Nobody today would object to that idea, and indeed it is irrefutable. Yet it became the source of trouble in 1957, when some other young Jiangsu writers and I were openly organizing a literary society called "The Explorers." We were condemned as an antiparty clique, and since I was the first "Explorer" to promulgate the objectives of the association, I had to stiffen my scalp, as they say, and make ready to wear the hat of "rightist," complete with a magic mind-control device in the hatband.[1]

Thus was I kicked out of the ranks of the writers, beaten down at "the age of thirty when I stood firm."[2]

How difficult it was to move forward on such a bumpy road!

IV

The injustice to "The Explorers" was ultimately rectified in late March 1979. With the passage of twenty-one years, I was back in the ranks of writers.

I'd left as a youngster. Now I returned, an old man.

During the early years of my exile, I'd broken all ties with the literary world. Many people thought I was dead. Lucky I am to be alive still today, long enough for history to have made amends and given me back my reputation.

For twenty-one years, however, my life in letters was a complete blank.

I felt sorry that so much time had been lost.

But I was also happy, because my forced retirement had helped me throw off all influence from the extreme leftist literary line. It was ossified and already at a dead end.

---

[1]Literally, "golden hoop incantation," something used by the Monk in the *Journey to the West* to control the Monkey King.

[2]A facetious quotation of the words of Confucius in the *Analects*.

So when I suddenly resumed writing, I was a realist again.

Furthermore, there really are no perfect vacuums in life. Even sealed up in a prison that never sees the light of day, one lives a real life. Everybody in the world goes at his work on the basis of his past experiences, doesn't he?

My life experiences and ruminations over the past twenty-one years therefore became the source of my literary creativity. I hope that it may in some small way be of value to the people.

I had tried hard to give up writing every year since 1957. My desire was finally dead and gone at the beginning of the "Cultural Revolution." I was content with other jobs and tried to do well in them. I reminded myself that, though my will to write had died, my will to serve the people must not die. As soon as the "Gang of Four" were removed, my desire to write was suddenly rekindled and got stronger as the cause of rectification proceeded. I discovered that the fire that burned in my heart from my younger days had not yet been quenched. Now, with fuel and oxygen, it burned stronger and stronger.

In May 1978, I knew I would soon return to the ranks of the writers. Alas, so many years had gone by. Once a girl is married out, she should come back to live with her parents only with grown sons and daughters of her own in tow. So what about me? Could I rejoin the ranks empty-handed, with nothing but a blush of shame on my face?

I took up my pen and began to write against time. By June 1978, I was buried in my writing. I worked with great difficulty at first, for I'd actually forgotten much of my vocabulary. Since I had few words with which to express myself, I had to spend time flipping through the dictionary. I read it through from beginning to end, copying down powerful words and phrases in a special notebook.

Summer that year was especially long and hot. I wrote for about eighteen hours a day. My physique, which was thin and weak to begin with, grew still worse. . . . I had always wondered about the meaning of "wholly emaciated." Now I knew. It's when your skin is so tight there's no slack in it. This was exactly my situation in those days. I was so pitiful that even the many swarms of mosquitoes mercifully left me alone, for I had too little blood. I cared for nothing other than my writing, and I did not even concern myself with family affairs. When somebody spoke to me, I nodded along without hearing a word. My family had never seen me write before, much less like this. My wife, fearing that I was going mad, occasionally snatched my pen away and berated me for "putting on an act." I couldn't explain it to her. After about three months of that, I'd completed a 180,000-word novel. I looked as if I'd come through a life-threatening illness.

A few more short stories, and I'd finally made ready a little come-a-calling gift for the literary ranks that I hoped to rejoin.

In 1979, I published eleven stories in national literary periodicals. I had resumed my life work.

V

I seem to be able to write with little difficulty.

One might think that I would have collected a lot of material and a trunkful of notebooks over the previous twenty years, more than I could ever use. In fact, I hadn't taken a single note. I wasn't experiencing life as an author back then; I was there to reform myself through labor. It simply didn't occur to me to gather materials for creative writing. My case was different in principle from those who "enjoyed flowers from horseback," "unhorsed to enjoy the flowers," or even "took up long-term residence."[3] By force of external coercion and inner awakening, I became a laborer who grew his own food. I only wished to be truly recognized as a peasant; I knew no higher honor. And I accomplished that. Not only did I make myself into a peasant, I raised an honest-to-goodness peasant family. Like all others, it was one cell in the body of a commune, a production brigade, and a production team. They all contributed their labor, their capital, and their fertilizer. They shared their food and their property. So we had the same things as all other peasant families: the necessary farm implements, a few animals around the house, and a piece of private land to cultivate. We left our mark on every facet of peasant life. I was there with the peasants during bumper harvests and crop failures, good times and bad, correct procedures and stupid ones, honest cadres and evil ones. When the policy was good and when it was bad, I felt the effects the same as all the peasants. My fortune became identified with theirs. . . .

I never consciously intended to "experience" the peasants' life during those two decades, yet their life became mine without my realizing it. I wasn't above them, below them, or to the side. I was in their midst. Perhaps that's why I've been able to write so fluently. I am not merely writing about and speaking for them, but for myself. "Li Shunda Builds a House" (*Li Shunda zaowu*), "The Debtor" (*Loudou hu zhu*), and "Chen Huansheng's Adventure in Town" (*Chen Huansheng shang cheng*) are objective accounts, and you can see me in them.

"Quzhe de lu" (The winding road), in Gao Xiaosheng, *Chuangzuotan* (On writing) (Guangzhou, 1981), pp. 42–52.

—Translated by Fung Mei-cheong

---

[3]These are references to authors gathering materials for their novels by visiting the countryside. Unlike Gao, they knew that they could go back to the city and write.

Gu Hua

GU HUA (pseud. of Luo Hongyu, b. 1942, in southern Hunan), like Gao
Xiaosheng, has demonstrated an exuberant talent for recording and relating the
plight of the Chinese peasant—a *xiangtu* (rural, provincial) literature worlds
apart in motivation and technique from the Taiwanese mainstream *xiangtu* (rural,
"nativist") literature. Since his famous 1981 novel *Furongzhen* (Hibiscus town),
which was made into a popular and controversial film, Gu Hua has written a
number of ostensibly pastoral novels that proffer a systematic historical treatment of rural life and reflect generally on China's slowly deteriorating social and
moral climate since 1949. Recent novels include *Zhennü* (Chaste women, 1987)
and *Rulin yuan* (The scholars' garden, 1990), the latter composed in Canada,
where Gu Hua has resided since 1988. His piece below is a fairly artless "literature and me" essay of the sort that Chinese writers and readers have enjoyed
writing and reading since the 1930s.

The Slow Maturation of My Craft
Tea in Cold Water Steeps Slowly

Gu Hua

1982

AT THE URGING of the editors, I have written this piece about "Literature and Me." The title, "Tea Steeped in Cold Water Grows Stronger Slowly," is a metaphor for how slowly I progressed as a writer. There truly is a bit of "Ah Q" in it.

1. The Planting of the Seeds

I was born in a small mountain village in the northern foothills of the Wuling Mountains of Hunan. The village, which had only forty or fifty families, was divided into northern and southern sections by a long, narrow cultivated gully. Said to resemble two elephants standing shoulder-to-shoulder, it was called "Two Elephants Village." On the western end of the "two elephants" were planted luxuriant cypress trees several rows deep, which formed a verdant protective screen.

Emerging from this screen of cypresses, a winding cobblestone road ran north and south. Flowing east to west was a small stream, ennobled as "Bigger than a Ditch." Each year in summer and autumn, it became the "River of Happiness" for us children. Once we'd all stripped naked, we learned how to jump in, dog paddle, dive, and splash each other, besides picking up conch shells, seizing fish and crayfish in our bare hands, catching crabs, and scooping up eels. Our tiny hands, fearlessly reaching deep into rock crevices, sometimes dragged out a slippery bream. The stream, continually pounded into jade green, flowed on until it was yellow and turbid. Yet, beginning from this tiny creek, some of my childhood friends ultimately became illustrious naval officers sailing the South

Seas and the Pacific. And who would have ever imagined that one of these bare-bottomed children would later come to write short stories?

Behind the small mountain village was a great stand of ancient trees, abundant and flourishing. Naturally, in bright daylight the old trees provided an even better playground for us. We searched for brushwood and grasses, raked up pine needles, plucked mushrooms, pulled up bamboo shoots, retrieved birds' nests, and learned to climb the trees like squirrels. When evening came, the old forest was full of fear and mystery for us. The sound of the wind, the rain, the billowing pine trees, bird calls, and wild animal noises scared me so that I buried myself in my quilt, head and all, where I dreamed of falling down the stairs, off the rooftop, out of trees, or from clouds in the daylight sky. Startled awake, I heard grown-ups say I must be in a growing spurt.

While climbing trees, I scraped my hands and feet, tore my clothes, and more than a few times got a hard spanking for it. Yet those lofty treetops, sweeping the blue sky and white clouds high enough to reach the stars and the moon, held a tremendous power of attraction for me.

In those days, remote mountain villages at the border were wholly backward in culture. A few times a year, itinerant performers from Henan and Anhui came with their monkeys to show off their tricks. Naturally, we couldn't enjoy the radio broadcasts, movies, and talk-plays that are now almost universally available in farm villages. Yet the ancient mountain villages retained some of the ancient culture. My hometown was praised as a center of Hunan folk songs. Popular among the women were traditional songs and dances to "Accompany the Bride." When a village girl was to be married, all her paternal aunts, brothers' wives, and sisters would gather indoors and sing on her behalf for three days and nights. What did they sing? Songs about the girl's reluctance to leave her old home, her hopes for married life, the sorrows of her family at the parting, and, even more important, her resentment of feudal ethics and the arranged marriage system. (After Liberation, musicologists who came to our area to collect folk songs recorded over six or seven hundred original lyrics.)

Another event in the small mountain villages that could be called a cultural movement was "Recounting of the Past" by elders. "Recounting of the Past," or simply telling stories, was a pastime for the older generation, and an unconscious means of transmitting cultural and historical knowledge to the younger generation. During that peaceful era, the village was mostly at rest during the night. It was relaxed and peaceful, without any small-group meetings or mass rallies. There were only birds chirping and dogs barking, or sometimes a disturbance raised by cattle thieves from outside the village.

Perhaps it was that creek that ran through my village, the stand of old trees out back, the sound of the songs to accompany the bride, the elders' recounting of the past, that unwittingly sowed the seeds of literature in my young heart and thick, impervious soul.

These seeds of course were most fragile and thin, and they seemed to have fallen into barren cracks in the earth. Without spring winds and rain, they never could have sprouted.

2. The Nutrients

I'm embarrassed to say so, but I first came into contact with literature through martial arts fiction. In the early years after Liberation, when I was eleven or twelve years old, books that had lost their covers and even some of their beginning and ending pages used to circulate in the countryside, like *Three Knights-Errant and Five Gallants, Most Incredible Marvels among the Swordsmen*, tales of court cases, and the like. I was obsessed and enraptured by the knights-errant who leapt up on roofs and vaulted over walls and courtyards to extirpate evil and help the poor, and also by the limitless magical powers of the sorceresses and Daoist adepts who mounted the clouds and rode the mist, or changed stone into gold. It's a good thing I wasn't led astray, for those books all have the same formula. One way or another, the knight-errant gets into a terrible spot, and when no other resolution is possible, the Goddess of Mercy or the Venerable Mother of Pear Mountain inevitably appears to save the situation. I think such writing is one of the historical roots of our [current] literary practice of writing everything according to the same formula.

My reading interests were broad. I read a little of everything, from Tang dynasty stories of the strange and marvelous and Ming-Qing romances, to the New Literature of the May Fourth period and works of critical realism from eighteenth-century Europe. I was particularly fond of *The Dream of the Red Chamber*; I read it five or six times all told, sometimes as a textbook on how to write, yet even now I haven't grasped all of its subtleties. Truly it is a vast and profound literary treasury.

3. The Soil

As peasants manage their land, writers manage their own lives. Life is the soil of literature. From the time I was small, I lived in a farm village in Hunan. When I was eleven or twelve, the poverty of my family got me prematurely caught up in the contradiction between seeking knowledge and seeking sustenance. For the sake of eating, the spirit naturally had to give way to material needs. I learned to make straw shoes to sell, chop bamboo, tote charcoal on a shoulder pole, even take people's cows out to pasture. The area around my hometown was very poor, so a lot of people bore charcoal on shoulder poles to sell in neighboring counties. In the blistering heat, the flagstones of the road were hot enough to keep you jumping as you went. Your sweat turned into a mist. In the rain and snow, you wound twine around your shoes to prevent slips and falls. On frosty days, your hands and feet were so frozen they split open like broken bricks, bleeding and exposing the flesh. Yet among charcoal sellers, the poor helped the poor and neighbor helped neighbor. Stopping along the way to rest their feet and wipe away the sweat, they never left a companion behind to fend for himself. If one day the charcoal or bamboo sold for a good price, a three-ounce cut of fatty meat would be brought back, stewed in an earthenware pot with black beans until it was fragrant and tender, then shared equally, so that all could beam with joy as they broke their fast together. This life allowed me to understand how precious it is to be able to support oneself. It let me empathize with the hardships of manual laborers, and feel for myself the laboring people's pure and precious willingness to share their good fortune along with their hardships.

Three years later I was able to go on to middle school, though I returned to the countryside each winter and summer vacation. During the Great Leap Forward, my studies were interrupted for a year. I taught in a local citizen-run primary school, where I participated in the making of charcoal and steel, launched all kinds of high-yield satellites,[1] and ate in the communal mess hall of a people's commune. The following year, I passed the entrance examination to a prefectural agricultural school. Then came the so-called "days of hardship." The collective was sent down to a poor district in the countryside, to undertake large-scale agricultural work.

In the winter of 1961, the school was ordered to disband and I was sent to a prefectural agricultural station as a farm worker. I lived next to a small town for the next fourteen years. During that time, we experienced the "Four Clean-ups" campaign and the "Historically Unprecedented Great Cultural Revolution." I planted vegetables, managed orchards and nurseries, planted rice in flooded fields, repaired farm tools, oversaw granaries, and so forth. I basically learned all about agricultural life. In those fourteen years, I never suffered from hunger or cold, but I was tired to my very bones. It allowed me to immerse myself in life at the grass roots, experience the illusory vicissitudes and storms of the times, and become intimately familiar with local conditions and the customs of the common people in rural Hunan. Moreover, all this provided the local color of my later fiction. One can sum it up with a little joke: Though Heaven entrusted no great task to me, it "exhausted my frame, made me suffer starvation and hardship, and tested my resolution."[2] I am thankful to life for tempering me.

I feel that if life is the soil of literature, there is a dialectical relationship between its breadth and depth, and between specific locales as opposed to the whole terrain. If an author, having written works of a certain quantity and qual-

---

[1]After the USSR launched the world's first space satellite in 1957, China tried to contribute to the socialist camp's victory by "launching" experimental fields ("satellites") in agriculture.

[2]*Mencius*, trans. D. C. Lau (Harmondsworth, 1970), book VI, part B, verse 15. This quotation is ironic, for these are the tests by which Heaven actually makes great kings and public figures.

ity, still limits his life to a certain village or stays at a certain level for a long time, that will surely influence his outlook on life and artistic viewpoint. His writing is bound to evidence a certain unimaginativeness, like an overly "self-conscious country cousin." He'll be unable to bring into play, unearth, or refine many of the precious elements of life. The problems we writers who hail from the grass roots confront, particularly those of us known as "*xiangtu* (rural) writers," are totally different from those of writers who rarely come down to the basic levels and rely on collecting materials and interviewing for their creative work. The latter kind of comrade ought to get involved at the grass roots (as our literary and artistic leaders have long stressed), and the former ought to create the conditions and opportunities for broadening themselves. They ought to go visit the great rivers and mountains of our motherland, and our famous ruins. They ought to participate in some literary gatherings, or read a few noted works by foreign and domestic writers. I have my own experience to speak of. Right after the smashing of the "Gang of Four," the Chinese Writers' Association and related units offered me the chance to visit the Southwest, East China, the North, Manchuria, and other places, where I could see our famous mountains and great rivers to my heart's content. Moreover, they arranged for me to leave my job for a time and study at the Chinese Writers' Association Literature Institute. We read some famous literary pieces and heard a lot of old writers and scholars speak. It expanded my living and artistic horizons. I think that the new breakthroughs in my own writing these past few years are very much related to these travel experiences.

4. The Seedlings

I wrote *Hibiscus Town* in July 1980, in a peaceful and secluded forestry project in the Wuling Mountains. As is my habit when I write a comparatively long piece, I followed normal working hours during the day and in the evenings simply found people to talk with, listened to the news, flipped through books and newspapers, then went to sleep at the usual time. One evening a friend from the school for the foresters' children came to chat. He mentioned that the head of a commune in his county, having clashed with a brigade cadre, had sent select militiamen to surround the latter's village. The villagers all signed a petition of complaint, which was forwarded to and approved by higher and higher levels, until it was like a document on a holiday trip. The matter was resolved only when the document got to a responsible person in a ministry of the central government who had relatives in the village. This affair reminded me of a discouraging but widespread phenomenon in our lives a few years earlier: although lots of people were in communication with higher organs at various levels to file a complaint, an appeal, or a request for a hearing, it would go unresolved for a long time. Because of overlapping agencies, overstaffing, and low efficiency, the buck would be passed up the echelons and then down again. How could government in a country governed by the people and under the leadership of the party allow these phenomena to exist so long?

Then I thought of yet another affair. In 1977, when I was in a different county collecting materials, I heard that the head of a production team was going against his commune's orders to institute uniformly "double cropping of rice." He had planted twenty acres of midseason rice without authority. When the commune head discovered it, he brought a group of people to pull the seedlings out of the ground and transplant early rice there. Commune members under the offending team leader were opposed to that, and they got into a fight with the people doing the transplanting, right there in the rice fields.

Afterward, the team leader was sent to prison for the crime of "assaulting cadres of the revolution."

I kneaded these two incidents from different counties together into a story about an old farmer who cried out against the injustice done to his son in prison. He filed complaints to higher and higher levels, but not until a leading cadre in a ministry personally looked into the matter was there any hope for a resolution. I used this story to extol the correct line of the party central and the flesh-and-blood closeness of the old cadre to the common people, and also to chastise the work style of certain bureaus that did not work on behalf of the people.

Transforming, polishing, and filling out a real-life story into my 1981 novel *Hibiscus Town* was a large task. It all began with the case of a falsely accused "rich-peasant widow" that I heard about in 1979 when I went to a large county in the mountains to gather information. The original story is chilling and sorrowful. It is said that an industrious young woman earned some money selling rice-beancurd during the "days of hardship" after the Great Leap Forward, enough that she built a house for herself on the eve of the "Four Clean-ups" movement. During the campaign, she was tagged as a "new rich-peasant element." Her husband, a pork butcher, was so cowardly and intimidated that he hanged himself. His young wife, her head full of feudalistic superstition, thought her fate was so formidable that it overpowered those around her, and that she was a fatal jinx to any husband she might take. Hence she often cried at his grave in the night. Later on, a prospecting team came to the village and she was ordered to put them up in her house. One member of the team was an unmarried technician in his thirties. Simply because some young workers in the team joked that they were willing to act as matchmaker between the young widow and the technician, misfortune came again.

In 1969, during the campaign to Cleanse the Class Ranks, they were repeatedly dragged up on stage together for criticism and struggle. The technician couldn't rid himself of the shame, so he also committed suicide. Thereupon the rich-peasant widow felt even more strongly that her fate was overpowering, and that her jinx had put to death yet another innocent male. Now she secretly went to two gravestones to cry in the night.

Only in early 1979, after the Third Plenum of the party's Eleventh Central Committee, when misjudged verdicts were overturned nationwide, was the new rich-peasant widow acquitted and rehabilitated. So her fate wasn't so formidable after all.

This story continually preoccupied me. If I had written the story as it was originally, it would have been easy to fall into the old clichés, for through the ages there have been so many, many stories about woman's fate. I thought about writing it several times in 1979, but in the end I never started. Finally, in 1980, when I was studying at the Chinese Writers' Association Literature Institute, this story came together with my long-standing plan to write a long novel. Thereupon, I seemed to see a light through the clouds, and I began to come alive; I finally hit on the following idea: I would write about life in a small mountain town. Characters from four different generations would act out their own lives, reflecting the social customs and ethos of small-town life in the mountain regions of the South.

I would use a small community to reflect the larger society in a time of turbulence and flux. That would of course be difficult, and if I didn't take care I would surely fail. It called on me to bring into play nearly all of my thirty years' experience living in the countryside. It was another big test of my ability to use language and delineate character.

Several of the main characters in *Hibiscus Town* are based on real people, but changed for the story: Sister Hibiscus Hu Yuyin; the Soldier from the North Gu Yanshan; the brigade secretary Li Mangeng; the cynic Qin Shutian; the "Campaign Cadre" Li Guoxiang; the owner of the stilt-house Wang Qiushe; and others. Some are based on several different life models. I lived and worked with these people for a long time, observing their ups and downs and their joys and sorrows, so parts of them reflect my own experience, too.

An old comrade in a Peking publishing house once asked me: You aren't very old, and haven't experienced any great rises or falls in your own life, so how did you come by the moving feelings of Sister Hibiscus, a woman full of hidden anguish [over her thwarted love life]? I answered: Sister Hibiscus's feelings come from me. For a long time I have been a weak person, and I've been bullied. The strong look at the weak as pitiful wretches, while the weak, who commiserate with each other and stay together, naturally can appreciate feelings that are lost to the strong. The weak have no difficulty comprehending the feelings of the strong, because they constantly have to deal with them, or even rely on them.

Thinking back on the creative path I have taken these last twenty years, I really feel guilty and afraid. Yet most writers do not like to expose themselves before their readers. This essay may be considered a work of self-consolation and self-encouragement; of self-mockery and self-analysis.

"Lengshui paocha manman nong" (Tea steeped in cold water grows stronger slowly), in *Wenxue zhi lu* (The path of literature) (Changsha, 1983), pp. 118–29.

—Translated by Linda Greenhouse Wang

Jia Pingwa

JIA PINGWA (b. 1952, in Shaanxi) relies on the remote hills of Shangzhou in the province of Shaanxi as the source of his inspiration, much as Lu Wenfu has chosen Suzhou, Feng Jicai Tianjin, and Gu Hua southern Hunan. Jia Pingwa convinces by preserving an awareness of the former greatness of his region even as he shows his desire for closer interaction with the outside world, including the West.

Jia Pingwa's prose emphasizes the rapid changes taking place in the country-side. The land reform and collectivization movements provide only a far-away background for the impulsively thoroughgoing changes of the 1980s that resulted from the flexible economic policies of the Peking reformers around Deng Xiao-ping and Zhao Ziyang. His major novel in this vein, *Fuzao* (Turbulence, 1987), won a Mobil Oil Pegasus prize in literature, after being selected by a committee from the Chinese Writers' Association. How rural stasis and rural change have come to inform his fiction is the subject of his essay below.

Life Is Changing
Even in Hilly Shangzhou

Jia Pingwa

June 9, 1984

How am I going to write this "Afterword"? At the moment, I'm revising a piece called *Shang Prefecture* (*Shangzhou*) and my head is filled with the people and events of Shangzhou, so why not write about that? But this smacks of "Old Wang selling melons" [praising one's own wares]. Yes, the Chinese have a proverb that says: "Everybody claims that his hometown is the best." I am no exception. Probably an outsider couldn't care less about the place. Even in Shaanxi there are people who turn up their noses at the mention of Shangzhou. It is small, isolated, and poor. If you look for it on a map of Shaanxi, you will see that it is triangular in shape and located in the southeastern corner of the province. It is the gateway to the eight hundred miles of Qinchuan [Shaanxi and Gansu, China's ancient Northwest], but it is not part of the central Shaanxi plain; nor does it have the Qinchuan breed of cattle. It borders on Hubei Province in the south and Henan in the east, yet it is not really part of southern Shaanxi proper. It does not have the warm, wet climate of Ankang or Hanzhong. The Dan River is its main waterway, and the Changping Highway its longest official road.

The seven counties of Shangzhou are Shang, Danfeng, Shanyang, Luonan, Shangnan, Zhen'an, and Zhashui. The terrain is seven parts mountain, two parts water, and one part farmland. The people cultivate the five grains but do not grow them in great abundance. They mainly eat corn, which is ground into a kind of porridge and called *zhoufan*.[1] The people have a saying, that "We've but potatoes, corn porridge, and dough drops to put on, but I'm happy as any god in the pantheon." You can see how hard is the life of the people. But the hard life

---

[1]Literally, "prefectural food," which may be taken as a pun on "rice porridge."

does not necessarily mean spiritual hardship. There are pleasures even in this hard life.

I lived in a place like this for nineteen years, after which time I moved to the city. But I return at least three or four times a year. Moreover, after I moved to Xi'an, my home there practically became the Shangzhou people's embassy at the capital. My fellow townspeople would visit me whenever they came to Xi'an, often bringing local produce such as walnuts, persimmon cakes, wood ear fungus, beans, yams, and ground corn. Some came to sightsee, others to do business or see a doctor; some even came to get married, or to settle a legal matter. In the past three or four years, I have written five or six legal briefs for my townspeople.

These folk have their own ways. Even though I live in the city now, they do not regard me as a city dweller. I must have on hand a set of large rice bowls for filling to the brim whenever my townsfolk come to visit. I needn't prepare a lot of dishes for them; the important thing is that the salt must be salty, the vinegar sour, and the peppers hot. You must let them throw their cigarette butts on the floor; after they spit, you must not wipe up right after them, and you must by all means speak in dialect. Because of all this, they do not regard me as having "changed." They're at ease and I'm at ease. There is no barrier between guest and host. We sit where we wish, there being no seat of honor. When there is wine, we all drink. When there's no wine, we just sit around, sharing everything under the sun and oblivious to all. Therefore, even without having returned home, I know everything that goes on there. I am like the scholar who "knows the whole world without ever going out," except here the "world" is Shangzhou.

My hometown folks only know that I "make books." When they leave, they always ask for some books or magazines, saying that these are for their sons and daughters to "study." But I never give them my own writings, because, as I've said elsewhere, I often change my subject. Several years ago, this kind of changing around was like waging "guerrilla warfare"; what I wrote was not worthy of being shown to my townspeople. This kind of guerrilla-war style of writing lowered my status from writer to that of bandit writer. After having suffered much hardship, I slowly realized the importance of establishing a "home base," even as a writer.

Last year, I finally decided to return to Shangzhou. At the time I was not actually set on writing anything in particular. I just brought along a map of Shangzhou and visited each county in it. Only after the trip did I realize how little I knew about the place, and that my earlier pieces about the mountain districts were very superficial. Actual experience changed my world view. I hadn't expected that this "purposeless" [wuwei, a word with classical Daoist overtones] trip would become so "purposeful" [youwei] for my writing. Every place I visited provided an educational experience and stimulated me. At night I hastily wrote down my impressions. They were real and vivid. My recording of these events came naturally; I did not ponder my words or try to be fancy. After a few changes, this became my very first piece of writing about Shangzhou, called "First Impressions of Shangzhou" (*Shangzhou chulu*). I had it published in [the Nanjing literary journal] *Zhongshan*.

The reaction to the piece went beyond my expectations. Many readers and writers wrote to congratulate me, saying that I had "found a new, Chinese-style path for literature." They encouraged me to keep on writing in that style. I was really intimidated, but at the same time I gained self-confidence. I realized that I could spend a lifetime writing about Shangzhou, and it seemed that new things were surging into my mind every day, every moment. Thereupon, I returned to Shangzhou a second time, a third time, and a fourth, always visiting the various districts and feeling at one with [the Tang poet] Wen Tingyun, who once lived there and said:

> The cocks crow as the moon rises above the rustic inn,
> only footprints are left on the frost-covered bridge

Each trip was more fruitful than the last, and in quick succession I wrote "Before the 29-Day Month" (*Xiaoyue qianben*), "The People of Chicken Nest Hollow" (*Jiwowa de renjia*), "The Turn of the New Year" (*Layue, Zhengyue*), and the piece that I am finishing now, called *Shang Prefecture*.

It is true that Shangzhou is poor, but as time progresses and society moves ahead, Shangzhou, like all other places in the country, is changing. What is unusual is that Shangzhou's changes differ from those elsewhere. They bear Shangzhou's special characteristics and local color. This preposterous thought then occurred to me: Take Shangzhou as a point of reference; carefully investigate and study it, and gain from it an understanding of the historical development of Chinese village life, of the evolution of society, and of the course of change in the life, feelings, and psychological make-up of mankind in this great world of ours.

Chinese literature today can be said to be a Chinese and Western hybrid. Under these circumstances, how does one tread a path that is properly one's own? I believed that I should approach the question by investigating the geography, history, customs, and habits of Shangzhou, proceeding from the perspectives of ethnography and folklore studies. China is just now in a period of revitalization. It is reforming and discarding what has been protecting our backward economy, and pursuing a balanced policy. It is also adopting measures that support a progressive economy, that develop commerce and finance. It should be said that the party is wise and that its policy is correct. But in China, ever since the rise of its historical tradition and concept of morality, such revitalization has necessarily brought on many, many problems.

Let us take the actual case of Shangzhou. Though it is remote and isolated, the problems that occur there are no longer simple, but intricate and complex, as elsewhere. Take its attitudes toward land and morality. The older generation of peasants differs from the younger generation, and even among the latter there are differences of opinion. These issues penetrate into each county, village, and even to every individual in Shangzhou, creating a completely new mode of change. At the same time, Shangzhou differs from other places. There are many new problems that need to be considered: Will historical progress bring about a decline in moral standards, and the spread of superficiality? Are simple, straightforward human relations suitable only in an isolated, natural economic environment? Will the movement toward modernization bring about a deterioration of the good old ethical concepts and encourage a worldly trend of profit making? I am troubled by these questions, but at the same time very stimulated by them. Therefore, from "First Impressions of Shangzhou" to the novel *Shang Prefecture*, I have tried to think through these problems and find a solution.

Unfortunately, I am not talented. All of my efforts are superficial and immature, if not fragmentary or simply wrong.

I am fully aware of my defects and also chagrined that my learning is insufficient. In Shaanxi my literary friends and I have discussed the merits and defects of our works deep into the night. We are of the opinion that three differences between ourselves and writers from other places probably account for why we haven't made any breakthroughs in our writings.

The first difference is geographical. Shaanxi is the place where thirteen dynasties have established their capitals, from the Zhou to the Ming. In the north there is the Yellow River, in the middle the Wei River, and in the south, the Han. The confluence of these three rivers brought together the genius and excellence of our ancestors, producing the splendor of the Han and Tang dynasties. Unfortunately, after the high Tang period, a conservative and arrogant mentality set in, affecting the customs and mores of the people. Hence the politics, economy, military affairs, and diplomacy of the region all deteriorated in successive dynasties afterward. Naturally, culture and the arts were also affected. In these regards, the culture of the Han was the most powerful and magnificent. It was more inspiring than the elegant and aristocratic culture of the high Tang period. As the capital city was moved to the east and north, the Shaanxi region became more and more remote and isolated. But hundreds of royal tombs of the emperors remain to nourish the dreams of past glory.

If we closely examine the customs and mores of the people of Shaanxi, we will find that they no longer have the strength and power of the Qin and Han dynasties. Especially on the central plains of the province, the people are content to discuss the merits of the Qinchuan ox. One cannot help but think of the sculptures of the six majestic steeds in the Museum of the Steles [in Xi'an], and then imagine the ancients' pride and joy in acquiring those excellent thousand-mile steeds. When today we gaze upon the slowly moving oxen carrying their heavy loads, we can only sigh. As history marches through the 1980s and society enters the information age, our region remains hemmed in by the four passes: the Jinsuo Pass in the north, the Dasan Pass in the west, the Tong Pass in the east, and the Wu Pass in the south. Within these four mountain passes, all is directed toward glorifying the past. The orientation of the people changes from one of openness to closed-mindedness. Naturally one cannot expect this region to be in the forefront of change.

The second difference is in life-style. That life is the wellspring of literature is the oldest and the most fashionable slogan today; no writer can afford to ignore it. As for me and my literary friends in Shaanxi who write about village life, we are peasants in background and experience, or cadres who have lived among the peasantry. It is not that we know less about peasant life than writers from elsewhere, but our writing is as not good as theirs. This, then, should be called a problem with our life-style. Precisely because of the regional differences, we felt intimidated and pressured. Therefore, we abandoned the territorial "base" of our lives and became literary highwaymen. Being roving literary bandits taught us a lesson, however, so we retreated back to our original territory, where we focused our attention on each village and hamlet, wrote about the peasants, and mixed with them. Yet this ultimately shackled us, too, because we adopted an attitude of simply writing about things the way they appeared to be. Because of our peasant background, we can be peasant writers, but we cannot become writer-peasants. We are writers with peasant consciousness.

The third difference is in training. Precisely because we began as peasants, or perhaps evolved from peasants into cadres, we have some natural advantages, but we have natural disadvantages, too. It is often said that "a writer cannot be trained in a university." This certainly is true. But because of this, we slight systematic training even in the basics of culture and the arts, and this has severely handicapped our writing. . . .

In my opinion, these three problems all desperately need a solution.

The profundity of a work does not depend on the writer's boldness, literary talent, or loudness. However different their styles, the major writers in China's several thousand years of literature, such as Tao Yuanming, Sima Qian, Bo Juyi, Su Shi, Liu Zongyuan, Cao Xueqin, and Pu Songling, have inherited a tradition of expressing the openness and spirituality of nature, society, life, and the mind. Openness and spirituality are treasures of Chinese literature.

How should we revitalize Chinese literature? Many writers are now pursuing this question. As I mentioned above, if we want our literature to develop, we must cross-fertilize Chinese literature with Western literature. Some writers have adopted Western literature in toto but have not digested it or harmonized with it. Therefore, they have either ignored or forgotten the merits of the Chinese spirit. This is a case of trying to achieve too much too fast. Other writers have totally rejected anything foreign. Thus, our people are either too haughty or too humble; too quick or too slow.

In recent years, we have been making great efforts to compare China with the West, beginning with philosophy, aesthetics, painting, and drama, in the hope of finding similarities and differences, and thus the direction that our own writings

JIA PINGWA   105

ought to take. We have expended much effort but achieved little. In using the traditional Chinese ways of expressing beauty to depict life and emotions in China today, I often wonder whether a work can have a kind of "distant goal" (*zhiyuan*). Can this "distant goal," built on the foundation of "starting from something close at hand" (*zijin*), give our works a sense of openness and spirituality rather than emptiness and triviality? Can it give them added depth?

At the same time, I often ponder another problem, that of magnanimity (*dadu*), which can also be considered a question of strength or power (*li*). Many of the Chinese writers famous now can be considered thinkers, or people of profound thought. Of course, "thought" should not be a narrow concept, or it might lead to the error of "making thought greater than events." Instead, it should express the power of magnanimity. The ancients said that there is melody even in a hammer, and toughness in a flower. This pertains not merely to the surface of a literary work, but to something internal. It is because of this that I earlier spoke of promoting the spirit of the Great Han dynasty. As I look at the stone sculptures in front of the tomb of [the great Han general] Huo Qubing, I feel that the art of the Han dynasty is the greatest in history. With a few finely sculpted lines, the artist made the image of his object stand out. Now that is the pinnacle of art. Therefore, as we revitalize our national literature in the course of revitalizing our whole nation, I admire the spirit of the great Han dynasty and despise the precious cloisonné objects from the end of the Qing dynasty [in the late 19th century]. When I read Latin American literature, I feel the same way. I can identify with it. I suddenly understand many things.

"Biange shenglang zhong de sisuo—*Layue, Zhengyue* houji" (Thoughts amidst the clamor of change—Afterword to *The Turn of the New Year*), June 9,1984, in *Pingwa wenlun ji* (Collected essays of Jia Pingwa) (Xining, 1985), pp. 21–31.

Translated by Peter Li

Zhong Acheng

ZHONG ACHENG (b. 1949), typically known simply by his given name, is the son of the film critic Zhong Dianfei, who died shortly after this interview. He became famous overnight with his short story "Qi wang" (The chess king, 1984). Like Acheng's other two best-known stories, "Haizi wang" (King of the children, 1985) and "Shu wang" (The king of trees, 1985), it is based on experiences and visions of China that molded his literary perspective when he was a sent-down youth following the Cultural Revolution. "The Chess King" remains his masterpiece, probably because it succeeds in conveying a kind of Daoist, dialectical view of the social upheavals in which the author and his generation found themselves. The story created a sensation on the mainland and, when reprinted in Taiwan, proved instrumental in making contemporary mainland literature acceptable to readers there.

Since 1987, Acheng has traveled extensively in the United States. A keen observer, he also paints and makes films. The following interview, in which the author sometimes appears rather reticent—as is his nature—was recorded and revised in written form by Acheng expressly for this anthology.

The First Half of My Life

A Boy from the City Struggling for Survival in Far-Away Yunnan

Zhong Acheng

January 31, 1987, in Berkeley, California

Martin: Acheng, we who translate Chinese literature and introduce it to those outside of China, whether in Germany or America, usually face this problem: the function of literature in Chinese society is very different from that in other countries. Do you feel that contemporary literature has a greater role in Chinese society than elsewhere?

Acheng: It seems to me that China traditionally has made an all-encompassing demand on composition (*wenzhang*: literary works in general). It is that "writing must convey the principles of truth" (*wen yi zai dao*). China is a country where morality (*daode*), which is to say, the True Path as it has been passed down to us (*daotong*), is required of all things. Literature is no exception. I feel that this is an important difference between Chinese literature and Western literature.

Martin: Can contemporary Chinese literature develop under an inherited orthodoxy?

Acheng: I think we can still ask that literature "convey the principles of truth." But the "principles" cannot be overwhelmingly social, because art has its own principles.

Martin: I'm driving at something else, too. I feel that the intellectuals in a society have a leadership role. If, for whatever reason, intellectuals are unable to carry out this function, then literature can serve to express their opinions indirectly. Currently in China there are limits to freedom of the press. Freedom of the press in Taiwan is insufficient, too. The function of literature, then, is all the more important.

Acheng: Yes, that's so. In China, literature shoulders the burden of the press, of education, of the law, and so forth. Chinese literature is weighted down with more burdens than it ought to be responsible for.

Martin: There are other Chinese writers with similar opinions. Liu Xinwu, for example, says that the burden is too heavy and that Chinese writers cannot continue in this manner.

Acheng: I think he's right.

Martin: It seems that you feel that each individual writer ought to have his or her own unique literary ideals. Does literature have a special definition for you?

Acheng: To me, it is clear and unequivocal. Literature is a concrete rendering of one's aesthetic judgment. A writer's sense of duty, and his actual responsibility, call for him to make something from his sense of the beautiful.

Martin: This is your first visit to the United States. Within these last three months, you must have witnessed many things that most Chinese could never imagine. There must have been certain social phenomena that you'd heard about but never fully understood. Now that you've experienced these new things, do they have any special significance for you?

Acheng: Very much so, because I am particularly interested in the "subjective quality" (*zhigan*), the "feel," of things and events.

Martin: I'm afraid I must ask you to explain "subjective quality."

Acheng: Subjective quality is the feeling for the essence of an object or event that distinguishes it from another object or event. For instance, in China, what we see of the rest of the world is by way of photographs. A photograph does not readily reveal the essence of its subject. If one were to talk about Manhattan, New York—I've seen photographs of it, but when I am actually walking in Manhattan, the streets become tangible. I then discover that the streets of Manhattan are neither level nor wide. They have been patched in many places. Furthermore, when observing people walking the streets—their pace, the spring in their step, the texture of the walls alongside the street, the lighting, whatever—what I am after is the subjective quality. When I see a photo, I seek to come up face-to-face with the real object. Another thing—there is something here in the United States that I find very elating. And it is something of utmost significance. I am an artist, you see. But all the world-renowned paintings I'd ever seen were reproductions. I was extremely happy to be able to come face-to-face with quite a few original works here.

Martin: I don't want to ask you what you are in the process of writing now, or what you plan to write, but may I ask you this—what do you consider to be of importance to you now?

Acheng: The most crucial thing now has to do with me personally: my freedom to think, or, perhaps, my ability to think free thoughts. That includes everything that goes into the making of my thoughts.

Martin: I'd like to move into more specific questions about you. You were born in 1949?

Acheng: Yes.

Martin: That was just when the country was liberated. I came across the name of your father several times previously, when I was editing Chinese political materials. But because I was not doing work in film, I was not very knowledgeable about him. Can you talk a little about your family background?

Acheng: My father became a member of the Communist party. It was during the War of Resistance against Japan. He's a critic, a critic of the arts. I consider him a very intelligent person. He was an artist while at Yan'an, a student at the Lu Xun Art School. Then he became a teacher there. Afterward, he went to work in the Jin-Cha-Ji base area. He's also a film critic.

Martin: Is that why so many friends of your family are in the film profession?

Acheng: Most of my father's friends fall into three categories—artists, writers, and filmmakers.

Martin: I'm not very familiar with your father's writings in the 1950s.

Acheng: In 1957, when I was seven years old, he wrote an essay entitled "Gongs and Drums in the Film Industry." Mao criticized this essay by name. My father was one of the first high-ranking persons to be called a rightist, and for that reason they dealt with him rather severely. To tell the truth, I have yet to read that essay.

Martin: Really?

Acheng: In fact, it was this very matter that got me into trouble when I was in school. The teachers kept at me to criticize it. They wanted me to write about what I knew regarding my father, and I told them I had not read anything of his—his things had been confiscated! Even they couldn't find anything he'd written. The words of the rightists couldn't be disseminated.

Martin: How was your father dealt with after being labeled a rightist?

Acheng: He was sent to Tangshan for reform through labor.

Martin: Just like Liu Binyan and other rightists; in one flash, twenty years were gone. What did he do after 1979?

Acheng: He went to work in the Institute of Literature at the Chinese Academy of Social Sciences, where Liu Zaifu is. He was also president of the Association of Film Critics.

Martin: Did you feel cut off from your peers and teachers?

Acheng: No, I wasn't completely alone, although there were some activities from which people with the wrong class background were completely excluded. Someone of my background had no hope of attending college. It was during my first year of senior middle school that the Cultural Revolution began.

Martin: Prior to the Cultural Revolution, what friends, what books, what sorts of things were important to you?

Acheng: Prior to the Cultural Revolution, I read a great variety of books after class. In those days, the Peking bookstores were still fairly good. You were able to get the books off the shelf by yourself. The older bookstores had a good selection. Actually, books on art had the most influence on me. But I read other books, too. For instance, there is this one book. Originally I thought the author was German. It wasn't until later that I found out he was American. It was Hendrik Van Loon's *The Story of Mankind*. There was also *Van Loon's Geography*. Not long ago, the Joint Publishing Company came out with a little book of his, *Van Loon's Lives*. These were not novels; nor were they the kind of history books we were using. It suddenly made me realize how dull and dry our history books were. For instance, in his preface, Van Loon says, "In Europe today, Napoleon is being depreciated for having revived autocracy. Yet, even as I write this book, if I heard the sounds of drums calling outside my window and saw that it was Napoleon's army recruiting soldiers, I would cast my pen aside, dash downstairs, and enlist." His history is not just factual, it's expressive, too.

Martin: At that time, we felt that China was very distant. It was during the period of the cold war. All Western governments perceived China as an enemy. For us, China was like the moon. It was a distant and mysterious place. Your government had a closed-door policy. Did you have this same feeling, observing the outside world from inside China? Or did you think that since China was so huge, it was not necessary to be concerned about the outside world?

Acheng: No, I didn't think that way. But there is a logic in that: if you don't understand the wider world to begin with, you have no way of knowing that your own doors are closed. Therein lies the tragedy, I think.

Martin: How has the Cultural Revolution changed your life?

Acheng: Me, I think the Cultural Revolution affected me differently than it did my contemporaries. My family suffered political misfortune very early on. The Cultural Revolution was simply another movement following a string of others, except that it was especially broad in scope. I was about sixteen then. To me, the Cultural Revolution was not something that sprang up suddenly. What was different about it was that people got killed. I hadn't seen bloody beatings and killings before, but I sure did then. I left Peking in the early part of 1968. First I went to Shanxi, then to Inner Mongolia.

Martin: Were you sent?

Acheng: No, I went of my own free will. I thought that since it was inevitable that I would be joining a production team, I might as well go with classmates who were already my friends.

Martin: Did all of you buy tickets? Or were you assigned by your work unit to enlist?

Acheng: Back then we didn't have any money to buy tickets. We just hitched a ride on a train on the sly.

Martin: What was life like then?

Acheng: We worked during the day and came back in the evening. We'd light our oil lamps and sit around chit-chatting. When we were tired, we went to sleep.

Martin: Your account of it now makes it sound like nothing unusual. If it were I going to a place like that, I couldn't have stood it.

Acheng: That period is over now. There were a lot of feelings associated with it back then, but now all those feelings have dissipated. What it leaves me with now is a lot of things to think about.

Martin: The life of young intellectuals is a major theme in Chinese literature. Writers approach it from their own different perspectives. Recently, I read an essay by Kong Jiesheng, very well written. It expressed the post–Cultural Revolution generation's feelings about their predecessors [i.e., Acheng's generation]. They're quite similar to those of young Germans of the post–student-movement generation, writing about the generation of the student demonstrators. The term "old intellectual youth" (*lao zhiqing*) seems to begrudge their going on and on about the old days whenever they get together. Some of the younger people find this a great bore. Do you think that your experiences are worth writing about, and that the following generation should know about them? Or do you feel that these emotions should stay within your own generation, that you ought not to talk about them too much?

Acheng: I feel that those in the next generation have their own lives to lead. Our experiences have come from our lives, and theirs will come from their lives. The one experience cannot take the place of the other. The literature of the young intellectuals has some elements that are part and parcel of their unique experience, and some that are coincidental. Young intellectuals are educated. When they write about their own lives, they necessarily write about that period. When Mao sent us down to the countryside, perhaps one of his goals was for us to understand the peasants. But he had no way of controlling the implications we drew from our understanding. He probably hoped we'd all come to the same conclusion.

Martin: I feel that there is another angle from which to view it. Currently, the thinking of a lot of writers is in tune with the slogan "Finding Our Roots" (*xungen*). I think the "roots" they are searching for are related to their experience of going down to the countryside. If they hadn't had this experience of being young intellectuals in the countryside, this term "Finding Our Roots" might not even have appeared. Do you think there's any truth in that?

Acheng: The slogan "Finding Our Roots"—

Martin: Did it come from Jia Pingwa?

Acheng: Jia Pingwa is a special case. He came straight from a peasant background. I don't think he originated the idea of "Finding Our Roots." On the contrary, it originated with writers of young intellectual background.

Martin: Han Shaogong?

Acheng: I think Han Shaogong was the one, all by himself, but I'm not quite sure.

Martin: The term of course can have many different meanings. I feel that for this generation, including you, Bei Dao, and some other relatively well-known young intellectuals, the experience of going down to the countryside was extremely important. It was like entering a new world for you. When you went down to the countryside, was literature something you gave any thought to?

Acheng: No. In general, we simply had no books. Therefore I read everything twice, in two opposite frames of mind. I'd take any book I could get my hands on, first read it straight through to get its face value, then compose a counterpoint to it, in other words, read it in the opposite light. That way I could read one book as if it were two. But since counterpoising can be done from more than one perspective, one book can actually be read as if it were several books. In the process, I changed my views of literature. Ultimately, I came to feel that literature was the rendering of one's aesthetic judgment.

Martin: I've discovered that under similar circumstances, when there is a book that you practically are forced to read, there are two attitudes you can take. One is to read it very grudgingly, in which case you don't remember much of it. The other way is to read with special thoroughness. Zhang Xinxin, for example, has done it that way and consequently is remarkably at home with Marxist slogans and ideas. Which attitude do you choose?

Acheng: I read very attentively. I have ample time to read attentively.

Martin: Does the content of those books stay with you forever? Can you recall them at will?

Acheng: Yes, I can. They remain crystal clear in my mind. In those days, my memory and ability to comprehend were at their peak. Now, my memory isn't any good.

Martin: It probably won't be the same for the next generation, do you think?

Acheng: They have so very many things they can read now.

Martin: Prior to 1976, did you go anywhere else?

Acheng: Since I couldn't settle in Shanxi, I went to Inner Mongolia. I couldn't transfer my residence permit to Shanxi; the locals wouldn't take me. It was the same situation in Inner Mongolia, so ultimately I went to Yunnan. Inner Mongolia was a bit better than Shanxi. There was meat there, but we were still impoverished.

Martin: You basically did not have enough to eat?

Acheng: You could say that.

Martin: Was it your own decision to go to Yunnan, or were you assigned there?

Acheng: I decided on my own. I went to the Xishuangbanna region. It was a very beautiful place, but scenery cannot fill your stomach. It was opened prior to the fall of the Gang of Four, but foreigners were restricted in what they were shown there. The place I stayed was a day's travel from Jinghong. It was very different, going through those thickly forested mountains. There was one small stretch for motor vehicles, but for the most part, you had to travel on foot along mountain trails.

Martin: What was life like in Yunnan?

Acheng: I had a specific problem: Unlike the others, who had something to go back to in Peking, I had nothing in Peking. So for me, it really made no difference. Nevertheless, when you've lived somewhere for a long time, you have a lingering fondness for it, so I still wanted to go back to Peking. I was really more accustomed to it than to any place else. But, as I gradually got used to Yunnan, I didn't want to go back so much. I felt that I could live in Yunnan for the rest of my life.

Martin: I've read a good many writers' memoirs in which they express a desire to go back to visit the countryside where they were sent down. Those by Kong Jiesheng and Wang Meng, for example. Have you gone back to Xishuangbanna?

Acheng: No. I'm always wanting to see new places. A place I've already been to, and even spent ten years of my life in, I have no desire to see again.

Martin: You don't feel like you have a special rapport with the place, as if it were a second home?

Acheng: Perhaps I do. It gave me a great deal. But all in all, I already know the place. What I want to understand are the things I don't know yet.

Martin: How did you get back to Peking in 1979 ?

Acheng: Young intellectuals held a massive strike in Yunnan in 1979. The tens of thousands of us sent a delegation to Peking to make appeals. On account of that strike, the government allowed all us young intellectuals to return to own original place of residence.

Martin: In other words, the policy of sending intellectuals down to the countryside was a failure?

Acheng: Generally speaking, it was not a success. In China, the difference between urban and rural life is great. It is especially difficult for young intellectuals to endure the lack of cultural activity.

Martin: Did you aspire to be a writer during those ten years, or was it later?

Acheng: No, I really didn't think about writing at that time. It's only now that I truly feel I have a career in literature. It all seems to me like such an accident. It was only because I didn't have many people to communicate with then. For a long while, I just talked with myself. Then I discovered that I could set down those dialogues I had had with myself. After the passage of time, when I reread what I'd written, I might well feel like contradicting myself and throw it all away. Another alternative was to write fiction. That was having a dialogue with myself. I retain that habit when I write even now. I use my writing to satisfy myself. In fact, writing is the act of satisfying oneself.

Martin: I was surprised to hear you say this at the lecture you gave at the University of California at Berkeley, especially when you used the term *manzu*, to satisfy.

Acheng: Only after I feel satisfied with my writing do I consider it completed.

Martin: What did you do in 1979, after returning to Peking?

Acheng: When I returned to Peking in 1979, the first thing I ran into was the emergence of the Democracy Wall at Xidan. It was right at the time when activity at the Democracy Wall was at its peak. I was living with my parents then, and they just happened to live across from the Wall. Since I had nothing to do every day, I went over to see it. I had no job at all. After returning to Peking from Yunnan, I discovered that I could not adapt to urban life. Take crossing the street for instance. After a long while, I still couldn't get across. I was mortally afraid of motor vehicles. The pace of Peking city life was much faster than that of Yunnan. I had become a peasant. I couldn't adapt. My speech was extremely slow, too. People were not accustomed to it. My ability to express myself had declined. So the first thing about returning to Peking was that I could not adapt to city life. Second, I was already in the habit of talking to myself. At Democracy Wall, there were so many people talking. I discovered that the world was actually very dynamic.

Martin: At that time, I was at the University of Michigan, proofreading my book *Cult and Canon*. It has a section on the developments from 1976 to 1979. That was how I came to read some of the nonofficial magazines. On the one hand, we felt that the phenomenon was very good. On the other hand, we felt that the content was very naive, with the discussions on how to change the world in three months and so forth. Did you have this feeling at the time?

Acheng: I did feel that some pieces were naive. They were solely concerned with their own logic and whether or not it was supportable, not whether it fit into a larger system and followed from the whole. Most of the arguments were about morality. I'd already discarded that.

Martin: Do you mean the "inherited orthodoxy" and "political morality" that we were discussing at the beginning?

Acheng: Yes.

Martin: You didn't feel any inner need to participate in these discussions?

Acheng: Right.

Martin: But wasn't it through this movement that you acquired several new friends? Bei Dao, for instance?

Acheng: By then, the poems of Bei Dao, Genzi, Duoduo, and Jiang He were already well known among us young intellectuals.

Martin: In other words, you'd known them by name for some time, but only now came to know them in person?

Acheng: Yes.

Martin: Did you feel that they were endangering themselves by these activities?

Acheng: No, I did not feel that. Since I had lived in Yunnan for a long period, I wasn't familiar with that kind of life. At the time, I didn't feel that they were engaged in anything dangerous.

Martin: Then you didn't feel that it would turn out badly?

Acheng: No.

Martin: What were your plans for your own life at the time?

Acheng: They were very concrete. I wanted to find a job and earn money, so I could go on.

Martin: You would have accepted any kind of work?

Acheng: Yes. All young intellectuals in Peking then had to pass an examination to get work. I was assigned to work at the Zhongguo Tushu Jin Chu Kou Zong Gongsi, the head office of the China Book Import and Export Company. It was a company that imported foreign books. We never got to see the books, however. We just transported and distributed them. I worked as an artist and writer for the company's magazine, *World Books* (*Shijie tushu*).

Martin: How long did you work for this company?

Acheng: Four years. The job gave me a lot of experience, experience that was entirely different from what I got in Yunnan. What vexed me the most, however, was the fact that I had no way of controlling my own time. A lot of time was wasted. I was already thirty-five. I felt I had to make something of the second half of my life, take control of it. So I resigned.

Martin: And that was the conclusion of the first half of your life?

Acheng: There are only about seventy years to a person's life. After that, I worked as an architectural interior designer on a free-lance basis.

Martin: Were you still able to read and write with part-time work like that? How did you begin to write?

Acheng: At that time I had already finished writing. I didn't write.

Martin: Then when did you begin writing?

Acheng: In Yunnan.

Martin: Oh! So that's it! So "The Chess King" (*Qi wang*) and "King of the Children" (*Haizi wang*) were written then? Really?

Acheng: I wrote a lot in those days. That includes all the writing I did when I was running around everywhere. A series of my shorter writings now being published under the title *Scattered All Over* (*Biandi fengliu*) was also begun at that time.

Martin: It was after *Shanghai Literature* published "The Chess King" in 1984 that you became known to the public.

Acheng: Originally, I didn't think anyone would read it. What's even more surprising is that it still has a considerable readership. The response has been enthusiastic. I was caught unprepared. The fuss it stirred up has had an annoying effect on my personal life.

Martin: Can you be more specific about this "fuss" you've referred to?

Acheng: A lot of people came to invite me to meetings.

Martin: What was your relationship with the Chinese Writers' Association at that time? Was there a distinction between professional writers and spare-time writers? Did they invite you to become a member of the association?

Acheng: Yes.

Martin: And they had not done so previously?

Acheng: Correct.

Martin: Did you apply for membership, or was it by invitation? Did they come to request your participation?

Acheng: Right. It was exactly as you have worded it. It was Feng Jicai and another person—Aying's son-in-law—who came to seek me out.

Martin: Did your new friendships with other writers provide a new impetus to your own writing?

Acheng: No, there was no new impetus. In fact, my writing was already finished.

Martin: What are some of the other things you spoke of as "fuss"? Do they include having strangers come to your home at all hours?

Acheng: Yes. There were a lot of them. I invited them in for tea.

Martin: Why didn't you post something outside your door, like "Acheng is ill."

Acheng: I think you have to have reached a certain level before you can do something like that. I'm still not there. It took a long time before I figured out what they wanted. Some of them came only to see what I looked like.

Martin: Did any young women come to express "interest" in such a terrific fellow?

Acheng: I'm not the sort of guy women would really be interested in.

Martin: Were you sought out by a lot of young writers wanting to emulate your style? There must have been some interesting visitors, too, weren't there?

Acheng: On the whole, I feel that those who came to seek me out never presented the interesting side of themselves to me. If they'd acted like real, ordinary people and just communicated person-to-person, then it might have been pretty good. But people who came to seek me out just wanted to have literary exchanges. That gets very tiresome. Think about it. You'd be talking about literature unceasingly. There are other things to talk about, like eating.

Martin: Your writings have spread abroad so fast. Have your friends done any of it?

Acheng: I don't think they've been spread abroad so quickly.

Martin: It has been very fast.

Acheng: But I personally don't understand it. I'm still doing my own things. I was told that my stories had been specially published by Hong Kong's *Mingbao* and *The Nineties.*

Martin: Do you know Michael Duke? He is a very talented scholar who teaches in Canada and is now working in Peking. He wrote a research article on "The Chess King" that was published in *The Nineties.* We who do research on China really ought to read China's own journals. Our understanding of China really ought not to come from Hong Kong periodicals. But because there are so very many things to read, if one were to get all one's materials at the source, one would have to be highly specialized. Reading the secondary Hong Kong magazines is a way of making up for it. Once your stories were published in Hong Kong, everyone began to discuss them. Furthermore, several Chinese writers introduced your work. Zhang Jie, for instance, expressed admiration for your writing while she was abroad. So you became popular overseas first from the Hong Kong magazines, and second, through word-of-mouth recommendations of other writers. These are our main avenues of approach. And that is why I looked you up in Peking when I went there in 1985. This is basically how the French and Americans study contemporary Chinese literature, too. This is why the response outside China has been so quick. It really is to the credit of these Hong

Kong periodicals. I feel that it is very important to be able to meet with writers directly. So I was very pleased that the Jinshan Conference just outside Shanghai enabled us to meet so many Chinese writers.

I would also like to talk about the good reception of your work in Taiwan. I think you yourself didn't expect it.

Acheng: To me, it was all quite strange. It didn't make sense to me, for when I went to Hong Kong, I discovered that this was a society that had never experienced hunger.

Martin: You thought that people in Hong Kong wouldn't be able to understand you?

Acheng: Yes. Everybody claims that "The Chess King" is well written. Do they see something else in it?

Martin: How do you view it now?

Acheng: I now feel that perhaps it has to do with the Chinese language itself. There is one acknowledged aesthetic judgment within this very system.

Martin: Taiwan cannot avoid discussing the literature of the mainland. I personally think that it is a significant event that some intellectuals not connected with the government published three of your stories in Taiwan, and at some risk to themselves. This is the first book in Taiwan to introduce post-Mao mainland literature with its literariness in mind. Previously the "Literature of the Wounded" was introduced, but for quite another reason. The selection was very narrow. Your work represents mainland literature to Taiwan.

Acheng: We will have to wait and see how things develop.

Martin: It was the same when Zhang Jie's *Heavy Wings* (*Chenzhong de chibang*) was published in West Germany. It was the beginning of something new. Most West German intellectuals were familiar with the book, and so to a certain extent it represented contemporary literature to them.

I feel that the recent developments in China really represent the clash of two value systems. Do you feel that you should be concerned?

Acheng: I don't need to be. In actuality, Liu Binyan is still turning around in circles amid the old moral tradition and orthodoxy, so you get this intense clash. In my own literature, I've already rid myself of this orthodoxy. My literature has become my own affair. You meet with conflict only if you are inside that system. I'm long accustomed to living for myself, instead of other people, and to me, all this excitement belongs to the periphery. Being relatively stubborn, I've already come to see my writing as *my* business.

"Acheng de qianban sheng" (Acheng's early years), interview by Helmut Martin in Berkeley, California, February 19, 1987. The Chinese transcript of the interview was abridged and edited by Acheng, March 6, 1987, and printed in *Baixing banyuekan* (Pai hsing semi-monthly, Hong Kong) 163: 54–55; 164: 41–43; 165: 34–36 (March/April 1988).

—Translated by Linette Lee

Zhang Jie

THE NOVEL *Chenzhong de chibang* (Heavy wings, 1981) by Zhang Jie (b. 1937, in Peking) became famous in Germany because it captured the mood and psychology of Chinese bureaucrats, managers, and workers during the first phase of Deng Xiaoping's reforms. German readers came to view the novel as representative of the new literature coming from mainland China in the 1980s. And Zhang Jie has continued to develop as a writer. Stories of hers like "Ta sheng de shenme bing?" (What's wrong with him? *Zhongshan*, 1986, no. 3) create an ironic mosaic of contemporary society through satire. Since 1985, Zhang Jie has frequently visited the United States, Germany, and other European countries, where her novels and satirical stories have been well received because of her outspoken social protest and moral courage. Her novella *Fangzhou* (The ark, 1981) has also attracted much favorable interest, as a rare Chinese novel with feminist or protofeminist consciousness. Her confession-like openness brought scathing official criticism down on her during the 1983–84 campaign against "spiritual pollution." The essay below, an early piece by the author, captures only a part of her talent for describing the moods and thoughts of her protagonists, for Zhang Jie, like Acheng, has been reluctant so far to write much about her own situation.

The Boat I Steer
A Study in Perseverance

Zhang Jie

July 1981, at Beidaihe

HUMAN beings, the most intelligent of all animals, are sometimes foolish. Otherwise, why would they travel long distances to places like the Penglai Peninsula [in Shandong] just to see constantly changing mirages? Though people know such things to be illusory, they still eulogize them and are reluctant to part from them. It shows that the human yearning for beauty has not been quelled by the bloody struggle of life and death. This is perhaps the most fundamental difference between human beings and animals, although they share the instinct for survival.

I more or less had this feeling of viewing mirages when I first began to read works of literature. It seems to me that literature gives more to people than real life does. It expresses what people love and what they hate in a more concentrated form. At the very least, the feelings it evokes are unique. Chernyshevsky once said that no work of art is ever as beautiful or as noble as reality. I consider his view too extreme. God created man in his own image, and writers create their characters in the image of their own souls. Through the various art forms, human beings express the beauty of *creation*.

Through their music, their sculpture, and their painting, artists are in dialogue with society.

I have always wondered why artists must use such painful and difficult forms, why they must grind their hearts on millstones, pouring out their souls. Is it because, like us, they sometimes feel a profound loneliness, and therefore hope to gain the understanding and forgiveness of humankind?

I believe that many human misfortunes are caused by our inability to understand and to communicate.

Because of this, I feel closer to literary characters than to real people. I find the characters easier to understand; I wish I could just live my life in books, and never come out again.

It was literature that awakened in me previously dormant ideas on all manner of social phenomena. Many of these ideas, unscientific and imperfect though they may be, go some way to explaining why I have been so battered in this world. But I have no regrets; people are never that objective or rational when deeply in love with something or someone. You must always pay for what you love, and sacrifice for it—if indeed that can really be considered a sacrifice. I rejoice that literature has made me a human being, a living human being with defects, a human being with feelings. Otherwise, I would not be able to write a single line. Tolstoy once told one of his brothers that he had all of the virtues of a writer but lacked an essential defect: he did not go to extremes.

It is rather amusing that in the past, whenever we were asked to summarize our ideological remolding and I was supposed to try and uncover the class and social origin of my long-standing and unreformable bad habits—lack of a sense of class struggle, low political consciousness, and slack discipline—I always heard people comment with exasperation, "The problem with Zhang Jie is that she has been too deeply poisoned by eighteenth- and nineteenth-century novels from the West."

I secretly congratulate myself that if I retain an iota of human feeling, if I never moved up in the world by stepping on and defaming other people for my own advantage (and I am somewhat proud of this), then it must be largely due to the influence of the human feelings, the character, and the humanism in classical literature.

History unceasingly discards dross and develops what is good. We do not curse food because we have to excrete. Being such thorough-going materialists at the dinner table, why do we pretend to be idealists when it comes to spiritual sustenance? We are afraid of everything except our own regression to bestiality. Has our twenty-million-year evolution all been for nothing?

For me, literature increasingly represents not just a pursuit for driving away monotony and sadness, but a longing for all manner of unrealized ideals: I wish life were more the way people want it to be.

Why can't it be so?

Nothing apart from literature can interest me and hold my attention over a long period. I once felt myself like a darting dragonfly, with no goals in life and no substantial pursuits. Only through literature did I discover myself. Successful or not, I am still very persevering. I don't know how other people deal with this problem, but I often feel that to be able to find oneself is a difficult thing. Some people can spend a whole lifetime and still not find or understand themselves. Others, of course, have a much easier time of it. For me, it took all of forty years. It was a little too late, but I treasure it all the more.

A life unfulfilled arouses us to dream of making it complete. Beauty, despondency, joy, ugliness—all manner of social phenomena weave themselves into one story after another in my mind; if this happened, then it would come to pass that—. Like an artless tailor, I cut my cloth unskillfully, according to old measurements. The result is like the factory clothes sold in department stores that come in only five standard sizes and styles.

Because of this, my rather undistinguished works always arouse suspicion in some quarters. "Were her pieces copied from a size three or size five pattern?"

Some say, "That story is about Zhang Jie herself," and they take it upon themselves to make investigations—in a certain month of a certain year there was such-and-such a person, such-and-such an event—all so authoritative that it seems true. . . .

It is common knowledge that the characters and events in literary works may be composites of several people and events in real life. They may well be wholly fictitious, made up by the author through logical reasoning.

Literature is more concentrated than life. It is more abstract, and more compact; more perfect, and more repulsive.

The truthfulness of literature and the truthfulness of life are two entirely different things. Yet there are people who insist on confusing them. Is this just stupidity, feudalism, or backwardness? Not at all; it is a kind of weapon.

Madame Bovary brought Flaubert ten years of litigation.

Xu Jun was decapitated by the Qing government for his words, "Why turn the pages when the clear wind cannot read?"[1]

Comrade Wu Han was persecuted to death for writing *Hai Rui Dismissed from Office*.

What made me think about all of this so seriously was one persistent question: Why is it that writers, foreign and Chinese, past and present, get into trouble over their work? I keenly feel the contradiction between the social responsibility and conscience of a writer, and the treatment he or she receives from society.

When the Guangdong People's Publishing House printed a second edition of my story collection, *Love Must Not Be Forgotten* (*Ai, shi bu neng wangji de*), I designed the cover: two white medieval boats sailing on a dark green background. But because the selection was part of a series, the publishing house wanted a uniform design and it was not used.

Can it be that my boat is now already stranded, that I can only listen at a distance to the pounding waves deep into the night? In the past, I had the courage to struggle against fate.

Do I give up easily? No, I wouldn't be me if I did.

If I did, I would be letting my readers down, too.

---

[1]In Chinese, "clear" (*qing*) is homophonous with the name of the Manchu (Qing) dynasty, which was sensitive to any possible reference to its incompetence or "barbarian" origins.

Many of my readers have written to say, "If misfortune should befall you one day, come to me."

What greater reward can a writer expect than a just hearing?

Apart from getting old or falling ill, about which I can do nothing, I don't expect to encounter misfortune; life, after all, must go on.

Of course there are readers who curse us, too. I would estimate about 1 to 3 percent.

These figures lead me to wondering: for whom do I write? For whom do I live?

So I've come to Beidaihe beach. I've been laughing away, talking nonstop, and swimming to my heart's content. Like a boat drifting about on the waves, I have cast self-control aside and let myself be buoyed up by a state of happy abandon. I have taken the sea to my bosom, let the waves lap at my feeble heart. My skin gleams like bronze in the sun, and when I look in the mirror, I see the red face of an [American] Indian. My teeth gleam when I smile. I seem to have recovered my health and strength. And so I renovate my boat, patching and repainting where it needs it. My boat will last a little longer. Heave ho, I've weighed anchor once again. The people, the houses, the trees on shore become smaller and smaller and I feel reluctant to leave them. But my boat cannot stay beached forever: What use is a boat without the sea?

In the distance, I see waves rolling toward me. They surge on, without cease. I know that one day they will smash me to bits, but that is the fate of all boats—if the end does not come here, then where?

"Wo de chuan" (My boat), Beidaihe, July 1981, in *Wenxue zhi lu* (The path of literature) (Changsha, 1983), pp. 144–50.

—Translated by Yu Fanqin

Wang Anyi

THE THEMES treated by Wang Anyi (b. 1954, in Nanjing, now long resident in Shanghai) predestined her to become widely recognized as a speaker for China's younger generation, and now, a breaker of the taboos that hide sexuality and carnal love from view in the modern Chinese context.

Wang Anyi grew up in Shanghai but was sent down to the Anhui countryside for the better part of a decade, beginning in 1969. She gained fame in post-Mao times by writing extensively about her own rusticated Red Guard generation and its frustrations getting reaccustomed to urban (particularly Shanghainese) life. In 1983, Wang Anyi and her mother Ru Zhijuan, another major writer of the post-Mao period, participated in the International Writing Program at the University of Iowa. Chinese literary critics recognize Wang Anyi as a talented and versatile writer with a special humane sensitivity, an idealist in quest of a friendlier, more civilized, and egalitarian society—among the classes and among the sexes, who must coexist in China's modern megalopolises. Her newer, more fabular works, such as *Baozhuang* (Baotown, 1984), *Huangshan zhi lian* (Love on a barren mountain, 1986) and *Xiaocheng zhi lian* (Love in a small town, 1986), represent for her a new departure, the latter two having love themes that explore fatal sexual attraction and tensions between deep emotional love and dull ordinary marriage in ways that are challenging and, to her Chinese public, unusually explicit. Although translations of these novelettes were well received in the English- and German-speaking worlds, they alienated many Chinese readers and infuriated semi-official critics because of their cool, existentialist spirit. Her talk below, which she delivered at a much higher emotional pitch, exhibits her note-worthy spirit of self-questioning.

Needed

A Spirit of Courageous Self-Examination

Wang Anyi

August 25, 1986, in Shanghai

My TOPIC is: We are our own worst enemy.

As I stand before you in this international forum, able openly and confidently to present a subject so charged with my extremely individual consciousness, I cannot help but think back upon the endless yet brief journey taken by China's old, and, at the same time, youthful contemporary literature. Beginning with the first seventeen years since 1949, through the handful of approved model works of the Cultural Revolution decade, on to the post–Cultural Revolution "Literature of the Wounded" and "Literature of Self-Reflection," up to the "Literature of Finding Our Roots" and of "Seeking Urban Consciousness" today, one realizes how rare and precious this moment is.

I have always considered myself a writer removed from all literary movements, but in fact I have benefited from every one of the gains made in those movements. Each time another "forbidden zone" is breached with death-defying foolhardiness, a new creative path has been cleared for me. Absolved of all obligations and restraints, I, then, can roam with perfect freedom over the battlegrounds of the past. I am a very fortunate young woman. Thanks to the cover provided by my colleagues and predecessors, I can afford now to devote time to my own problems.

I must admit that during my first few years of writing, I was engaged not so much in rational thinking as in mechanical groping, with just a vague idea, invisible and inexplicable, to urge me on. It was not until much later that conscious reasoning began to reveal itself to me. Then, like a flash of lightning, it illuminated both the road ahead and the road behind. I advanced by this brief yet brilliant flash of light, though without full understanding, and with a sense of fatalism. Now, it appears that the moment has arrived again for the light of reason to shine forth, and I discover that I have a theme for my writing:

We are our own worst enemy.

My original intention was to illustrate this theme with the experiences of a young woman who lives in comfort and lacks none of life's necessities. The conflict between her and the external world can be said to have eased, yet she is far from being at peace. On the surface, she is calmness itself, but inside, she is beleaguered and constantly at war. She indulges in self-torture by creating vexations for herself, but she also is able to draw from the crowd a small measure of good will to warm and pacify her agitated heart. For a long time, this young woman represented me; she was a symbol of myself. Thus, her life closely parallels mine. My childhood was quiet and peaceful but also filled with hours of loneliness and solitude. Therefore, when faced with sudden changes in life, I was totally incapable of action to contend with the outside world. Instead, I retreated still more into meditation and quiet contemplation; the battle within me grew fiercer and grimmer than the one without. I am much more knowledgeable and experienced in that kind of war, and well aware of its consequences. Sometimes I even believe that one's fortune hangs on the victory or defeat in this war. However, since we live in a time filled with tumult and unpredictable changes, it is inevitable that we divert a great deal of our energy to mundane affairs, to improve our circumstances. Thus we put an end to our wild flights of fancy.

That was what happened at one stage in my life. While I continued the painful task of writing about the young girl's restless inner world, the swift torrents of life roared on behind me. Sometimes I would look back, only to see those innumerable lives that were still obliged to contend with the outside world. I felt ashamed. Compared to theirs, my life seemed to be too leisured and self-indulgent. And so I gave up that symbol I held so dear, to link hands with all those ordinary people facing a very real fight for survival. I tried my best to understand their hard struggle in these trying times. This was a new start, followed by a long trek in my writing as in my life, but one that offered me temporary release and respite from my internal torments. For a short time, I lay down my arms in that exhausting psychological battle and concerned myself with a larger war fought in the greater arena of life and the world. For the sake of their survival, and ideals, people were engaged in a nonstop struggle with the outside world. I found myself becoming passionately involved. Faced with such struggles before, I in my timidity and cowardice had only covered my eyes and run away, curling up in my little shell to wait for divine intervention. Now, safely at the outer perimeters of the fight, I could open my eyes with confidence and seek out the thick of the battle. It was then that I discovered the truth. The external struggle was so closely linked to the internal war that they were actually one and the same. This is how the battle lines appear to me: the individual confronts two opponents simultaneously. One enemy is fate and circumstances. The other is one's self. The opposing self often becomes one with the battling self, yet just as often turns traitor and conspires with fate. The individual is in fact under attack from both front and rear. Life is truly a bitter struggle. Then, as I recalled my life's experiences, I began to see through the many illusions and misunderstandings. In one's intense combat with one's self, the forces and counterforces of the outside world are ever present. Only when one's internal opposition links up with outer provocations are flames of war ignited from within. Conversely, the forces and counterforces of the internal world are part of the external struggle. When the balance within is upset, war erupts without. Allow this condition to spread and grow, and the result is the Cultural Revolution, whose ashes are still warm. Let those who have suffered look calmly and searchingly into their own souls; not one of them can deny culpability. One may trace the origins of this conflagration, which raged on for an entire decade, to eight hundred million individual sparks. Now, bring the experience down to the level of an insignificant fate, like mine. If I had given in, one night, many years ago, when doubts momentarily beset me as I sat at my desk, then all my struggles to become a writer would have been just a frivolous dream. The self in each of us does make an impact on our destiny; the self in each of us does shape our circumstances. None of us can really escape the self. As a result, that struggle with one's self is a painful, never-ending one.

On returning to my inner world, however, I discovered that the war within was no longer the self-induced adolescent anxiety of a few years earlier. After facing itself squarely, in the light of broader and profounder issues of the human world, the struggle has taken on more meaningful questions. It is a struggle relevant not just to a leisure class spared from material and mundane worries, but to all humanity, from the lowest to the highest levels. It is a struggle belonging not to a minority, but to all humankind. Whether we realize it or not, we are bound, from birth, to face up to our self, to confront our self. I have a feeling that this struggle before me has suddenly escalated to a higher level, and even acquired a certain nobility.

An individual facing the world also faces unpredictable calamities and upheavals: volcanic eruptions, avalanches, wars, pestilence, famine, and disease. We can all link hands and fight these disasters shoulder-to-shoulder. Yet when it comes to facing the internal world, the individual is alone. People on the outside are powerless to help, and those who have passed on cannot provide inspiration. It is up to the individual to fight and grope for a solution. Already, one's internal world is plagued by many arduous trials: selfishness, feelings of inferiority, pride, cowardice, cruelty, timidity, childish ignorance, the stirrings of puberty, sexual awakening and repression, and so on. How many more trials by fire must human beings go through before they emerge as steel from the flames? This is an eternal conflict. Human civilization, however advanced, cannot hope to escape it. In fact, it will only grow more intense. There is, however, one consolation. While one continues the lonely battle with one's self, all other people are likewise engaged. So one is not entirely alone. This battle is a common one fought by humanity on countless different battlefields. We can share experiences and offer each other comfort. Though it is not an easy task, I believe my writing may provide these lonely combatants a channel for communication and exchange of information. My writing will tell them that they are not alone, that all humankind is behind them. At the same time, I myself may gain the strength and wisdom for victory in my own internal battle. A wild hope perhaps, but that is what I am striving for.

This is a world beset by disasters and suffering. We have many, many unsolved problems. Even as I speak, tens of thousands of refugees are adrift in our world. Deserts encroach upon fertile land. Wars are fought on and on. Earthquakes threaten the world. Women call for equality. Though I am engrossed in internal struggles, that does not mean that I am turning my back on these other problems. I firmly believe that an individual, and a people, must possess the insight and courage to engage in self-examination. This spirit of self-examination is what guarantees that individuals will become real human beings, and that a people will develop into a strong and worthy nation. We must first face up to our inner self and struggle unremittingly against it if we are to become truly strong and healthy, and endure for generation after generation, through every challenge put to us by nature.

"Miandui ziji" (Facing oneself), Shanghai, August 25, 1986, essay for the International Conference on Contemporary Chinese Literature, Jinshan, Shanghai, November 1986. From the conference volume.

—Translated by Ellen Lai-shan Yeung

Liu Binyan

LIU BINYAN (b. 1925) is China's most famous investigative journalist, purveyor of *baogao wenxue* (reportage literature), and, perhaps now with the exception of Fang Lizhi, high-moral-profile dissident. His following essay about reportage may be read as a self-reflection on his whole career.

Having a fluent reading knowledge of Japanese, English, and Russian, Liu was already an accomplished Communist party journalist and member of the new establishment when he was purged as a rightist in the campaign of 1957, not to be rehabilitated until 1979. He reappeared on the literary scene with a vengeance in his long reportage piece *Ren yao zhi jian* (People or monsters? 1979), about pervasive corruption in Manchuria. As special correspondent for the *People's Daily*, Liu Binyan became the "conscience of the nation" because of his willingness to speak the truth. In the years following, he remained constantly under attack by the old guard. Ultimately, he was expelled from the Communist party (and its organ, the *People's Daily*) in January 1987, called a spiritual coinstigator of the student protests for democracy in December 1986. Nevertheless, he retained his position as vice-chairman of the Chinese Writers' Association (*elected* by the membership of writers instead of appointed from above, in a leadership selection process that was itself a sign of the liberalization of the times). Due to all the official criticism of his activities, Liu Binyan's writings were never assembled for republication in China; in 1988, however, Hong Kong's Xiangjiang Press brought out a two-volume selection entitled *Liu Binyan yanlunji* (Speeches and articles by Liu Binyan) that if anything portrays Liu Binyan in an even more revealing way than do his famous reportage pieces.

In 1988, Liu Binyan left China to become a Neiman fellow at Harvard University. Since then, he has taught at Trinity College, Connecticut, and Princeton University and toured worldwide, lecturing on problems of Chinese law and government ranging from press censorship to environmental pollution.

Is Reportage to Be Excluded from the Realm of Literature?

The Function of Warning Bells

Liu Binyan

LET ME begin with some extraneous remarks. I think you can say this, can't you—that a particular kind of era will have a particular type of literature. In other words, what an era supplies, an author can write about. When the two elements come together, they create a literature characteristic of the age.

We will shortly reach this nation's thirty-fifth birthday. Looking back over these thirty-five years, we see that the country has constantly been in the midst of huge changes. First there was land reform, then the Suppression-of-Counterrevolutionaries revolution, the Elimination-of-Counterrevolutionaries revolution, collectivization, communization, the Antirightist movement, the Anti–rightist tendencies movement, and so on, right down to the "Great Proletarian Cultural Revolution." These all supplied literature with extraordinarily rich subject matter. Still, even over this long period, our literature was not able truly and penetratingly to reflect these historical changes. Looking back on the literature of the 1950s and 1960s now, we can see that many works were about history, such as *Keep the Red Flag Flying*, *Red Crag*, *The Song of Youth*, and so on. All these famous novels were about history, not the era in which they were written. At the same time, when we look at the works that were about their own times, we see that they, too, constantly evaded the real and important social conflicts that were going on. They presented a false, even an upside-down image of social reality. Beginning in 1957, literature became increasingly narrow, until it evolved into the "Gang of Four" period's literature of conspiracy. Particularly after 1963 and 1964, the opposition to writing about "characters in the middle" and so forth made it impossible for the majority of us citizens to appear as characters in literary works. Literature could only portray two types of people:

heroes and enemies. Actually, for a long time, even our literary heroes and enemies couldn't be authentic; the struggles portrayed were among fake heroes and fake enemies.

The fate of reportage was the same as that of other literature. Perhaps, in a certain sense, from the 1950s on, the literary characteristics of the era were still more evident in reportage literature. In the early 1950s, I was already working for a newspaper. For various reasons, there were many things then that couldn't be printed, just couldn't be publicly known, particularly certain social contradictions and problems. From 1951 to 1956—or perhaps from 1949 to 1956—some very good reportage appeared, mainly about advanced persons and the constructive achievements being made on every front. Although these things needed to be and should have been written about, deep changes in people's lives were also starting to appear throughout society, gradually sharpening the contradictions, and there were all kinds of new needs in every sphere of life. Either writers and reporters didn't notice these things, or they noticed them but could not write about them.

Thus, when we look back on the literature of the 1950s and 1960s—on up to the 1970s—on the one hand we see that many excellent works appeared; but on the other hand, literature as a whole was quite unnatural. Our lives from 1950 to 1970 witnessed a multitude of things both good and bad, but the reflection of them in literature was unrecognizable. In sum, my own opinion is that the literature of that era does not truly or deeply reflect the history of that period. In 1956, there was a change: works of reportage literature appeared. They raised relatively real and hard questions. That this happened in 1956 was not accidental, because in the several movements up until then, struggles between the people and the enemy had been relaxing, while contradictions among the people were starting to become the principal contradiction in our lives.[1] This is one thing. For another, the policy of "let a Hundred Flowers bloom, let a hundred schools of thought contend," proposed by Comrade Mao Zedong, was beginning to be carried out in literary circles. Today it is over twenty years since 1956; only in 1978 or 1979 did reportage literature again enter a new phase. One could that say it is experiencing unprecedented prosperity. This is because our party's Central Committee, in summing up lessons from history, has enacted a correct line and set things right. The whole party and nation are reevaluating history. At the same time, our real-life contradictions have become unprecedentedly rich and complicated. We want to carry out reform; the reforms have produced many glorious reformers and outstandingly successful people worth writing up, and the struggles between reformers and antireformers have sharpened. Consequently, the following situation has appeared: under the Central Committee's policy of liberating thought, the creative force of us writers has been greatly liberated, and for

---

[1] Liu Binyan is alluding to the rise of class struggle against social elements previously considered loyal, using the terminology of Chairman Mao's theory of contradictions.

this very reason, more and more writers are able squarely to face life's contradictions. They can see the outmoded things in our lives, our thoughts, our organizations, and our social order. They can see all sorts of people and things in society that do not conform with the needs of the "four modernizations" or the spirit of the reforms, and make them rise up before our eyes, like a vast tide. Many writers are inspired—impelled—to take up their pens and reflect these newly arisen people and events—whether heroic or lamentable—and the many new kinds of struggles in our lives. Reportage literature is the genre they use to deal with these things.

Compared to other types of literature, reportage is more timely and direct in revealing life's many problems; and, compared to other genres, it is freer in its techniques of expression and structure. For example, reportage does not require a complete story. The writer has more opportunities to express his or her own views and feelings. It is a form of literature between journalism, fiction, and the essay. In recent years, reportage literature has reached a new high. This is because life itself, and readers, require it, as I said previously, and also because writers now have more freedom to create. Thus, these last few years, reportage has been able to reflect life more fully and realistically than at any time before in the past thirty-five years. The breadth, width, and depth of its influence on readers has been astonishing. But considering the needs of the times—of the reforms—and in comparison with the richness and complexity of our lives, reportage literature still has not done enough. Many social phenomena and problems requiring solutions, and all sorts of character types representing them, have yet to be reflected in our reportage literature. There are, in my opinion, two reasons for this. Objectively speaking, whether or not various problems and other phenomena in our lives can be published, and whether it is advantageous or disadvantageous for us if they are, is a theoretical problem that has not yet been completely resolved. In recent years, our newspaper reporting and depiction of life in reportage literature have greatly expanded. But opinions differ as to whether they need to be expanded further.

Our nation has experienced several decades of war, and many habits and practices of the war years are still in evidence today. For instance, war required total centralization and a high degree of secrecy. It required each person to make the ultimate sacrifice for victory, especially inasmuch as we were always at a disadvantage before the enemy throughout our protracted revolutionary war. Under such conditions, we didn't begin to speak of individual needs. Yet these things, to one degree or another, still influence our lives and thinking today.

In my personal opinion, journalism and reportage literature have long been allowed merely to reflect the final decisions of a party committee of a certain rank, if not of our Central Committee itself. But life is vaster and richer than any policy document or resolution. It continually progresses, too, and always ahead of our policy. So should we write about this multitude of new matters, to keep our people and our party on top of things? Or should we wait until a problem has a solution, a correct solution, before we can raise it? This question was never solved in past history. Now the situation has already changed. Our newspapers reflect life's trends more fully every day, but the question has not yet been solved theoretically. For example, besides propagandizing the party's policies to the people, is it or isn't it proper for newspapers to turn around and provide information to us party cadres and to party organs? Questions of journalism like these have not been entirely resolved. These conditions are bound to influence the subject matter and development of reportage literature. The most prominent question is whether open publication of articles containing criticism and exposure is to our advantage or not. This is a very old question, already raised back in the mid-1950s. This question can be said to have been solved in part, but I believe that it still has not been thoroughly resolved.

A traditional concept holds that we still need to write of good things, of our successes, good deeds, and advanced characters. This will benefit us, as these things can inspire the people and arouse the masses to work still more vigorously and with unity of purpose, to bring about the "four modernizations." Gloomy and negative things had best not be made public. To write of them might cause people to lose heart, increase their worries, fill them with disappointment, and so forth. I think that for many of our comrades, this point of view has not been thoroughly dispelled. However, according to my own experience since I wrote *People or Monsters?* (*Ren yao zhi jian*) in 1979, only the bold, intense works that impinge on the contradictions in our lives can elicit the masses' faith in our future and strengthen their trust in our party and socialist system. Probably ninety to ninety-nine point some percent of the letters I receive from readers are supportive. They say: Reading your work solved a dilemma for me. At first I didn't want to speak, express my desires, or bring up the problems I observed. But after reading your article, my attitude changed. Why? I think the very fact that our press today allows the printing of this type of essay clearly shows that our party has the courage to face reality and the determination to transform the status quo. That's how they see it.

Still, even among writers of creative and reportage literature, attitudes toward this problem are not unanimous. After my "rightist" problem was rectified in 1979, my very first article addressed "The Question of Writing about the Dark Side of Life and Delving into Life." Now, it's no surprise that most people don't agree on this question. Not long ago, possibly in 1981, a reportage author wrote that the slogan "delving into life" (*ganyu shenghuo*; "intervening in life") was intolerable. Can it be that only capitalist countries need writers to come out and speak for the people? Do we in a socialist nation have no such need? Is coming out and delving into life now a disparagement of the party? We first heard this argument over twenty years ago. They may or may not have used the words "delving into life." But this question relates to the problem of a writer's attitude toward life. Do you passively record life and write about things wholly unrelated to life's mainstream, or do you fill yourself with political enthusiasm to extol what should be extolled and denounce the phenomena that should have been eliminated long ago? Comrade Mao Zedong often said: One's standpoint, attitude, and feelings are a question of on whose behalf they are. This question deserves our attention still today.

Just this past year, I saw a sign that I regard as very positive. There are quite a number of leaders, even senior ones, who entreat us journalists and reportage writers to take hold of a particular problem, or to elucidate and report on a particular event. This has led me to a clearer and more profound appreciation of something. Journalism, including reportage literature, really does have a special social function. When there are problems that political organs and the judiciary are unable to resolve, newspapers, including their literary authors, can sometimes assume the task. This is certainly not to say that we are wiser than our party committee leaders. It's just a social division of labor. . . .

Whether a writer living in our era should adopt a progressive attitude toward the problems surrounding us or a passive, conservative attitude ought to be a very simple question, yet it still has not been entirely resolved. This is the first obstacle in the progress of reportage literature I wish to point out.

The second problem is that of us writers' own abilities and vigor. I touched on this problem earlier, which is whether a writer—a reportage writer—should have a sense of mission, of social responsibility. In recent years, I've felt that many of our literary works avoid our society's great contradictions. The authors are more interested in writing about soft things like romantic love and the ups and downs in people's personal lives. These things can be topics for literature, and in fact they should be, for some time to come. But when there are too many of these works, when so many writers spend most or even all of their energy writing this kind of thing, that's clearly not very well suited to the times. Some writers' works are, to put it bluntly, written from an ivory tower. They concentrate on one-upsmanship in technique and modes of expression. This certainly is not impermissible. Our literary creation faces the problem of needing innovation in form. The form of some works has clearly limited their content, but if one focuses one's effort on form and doesn't observe, analyze, study, and reflect on some things in the mainstream of our lives, then I believe that we cannot complete the mission that our age has bestowed on us. Of course, many young writers have been limited by their environment. These comrades are unable to travel freely and extensively like the reporters from national newspapers, or professional writers, and so they only come into contact with a narrow and specialized range of experience; this is a problem. I think it is up to both the leadership and the individual to work to overcome this. Further limiting the level of literary works is the insufficient interest some young people show toward theory. Due to the Ten-Year Calamity under Lin Biao and the "Gang of Four," some people lost interest in Marxism. False Marxism undermined the reputation of real Marxism. Thus, their interest typically was no longer on how to cultivate their theoretical understanding, stand a little taller, or see a little farther, but on some person or thing. Yet, if our authors do not stand a little taller and see a little farther than our readers, their works will be of limited value. Another problem is understanding the relationship between literature (including reportage literature) and politics.

Our Central Committee has now repudiated the slogan "literature must serve politics." This I completely agree with. But does that mean that our literature can be oblivious to politics or wholly unrelated to it? I have some opinions on this; indeed, historically we have not managed this well for some time. But I think we should divide this problem into two aspects. First, what kind of politics is at issue? When the political line is wrong, this will naturally influence the lifespan of any literary work following it. The work can even lose all justification for its existence. Consider the "Great Leap Forward" and "people's communes" of 1958. Any work about the "Great Leap Forward" and "people's communes" that was written fully in accord with the propaganda needs of the time—that went all-out to praise and eulogize them—has no value whatsoever today. Even at the time, it could only have had a bad influence. But when the political line is correct, there's nothing wrong with speaking up for it and praising it, I feel. In fact, it is very much needed. Since ancient times, most writing (not to say all) that has been handed down to posterity has reflected great social problems of its era—problems of the sort that affected the fate of thousands and millions of people. I must add that our concept of politics is relatively broad. Our politics includes the social within it. In that sense, to say that literature has abandoned social contradictions is not to judge the works' value or lifespan, but to ask if there might not be a problem with their value and lifespan.

Nineteenth-century Russia provided the high point in world literary history. That was the era when the czar's dictatorship was extremely cruel and the serf system fettered tens of millions of the Russian people. There were writers at the time from noble families such as Tolstoy and Turgenev whose thought was largely reactionary, and yet they still wrote immortal works. I believe a very important reason for this was that they paid close attention to the fate of the masses and had a strong interest in politics and society. Some works by Turgenev, for example, resemble our reportage literature a little. I am referring to their topicality. He often wrote about things as they were going on, and published them in the same year. Hence, in that very year, they would become popular throughout Europe. *Fathers and Sons* is one such work. This work is strongly political and social; its character Bazarov is such a model type that his name later entered the vocabulary of many foreign languages, just as the Russian word for nihilism has been adopted in English, French, and many other languages to express the idea of nihilism. We Chinese have not transliterated the Russian word, we use a traditional root of our own, to describe people like Bazarov. So what do I consider strange? When our political line and policy are in error, we absolutely insist that writers follow it and go all-out to describe a particular movement or event. Today, when our political line is correct, such demands happen not to be so strong. Quite a few writers now lack sufficient interest in politics; I don't consider this a minor problem.

To conclude, I would like to say a little about technique. The question is, what is the difference between reportage literature and journalism? The boundary between them is not very clear, either in China or in other countries. Some languages do not even have a word for reportage literature. For example, in America, "nonfiction" means all works that are not the product of imagination. This includes all kinds of writing except fiction and is too broad. Yet you can see a trend in many countries, including the United States and some European nations, of increasing indifference toward fiction, while the market for works about real people and real problems grows larger and larger. . . .

"Baogao wenxue yu shehui shenghuo" (Reportage literature and social life), 1984, in *Dangdai zuojia* (Contemporary writers), ed. Chinese Department of the Central Broadcasting and Television University (Beijing, 1984), pp. 262–80.

—Translated by Carolyn S. Pruyn

Zhang Xinxin

ZHANG XINXIN (b. 1953, in Nanjing, but raised in Peking) was sent down to the countryside during the Cultural Revolution instead of receiving a regular high school education, a disillusioning experience that influenced her early short stories. "Zai tongyi dipingxian shang" (On the same horizon, 1981) depicts conflict among married artists striving for self-realization, told from the perspective of the woman; "Fengkuang de junzilan" (Orchid madness, 1983) aims Absurdist satire at the sudden explosion of materialism that has engulfed China since the 1980s. Her fiction was consequently savaged because of its subversive modernist tendencies during the 1983–84 campaign against "spiritual pollution."

Unable to publish throughout 1984 (and denied her diploma at Peking's Central Academy of Drama, although she went on to become a director at the Peking People's Art Theater when the movement was over), Zhang Xinxin in a fit of defiance decided on a new tack. She and a collaborator, the young journalist Sang Ye, toured China to produce a book of oral history in the tradition of Studs Terkel. They called it *Beijingren* (Peking man, 1985, titled *Chinese Lives* in the authorized English translation). The work won them overnight worldwide fame. The chaotic and unidealized images of "real life" in the book were a sharp retort to Zhang Xinxin's critics in the Communist party who wanted China's new authors to continue as propagandists, only now for Deng Xiaoping's reforms instead of Mao Zedong's utopianism. Zhang Xinxin has since then written a good deal for the Chinese television and film industries, even while continuing her avant-garde experiments in fiction. She has traveled widely abroad, spending much of her time since 1988 at Cornell University and the University of Georgia. The satiric and self-satiric bite of the mock interview below go far to explain her appeal to critics of smugness both at home and abroad.

A "Bengal Tigress" Interviews Herself

A Panorama of Our Times from Within

Zhang Xinxin

January 13, 1985

DURING and also before and after the Fourth Congress of the Chinese Writers' Association, reporters and colleagues kept asking me questions. Some of these I need to answer in my fictional works: through their structure, atmosphere, characters, action, and the effect produced by paragraphs colliding with each other. Other questions I ought, as a young person, to answer frankly and without reservation—to the extent that our era permits it. There are other questions, of course, that should be allowed to settle and rest for a while.

In general, you can collapse the questions into the several that follow.

Q: Since the smashing of the Gang of Four, our policies on literature have gone through several evident stages of relaxing and tightening, and yet Comrade Wang Meng said today: The golden age has truly arrived. As a specially invited delegate to the Fourth Congress of the Chinese Writers' Association, what are your views?

A: The basic policy of the party toward literature has not changed. Neither has the basic responsibility of the writer.

Q: What kind of future do you see for literary and artistic creation in China? What kinds of works are needed most? What are your own plans for writing?

A: I never put my writing plans down on paper, for fear that I'll be unable to carry them out and thus disappoint my editors and readers. Most important of all, I am superstitious. My past experiences certainly have borne out my fear, not just once but repeatedly, that whatever I want most, once I say it out loud, I'm bound not to get. Anyway, I feel we live in a world of great color and beauty. Even if I were to experience and think about it all the time, and write on and on about it without cease until I died of exhaustion, I still wouldn't be able to keep up with this world of ours. To be a writer, one must first and foremost have a conscience, and write with sincerity about one's own perceptions and feelings, reflecting one's own times. Today, however, it is equally important to provide the people who create this rich life of ours with some entertainment that they can enjoy to the fullest: not merely disguises for moral teaching, but honest, unadulterated entertainment. We must allow those who build for us and protect us to work like human beings and play like human beings. The richness of life and the heightened tempo of living, the increasing variety of ways to express feelings and to communicate, all demand a corresponding diversity in art forms. This is an age that challenges the writer's imagination and adaptability. At the same time, our era asks of us panoramic works similar to *Blockade*, which delineates a great epoch by depicting everyone from ordinary soldiers on up to Stalin.[1] There are already works that tell of the violent surface pulsations. But works that aim truly to interpret and recapture the full spirit of the times have yet to be written. A process of settling out, reflection, and arduous struggle is still needed.

Q: Are you planning to write something like *Blockade*?

A: Blockade talks about the Second World War, but from the perspective of the 1970s. It involves only Leningrad and one-hundred-odd living and thinking individuals.

What is needed is a real and concrete space. Within this crucial space, the times call for mobilization on the battlefield, clapper tales, street theater skits, even catchy propaganda verses.

Q: Do you usually complete a manuscript in one attempt? How many revisions do you go through? What kind of pen do you use? What kind of paper?

A: Sometimes I can plot out my novellas in a flash. I can write very fast when I put on my earphones and surround myself with fast-tempo music. But as soon as I feel that I can't think clearly, and particularly when I'm not sure what I intend to do with the characters and the action, I stop, unwilling to proceed a single word further. A short story, on the other hand, can sometimes take me months. Take, for example, "Orchid Madness" (*Fengkuang de junzilan*). I just happened to hear a joke during a conversation. It inspired the theme, opening, and ending of that story. But I didn't actually start writing for quite some time, because I didn't want it to be simply a criticism of money-worship. Instead I saw [the present behavior] as a "logical reaction" against what went before. I began to write only after I thought I'd grasped the trauma and anguish experienced by intellectuals, who, faced with a new set of moral principles, have had to make difficult choices relating to human integrity. Even now, I don't think of it as a finished piece of work. . . .

---

[1]Aleksandr Chakovsky's *Blokada* is a multivolume novel about the siege of Leningrad. Its serialization began in the USSR in 1970.

Q: During the past year, when was your prime creative period? When the most difficult? . . .

A: I was considered at my peak in 1983, but I was interrupted at the height of it. Actually, I have always been affected by all sorts of things and people. Since I write slowly, I become ever more agitated. If I really have to identify a few days from the past year as my best time, then it is probably when I was writing "⊗ O ⊕." I have to keep explaining this title, which is really *Envelope, Postcard, Block-of-Four (Feng, pian, lian)*. These three symbols are well-known among the stamp collectors of the world. Unfortunately, not all our readers and editors are philatelists, nor am I one, for that matter. This could be called a story that merges popular and high literature—a contemporary collage of deductive reasoning, detection, and history. I wrote fourteen thousand characters of it in one day. That was immediately followed by my most unproductive period. I was facing problems in my postgraduation job assignment more difficult and more delicate even than those that people ordinarily face.[2] I don't really demand a lot from life—just the freedom to exercise my imagination. This freedom, however, has repeatedly been suppressed. . . .

I've always considered myself relatively calm when faced with setbacks, for I can usually predict them. Still, amid my calm, I sensed something terrifying—that this unfettered, invisible thing in me called imagination was degenerating. Thereupon I traveled to Sichuan, Guangdong, and other places, to continue my search for *Peking Man (Beijingren)*, which I wrote about with Comrade Sang Ye. Our plan was to write the autobiographies of one hundred ordinary Chinese, in the form of oral history literature. We would collect them under the title "Peking Man," after the apeman that inhabited Zhoukoudian, where more than six hundred thousand years of culture has accumulated. The book is now basically finished. Afterward, I went back to my ancestors' village and wrote a 40,000-character essay, *Back Home (Hui lao jia)*. Come to think of it, 1984 was a relatively productive year for me, because I failed to get a job assignment and had so much precious leisure. My low point has to be the beginning of 1984, when I took the student reexamination. One of the questions was the same as in the college entrance examinations: Tell a story. We were given a topic and half an hour to make up a story to tell to the examination committee. After close to one hour of rumination, I still couldn't think of a story. My grade was a zero.

The title I was assigned that day was "The Fragrance of Plum Blossoms Comes from the Bitter Cold [That Precedes Them]."

Q: When it comes to writing, how would you rate your ability at extemporaneous expression? Do you need to talk over the plot with another person, or draft an outline?

A: Probably because I love to talk so much and can't wait to tell people about

---

[2]This refers to the official persecution of Zhang Xinxin in 1984, after the campaign against "spiritual pollution."

the books and things that excite me, I'm always telling people stories despite myself. As I tell them, I also begin to put together elements of plot, thinking, and logic that never occurred to me before. This process intensifies my feelings as a writer for the immediacy of the work.

But real life, and the problem basically rests with me, sometimes forces me into a corner where I can't find anyone appropriate to tell my stories to. . . .

Still, I have been very fortunate. All my teachers were fine, decent people. Time and time again, they treated me generously, counseled and made allowances for me, making sure that I would never fall so badly that I could not pick myself up again. I learned from my teachers not only book knowledge, but how to live. And then there were my schoolmates, Dragon Junior, the Dove, Small Peace, and the others. We were the last group of "old" college students, for we were well over thirty when we graduated. Each of us had experienced his or her share of setbacks, and each of our families had suffered during either the Anti-rightist campaign or the Cultural Revolution. Consequently, we learned to treat others with understanding and sympathy. I'm grateful for that. When I thought I was all alone under my lamp, quietly writing away with my earphones on, I was actually creating a rustle with my manuscript paper that kept my roommates up with me in silent vigil half the night. . . .

Q: How do you view the "projection of subjectivity"?

A: Nowadays I prefer to use the term "projection of inner feelings," or "projection of an inner world."

I read *The Dream of the Red Chamber* once when I was thirteen and haven't touched it since. In writing about the thoughts, or inner worlds, of a group of young men and women and their vacillating and contradictory life-styles, Cao Xueqin was announcing explicitly and conclusively the death of an old era and the inevitable coming of a new one.

I feel that my work so far falls woefully short of creating an "inner world." Still less have I "projected" anything. The "inner world" of an individual in a group has to be dug out again and again in order to survive. Even if we do "truly enjoy complete freedom to express our emotions," I feel we must first continuously confront, root out, examine, and broaden our experiences, our so-called inner world. Only then can we communicate a contemporary consciousness from a self-reliant Chinese people that stands out among the world's nations—which is not the same thing as catching up to and overtaking some "contemporary world literature," or competing for a Nobel Prize, which hardly encapsulates literary excellence.

During the war years, a quite unusual period, there was not just self-criticism, but isolation and exclusion within the revolutionary ranks. Self-reflection was applied not only to our writings, but to our lives.

Q: If that's your opinion, how do you ensure unity of purpose?

A: That's a very vague question. When I was interviewing for *Peking Man*, often I myself raised questions, consciously or unconsciously, that could be taken two ways. But your question is going to get me embroiled in an unfair competition.

If by "purpose" you mean the winning of prizes, and by "unity" a consensus of editors, readers, writers, critics, and the broadcasting media, then my purpose is definitely not to win a prize.

During the interviews for *Peking Man* this year, I was always talking to people, listening to their life stories, their experiences, personal desires, and aspirations for their country's future. Naturally there were differences between my subjects and me, on account of our dissimilar lives. Our inner worlds and the ways we reveal them were not necessarily similar, either. And yet, beneath all those differences, I sensed a unity of purpose. For example, when I interviewed Comrade Yang Sixian, a peasant in Guan County, we sat up in his tiny, two-story house made of cement and prefabricated boards and talked deep into the night. He recounted the life of the simple but intelligent peasant these past several decades, and how he "made it" during the recent call to "get rich and prosper." He not only narrated, he analyzed and worried over it. He wanted to be an industrialist, concerned with production rather than commerce. I could tell, from our feelings and analyses, that we had a lot in common. . . . Don't you think there's a certain unity in all this?

Q: Some newspapers abroad have serialized your novels, and also printed reviews. For example, someone equated you with a Bengal tigress, even using that as the title of an article; then there was someone who claimed that "Orchid Madness" beat the *People's Daily* by two horse's lengths.[3] What do you think of all that? And, oh, did you know that a Hong Kong publisher has put out an anthology of your works?

A: They didn't bother to pay me any royalties or ask for my permission, so of course I didn't know. As for those critical articles, I really can't comment, since I've never read them. And what does it mean to be ahead by two horse's lengths? I'm not a horse, and I can't compete with the *People's Daily*. The *People's Daily* isn't a horse either. The funny thing is that what I write can't be considered news or even factual. Imagination and take-offs can never keep up with reality. That part about the "Bengal tigress" is really funny. I write a few articles, and people get the idea that I'm incredibly domineering, or at least shrewd and calculating. In real life, I'm not very good at sparring or even holding my own against other people. This business of the difference between a writer's works and her life, and between her writing and the criticisms of it, could fit into your earlier question about unity, don't you think?

Q: Are you a writer of the "modernist school"?

---

[3]This would be an article by Bi Hua in *The Nineties* 175 (August 1985), which pointed out that in writing about China's scandalous and "mad" trafficking in orchids, Zhang Xinxin had simply chosen a subject that appeared in the *People's Daily* itself—and scooped it to boot.

A: In the eyes of the mass media, the modernist school was defeated in the debate about it that took place after October 1983. During that criticism, some of my works were also labeled "modernist." The past few days, however, several journal editors have been saying that they want some "modernist" works to go along with the others.

I remember asking someone in 1983: What *is* the "modernist school"?

Today I find myself still asking that question. What on earth is the "modernist school"? This concept of "modernist school" that we use—does it include "modern literary thought" and "modernism" as such? And one more question, about contemporary world art and literature: just how much do we know about the big picture and where they're headed? And how many of these issues have even been introduced here? Yet we're pretty adept at taking one after another of these imprecise concepts and using them as soap boxes from which to preach our own positions, or barriers to rope ourselves off.

I'm an individual living in modern times. I can only say that I will try my best to use what I consider to be the most convenient and effective forms to communicate whatever I feel to be most interesting.

Q: Do you believe in "literary genius"? What are your favorite authors and works?

A: I've accepted that there are differences in intelligence ever since I learned about "IQs." When writers are naturally gifted, I feel it in their works and can only bow my head in resignation for myself. I have to keep on acquiring experience and skill, inching forward, bit by bit, across my writing desk, as through life. Some brilliant writers come out to me as I read. There's a very skillfully written book from the United States called *Centennial* [by James A. Michener]. Begun as an "authorized" work to celebrate the bicentennial of the United States, it turned into a birthday card steeped in poison. Yet it still earned the approbation of patriotic readers and critics, who thought that it truthfully chronicled the pioneer spirit of the American nation.

I can't really say I like Ba Jin's works, with their childlike innocence and high-minded, self-probing attitude, but I do deeply respect them. I also greatly admire Liu Binyan, who, for the sake of his country and his people, admonishes the authorities with total disregard for his own safety. And [I admire] many other writers of the past, and of my own generation, including some who may have written only one essay or poem or novel, or have not been able to publish, yet still possess a unique appreciation of the spirit of our age.

I'd also like to say here that I have a high regard for the Hong Kong writer and veteran newspaperman Mr. Zha Liangyong, who did not attend this congress.[4] I love reading the knight-errant novels he's written under the pen name Jin Yong. I admire his plot-making ability and the patriotic Chinese spirit that comes across the page so vividly. Furthermore, I find that his

---

[4]A piece by Zha Liangyong appears in this volume under his pen name, "Jin Yong."

knight-errant novels express a certain nobility.

It would be too much to list each of my favorite works by foreign authors.

Q: Could you talk a little about your own life?

A: The life experience I've listed on my résumé isn't that different from that of my peers. The Cultural Revolution began when I was in the sixth grade. At sixteen, I joined a production and construction military corps in Heilongjiang and participated in labor. After that, I served as a soldier, a nurse, and a full-time cadre. Then, because I wanted a diploma, I managed to pass the college entrance exam and get myself admitted to the Central Academy of Drama.

If by my own life you mean my private life, however, then there really isn't anything worth talking about.

I only want to say that being a single and, for whatever reason, somewhat famous woman is not such a difficult thing, provided one remains true to one's integrity. What's difficult is being an ordinary person no one talks about. . . .

I'm well aware that "On the Same Horizon" (*Zai tongyi dipingxian shang*) attracted several rounds of criticism and influenced the "image" of my later works, bringing about a whole chain of "dramatic" events that quickly catapulted me into "personality" status. Still, I have no regrets about writing that piece. By now I've adopted a "what's past is past" attitude toward it all. In fact, this was the title of a short autobiography that I wrote for the third issue of *Writers* (*Zuojia*) magazine in 1985. . . .

Q: You're a young writer, and a woman. During your childhood and your teens, that is, when you began to understand life, who and what influenced you most? . . .

A: In my teenage years, I was influenced most by my father.

I believe that classifying authors by sex is pointless. It's a little like the way we view women's soccer nowadays. I'd rather stay under the heading of "writer" but remain unclassified. If women's intelligence and physical stamina really were inferior to men's, they wouldn't have ventured into soccer. I have always empathized with Comrade Ding Ling. During the 1930s, she refused to contribute to special "women writers" issues of magazines. Of course, I am not trying to make any comment on the present magazine *Women Writers* (*Nü zuojia*). On the contrary, I believe that that magazine has, to a certain degree, contributed to the study of contemporary Chinese women from a sociological point of view—in particular, to the study of the psychology of women intellectuals. In my opinion, those who specialize in the study of women writers are primarily sociologists rather than literary critics in the pure sense. . . .

Q: Do you feel that there are conditions conducive or damaging to the creation of literature? Is there such a thing as a profession that is helpful to writing?

A: Chekhov was a physician, while Kafka was a lowly clerk all his life. That should take care of the question of a helpful profession. However, that still leaves us with a big, confusing question. Concentration and tenacity produce a unique personality that should be favorable for writing. Yet a lunatic is also self-absorbed and tenacious. Probably the brink of madness is also the peak of creativity, except, of course, for complete breakdowns. Van Gogh is an example. Labor camps at thirty degrees below zero produced several outstanding writers, while also imposing a certain limit on their creativity. I say limit, not in a derogatory sense, but to mean that it causes them to write a particular type of literature. Poor cultural soil and lack of elementary education have prevented countless highly gifted peasant youths from becoming writers—I always wonder just how many people are capable of becoming writers. Between the nurture produced by suffering and the debilitation produced by peace and prosperity; between facing life with sophisticated composure and maintaining a childlike and foolish enthusiasm—how many can survive every calamity and learn to treat joy and sorrow with equanimity? . . .

Q: Do you give much weight to the opinions of critics? Are you interested in them? Are you affected by them?

A: I try to accept opinions from all quarters. I feel that our literary criticism has no shortage of people with valid, objective judgment, and that there is also a new generation waiting for the chance to display its talents. At the same time, there are criticisms, including complimentary ones, that I just don't understand. . . . But I take criticism to be an art form itself, a form of creativity. . . .

We writers are always speaking of working for the values of "pure literature."[5] I wish there were such a thing as "pure literature." . . .

I have long felt that one should write according to one's audience. That's why I treasure letters from readers who live in places I've never visited. This, I take it, is another "unity"? . . .

Let me add that I, too, oppose critics who, provoked or not, give in to exaggeration—exaggeration of the damage that literature can do to society.

Q: What are your views in the debate on the "opposition of two principles"?

A: I read in an essay once that literature is the crystallization of a high-level sociocultural consciousness, and yet the writer is not necessarily a philosopher. Consequently, there exists an antinomy between the writer and his or her work.

What Kant meant by antinomy was the contradictory state arising from two propositions that are mutually conflicting and validating at the same time. He listed four sets of contradictory phenomena—the universe, freedom, and so forth. But the antinomy as used here probably only refers to literary phenomena that are at once conflicting and validating. In these days when "field theory" is practiced, if not for the critique of philosophy, then what need is there for the "opposition of two principles"? I'm afraid I don't understand.

There are in fact authors who, despite their imperfect world views and theories, and deficiencies in their education, produce good writing. Regardless of

---

[5]"Pure literature" is "literature," as defined by Chinese intellectuals and professional "writers"; excluding popular fiction and propaganda, it tends instead toward works that eschew entertainment and utilitarian values altogether.

how many such people there are, there isn't any sense trying to come up with a percentage, in order to formulate some theory about it, because the law of creativity is unique unto itself. Creative individuals also differ from each other. Yet, in our present age, one who wants to persevere at producing good writing must absorb as much of the best of world civilization as possible. After all, one does not read merely to learn. One reads for pleasure! Our problem is that not many books are available to us.

Q: Are you now swamped with requests for manuscripts?

A: This is how my schoolmates described me during our graduation party: Zhang Xinxin in 1984: You could catch sparrows on her doorstep [nobody comes to visit her]. This is really a comment on my relative "popularity" before and after. Actually, in 1984 there were still a number of friends and editors who came to see me, and editorial departments who solicited my works. Last spring, the *Encounter Monthly* (*Wenhui yuekan*) asked me to do a piece of reportage for them that I still haven't written, for lack of time. But I keep to my old principle of not making empty promises, so as not to create false expectations among my readers and editors.

To some extent, criticism can make a writer famous. But who recognizes the role of the editors? They quietly slave away, getting our writings ready for publication. Not just outsiders, we ourselves don't appreciate their labors enough. Once a piece of writing is criticized, the editors get criticized, too, and they have to write self-criticisms. But who raises enough ruckus to rehabilitate these editors when it's over? They have nothing to crow about, nor do they wish to crow. All it takes to fill their hearts with joy is for them to see their authors, who may not even be talented or genuine writers, able once again to get their works published, free of worry and restraint. Indeed, true editors, despite their different personalities, all seem to share this trait. I am not exactly naive. I know that I have no power to save myself, much less anyone else, but I still want to say this: If any more reversals should occur, please leave our editors alone! Let the authors be responsible for what they've written. Knowing full well that all this talk won't be of any use, I still want to reiterate it, and to keep reflecting on the fact that such editors, such human beings, do exist.

Q: Is there anything you want to add to any of the questions?

A: I'm very sorry I didn't satisfy you the first time around.

I'm going to treat this request as another question to be answered, and provide an overview of the answers to all the foregoing questions.

Several of my works subjected me to criticism for a time, and they will probably do so again. Self-analysis has led me to discover that this phenomenon I call "myself" is the result of the collision between elements inherent in me and others exterior to me.

This much-publicized "I" is just a chance creation.

I just happen to be a lucky gal.

Compared to the older writers, who have suffered longer and harder; to those who were buried in silence on flimsy pretexts; to the many gifted individuals who were planted in poor soil; and compared to my peers, I'm a drop of water that had the good fortune to be borne on the crest of a wave—even if I end up down in the valley the next instant.

Hans Christian Andersen passed his entire life in frustration and loneliness. In his twilight years, he wrote a novel called *Lucky Peer*, in which he bestowed all of his own unfulfilled fantasies on the person of his youthful protagonist: his love of dancing, singing, and reading, and his dream of falling in love with a young girl who returns his love and lives with him happily ever after. I couldn't hold back my tears as I read this enchanting story.

Compared to so many others, what I have gone through is really not so much. Hence my fear that I may be only a shallow person who was favored by fortune. And yet, it's my earnest wish to avail myself of the east wind of "Unity, Enterprise, and Prosperity" and really make a contribution. . . .

"Xingyuner—dui 26 ge wenti de huida" (Lucky me—my answers to twenty-six questions commonly asked about me), January 13, 1985, in *Wenhui yuekan* (Encounter monthly, Shanghai) (February 1985): 12–17.

—Translated by Ellen Lai-shan Yeung

Han Shaogong

LIKE Zhang Xinxin, Han Shaogong (b. 1953, in Changsha, Hunan) was once upon a time an enthusiastic Red Guard. Employed at a local cultural center after 1977, he soon won recognition as an outspoken new literary talent. His early stories attacked the ultraleftist degeneration of China during the Mao era; they tended to slight "modernism." Yet Han Shaogong reemerged in the mid-1980s as the leader of an avant-garde school of "Finding Our Roots." The following essay gives a lucid introduction to many young Chinese authors' reaction both against foreign literary influence and the major old-line Chinese trends of social realism and socialist realism.

Readers of Han Shaogong's fiction cannot fail to note that he has himself been influenced by Kafka and by the "magic realism" of García Márquez. In 1987, the young author published a Chinese translation of Milan Kundera's *The Unbearable Lightness of Being*. PRC writers have not been so polarized into modernist versus rural, provincialist "camps" as the Taiwanese writers whose essays appear later in this anthology.

Partly to escape the dearth of economic and cultural opportunity in his native Hunan, Han Shaogong journeyed in 1988 to China's underdeveloped and newly established tropical island province of Hainan. There the local Communist party organization, in a conscious effort to create more journalistic autonomy in the interest of the Chinese reader, allowed him to open a journal called *Hainan jishi wenxue* (Hainan documentary literature). The magazine was enormously successful, continuing to sell copies even after it was officially closed down for investigation after June 4, 1989.

Han Shaogong and other Chinese writers visited France in 1988, at the invitation of the French Ministry of Culture; Han was invited back in 1989 but was denied permission to leave China until 1991.

After the "Literature of the Wounded"

Local Cultures, Roots, Maturity, and Fatigue

Han Shaogong

February 1987

XIA YUN *[Helen Hsia]:* Could you tell us a little about the school of "Finding Our Roots" (*xungen pai*)?[1]

Han Shaogong: There is a "Roots" tendency, but I'm afraid I wouldn't call it a school. The word "school" creates the impression of a camp or a movement. True literature is a little like talking to oneself; it's not much concerned with the commotion of those other things.

The writers who favor a Roots approach differ from each other in a thousand ways, so putting one label on all of them is a little awkward. Roots is but one of the many questions we have pondered. We do speak of roots, but we also speak of leaves, branches, and trunks.

My putting forward of the Roots idea is directed at the present state of Chinese literature. Nowadays, there are primarily two strata of active writers: middle-aged and young. To look at it historically, the middle-aged writers received a fairly big dose of Russian influence. They were nurtured on Tolstoy, Chekhov, Vsevolod Kochetov, and so forth, and they are moved just to hear Soviet popular songs from the 1950s. Zhang Xianliang has called Russian literature the world's best literature. That statement is quite characteristic. In the field of literary theory, such concepts as populism and beauty-in-real-life are also derived from Belinsky, Chernyshevsky, and Plekhanov.

The situation for the younger Chinese writers is different. They were in

---

[1]See also the pieces by Bai Hua and Zhong Acheng in this volume.

school just as Sino-Soviet relations were turning sour. Most Russian books were proscribed and criticized. Since the fall of the "Gang of Four" and China's opening up to the outside world, the bookstores have contained primarily Western, Euro-American literature and literary theory. To young people, the modernist, avant-garde works seem especially new and attractive.

Foreign Influence

Xia: Many overseas critics feel Kafka has had a large influence on contemporary Chinese literature. Is that so?

Han: Yes, it is. His books have gone through many editions. In addition, the Americans Hemingway and Faulkner, Joyce of Britain, and later, the South American García Márquez, the Italian Calvino, the French "New Novel School," the Japanese Kawabata Yasunari, and so on, all have gone through very lively periods of popularity. Twenty-year-old college students today discuss these authors as if they were members of their own family, but they are strangers to Tolstoy, Chekhov, and Gorky, who were so familiar to the older generation. All these young people seem to have written some surrealistic "misty" (*menglong*, "obscure") poems or a couple of stream-of-consciousness novels, works you can't tell from the original things. This is a generation molded by new life experiences and new reading experiences.

I am happy about both the Russian and the Euro-American influences. I feel these influences are still insufficient, that broadening our field of vision still further is a fundamental requirement for the maturation of contemporary Chinese literature. But people who eat beef do not become cows, and people who eat dog meat do not become dogs, even if they want to. Any copy is inferior to the original work, so I don't agree with copying the Russians or Americans. In my essays, I argue for "releasing the energies of modern ideas, recasting and broadening the self among our people," and uniting global consciousness with consciousness of one's roots. I've advocated that Chinese literature and other people's literatures "march forward together along separate roads."

The Roots Writers

Xia: Could you tell us a little about the similarities and differences among the Roots writers?

Han: The term refers to a group of writers who are roughly thirty years old, with a few who are middle-aged. These writers have been through the Cultural Revolution, gone down to the countryside, and written several years' worth of political fiction. Dissatisfied with literature that was the equivalent of political propaganda, they wanted to make breakthroughs in the philosophy and aesthetics of their work, and expand literary horizons. This was the point on which all agreed. Only after that groundwork was laid was there a discussion of modernism, and later a discussion about Roots.

To make a comparison, some writers stress the people's cultural psychology as the objective target of their writing. This solves the "what to write about" problem, as when Jia Pingwa writes of the various aspects of history, geography, human nature, and society in Shangzhou.[2] Other writers stress the people's cultural mentality as a subjective spirit. That resolves the "how to write" question. One example is the Daoist spirit and flavor that some have already noted in Zhong Acheng. Each writer has his or her own particular emphasis, be it style, atmosphere, language, theme, or regional color, and all have produced good results.

Local cultures have of course influenced Chinese writers, too. Consider the influence of Islamic culture from the Northwest on Zhang Chengzhi, of the Qin and Han realms on Jia Pingwa, of the Manchu culture of Peking on Chen Jiangong, of Wu-Yue culture [from the Southeast] on Li Hangyu, of Chu culture from the Southwest on He Liwei, Cai Cehai, and Sichuan's "Ba Shu Poets."[3] All of these influences have left a distinctive stamp, a whiff of exoticism. The many regional colorations are very difficult to put into words. But I don't attach much importance to external local color; I attach more importance to the inner spirit. The old *xiangtu* (local, nativist) literature also had local color, but it was anemic in spirit. It did not possess true Eastern spirit.

Views on Liu Xiaobo

Xia: How do you feel about Liu Xiaobo's critique of the Roots school? Do you agree with him?

Han: We strongly agree with the urgency and rebellious spirit with which Liu Xiaobo criticizes the Chinese feudal tradition, including some of his specific ideas. Here's the problem: If criticism of Eastern feudalism means denial of the whole of Eastern culture, then doesn't criticism of Western feudalism necessitate denial of the whole of Western culture? Does criticism of the oppression of humanity by religion write off religious art with a single stroke? This is just too simplistic. Looking to the past for subject matter may look like spiritual regression, but it's not the same thing. The art of the European Renaissance drew heavily on Greek and Roman mythology, but it would be very difficult to say it was a regressive movement. Further, in speaking of literature, can we even use words like "evolution" and "regression"? If we fail to understand that the utilitarian and aesthetic outlooks are two different yardsticks and demand that literature be an appendage of utilitarianism, then even if we use a completely modern

---

[2]See the essay by Jia Pingwa in this volume.

[3]Qin, Wu, Yue, Chu, Ba, and Shu were regional kingdoms in the territory that is now China, prior to 221 B.C. The Kingdom of Chu was centered around present-day Hunan and Hubei.

utilitarianism and manage to unify all of literature, that in itself would be un-"modern." It would diverge greatly from modern pluralistic thinking.

Another of Liu's drawbacks is in philosophy, especially his lack of understanding of Eastern philosophy. He says traditional Chinese culture is "rationally based" and therefore must be completely abandoned. As to his extreme attitude toward rationality, for now let's say his judgment is only suitable for a Confucian. Chinese Daoist and Zen Buddhist philosophies were not rationally based. Traditional Chinese culture was Confucian-Mencian on the outside, as in governance, and Zen-Daoist on the inside, as in moral cultivation. Zen-Daoist philosophy contains the idea of relativity. Its concepts of intuition and holism are great treasures of the humanities today. Few Chinese and even fewer Westerners understand them. Only great scholars like Einstein, Leibniz, Bohr, Heidegger, and so forth have wholeheartedly marveled at the wisdom of Eastern philosophy. What we want to do is study how this wisdom became a hollow and useless spiritual opiate in modern China. We want to study how Zhuang Zi became Lu Xun's [literary creation] Ah Q. And after solving this problem, we want to transform its negatives into positives. But I feel there is no need to punish Zhuang Zi as an accomplice just because China produced Ah Q, nor any need to feel that everything is inferior.

Liu Xiaobo extends the normal desire for social-political modernization into a proposal for wholesale cultural Westernization. This is going too far, an obsession with a pet theory. When he says, "Chinese traditional culture is entirely worthless dregs," how far does he mean to take it? Make one billion Chinese give up the Chinese language and use a Western one? Or ban Chinese medicine and solely honor Western medicine? I doubt this is Liu Xiaobo's real intention. He's only using those extreme views to amplify his own voice. We don't have to take that too seriously.

Dilemmas

Xia: Much attention has been focused on your novellas, *Woman, Woman, Woman (Nü, nü, nü)* and *Dad, Dad, Dad (Ba, ba, ba)*, but some people say they don't understand what you're are getting at in these pieces. When you are writing, how do you handle the question of theme?

Han: I feel that theme can be thought, taking the form of lines; and that it can also be feelings, having dimensions. Of course, both can be tied together, alternately clear and misty. *Dad, Dad, Dad's* starting point is social history; the decline of a race as seen through the prism of Chu culture. The rational and nonrational have both become absurd, and all ideas, old and new, lack the power to save the situation. *Woman, Woman, Woman's* perspective, on the other hand, is individual action—the fluctuations of good and evil within the individual, the shifts between bondage and freedom, and the danger to human survival. But these themes are not final opinions; they are shifting equivocations. Therefore, like my readers, I feel these themes are difficult to grasp. Of course, there are some modernist writers and readers still saying that my themes are too clear.

These novels are my dilemmas. The Daoists have a saying, "The Unity of All," and the Buddhists have "The Invisible Way." These are also dilemmas. Once, in Shanghai, I said that in the process of representing his meaning, the writer should succeed once and fail once. In finding himself lost, the writer also draws the reader into a loss of bearings. But this loss is not all bad, for it is the starting point and impetus for new exploration. At the very end of all philosophy, science, and literature, you always discover yourself facing a strange and unfathomable equivocation. That ambiguity is at the terminus of logic and knowledge, but it is also a freeing of instinct and wisdom. Then begins a new logic and knowledge. Kant is this way, and so are Bohr, Cao Xueqin, and Kundera.

I don't favor the currently popular "New Wave" style that is obscure and depressing. But sometimes, in order to express more strongly one's thought and sentiments, it is necessary to sacrifice a little clarity. Personally, I regret that. I try hard to write stories that are understandable. Let's say the reader understands the story, and though he has a general feeling that its implications have some value and interest, he doesn't fully grasp them. Then, together we can make an effort to understand them. Of course, many readers will not, I fear, put in the necessary effort. They have many important things to do, and their time is very precious.

Chu Culture

Xia: You have twice mentioned "Chu culture." Could you explain this a little?

Han: Chu culture is primarily scattered among the minority peoples of Southwest China and Southeast Asia. Historically, as these southern peoples suffered repeated military defeats, they were drawn into the orbit of the advancing Confucian-Mencian culture of the North China plain. At the same time, they suffered rejection and discrimination. Therefore, theirs is an unorthodox, nonstandard culture that even today has not been codified or intellectualized. It's been mainly concealed and saved among the people. It is a half-primitive culture, whose religion, philosophy, science, and art are not yet fully differentiated. The rational and instinctive are mixed together as one. When he created *On Encountering Sorrow, The Heavenly Questions, The Nine Songs,*[4] and so forth, Qu Yuan used elements of the mystical, the unrestrained, the strangely beautiful, the angry, and the profound. The unity of people with the gods in his works, and their mixing of time and space, were derived from this culture. This is one part of Eastern culture. Because of its relationship to locality, certain Hunanese writers have taken the lead in excavating it.

---

[4]Books of the *Chu ci* (Songs of the South).

Instinctive Thought

Xia: What is the relationship between this type of culture and literary production today?

Han: I feel that all primitive and half-primitive cultures merit the attention of writers and artists. Literary thought is a kind of direct or instinctive thought. Now I'm not referring to concrete literary works, for they are always permeated with rationality; I'm referring to the literary quality that is the essence of the piece, just like the alcohol in the wine. This type of basic literary element or literary substance is instinctive. Primitive and half-primitive cultures are specimens of this type of direct thought. As humanity has entered the scientific and industrial era, the entire spirit of mankind has tilted toward the rational. Instinctive, nonrational thought has been cast off by the busy, busy people of today. It has entered a concealed, subconscious realm, where it is fast asleep. Only during drunkenness, dreaming, insanity, or youth—in short, when rationality is weak or out of control—can people even begin to get a hold of fragments of this type of thinking.

Early on, the ancients realized that there were close connections between literature and wine, literature and dreams, literature and madness, literature and youthful innocence. But they didn't investigate the issue deeply. Lévy-Bruhl's studies on primitive thought, Piaget's research into children's thought, and Freud's studies of subconscious thought have all produced outstanding results. But their relationship to artistic thought hasn't been given attention. In fact, there is a line that can completely interconnect them: instinctive thought.

Primitive times were the youth of mankind, and youth is the primitive stage in the making of an individual. Those years have not vanished completely; in the present day, they have sunk into mankind's subconscious. The significance of digging out primitive or semiprimitive culture is that it digs out humanity's youthful innocence and subconscious. This is precisely what art should do.

I feel that in scientific and industrial society, people are generally uncertain and insecure precisely because of alienation from the self and from others. People have been ordered around and divided up into professions, statuses, sexes, interests, age groups, and ideologies. Therefore, they need a sort of counterforce, a counterwholeness. In the daytime, people see much too clearly; they need the mist, obscurity, and numbness of the night. When people become adults, life becomes hard, and they need to revive the sweet dreams of youth. This is how art is born. Art is a countercomplement to science.

Rationalism and Nonrationalism

Xia: Do you mean to advocate nonrationalism, then?

Han: In China, there are some in my field who are indeed giving high praise to nonrationalism. But in speaking of an "ism," it is relatively easy to oversimplify, to go too far. In fact, I'm a strong advocate of rationalism. The problem is that in the past, rationalism and nonrationalism have frequently been used on the wrong occasions. For example, to those in conventional economics or science, rationalism is very necessary. But the slogans formerly used, such as "the land's production will be as great as the people's courage," "long live so-and-so," "reach for the perilous peak," "chase the remnants of the enemy," and so forth, were like poems and religious superstition, very nonrational. Yet people in literature and the arts in those days were required to follow official editorials and documents, try to understand political theory, and make their work follow the proper ideological recipe. There was absolutely no room for nonrational thinking. It was the mixing of fire and ice, a freak accident. Other people say the Chinese people's collective consciousness is too strong, that they are used to unity and uniformity. Since individual consciousness is too weak, individualism should be advocated. I, however, have many doubts about this. Do the Chinese people, in fact, have too little individualism? Look at the zeal with which people mistreated people during the years of internecine strife. Look at the phenomenon of people in public screaming and pushing others out of the way to be the first in line. What kind of "ism" is that? The problem is that the private is not private, and the public is not public; private life has become too public, and public life has become too private. Black and white are mixed—everything, indeed, is a freak accident. Therefore, I think the problem of Chinese cultural psychology is not the cultural psychology itself, necessitating criticism of Confucianism, rationalism, or some so-called social consciousness. It is a problem of changing the cultural structure.

It's the same for literature. Having gone through the ten years of the Cultural Revolution, Chinese writers now need to strengthen both rationalism and non-rationalism, to nourish the yin and strengthen the yang. Most important, these things must not be used in the wrong places.

Xia: There is a relationship between literature and life, of course, but literature does not merely recreate real life. Could you speak about your views on "truth" in literature and "truth" in life?

Han: A completely objective truth probably does not exist. This has already been proven by physics. I agree that when talking about truth, it is necessary to pay attention to layers of truth and to use different measurements. For example, if we speak of subjective as well as objective truth, Balzac and García Márquez can both be considered to have written the truth. The great dynastic histories and the common myths are both true. Otherwise, we can't resolve this. In my writing, sometimes I make strange parts of life familiar, and familiar parts of life strange. *Dad, Dad, Dad* is an example.

Xia: Please say a little about how you decided to pursue a career in literature.

Han: I was a Red Guard for three years and a [rusticated] "educated youth" for six. During my time in the countryside, partly as a means of livelihood, and partly for my own spiritual freedom and the benefit of China, I began to write a few little pieces. Later, in university, I studied four years in a Chinese department and another year of foreign languages. It looked as if I couldn't do anything else except write.

Xia: How do you feel about the future of our Chinese literature?

Han: The period of what's been called the Literature of the Wounded has long since passed. The to-do of one-upmanship in the realms of theme, daring, ideas, and techniques has either already passed or soon will. Neither storming the barricades nor putting on exhibitions of technique are sufficient to supply fresh blood to our culture any more. Within the last ten years, Chinese culture has scrambled to do what other countries have done over the course of centuries, so our culture is now facing a period of fatigue and maturation. In my estimation, many writers will mark time in their present styles, and even more will go into popular or journalistic genres. A few may form their own philosophic and artistic styles and go on to become truly outstanding.

"Zhimian beilun de Han Shaogong" (The frank and unconventional Han Shaogong), interview of the author by Helen Hsia, *Meizhou Huaqiao ribao* (China daily news, New York), February 27, 1987.

—Translated by David Wakefield

Wang Zengqi

THIS ESSAY by an older writer sheds light on the crucial relationship of the contemporary Chinese author with traditional literary and artistic forms. Only Jia Pingwa, Han Shaogong, and Zhong Acheng have shown in their writings an awareness that, beyond "coming to terms with the past" (meaning the recent, Communist, past), the contemporary Chinese intellectual must rediscover the more remote past and relate to it anew, as part of his or her quest for identity.

Wang Zengqi (b. 1920, in Gaoyou, northern Jiangsu) was a talented young fiction writer—and a modernist—already in the 1940s, while studying creative writing under Shen Congwen in Kunming. When the People's Republic was founded, Wang Zengqi became yet another unfortunate intellectual condemned to be a rightist. After 1962, his profession was writing librettos for Peking operas and subsequently, for Jiang Qing's reformed model operas. In 1980, after a tense period following the fall of the Gang of Four, he reemerged, phoenixlike, as a writer of pastoral, nostalgic fiction seemingly in the image of Shen Congwen, but with cleaner social lines and a subtle political edge, as in "Shoujie" (Ordination), "Da Nao jishi" (A tale of Big Nur), and "Chen Xiaoshou" (Big Hands Chen). Acknowledged nevertheless by young readers as perhaps the first author in the post-Mao period to write thoughtfully and lovingly of the "old (pre-1949) society," Wang Zengqi surprisingly became a retroactive spiritual godfather to the Roots school of young people such as Han Shaogong. Wang Zengqi's subsequent concentration on short, familiar essays about customs, shrines, places, and usages in traditional China has reinforced his role as a scholarly interpreter of the old Confucian temperament and its high cultural taste, a side of China that has now nearly lapsed into oblivion.

We Must Not Forget Our Historical Roots
Popular Literature, Peking Opera, and Modern Prose

Wang Zengqi

September 17, 1982, in Lanzhou

I'M AMBIDEXTROUS: I write fiction and opera, too. I began with fiction; composed plays for a Peking opera house during most of the last twenty years; and then, in the past two or three years, wrote a few more short stories. An old friend who ran into me and heard I was writing opera asked, "How can you write opera? You're a writer of short stories—'foreignized' ones at that." He couldn't believe it. When some new acquaintances saw the short stories I'd written recently, they said, in all earnestness, "You're better off writing fiction. Why bother with opera?" All agreed that fiction and drama—Peking opera—were two different things. They also felt, each in their own way, that I was wasting my time composing Peking opera. They felt sorry for me. It was gratifying that they cared. But some old-timers in the opera world wanted me to stay on as a lyricist. They were delighted when I announced that I had no intention of leaving the field. It was gratifying that they cared, too. Comrade Cao Yu once said, "Go ahead and paint with both hands." I took him up on it.

When I was little I'd never thought of writing plays, or stories, either. I liked to paint.

My father painted. He achieved some little reputation for it in our district. I loved to watch him paint from the time I was little. It elated me every time he opened the door to his studio (he painted rather seldom) and propped open the windows. I watched him mix his colors, grind ink from his inksticks, and spread out his paper. He would think a while as he smoked, staring at his snowy-white

Anhui paper for the longest time, and then, making scratches on it with his fingernail or the opposite end of his brush, sketch some lines by way of an outline. Then he'd paint a few blossoms (Father was a freehand painter of flowers and plants), then branches, leaves, knots in the branches, rocks, and mosses, and finally "tidy it up," inscribing his name and stamping his seal on it. He would tack it up on the wall and stare at it endlessly, still smoking. I watched the process intently. Each step held my interest.

I was "crazy about painting" from primary school through middle school. My father had some painting manuals with lithograph and collotype prints, and I knew them all by heart. On my way home from school, I'd always enter a picture scroll-mounting shop to have a look.

I wanted to take entrance exams for art school after graduating from middle school.

In my forties, too, I wanted to change my line of work completely and take up painting again.

I've felt all along that pen-and-ink is the most direct and enjoyable way there is of expressing one's thoughts.

But I did not ultimately become a painter.

Today I still love to watch people paint, and I still go to art exhibitions. Sometimes, when I felt like it—particularly in the midst of a political campaign, when people were coming down on me—I'd get into the habit of making a few passes with my brush again, to work off my anger.

An affinity for painting is useful to me as a fiction writer. For one thing, when I work out the composition for a story, it bears some resemblance to the way my father painted. First there are lyric feelings—ideas. Then comes the composition, drawing the "blossoms," branches, leaves, and knots. Another resemblance is that one trains one's own sensitivity to shape, color, and the spirit of things.

How did I start writing fiction?

Besides my painting, my grades in Chinese class were always good. From fifth grade until I was a third-year student in junior middle school, my Chinese teacher was Mr. Gao Beiming. To commemorate him, my short story "Migration" (Xi) uses Mr. Gao's own name. His character, learning, and teaching methods were just as I described them in that story—though naturally not in every detail, for some parts are fictitious. Of all the works I read under him, the ones that made the deepest impression on me were Gui Youguang's Notes from the Neck and Back Studio (Xiang ji xuan ji) and The Story of My Deceased Mother (Xian bi shi lüe).

There were several summer vacations during which I studied with Mr. Wei Zilian. Mr. Wei specialized in the Tongcheng school. Following his lead, every day I memorized an essay in the ancient style of the Tongcheng writers—Yao Nai, Fang Bao, Liu Dakui, and Dai Mingshi. Altogether, I learned no fewer than a hundred pieces.

You can see the influence of Gui Youguang and the Tongcheng school in my stories still today. Gui Youguang wrote of ordinary human feelings with delicate strokes, and I like that (though I don't care for his traditional thought). I believe that in some ways, he very much resembles Chekhov. I consider the "Tongcheng purpose and mode of expression" to be correct. The Tongcheng school was particular about the capacity of a piece of writing to uplift, and to release; its abstinence, its connectedness, its quickness, and its steadiness; its pauses and its divergences. The school spoke of *wenqi* ("literary spirit" or "emotional impact"). Chinese painting, likewise, uses phrases like "the blood circulates" and "the spirit is lively." I think "literary spirit" is a more intrinsic property and a more profound concept than "structure," and also more organically bound up with content and thought. It's a superior, very advanced concept, one that's more modern than many of the concepts of modern Western aesthetics. Literary spirit is a direct form of thought. I hope that critical theorists will introduce the "theory of literary spirit" into criticism of fiction and use it to criticize fiction from other countries.

I seem to have been destined to become a pupil of Mr. Shen Congwen.

After I'd finished my second year of senior middle school, the Japanese invaded the districts near my home. I took refuge in the countryside, in the small monastery described in "Ordination" (*Shou jie*). Besides my high school texts, I only brought two books with me, *Tales of a Sportsman* by Turgenev, and a pirated book of *Selected Stories by Shen Congwen* printed by some fly-by-night shop in Shanghai. I read those two books over and over.

I went to Kunming for college and entered the Chinese literature department of the Southwest Associated University, precisely because Mr. Shen, Zhu Zi-qing, and Wen Yiduo were there.

I enrolled in three of Mr. Shen's courses: "Writing Exercises in Various Genres," "History of Chinese Fiction," and "The Practice of Creative Writing."

I followed Mr. Shen for many years and learned a lot from him, but two phrases of his made the strongest impression on me.

The first was: "Remain in touch with your characters."

What he meant by that is not so simple. According to my understanding, there are several layers of meaning.

First, fiction is about its characters. The characters are primary—they go first. All else is secondary, derivative. The author must like the characters he is writing about. Mr. Shen once said that he "felt an inexpressible warm passion" toward the soldiers and peasants he wrote about. "Warm passion" strikes me as just right. That phrase, I believe, more accurately explains the relationship between an author and his characters than does the usual phrase "hot passion." An author must be full of tender humanitarian feelings for the people he writes about, and he must feel poetical sympathy.

Second, the author must side with his characters and treat them as his equals. Except in satirical fiction, he ought not to take an Olympian view of them. He should attach his heart to theirs, taking their grief and happiness to be his own.

Only then can he merge with his characters through most of the creative process, so that when he speaks straight from the heart, it is also straight from his characters' hearts. Only then can he avoid descriptions that are superficial, unreal, too generalized, or imitative. This is the only way that a work can take form naturally from the logic of the characters' actions. The work will "flow" instead of being "manufactured," and the characters will not have things imposed on them from the extraneous designs of the author.

Third, the other things in the story are subservient to the characters. The setting and surroundings must be in harmony with the characters and take their coloring from them instead of going off on their own. All settings, surroundings, sounds, colors, and odors must be such that the characters are capable of experiencing them. Describing the scenery is writing about people: the way the characters feel about the world around them. Only thus can the work's characters permeate it and diffuse their flavor. Characters are present even in the parts that do not write about them.

His other phrase was: "Don't ever be cynical."

This is an attitude toward life as well as toward writing. Being poor and abused under the old, pre-1949 society, and having read some works of Western modernism, I acquired a mocking and cynical attitude toward life that was colored by my pessimism. I was dissatisfied with my lot and had nothing to look forward to. You can see it in some of my works. Mr. Shen discovered it and told me so, in Kunming. After I'd gone to Shanghai, he wrote me about it yet again. What he demanded was "persistence" in life, being full of passion for life, even in the face of grim reality. One must not feel that "life has nothing to give me, and I have nothing to give it." Each person ought, through his or her own work, to make the world a little better, to leave behind a little that is good. Not even in adversity ought one to forsake one's poetical interest in life—or lose one's love of it. When Mr. Shen was sent down to cadre school in Xianning, Hubei, he wrote the artist Huang Yongyu, in a letter, "The lotus blossoms here are wonderful!" Mr. Shen, now eighty, still works more than ten hours every day. He was able to finish such a giant project as his *Researches into Ancient Chinese Costume* precisely because of his persistence and passion for life. That admonition of Mr. Shen's has influenced me deeply.

How did I come to write Peking opera lyrics?

Ever since I was little, I had loved to watch Peking opera, and also sing. My father could play the fiddle (*huqin*), and in my first year of junior middle school, I sang to his accompaniment. I sang the parts of the older male characters, and also those of the female leads. I was still singing when I entered college. When a Cantonese classmate heard me, he said, "God damn you, you sound like a screeching cat!"

Since I was in the Chinese department, later I learned to sing Kunqu opera [an archaic Shanghai-Suzhou opera], too.

I liked dramatic performances. I liked to watch Peking operas, and also local operas, particularly Sichuanese operas.

But I never gave a thought to writing opera lyrics.

I became an editor, of *Storytelling and Singing* (*Shuoshuo changchang*), so I wanted to write myself, but I couldn't get into the spirit of it. I didn't have a true feeling for life, and I couldn't keep from complaining. That year happened to be an anniversary for commemorating the famous eighteenth-century world author Wu Jingzi, so someone suggested that I find a theme in his novel, *The Scholars*, and use it as a basis for a Peking opera. Hence I wrote *Fan Jin Passes the Exam* (*Fan Jin zhongju*). It was actually put on, and a performance of it before a Peking municipal theatrical assembly was awarded a prize.

In 1958, I was sent down to do physical labor, wearing the cap of "rightist." When I was uncapped and wanted to return to Peking, the Peking Opera Troupe of Peking just happened to have an opening for a scenarist, and that's how I transferred into that unit. I've remained there until this very day—twenty years.

People in the field of literature don't have a very high opinion of Peking opera.

That's not hard to understand. The literary quality of Peking opera is indeed rather low. Many lyrics are simply nonsense. When I was in Peking a few months ago, I went for a daily stroll in Yuyuantan. Every day I got to hear an actor practice the lead's entrance soliloquy from the Peking opera *The Pearl Curtain Command Post* (*Zhulian zhai*):

> *Li Bo has a great capacity for drinking and poetry,*
> *he slept in the wineshops of old Chang' an.*
> *When the emperor's brother-in-law met his end,*
> *the Prince of Tang angrily demoted the one responsible to*
> *the northern march.*

But what does the imperial Li Keyong have to do with the poet Li Bo? There's also a lyric in the opera *Romantic Complications* (*Huatiancuo*) that goes like this: "Peach blossoms are no yellower than apricot blossoms." But peach blossoms aren't yellow, and neither are apricot blossoms.

Still, Peking opera is part of our cultural heritage. And even Peking opera has a lot to contribute. For instance, I need hardly mention how the familiar *The Four Metropolitan Graduates* (*Si jinshi*) creates a distinctive character in the role of Song Shijie, using all sorts of telling details. I believe that this play could hold its own among the masterpieces of world drama. Another example is the dialogue between Xiao En and Gui Ying when they leave home in *The Fisherman's Revenge* (*Dayu shajia*).

Xiao En: Open the door! (*Goes out*)
Gui Ying: Father, please come back.

Xiao En: What's the matter, daughter?
Gui Ying: We haven't locked the door yet.
Xiao En: It doesn't matter if we leave it open.
Gui Ying: There's lots of furniture inside that can be carted off.
Xiao En: Silly girl, I don't want the door, much less the furniture!
Gui Ying: You don't want it?
Xiao En: You'll be the death of me yet!

I consider this fiction—good fiction. I think a fiction writer can learn a lot from drama.

Some of the techniques of traditional opera and Peking opera appear to be quite ancient. But what's old in China may be new in other countries. For instance, the operatic device of the opening lines in which a character announces who he is is much more economical than using a whole act of modern drama to introduce him. And Brecht's theory of *Verfremdungs-Effekt*, the aesthetic "distancing effect," was inspired by Chinese drama. Now that is something very new.

I feel that we ought not to underestimate our own resources or be familiar with everybody's history but our own. We ought to "put the old at the service of the new": find new things within our heritage. I particularly recommend that comrades absorbed in Western modernism read some classical works and use the comparative literary method to study ancient Chinese literature. I'm always looking for a fusion of the ancient with the modern and of the native with the foreign.

In writing Peking opera, my idea is to elevate its literary level and readability; to make it into a kind of modern art that can be placed alongside modern works, so that, except for the differences in form, people will think it comparable to the fiction of Wang Meng, Gao Xiaosheng, Lin Jinlan, and Deng Youmei.

Another good thing about writing Peking opera is that you learn that drama and fiction are different things (though of course they have resemblances, too). Drama prefers the exaggerated and the highlighted; fiction, the veiled and the understated. According to Li Liweng, poetry doesn't allow one to express everything; of ten parts, you can only make two or three explicit. In drama, though, you must say it all; if there are ten parts, you must state all ten of them. That is very insightful. Tolstoy said that people don't converse in epigrams, but he was speaking of fiction. Characters in drama can do that. Hence, fiction can't be written too much like a drama; you can't have too much plotting or dramatizing. If you write a very dramatic short story, you might as well have simply written it as a play.

All this is the apology of an ambidexter.

Besides drama, I've worked with folk ballad and storytelling forms, and edited *Storytelling and Singing*. I've also worked with folk literature, and edited the journal *Folk Literature* (*Minjian wenxue*) several years. The first piece I published after the "Great Cultural Revolution" was not a story, but an essay on folk literature, "Rules of Versification for *Hua'er* Songs," about a folk song genre of Gansu. I feel that these fields are useful to the writing of fiction. Folk literature in particular is a treasure house. I'd go so far as to assert that one cannot become a good novelist without reading some folk songs and folk tales.

What kind of lessons can a "mixed species," an amphibian like me, offer up? One is that we must respect, and love, the literary and artistic traditions of our motherland. Another is that we must take in things from everywhere, to broaden our interests and expand our knowledge.

I hope there will be even more ambidextrous people in the future. I hope that both poets and novelists will try their hands at drama.

"Liangqi zashu" (Rambling thoughts from an amphibian), Lanzhou, September 17, 1982, in *Wo shi zenmeyang zoushang wenxue daolu de* (How I came to take the path of literature) (Beijing, 1984), pp. 218–26.

—Translated by Jeffrey Kinkley

Zhang Xinxin

THIS second piece by the multitalented Zhang Xinxin, added to the volume in commemoration of the Peking massacre and attendant tragedies after June 4, 1989, marks the death of the "New Era" in PRC literature and of the expansive new trends in thought and society that had accompanied it in the 1980s.

By presenting a probably fictive letter from "a writer friend in Peking" (quite possibly it is a creative amalgam of several such letters), Zhang Xinxin here makes yet another contribution to the always fluid genre of "reportage literature." This piece, announced as the first in a series, was written in the United States for publication in Taibei and Hong Kong.

The "June 4 Syndrome"
Spiritual and Ideological Schizophrenia

Zhang Xinxin

December 1989, in the United States

Dear Xinxin:

I'm so lonely that I get much more out of your letters and telephone calls than the things you actually write and talk about. Ever since "June 4," the sinews of class struggle have been closing in on us. "Clean-up investigations" (*qingcha*)[1] have escalated step by step. The vapid self-censorship among acquaintances on the street and the new guardedness in personal relationships are a sickness that increasingly pervades all public life. The standstill in the economy, the stifling ideological climate, the high-handed measures of political control—they've brought our whole society to such an oppressive state that time and space themselves seem frozen. We'd grown used to the liberalization during the past two years. Now we have to suppress and disguise habits that were already second nature. It's worse than if we'd never tasted freedom to begin with! We're so suffocated we can't even breathe. We want to cry and scream, anything that will give us some relief. On the October 1 celebration of the founding of the People's Republic, a group of us back from study in America and England got together and began singing our hearts out: "The Waters of Lake Hu Are Stormy," "Sailing the Seas Depends on the Helmsman," and even "Without the Communist Party There Would Be No New China." It was uproarious while it lasted, but when it was all over, we broke down and cried.

---

[1]An inquisitorial activity carried out in each workplace or unit by the leaders. Each person was required to account for his or her activities during every day of the 1989 democracy movement, typically by concocting a diary and verifying those of others. Most who had marched for democracy responded by corroborating each other's made-up alibis. For those who did not escape the net, the term was a euphemism for "purge."

The political "investigations" and economic "reorganizations" are progressing at a peculiarly slow pace, because nobody is enthusiastic about them, either at the top or at the grass roots. Those who consider themselves "old hands" at political campaigns say this is unprecedented within all the mobilizations of the past forty years. Instead of the usual concentration of pressure, with a climax and fall-off, there's only a kind of slow attrition going on. The original plan was for the "investigations" to be wrapped up after three months. That was extended to six months (until the end of the year), and then to one year (until June 1990). People are being called to account for only twenty days of their lives, from the middle of May to June 3, but even a year isn't enough for that. The Beidaihe Conference of August 1988 took place at the height of panic buying. August of *this* year found us in a profound economic slump. You can't get people to buy a television set even with a two- or three-hundred-yuan gift as a come-on. Electric power, always in such desperately short supply, was available in amounts exceeding demand this October! Some say that a billion people are putting on an act. Others ask how the government can win if one billion people are opposed to it. But pessimists liken China to a cancer patient that will decline slowly until it dies. Now, all of a sudden, I've come to a new appreciation of an old poem, "The Nirvana of the Phoenixes," by that past master of hack opportunism, old lord Guo Moruo. Let a great ball of fire pass over, fast and furious, so that when the suffering is over there can be a rebirth. Too bad it's only poetry. Our reality is a slow death through protracted suffering.

To borrow a phrase from America, which had a "Vietnam War syndrome," China now has a "June 4 syndrome." The guns held sway at Tiananmen, but the significance of that is hardly just the question of how many died. With one shot, the legal basis of the government was gone, and also the self-respect and cohesion of the people. It has thrown the whole nation into a spiritual and ideological schizophrenia. The phrase commonly used during the Cultural Revolution, "fully insulate yourself from and stand in ranks against so-and-so," has now been adapted to "fully insulate yourself from the events of June 4." Practically everybody in the whole country with education, including the workers and some of the peasants, showed which side they were on through their actions, their thought, and their conscience. The government knows that its basis of control is weakened, if not lost. So it feels ever more frightened and psychologically off-balance, and it relies even more on naked force and troops, on steamrollering its way forward. Most intellectuals, particularly young ones, have no power to struggle and don't want to die, so one after another they are figuring out ways of leaving. All the young people in my institute have already become "Tuo-ists," dedicated only to getting away.[2] It took the United States ten to fifteen years to

---

[2] A standing punning joke of the late 1980s held that students were divided into "Ma-ists" (usually denoting "Marxists," but here meaning "mah-jongg player-ists") and "Tuo-ists" (usually "Trotskyists," but here meaning "TOEFL taker-ists," that is, those bent on escaping to study abroad by passing the standard Test of English as a Foreign Language).

overcome its "Vietnam syndrome." It's unclear whether or not China has such a mechanism to overcome its "June 4 syndrome." If it doesn't, then June 4 will become the turning point in its losing battle with the cancer.

Here I've run on so long, all about unhappy things, but it's because I really can't find anything optimistic to write about. The idea of leaving here for a while and continuing my research elsewhere is becoming my secret hope, but this hope, too, is continually being beset by bad news, one piece after another. The policy here on long trips abroad is basically frozen. My supervisors have already clearly indicated that it's not realistic for me to think of going to the United States in February 1990. Right now I'm doing all I can to have people intercede on my behalf. I hope that once our Great Leaders have settled themselves down emotionally, they'll ease up a little, do you think? A person is just like an object, up on top of another object, set to be flicked off at the merest whim. . . .

"Zhang Xinxin jiashu" (Zhang Xinxin's letter from home), in *Zhongguo shibao* (China times, Taibei), December 21, 1989, reprinted in *Dangdai shishi zhoukan* (Contemporary, Hong Kong), January 6, 1990.

—Translated by Jeffrey Kinkley

II

Without a Regime
or a Regimen:
Entertainment Fiction

ENTERTAINMENT fiction provides a link between the writers from the PRC just anthologized and those from Taiwan to follow. Fiction of this type is written and enjoyed throughout the Chinese-speaking world, not least in Hong Kong, home of Jin Yong, which at the time of his writing was subject to neither the Communist nor the Nationalist regime. Jin Yong's specialty, the swashbuckling "martial-arts," "sword play," or "knight-errantry" novel (*wuxia xiaoshuo*), was the favorite Chinese popular genre at the turn of the 1990s, although it had yet to be "discovered" by scholars in the West.

Jin Yong

JIN YONG (pseud. of Zha Liangyong, or Louis Cha, b. 1924), publisher of the
Hong Kong *Mingbao* (Ming pao daily) and related publications, is an enormously successful writer of historical novels of the popular "martial arts" variety. One of the richest men in Hong Kong, he has currently dedicated himself to
local politics, attempting to smooth the path for Britain's return of Hong Kong to
China in 1997.

In recent years, the "martial-arts novel" has been elevated to an accepted
category of literature, or at least of "popular literature." So many articles have
been published in Chinese on the subject that some scholars speak of "Jin Studies," or "Jin Yong-ology." Late 1987 also saw the first international research
conference devoted to the genre. The following piece, which proffers fresh insights on twentieth-century Chinese literature from the viewpoint of an "outsider" close to popular Chinese traditionalist taste, may be considered Jin Yong's
own contribution to such studies.

In the extract below, Jin Yong discusses his philosophy of entertainment
fiction while being interviewed by a leading journalist from Singapore, Du
Nanfa.

Against the Authors of "Foreign Books in Chinese Language"

An Interview with China's Most Popular Writer of Adventure Novels

Jin Yong

DU NANFA: Everyone feels that one of the most prominent characteristics of your martial-arts fiction is that it is very closely linked with Chinese history. Why do you write that way?

Jin Yong: There are two reasons. First, martial-arts fiction to begin with is set in ancient Chinese society. The more realistic it is, the more interesting it is to the reader. Since it takes ancient society as its background, it can't stray too far from history. The other reason is that I'm interested in Chinese history.

Du: What do you think of your own martial-arts fiction?

Jin: That question isn't so easy. If you rate yourself too highly, it's not only embarrassing to you but displeasing to your readers. If you denigrate yourself, readers may get the wrong message. So what can you do? (*laughs*) It's like in *The Sneering Adventurer* (*Xiao'ao jianghu*, a 1967 novel by Jin Yong), when the Miao girl asks Yue Buqun's wife whether or not she's good with the sword. She finds the question difficult to answer. If she says she's pretty good, that might seem impolite, but if she speaks of herself too disparagingly, the other person could mistake humility for the truth. So it is best just to smile and not answer! (*laughs*) After all, we Chinese believe in modesty. . . .

Du: Well, then, how do you generally view and appraise Chinese martial-arts fiction, especially these past few years?

Jin: In appraising it, I think we should put aside for the time being whether it's high-level or low-level stuff. There is, however, one point I think is worth noting: martial-arts fiction is truly fiction for the masses. The leftist and rightist views of literature agree on one point: The former says one must serve the workers, peasants, and soldiers. The latter likewise says that the arts should be popularized and brought to the masses. Martial-arts fiction generally succeeds in that regard.

Modern Chinese fiction that is considered New Literature is really quite divorced from the Chinese literary tradition. It can hardly be called *Chinese* fiction. Ba Jin, Mao Dun, Lu Xun—they all wrote foreign fiction in Chinese. Actually, the true Chinese artistic tradition, as in Chinese painting, is the one that has come down from the Tang, Song, Yuan, Ming, and Qing dynasties. It's totally different from foreign painting. It's the same with drama: regardless of whether it's Peking opera, Shaoxing opera, or Cantonese opera, it's not at all like Western opera. Even poetry is directly descended from ancient verse and *yuefu* (ballads). Completely new forms and styles came only with the advent of New Poetry.[1]

Chinese art has its own unique techniques of expression, as in music. The Chinese pentatonic scale sounds completely different from the Western octave scale; they can be distinguished on first hearing.

Chinese fiction since the May Fourth movement has not been traditional Chinese fiction. People often ask me, why do you suppose martial-arts fiction has received such a welcome? There are lots of reasons, of course, but I feel the main one is that martial-arts fiction is a Chinese genre. And Chinese, of course, like to read Chinese genres.

Du: You say that martial-arts fiction is a Chinese genre. Is that based on its spirit, or on its style and form?

Jin: I believe the form is the key thing, since the spirit can reflect modern themes and ways of thinking. Still, in reality, "spirit" is not easily divided into modern or ancient. "Form" is different. Chinese art has its own unique forms, in music, painting, costume, drama, dance, poetry, and song. You can sense them at the first encounter; in fact, this is cultural. You can clearly tell Japanese art from Indian, or from that of another culture, right away. Art from a culture with a very ancient tradition is bound to have its own unique character.

What martial-arts fiction has inherited is the traditional form of expression of Chinese fiction. Its content, too, is not that far removed from that of *Water Margin.* Of course, whether it's well written or not is another matter. Still, the form is a Chinese form, one that carries on the tradition of Chinese fiction.

Ever since the May Fourth movement, intellectuals seem to have felt that fiction only exists in foreign forms, and that Chinese forms are not fiction.

Du: I sense that martial-arts fiction has always been enthusiastically welcomed by ordinary people, and popular even among high-level intellectuals, from the May Fourth movement to the present. Nevertheless, in standard evaluations, as for instance in most literary histories, martial-arts fiction is rarely men-

---

[1]"New Literature" and "New Poetry" refer to the modern Chinese vernacular literature that came into being only in the early twentieth century.

174 WITHOUT A REGIME: ADVENTURE NOVELS

tioned or given any sort of recognition. This is very strange and contradictory.

Jin: I believe that has to do with the fact that martial-arts fiction is poorly written, so it's understandable. However, that most intellectuals reject *zhanghui* [traditional "chapter-driven"] novels and canonize the fiction of Ba Jin, Lu Xun, and so on is due more to political reasons than to artistic ones, I think. It's because those men were all great intellectuals with political power or influence. Moreover, the whole literary arena in China was made up chiefly of people like them. Those who wrote fiction using traditional Chinese methods weren't taken seriously by the Chinese cultural establishment, or were even despised.

Even though martial-arts fiction has been around for some time, relatively well-written examples of it have come only recently. There are a lot of early works, but few of them are good, like the late Qing novel, *Seven Knights-Errant and Five Gallants* (*Qi xia wu yi*), which is already classified as well-written. Of course, if you're going to pass judgment on a work, you can't simply consider its form. Content is involved, too. If a work has literary merit, due critical appraisal and stature will come to it in time. Take *Seven Knights-Errant and Five Gallants*. Even Lu Xun had to mention it in his *History of Chinese Fiction*. The same is true of the *Tale of Heroic Young Lovers* (*Ernü yingxiong zhuan*). Principally, then, these novels have to be judged on their own merits. . . .

Du: You've raised the question of whether or not a work can move people and whether or not it has meaning. Do you believe, then, that these two points determine whether a work has literary worth or not?

Jin: Everybody has his own views on literature, but I personally believe that literature for the most part conveys human sentiments. Literature is not to be used to preach morality. . . .

Du: I've read some reviews of your work, all of which point out that your novels convey a strong sense of martial chivalry, and particularly of "loyalty" (*yiqi*).

Jin: Loyalty (*yi*) is a natural human drive. Some literary works in the manner of parables attribute human feelings to dogs and horses to make their points. We really don't know what animals' feelings are like. What these parables actually describe are human feelings and personalities.

A literary work is meant to show that all sorts of emotions are all right. Passionate love, passionate hate, that loyalty I spoke of, or in other words, special friendship—these are all human feelings. Of course, chivalry is a rather special category of human emotion.

Du: Did this spirit of chivalry originate with the literary traditions of chivalry in the biographies of assassins in the *Historical Records* (*Shi ji*) of Sima Qian?

Jin: Probably so, but of course it's not only China that has this tradition of chivalry; other countries have it as well. But the Chinese seem to attach particular importance to it. This has its own sources and foundations in society.

Du: Let's set aside the Chinese tradition of chivalric literature. Has Western literature ever had an influence on your work?

Jin: Some foreign fiction and films—especially foreign action movies—have a strong spirit of chivalry, too. The West really emphasizes action, so there are many similarities with martial-arts fiction. Singapore and Hong Kong, where I've lived, are both societies where East and West come together. They're neither purely Eastern nor Western. People are, of course, influenced by what they see and hear. Some new Chinese painting and music has been highly influenced by Western forms, and Chinese fiction is no different. It often uses Western forms of expression to write about Chinese people and events. I feel there's no reason not to experiment with using traditional Chinese chapter-driven fiction to portray contemporary men and events. Zhang Henshui's fiction, for example, has received quite a bit of praise.

Du: In your view, is martial-arts fiction just for enjoyment, or does it have some other influence or role in contemporary society?

Jin: Literature inevitably has a certain influence and function, but I myself don't wish to make literature into an instrument for influencing society. I believe that these are all side-effects, that art is basically still art and that it does not seek out any goal. It only seeks beauty. . . . Whether it's true or false, or good or bad, is another matter.

Of course, a lot of people do not endorse this argument. Many literary critics like to consider goodness and beauty together, forever mentioning one in the same breath as the other. They always like to discuss what sort of effect a particular piece of fiction has on people, or what kind of benefit that piece of music gives people. There's a joke to the effect that music can mold one's temperament. . . .

Du: Can we say that your fiction primarily tries to lay out fully the individuality of its characters, and to depict and mirror human feelings, in hopes of leaving your readers with a sense of reality and immediacy?

Jin: That's right. I only hope to write honestly and penetratingly, to uncover and express emotions that people don't usually pay much attention to. Of course, martial-arts fiction is basically fantasy; most people's lives aren't that exciting or dangerous. It's like the science fiction of Ni Kuang (*turning to Ni Kuang*). One is always encountering extraterrestrials in it, but none of us has ever seen any (*laughs*). . . .

Jin: I think [the idea that a novel has to be "interesting"] must have been invented by literary critics.

Du: Right. In fact, I believe that if Cao Xueqin had ever thought that *The Dream of the Red Chamber*, which he couldn't sell to anyone at the time, would finally become as influential as it is today, he certainly wouldn't have been able to write it.

Jin: Yes. If a writer single-mindedly sets out, even before he picks up the pen, to write a piece of "great" fiction, he certainly won't be able to do it. If he does get it down on paper, he surely won't be able to achieve the greatness he aspired to.

Ni Kuang: I believe, however, that traditional Chinese fiction is still on the whole quite interesting. For instance, the Ming dynasty *Common Words to Warn the World* (*Jingshi tongyan*), *Slapping the Table in Amazement* (*Paian jingqi*), and several other works, still bear reading.

Jin: I think this has something to do with cultural tradition. If you gave them to foreigners to read, they might not think them worth reading. It has, then, a lot to do with national temperament. It's the same as with Chinese popular tunes: what we find nice to listen to, foreigners may think vacuous and silly. Or take *The Dream of the Red Chamber.* Foreigners read it primarily for purposes of research; the average foreigner doesn't seem able to read it for fun. Consider those foreign housewives and office secretaries: how could they appreciate the novel in some translation in which even the love relationships aren't clear? . . .

Ni: (*Laughing and cutting in*) Hey, how can you be so sure of someone else's aspirations? Maybe you think even you are orthodox.

Jin: (*Laughing*) You're right. Usually, whether something is orthodox or not is related to whether or not it is popular. Most popular theories get recognized as correct.

Ni: No, no. What's popular isn't necessarily correct. Actually, though people who advocate that point of view may be very influential, ordinary people don't necessarily agree with them (*at this reproach, everyone nods in assent*).

Jin: (*Nodding*) Actually, those who uphold our viewpoint may in fact be more numerous.

Ni: (*Another quick attack*) Of course they're numerous. If you don't believe it, all you have to do is look at the market for fiction, right?

Jin: In today's *Mingbao*, there's an article by Xu Su entitled, "Where Has Hong Kong Fiction Gone?" The literature he speaks of doesn't even include the works we're discussing.

Ni: I think that Gu Long's phrase is most apt. He said, "Though we mustn't count on winning any literary prizes, we can still win kudos from the masses. If the masses love us, then all's well and good. What does it matter if the professors don't like us?" Isn't that the way to look at it?

Du: But Jin Yong's fiction has received much praise from professors and specialists!

Ni: Right, and therein lies the greatness of Jin Yong's fiction. From university professors and cabinet ministers on high, down to peddlers and go-fers, everyone loves it. You could truly say it suits both popular and refined tastes. That's one of the most difficult things to achieve, isn't it? It's exactly as in the saying, "Those who can appreciate it see there's a knack; those who can't, just see the attack." To have both is very difficult.

Jin: Most literary critics look at technique, the knack. Relatively few see the fun in the action. . . .

Du: Are you saying, then, that your concept of literature is actually very "unorthodox"?

Jin: Yes, my viewpoint is really the viewpoint of the masses. If I may borrow the Communists' admonition about the necessity to "serve the workers, peasants, and soldiers," how can workers, peasants, and soldiers possibly understand works of the sort that win Nobel Prizes? Take Mao Dun, who just passed away. If we were to give a worker, peasant, or soldier his novel *Midnight* (*Ziye*), together with a martial-arts novel, which of the two do you think he would take? He'd prefer the martial-arts novel for sure. Works like *Midnight* are naturally very well-written, but even though they're said to serve the masses or the workers, peasants, and soldiers, how many of the latter would really enjoy reading them? There's no doubt about the answer to that.

Du: Looking at it from that angle, then, most literary histories ought to reexamine [their neglect of popular fiction] and make some corrections.

Jin: It depends on what you're talking about. When it comes to reflecting society, or the profundity of the writing, *Midnight* certainly has its uses, as a depiction of the lives and living conditions of segments of Shanghai's old society. At the very least, it records the reality of society in those days, so much so that it might indeed have "served the revolution." Martial-arts fiction, of course, doesn't do that. . . .

Naturally, from one point of view, those literary works do have their strong points and their value, but if people keep saying they must serve the masses, that becomes dubious when the masses in the final analysis may not be able to understand them. What does this contradiction mean? We intellectuals can of course appreciate these works, but workers, peasants, and soldiers are wholly unable to. So, then, don't you believe that the most important thing about a work is that it be as acceptable as possible to the majority? . . .

Du: Let's turn to your newspaper and the running of it. I think everyone knows that even though the *Mingbao* isn't number one in circulation, everybody rates it at the top in quality and standards. How do you feel personally about this success?

Jin: I'm naturally quite pleased. Generally speaking, papers go to one extreme or the other. This is particularly apparent in England, where they have "quality papers" and "popular papers" [original in English]. Of course, the personal ideal of all those who run a paper is to put out a good one; circulation is really secondary. As for the *Mingbao*, I feel that the content is not good enough yet, and that there are still things that could be improved. That's the truth, not modesty.

Du: Recently, when I was in Taibei talking with friends, notably Shen Deng'en, the mention of you and the *Mingbao* started everyone to praising its quality and standards in the highest terms. We all inadvertently homed in on the same question: what force or sense of mission motivates you? What enables you to put out such a high-quality paper?

Jin: As soon I left school I went to work for the *Dagongbao*. At that time, it was the best-regarded paper in China (though its circulation wasn't that large), and it had quite a bit of influence on public opinion. I've liked that kind of newspaper since I was a student. Later, when I went to Hong Kong, I worked for the *Dagongbao* again. Afterward, however, it changed its political line, completely breaking its old tradition. . . .

Du: Now you've spoken of public opinion, ideals, and highest objectives. That reminds one of your universally acclaimed editorials in the *Mingbao*. Here, in the most simplistic fashion, I'd like to ask a question that interests everyone: why are your editorials so good?

Jin: (*Smiles*) I'm indebted to everyone for this high opinion. Hong Kong is a place where political struggles are sharp, and that's because it is a completely open society where every manner and type of political power exists. In other regards, the *Mingbao* isn't necessarily better than any other paper. We're successful, however, on another point: we are truly independent. If any power attempts to influence us, we absolutely resist it. Readers may not notice our attitude and position in the short term, but in time they come to see that we are truly objective, independent, and fair-minded. We've maintained these principles now for over twenty years. It wasn't easy, for the threats and blandishments were great. . . .

Du: I've heard that recently you've quietly been devoting your attention to the study of Buddhism. How did you become interested in that?

Jin: That question is not easy to answer, since religion is a mystical experience. If you believe in it, you believe in it; if you don't, you don't. It's not rational, but religious. I believe in Buddhism because I believe that this is the way human existence is.

As I just said, to write fiction is to seek beauty. When I write editorials, it's to seek what's true and what's false, whether an argument is adequate or flimsy, or whether a judgment is correct or faulty. Buddhism is in the category of religion, and it's a question of whether or not you have faith. There's no right or wrong to it.

"Changfeng wanli han jianghu—yu Jin Yong yi du tan" (A strong wind shaking the realm for a myriad miles—a conversation with Jin Yong), interview by Du Nanfa, *Nanyang shangbao* (Singapore), September 9, 12, 1981, in *Zhuzi baijia kan Jin Yong: Jinxue yanjiu congshu* ("Philosophers and writers of all schools" look at Jin Yong: A collection of "Jin-ology" research) (Taibei, 1985), 17:1–28.

—Translated by Marty Backstrom

III

Chinese Literature from Taiwan

ONE group of young writers in Taiwan in the late 1950s and early 1960s was profoundly influenced by modern Western literature, particularly owing to the "cultural desert" that kept Taiwan isolated from both modern Chinese literary works written in the 1930s and contemporaneous literary trends on the Communist mainland. To protect their intellectual independence, some in the group left Taiwan and took up residence in the United States and elsewhere. This anthology refers to them as semi-émigrés, for they continue to have an impact on the literary scene in Taiwan and overseas, and, since the late 1970s, also on the mainland. They constantly commute between the several Chinese realities (in the PRC, Hong Kong, and Taiwan) and their new homes abroad. Taiwan's "modernists" and "semi-émigrés" overlap, and so they are treated together in this section.

In the late 1960s and early 1970s, local Taiwanese writers, the so-called nativists (*xiangtu zuojia*), rose in protest against the Westernisms and rootlessness of the modernists. They chose to write about social realities in the countryside and later also in the cities, and about the many forms and shades of repression by the Kuomintang (KMT) government. These writers are here referred to under the heading "Native Realists."

By the 1970s, in the wake of a polemic about *xiangtu* literature, many Taiwanese readers came to feel that the much-suppressed nativists had actually come to dominate the literary scene. Some writers developed a strong tendency to become "social activists" and, in the intellectual field, ideologists. They tried to raise Taiwanese consciousness to a realm of more independence and self-confidence. Radicals among them withdrew for years to the countryside but returned in the late 1980s to voice strong protests against new cultural and other links with the mainland. Considering Taiwan to have a cultural identity all its own, they joined the newly tolerated political-cultural opposition to the KMT—not caring whether the ruling elite remained fixed in its old ways or represented itself as rejuvenated and inclined to reform. Because of the gamut of opinion among the nativists, they are here tentatively divided into three subtrends: "Black Humor and Other Experiments," "Ideologists," and "Alienation, Withdrawal, and Dissent."

"New Generations" represents those younger Taiwan writers who have tried to find a way through the strict borders and limitations of the modernist and nativist camps. It is difficult as yet to characterize and label the essence of their writings.

Bai Xianyong

BAI XIANYONG (Pai Hsien-yung, b. 1937, in Guilin, on the mainland) is the son of General Bai Chongxi of the Guangxi Clique, a major figure in modern Chinese history who was variously a subordinate and a political rival of Chiang Kai-shek. From the age of eleven, Bai Xianyong grew up in Taibei. His prose describes in a nostalgic way the eclipse of the scattered remains of the military and civil bureaucracy of the KMT, which fled the mainland but never really gave up the conviction that their residence on such an "insignificant" island as Taiwan could only be temporary. The publication of Bai Xianyong's short-story collections, *Taibeiren* (People of Taibei, 1971) and *Jimo de shiqisui* (The lonely age of seventeen, 1976), were major events in postwar Chinese writing. Using highly sophisticated language, Bai surprised his readers with narrative perspectives never before used in modern Chinese literature. Another major theme of Bai Xianyong's has been the fate of Chinese intellectuals "exiled" in the United States. His novel *Yu Qingsao*, also called *Youth in Guilin*, is based on semi-auto-biographical reminiscences of his awakening from boyhood. Another half-real, half-fictional novel, *Niezi* (Crystal boys, 1983), broaches the subject of homosex-uality. After being made into a film, it became very controversial in Taiwan and was banned in the PRC, where most of Bai's other works were warmly wel-comed amid the open climate of the 1980s. The novel's insinuated comparison of the homosexuals' dark corners in Taibei's parks with the hothouse atmosphere of "island Taiwan" as a whole proved quite unacceptable to Taibei's establishment, even though Bai Xianyong has generally remained a loyal supporter of the ruling KMT. Bai subsequently stood up and openly defended the right of homosexuals to acceptance in Chinese society.

Bai Xianyong is a professor of Chinese at the University of California, Santa Barbara, and thus is one of those who voluntarily emigrated to the United States to maintain his independence. This new form of self-exile, which does not pre-clude continued publication for Chinese audiences in Taiwan, Hong Kong, and

181

the PRC, nor frequent visits to those areas, is the real topic of the following essay. It defines Bai's own situation as well as the circumstances of fellow writers Chen Ruoxi, Liu Daren, Zhang Xiguo, and many others who reside permanently in the United States.

The Chinese Student Movement Abroad:
Exiled Writers in the New World

Bai Xianyong

1981, in Singapore

MODERN Western literature has a tradition of exile literature. Around the time of the world wars, a group of Western writers left their own countries and continued to write during prolonged stays abroad, leaving behind quite a number of works as testimony to their spiritual odyssey.

A number of Chinese writers lived and wrote abroad after the May Fourth movement, such as Lao She in England and Ba Jin in France; but they soon returned to China, and their major works were all written at home. So they cannot be called "writers in exile." The Chinese tradition of exile literature did not emerge until the 1960s and 1970s. It arose in the New World, mainly in the United States. This of course is closely related to the course of modern Chinese history. In 1949, when the Chinese Communists obtained control of the Chinese mainland, a small number of writers left for the United States. Zhang Ailing is a representative example. Zhang Ailing had already written *The Rice-Sprout Song* (*Yang ge*) and *Naked Earth* (*Chidi zhi lian*), masterpieces in the portrayal of early Communist China, while living in Hong Kong; after she arrived in the United States, her writings were for the most part nostalgic works. Following the Nationalist government's move to Taiwan, a new group of intellectuals was created. When in the 1960s it became the fashion to study overseas, they came to the United States in large numbers. Some of these intellectuals settled there and wrote for a living. Their works are rich and colorful. Though each chose a different political stance and separate subject matter, their stories were still about the Chinese, for all of them lived in a foreign land and longed for home. Examples would be Nie Hualing, Yu Lihua, Cong Su, Ouyang Zi, Shui Jing, Zhang Xiguo, and so forth. Some of these writers I shall overlook for now, even though their literary achievements are remarkable, since what they wrote about is unrelated to my topic.

The writers with whom I am concerned here can more or less be divided into three periods. Yu Lihua is of the early period. Having taken the trials and tribulations of Chinese foreign students as her major theme, she wrote about the rootless generation. In the early 1960s, when foreign students from Taiwan did not yet have a sense of direction, Yu Lihua's novels expressed their uncertainty and confusion.

Writers of the middle period are more numerous, and most of them graduated from the National Taiwan University. Among them is the versatile and talented Cong Su, whose allegorical novel *Blind Hunt* (*Mang lie*) relates the anxieties and fears of modern man. Recently, her style has undergone a marked change. Though occasionally she still uses allegory, her novels now are full of political satire that trenchantly criticizes the evils of authoritarianism.

In the early 1970s, Chinese foreign students in the United States launched a very important political movement—the movement to protect Diaoyutai. It had far-reaching consequences both for Chinese foreign students then in the United States and for intellectuals in Taiwan. When the United States returned sovereignty over the Ryukyu (Liuqiu) Islands to Japan, Japan claimed Diaoyutai as Japanese territory. This act of aggression against territorial sovereignty enraged Chinese students in the United States. They held demonstrations in major American cities, taking action and forming organizations in order to defend Diaoyutai. This could be called the first political awakening of Taiwan's students abroad, and a resumption of the patriotic tradition of the May Fourth movement's resistance against foreign power and struggle to defend the homeland. But this student movement, which originated from purely patriotic motives, later evolved into a polarization of left against right. That influenced the political identification of many Chinese intellectuals in the United States. Since the movement at its inception did not receive active support from the government [on Taiwan], some disappointed students abroad became radicalized in their speech and left-wing in their sympathies. But when, in 1972, Japan established formal diplomatic relations with the PRC, the problem of the Ryukyu Islands was purposely set aside and ignored. Hence, these veterans of the Diaoyutai movement, who had placed so much hope in the PRC, now suffered bitter disillusionment. Although the movement ended in tragedy, it had a profound impact on the political consciousness of students and intellectuals both in Taiwan and abroad, and of course it also had a tremendous impact on Chinese writers in the United States.

Zhang Xiguo is the principal figure in the third generation of Chinese writers in American exile. He is sensitive and original in his observations of the sociopolitical changes in China; though a scientist by profession, he has an irrepressible enthusiasm for literature. He has written several volumes of novels and short stories, but his full-length novel, *Yesterday's Fury* (*Zuori zhi nu*), remains his representative work. It has won a warm and sympathetic response from intellectuals in Taiwan and abroad. *Yesterday's Fury* tells of a group of Chinese intellectuals in the United States who, prompted by patriotism, take part in the Diaoyutai movement, only to meet with disappointment and disillusion in the end, each in his own way.

Many idealistic Chinese intellectuals have unfortunately been drowned and senselessly sacrificed in the torrent of modern Chinese history and politics. The entire career of Liu Daren, another writer of Zhang Xiguo's generation, is living proof of *Yesterday's Fury*. At the time of the Diaoyutai movement, Liu was a doctoral candidate at the University of California at Berkeley. He took an active part in the movement and even became a student leader. Like several of the intellectuals described in *Yesterday's Fury*, he gave up his studies and threw himself wholeheartedly into the movement. In the end, of course, he couldn't avoid the other characters' destiny—despair and disillusion. These last few years, Liu Daren has greatly revised the political views of his youth and started writing again. In a spirit of remorse and nostalgia, he is recording his spiritual journey. His first full-length novel, *The Nomads* (*Fuyou qunluo*), will soon be published in Hong Kong, the first volume of a planned trilogy. The story is set in Taiwan during the 1960s. Liu describes how several young intellectuals, all with a high degree of social consciousness, are gradually drawn into the windstorm of the political movement; Liu Daren clearly sought to set down the whys and wherefores of the Diaoyutai movement in an epic mode, as historical testimony for a whole generation of Chinese intellectuals in the United States. Since the May Fourth movement, the development of a New Chinese Literature has often found itself inextricably caught up in the tumult and unpredictable fluctuations of the political atmosphere in China. Chinese writers, especially those with a higher degree of social consciousness, are often severely tested in the course of choosing their political affiliations. This has permanent consequences for their creative work.

In 1966, Chen Ruoxi "returned" (*huigui*) to mainland China. She was thus destined to become a witness to the Cultural Revolution. After having stayed in mainland China for seven years and personally experienced the great catastrophe of the Cultural Revolution, Chen Ruoxi ultimately could not escape the workings of fate. After passing through many places, she ended up in the United States again, where she wrote several novels about the Cultural Revolution. In the late 1930s and early 1940s, a group of writers in China who longed for socialism rushed to Yan'an as if on a pilgrimage; Ding Ling's enlisting at Yan'an and Chen Ruoxi's "returning" to Peking are fundamentally very similar. But Chen

Ruoxi was much more fortunate than Ding Ling, for she had the opportunity to go into exile again, to write such stories as "The Execution of Major Yin" (*Yin xianzhang*) and "Geng'er in Peking" (*Geng'er zai Beijing*), as literary testimony to the Cultural Revolution.

Chinese writers living in the West cannot of course avoid being influenced by Western culture, and thereby coming to a new recognition and awareness of their own culture. Ma Sen studied in France, taught in Mexico, lived for several years in Canada, and wrote quite a few plays and novels. Deeply influenced by the modernist tradition in Western literary thought, his works are imbued with the flavor of existentialism. Ma Sen methodically seeks to analyze how Chinese abroad cope with the pressures of living in a Western technological culture. His latest novel, *Night Promenade* (*Ye you*), which is scheduled to appear in the Taiwan journal *Modern Literature* (*Xiandai wenxue*), is a work written against the social grain. The novel relates the adventures of a Chinese woman married to a professor from England. In her pursuit of self-emancipation, she has all kinds of experiences that do not conform to established social norms. In its subject-matter, this novel has made a rather daring breakthrough.

From the above brief introduction, we may draw four conclusions as follows:

1. Although the aforementioned writers in the United States and Canada live there year in and year out, the political and historical changes in Taiwan and in mainland China have had a decisive influence on them.

2. Although they live overseas, all of their works express a strong sense of love and concern for the future destiny of the Chinese people and their culture.

3. Because they live abroad, they enjoy greater freedom of thought and so can maintain an independent and critical attitude toward both sides of the Taiwan Strait.

4. Because most of their work is published in Taiwan, with a little of it recently being picked up and published in the newspapers and magazines of mainland China, too, these writers have had a tangible influence on the literary vogues of Taiwan and the mainland in return.

Given China's unusual politics and history during these last few decades, this tradition of a Chinese literature in exile will most probably continue to play a rather important role on the Chinese literary stage.

"Xin dalu liufangzhe zhi ge: Mei Jia Zhongguo zuojia" (The song of the exiles in the New World—Chinese writers in the United States and Canada), talk given in Singapore, 1981, in Bai Xianyong, *Mingxing kafeiguan* (Celebrity coffeehouse) (Taibei, 1984), pp. 33–37.

—Translated by Ding Naifei

Chen Ruoxi

CHEN RUOXI (Ch'en Jo-hsi, or Lucy Hsiu-mei Chen, b. 1938, in Taiwan) studied in Taiwan and the U. S., then established herself as a writer, perhaps a precursor of the *xiangtu* authors. She belongs to that tiny group of Taiwan intellectuals, including also Chen Yingzhen and the historian Wang Xiaobo, who are convinced that Taiwan's goal ought to be a new cultural unity with the mainland, ultimately through political unification. Chen has fought for a more tolerant cultural environment on both Taiwan and the mainland, and for uncensored intellectual and literary exchange. In 1966, therefore, she went with her husband to the PRC. After teaching for seven years in Nanjing, she left the country in 1973, her hopes and convictions shattered by firsthand experience of the Cultural Revolution. By writing about her experiences in short stories collected under the title *Yin xianzhang* (The execution of Mayor Yin, 1978), she became instrumental in the overseas reevaluation of Mao Zedong and his policies.

Chen Ruoxi has continued writing fiction about contemporary Chinese problems while living in Berkeley, California. She analyzes the "Chinese national character" in an age torn between different political camps somewhat as Lu Xun did decades before. She is also known for her essays and reportage, published in all parts of the Chinese-speaking world, for which she continues to serve as both a bridge and a conscience. Her essay below, like Bai Xianyong's, reflects on the situation of the overseas writers who came under vicious attack by Taiwanese regionalist radicals such as Song Zelai. Like Wu Zuguang, Chen Ruoxi is also distressed to see how influential the heavy hand of censorship remains in all parts of the Chinese world.

On the Miseries of Writers in American Exile
Sanitized Versions for Taiwan, Hong Kong, and the People's Republic

Chen Ruoxi

AN OVERSEAS Chinese writer's state of mind is often solitary and lonely.

I have always believed that writers cannot do without a homeland, just as plants cannot do without soil. A writer who lives in a foreign country is like a transplanted shrub. It is difficult for it to grow as vigorously and as luxuriantly as on native ground.

First of all, geographical separation and estrangement from everyday life are drawbacks that an overseas author has no way of remedying. Nostalgia is certainly one of the eternal literary topics, and stories about love affairs and pure emotion are not limited by time or space, either. But ultimately these themes tend to become narrow and divorced from reality. Literature about the lives of foreign students and their nostalgia for their youth and their native land flew under its own colors for a while on the Taiwan literary scene, but in the end it was considered a peripheral part of native literature that did not easily blend into the mainstream.

Many writers strive to return to their native country, in order to "refuel" and "recharge." Due to limits of time or opportunity, those who succeed are a very small minority. The majority of people face crises of a gradual loosening of familial and cultural umbilical cords between themselves and their native land. Even if one is lucky, able to return often to observe and experience things, one can't help being one step removed. It's like a dragonfly touching down on water and floating along the surface; or like dipping something in soy sauce—the outside is salty and the inside bland. There isn't a writer who doesn't love and embrace life. Those who write in Chinese typically are emotionally connected to both sides of the Taiwan Strait, but too far away to be of help. They suffer from having no way of participating. To those with high aspirations, this is truly a heart-rending sorrow.

Overseas writers have another opportunity, to advance in the literary world of the country they live in. This involves one's feelings of belonging, and one's ability to write in a foreign language. Both subjectively and objectively, there are limitations. What's more, local literary circles are invariably exclusive. To penetrate the inner circle is no easy matter.

Take, for example, the United States: the Chinese are a minority here; we have large numbers of excellent and talented people in every profession, but we still haven't got anywhere when it comes to power as a group. It will take much effort from all of us before we can be like, say, the Jews, and win the recognition and respect of American society for our culture, then have that reflected in the salability of our literary works, maybe even break onto the stage of world literature and win a Nobel Prize. So far, the few works of Chinese-American literature that have taken off have been distinguished by their descriptions of the mysteriousness and backwardness of old China. In the thirty years separating *The Flower Drum Song* from *The Woman Warrior*, the main improvement has been literary [not in the image projected of the Chinese].

Writers from both sides of the Taiwan Strait frequently envy the creative freedom of overseas Chinese authors. They can write whatever they want. Not only do they have no "forbidden territories" to speak of, they enjoy complete freedom from fear.

This is actually only a superficial thing—a small piece of the picture.

If creative freedom is not joined by freedom to publish, freedom is merely an empty phrase. Since the number of Chinese-language publications overseas is limited, a writer's main opportunity to publish still rests with one side of the Taiwan Strait or the other. So the editorial and press clearances an overseas writer must acquire are no fewer than for a native writer. Not only do writers have to censor themselves when they begin to write, editors contribute their own deletions and revisions, either from "national feeling" or some other scruple. That some overseas Chinese writers "submit one manuscript to two publishers" is more often because they are seeking to have their work printed right, and printed whole.

In fact, overseas Chinese writers have to cope with censorship by the post office, too.

Writers aren't so afraid of editors; they fear the postal inspectors most. They are high literary officials, armed with imperial swords of authority, who have the power to make a manuscript disappear without a trace. From time to time, one hears of unregistered mailings getting lost. These postal inspectors obviously are free from having to work overtime. This can be seen from the direct ratio between the length of the manuscript and the time it takes it to get delivered. Once a manuscript of mine over thirty thousand characters long still hadn't arrived in

Taibei ten days after I mailed it (usually it takes five days). It happened that I had only a partial draft with me, so I urgently requested a Singapore newspaper to transmit a photocopy to make up the difference. After two weeks, the manuscript I had sent finally showed up. The whole thing turned out to be a false alarm.

Editors from Taiwan often say: "Everybody has their own miniature internal security bureau inside of them."

Overseas writers have two.

The systems on either side of the Strait are different, and the demands they put on literary works are dissimilar, too. Writings that are acceptable in one place are seditious in the other. If a book is published in Taiwan, Hong Kong, and the mainland, it invariably comes out in three different editions. Take my work, *Breaking through Enemy Siege* (*Tu wei*). The Taiwan edition was the original. The Hong Kong edition edited out criticisms of Mao Zedong and descriptions that touched upon the attitudes of people in Hong Kong toward the 1997 deadline (when Hong Kong will be returned to the mainland government). The mainland edition followed the Hong Kong edition, further editing out the allegedly "sexy" parts. Each side takes what it needs, without disturbing the others. And the censorship system on the mainland makes obvious distinctions between authors inside the country and those outside. It doesn't allow foreign writers to criticize the system (this includes the dead), but it does nothing to inhibit the sale of works by domestic writers that make personal attacks on foreign authors. The "one country, two systems"[1] or, as some people say, "many systems" policy promoted by Deng Xiaoping has long been realized in the publication of literature.

Considering the vastness of the area outside of China, the number of Chinese writers there is relatively small. Those few are separated by great distances. Usually it is difficult for them to assemble, so they lack opportunities to study and improve through mutual discussion and criticism. Besides this inherent deficiency, Chinese overseas writers face man-made impediments common to all overseas Chinese groups. They are either collectively as tight and exclusive as a fortress on a mountain top or as loose as a pile of sand.

The long-standing division between the Communist and Nationalist regimes, along with the lack of a proper solution to the problem of Taiwanese political participation, has caused Chinese overseas to be divided for a long time, too. The leftists, the rightists, and the advocates of Taiwan Independence all reject the others, or sometimes use one group to attack the other in a style similar to the three-way confrontations in *The Romance of the Three Kingdoms*. If one adds to this the groups that profess neutrality, the splinter effect creates a replay of the Warring States era.

Take, for example, the largest groups in North America, the organizations of

---

[1]Facetious allusion to the disingenuous slogan by which the PRC hopes to induce Taiwan to unite with it, becoming one country, with Taiwan keeping its old "system."

Taiwanese. For some time now there has been a split between the two big factions, the "Compatriots' Society" (Tongxiang Hui) and the "Compatriots' Unity and Friendship Society" (Tongxiang Lianyi Hui). They stymie and attack each other, generally setting all the compatriots at odds. Recently, the "Compatriots' Society" has had its own distinctions, between chapters that are, or are not, controlled by the Taiwan Independence Alliance. It's got all the fellow-provincials' heads reeling.

Being "Ugly Chinamen,"[2] the Taiwanese have not yet overcome the defects of factionalism and disorganization. Authors are naturally no exception. In 1982, some enthusiastic writers of Taiwanese descent called for the establishment of an organization to facilitate cultural exchange and dissemination.

Many people responded; unfortunately, due to difficulties in bridging various differences, two different organizations formed within a month. This not only dampened the zeal of all concerned, it dissipated their energy. I straddled both organizations and for a long while rushed around every year attending their annual meetings. But my energy really wasn't up to it. The last two years, I could only harden my heart and attend no meetings at all, in order not to demonstrate favoritism.

The situation of a Taiwanese writer who is concerned about political and social issues is particularly difficult. If your writing criticizes the realities of the Chinese mainland, people sympathetic to that side will be sure to award you with the titles "anti-Communist writer" and "right-winger." If you say there are signs of progress and hope for the one billion people on the mainland, you'll immediately be capped as a "small-time leftist who refuses to admit the error of her ways." If you don't endorse the idea of a Taiwan nation and Taiwan nationalism, then your more extreme compatriots will curse you as a "traitor to Taiwan" and "assimilationist." If you say a few words on behalf of your tragic and heroic Taiwanese compatriots, then in a flash you'll become a "Taiwan separatist," subject to attack by both the left and the right. The mainland writers who keep harping on the theme of "peaceful unification" with Taiwan self-righteously take the offensive with their pens: "How can a person without a country, who rejects her own people, even talk about saving humanity?"

A Taiwanese who writes according to his or her conscience is worse off than "Pigsy" Zhu Bajie [a character from *Journey to the West*] looking in the mirror— from whatever angle we look at ourselves, we're not human.

Fortunately, things are improving. As both sides have gradually loosened up, so have the sharp divisions among overseas Chinese writers. In the past, North American writers took refuge in the newspapers, each group barricading its doors and minding its own business. Recently, publications professing neutrality have gradually raised their heads. Little by little, writers have cut across newspa-

[2]An allusion to *The Ugly Chinaman*, by the Taiwan author Bo Yang.

per lines and submitted manuscripts to different places. This is a heartening beginning, but there's still a long stretch of rocky road to go before we arrive at the "free and democratic" spirit in which the United States was founded. It is true that writers born and bred in America enjoy democracy and freedom, but this is not necessarily the case for Chinese immigrants. Writers repeatedly encounter difficulties getting a visa to return home to visit their relatives once their writings have criticized politics in their mother country. Some who have been informed on are unable even to return home to visit seriously ill relatives on special request. Only after repeated efforts may they return—just in time to mourn at the grave. Others, long denied entrance to their own country and unable to return to families they've left behind, sigh deeply over the fact that "the beggars have chased the abbot out of his own temple."

Such difficulties pale into insignificance when one's own life is at risk. In the fall of 1984, the author of *The Biography of Jiang Jingguo* [Henry Liu, or "Jiang Nan"] was murdered by a member of the United Bamboo Gang sent by the Taiwan [Military] Intelligence Bureau. Before he died, the victim's greatest reassurance had been that he lived in a free America governed by law and thus could escape terror. His death shattered the illusions of a great many writers.

Not long ago, a member of the United Bamboo Gang revealed that prior to the murder outside San Francisco, they had planned an attempt on another writer. Who *was* this writer who temporarily managed to avoid looking down the barrel of a gun? We writers, not yet recovered from the earlier fright, were once more plunged into terror.

The assassination also cast a dark shadow over the minds of American scholars and authors doing research on contemporary Chinese history. Sterling Seagrave, who for many years worked on the secret documents and correspondence of the Jiang and Song families, a few weeks ago published a book called *The Soong Dynasty.* Now he and his family have left the country for a while, to prevent any unfortunate occurrences.

Just when people were clamoring to denounce Taiwan's spy activities, the state chairman of the People's Republic of China publicly announced that after China was unified, Taiwan would be allowed to keep its secret agent system. This truly earth-shattering pronouncement depressed everyone who heard it. Now, not only overseas writers, but even the nineteen million people of Taiwan feel endangered.

Many Chinese writers envy overseas writers for their ability to be "free and easy and above the law." Or they denounce them for fleeing from their own nation's political struggle, since they consider those who have run to a free country "deserters." Actually, as long as you write in the Chinese language, it's all the same, no matter what corner of the world you happen to live in. How can a single nationality go two separate ways?

I would hope that we writers would not divide ourselves along lines of north and south, or left and right; nor make distinctions between those living in China and those overseas. Would that everyone could live together in harmony.

"Haiwai zuojia de kunjing" (The plight of Chinese writers abroad), *Jiushi niandai* (The nineties, Hong Kong) (May 1985):14–16.

—Translated by Kim Besio

Wang Wenxing

WANG WENXING (Wang Wen-hsing, b. 1939; originated in Fuzhou) is a professor of English literature at National Taiwan University and one of the few "modernists" of mainlander extraction to have chosen to stay in Taiwan instead of leaving for the United States. With Bai Xianyong and others, he edited the journal *Xiandai wenxue* (Modern literature), the cradle of Taiwan's new modernist movement after 1962. Wang Wenxing has remained a strong advocate of Westernization in Chinese literature; with the versatile conservative poet Yu Guangzhong, he furiously attacked the idea of *xiangtu* literature during the government-backed campaign against the tendency in 1977.

Wang Wenxing's oeuvre is small; he is known for his two collections of short stories and two novels, *Jiabian* (Family mutation, 1973) and the startling *Beihai de ren* (The man with his back to the sea, 1981). *Family Mutation* is a kind of *Bildungsroman* about a rebellious young intellectual in a claustrophobic émigré family milieu. It echoes the iconoclasm of the May Fourth generation of writers and became a best-seller, creating a stormy debate about Taiwan's generation gap, the clash between Eastern and Western values, and the possibility of changing the Chinese language, whether through a renewal of classical syntax or innovations in the characters themselves. The novel won Wang Wenxing the name of "Taiwan's Joyce," with its "anti-Confucianism," interior monologues, innovative use of stream-of-consciousness technique, and Freudian overtones about the protagonist's father, who in the end is "banished." *The Man with His Back to the Sea* (currently being translated into English by Edward Gunn) is still more shocking, due to its Joycean reinvention of language itself. Wang Wenxing's concept of literature has come under attack by Song Zelai from the viewpoint of the Taiwanese nativism that largely supplanted Taiwan's modernism during the 1970s.

Such a Symphony of Written Characters One Must Not Allow to Disperse

Wang Wenxing

October 16, 1978

Preface for the New Edition of *Family Mutation*

FAMILY MUTATION has been on sale now for five years. One might say that five years in the publishing history of a book can be fraught with danger. In fact, we could say that the publishing history of *Family Mutation* might be considered a history of astonishment. I was quite astonished at the outset, when *Family Mutation* became a best-seller. Honestly, in the beginning I only intended to produce some mimeographed copies as a present for "friends and relatives"; with that I presumed to be quite satisfied. The "concern" (how beautiful that word "concern") for *Family Mutation* among critics again gave me a kind of startling astonishment. The book, they maintained, was immoral; it had broken with tradition, the written words had ceased to be understandable—had become Ulyssified—everybody displayed his literary talents, exercised his thoughts, and let his fantasy loose as if participating in an essay contest. Moreover, many readers maintained that, "In *Family Mutation*, you may as well ignore the words, you only have to read it." This again astonished me very much. Then I realized how this threefold astonishment had come about: It had its roots merely in the special dispositions of the readers. The first stemmed from readers who had bought the book but not necessarily bothered to read it; the second came from readers who never bought the book and certainly did not bother to read it (they belong however to the readership; they have overheard other people discussing the book). The third stemmed from those readers who bought the book and actively read it, but much too quickly.

One can imagine that I owe gratitude mostly to the readers of the third category. But I hope still more that there might exist another, fourth kind of audience: Readers who buy the book and are prepared to read it slowly.

The fact is that I get ideas that show nothing but contempt for common sense. I feel that "With *Family Mutation* one can brush everything else aside and take only the words into consideration." I'm convinced that *Family Mutation* would cease to be *Family Mutation* if we decided to remove the written words. We might compare this with a red rose that has been stripped of its color: the rose would cease to be a rose. All components of a novel—its theme, characters, underlying idea, texture—are expressed with words. Period. The success or failure of a writer lies simply and exclusively in his written words. PERIOD.

As words are the whole basis of a work, one has read the essence of a work only if one has followed the text word by word. After all, you are not supposed to listen to a symphony of four movements by hastening to the end in ten minutes. The ideal reader should not skip a single note (written character), just as the ideal listener of classical music should not overlook a single rest (punctuation mark). The ideal speed of reading for any written work should be around one thousand characters per hour. One should desist from extending one's reading to more than two hours a day. Maybe writers are the most intolerably demanding people on earth, asking more of other people even than lovers do. Of course, they tend to be more reliable than lovers.

One thousand characters per hour. You are astonished? Now even you feel somewhat surprised!

"*Jiabian* xinban xu" (Preface to the reprint of *Family Mutation*), October 16, 1978, in Wang Wenxing, *Jiabian* (Family mutation) (Taibei, 1986), pp. 1–2.

—Translated by Helmut Martin

Qideng Sheng

QIDENG SHENG (Ch'i-teng Sheng, pseud. of Liu Wuxiong, b. 1939, in Tongxiao, Miaoli County, Taiwan) has always been a loner and so cannot be grouped with any of Taiwan's literary schools. His odd pen name recalls the Seven Sages of the Bamboo Grove, the poetical Daoist recluses of the third century A.D.

Influenced by Kafka and Faulkner, Qideng Sheng was considered a modernist in his early short stories, the best-known of which is "Wo ai hei yanzhu" (I love Black Eyes, 1967). Later, his writing was classed with the *xiangtu* group, and, like many of those writers, Qideng Sheng left the capital in 1970 to work exclusively among Taiwanese-speaking compatriots, as a teacher in his hometown. He has written much about the rapidly changing life in the cities of the island. In his peculiar way, Qideng Sheng has thus documented the tragedy of modern man and the absurdity of existence in a Chinese and Taiwanese context.

The essay below was written as a preface to his ten-volume collected works, published in 1977.

How Love Scatters
On the Publication of the First Collection of My Works

Qideng Sheng

July 10, 1977, at the old house in Tongxiao

> I look within myself; I have no business but with myself. I incessantly
> consider . . . and taste myself."
> —Montaigne

THESE ten volumes represent the first stage in my fifteen years of writing. I feel thankful to God and Father Time for helping me through those sorrowful months and days and finally letting me enjoy the rich love of true friendship. Now I can happily witness the publication of all my works by the same publishing house. I obtained no wealth through this, but I continue hard at my work. Who, at this moment, can be happier than I?

Because of this encouragement, I am also going to include in these volumes a chronology of my life and works, incomplete versions of which appeared in magazines this year. I would like it to be known that this version from my own hand is the most accurate and complete one. This might raise suspicions that I plan to conclude my creative life, but that is untrue. The message is rather that today's work is completed today; tomorrow is a new beginning. This is the principle I live by. I want personally to see through to the completion of all my endeavors. It is only natural to want to name this little collection of ten volumes my "complete works" and publish a chronology of my writing. . . .

I met F. Luo in the summer of 1983, while traveling in Taibei. Reminiscing with him, I described how I came to be attracted to the opposite sex as a schoolboy and how, because of my rather odd behavior, my attentions were never reciprocated. I slowly became depressed, to the point of completely ignoring my schoolwork. I threw myself madly into the pursuit of painting. I even went to a forlorn mining town to get away from it all, but my painting could not make me whole.

I spent the summer that year wandering on remote beaches like those where I grew up. I climbed tall mountains from dawn to dusk, just to watch the beautiful sunny days go by. In the chill wind and heavy rains of winter, I lived alone in my dilapidated garret. There I delved into studies of Beethoven and read Western novels. Sometimes Touxi, recently discharged from the military and utterly depressed, would come up to my garret, turn on the record-player, and start to cha-cha all by himself in those cramped quarters. He was a small but handsome man who moved and danced very gracefully. I would stare at him, imagining him to be an angel. His eyes were downcast in rapture, although occasionally he would raise his head and smile at me mysteriously. Two years went by this way, until I became so despondent that I felt I had finally hit rock bottom. I told myself that I must record something to pass the time. It was then that I wrote my very first short story, entitled "Poker, Unemployment, and Deep-Fried Squid" (*Puke, shiye, zha youyu*), which was published in the supplement of the *United Daily News*. It is now fifteen years since then.

F. Luo really tried hard to get close to me, but sometimes I found him extremely cruel. He asked, "Whom were you really in love with back then?" I hesitated before telling him. "Meixia, who was known as the prettiest girl in school." I experienced a sudden attack of shame after mentioning her name, because in those days, I was known as the loosest and wildest man around. This kind of mismatch, I'm afraid, is one of the sorriest things in the world. A chill went down my spine when I saw that inexplicable smile surfacing on Luo's expressive face. I had the premonition that a cruel prank was coming. He sighed, which increased my suspicion.

"Fate can really put one over on a person."

"Why's that?"

"Why? I don't know, but let me tell you this."

He noticed with disdain the foolish look that came over my face because of that girl with whom I am, to this day, still very much in love. I didn't mind his sneer. I told him I didn't know whether she was dead or alive; the last I heard was that she had married an aging diplomat and gone to Paris. I imagined that she must now be a wealthy and elegant lady, living the good life she had so longed for.

"That's not true, not true at all."

F. Luo interrupted, deliberately trying to ruin my mood.

"Then you know her?"

"Indeed. Not only do I know her, I'm an old friend of hers." He hastened to add: "It's a shame I met you too late." Luo was a famous scholar and I had known him personally only a short time.

"What happened to her? Where is she now?"

"Last year she made a trip back here from Canada. I was shocked." He stopped and looked at me before he continued.

"You really want me to tell you the truth?"

Although filled with doubts and concerns, I said, "Yes, I want to know everything."

"In that case, I need to start at the beginning."

His expression wasn't as frightening as it had been. He had wholly regained his earlier look of compassion.

He said that Meixia had been a friend of his family as far back as our school days. She went to visit his house every weekend and even stayed with the family during the summer and winter vacations. Among the many friends who gathered at the house, there was no lack of smart and handsome young men, nor of bachelors from wealthy families. Poets and painters met there to play bridge.

Meixia's natural beauty caught the eye of everyone there. She, however, had only one thing in mind, to get out of Taiwan as soon as possible, leaving her needy parents and younger siblings behind. They tied her down to a job just to support them. Hence she married an overseas Chinese college student from Vietnam, who was about to go to Paris to study art. His family was in business and was well-off. He, however, was small and skinny, several inches shorter than the tall and graceful Meixia.

"Oh!" I sighed over this sudden revelation.

Luo continued: "A short time after they arrived in Paris, his family in Vietnam went bankrupt. The couple's money was cut off. They moved on to Canada to work, where they have been ever since."

"You said she came back last year?"

"Right."

Luo's expression took another unusual turn and his voice softened into a heavy whisper: "When I held her hands, I was shocked, but she kept calm and a smile stayed on her face. I just couldn't believe it. Those rough, calloused hands belonged to a woman who had been doing hard manual labor for a long time. There was a difference of heaven and earth between those hands and the soft, tender hands I had held when I saw her off at the airport ten years earlier."

The event Luo had just related filled my heart with such indignation that I gulped down the huge glass of wine in front of me. It made me lightheaded. That evening, I wrapped up my visit to Taibei in a hurry and bade F. Luo farewell. No matter what sweet talk, honeyed words, and other temptations he might offer me, I couldn't stay a minute longer. On the train, amid the sound sleep of many exhausted travelers, I let my tears flow in quiet solitude. I regretted what I had done during my student days. Throughout the autumn, all those long-past events rushed back at me like a tidal bore. Each night, I stayed up, sober and unable to sleep, writing feverishly about those events, like a ghost trying to exorcise itself.

* * *

Sometimes, in contemplation, I am filled with joy. It comes not merely from being liked, but from the delight we all share in literature as an exploratory means of seeking knowledge of human history and the world around us. More precisely, literature enables us to peer into an interior world. In the pulse of that interior world we perceive certain emotional messages that link us spiritually and merge our ideals, so that we share the exultation of happiness as well as the burden of sorrow. My hope is that we may create beautiful verses and powerful prose, to reach even more people.

I think that literature is a specifically human world of existence. Any thoughts and emotions can be portrayed by these simple written signs. In this huge and complex world, one should not unyieldingly adhere to an uncompromising idea or uphold a certain fixed form. One should live like a nomad, a gypsy wanderer, a poor mendicant monk, or a romantic lover. These people, before they find themselves, accept and reject things as does a pure, innocent babe. Before we are fully equipped with the faculty for rational and critical thinking, we rely on our innate senses. They are our most accurate guides. Thus, in our wandering journey through life, the vaguely formed spirit from our beginnings will gradually be shaped into a concrete form by absorbing the essence of the day and night. We find ourselves not by relying on one path, but by walking all the paths. The hope of life will take us searching madly, wear us out, and give us pain, but when we are exhausted and fall by a pond in the marsh, thirsting, and thrust our face over that mirrored expanse, we shall see ourselves clearly. In that solitude, we can better know our true face. Let us not be intimidated by the hardships or mesmerized by the comforts of life and sell our body to those who would have us, for then we sell our soul as well. We should search for revelations from the great masters past and present, not ignorantly follow the impostors of the present.

Slander and malicious criticisms come from intolerance and ignorance. Evil persons do not necessarily know their evilness. Sometimes, we are not aware of heart and mind. They make it impossible for us to see reality, and so we judge everything from our own point of view. We have regrets afterward, but out of fear of being found out, we miss the chance to be forgiven by others, and let this heartfelt pain accumulate in the depths of our soul until it develops into an illness. This human world then appears filthy because of these hidden emotions. Indeed, since we cannot forgive or be forgiven, enmities develop and intensify, until there are mutually antagonistic groups. This is the cause of the evil in today's world. I, therefore, believe that literature is a way to salvation. Every person traveling this road of experience can gain complete liberation of the body and soul. At the same time, this message can cleanse the heart and mind of mankind. There is a condition, however; literary creation must begin with each individual's convictions about life, instead of submitting as a tool to some extreme system of thought. Only when our individual thoughts remain completely free and independent can we write to meter and rhyme, and through these trans-forming words of the heart obtain heartfelt resonance with other people of sensitivity.

Obviously there are some people today who falsely define the essence of literature. They want to derive a literary goal from the logic of economic philosophy. They want literary creations to obey a certain doctrine and march to the same beat. They consider everything Western to be decadent. They condemn the ancient Chinese and consider our ancient poets to have had bourgeois ideas. They condemn us today as nihilistic. Where do all these accusations come from? Let us consider this calmly. I feel my heart bleed when we have to suffer their heartless cruelty. I can only contemplate the whys of their insensitivity. We must never again become instruments and slaves of the giants in history. We must not consider the heaven-conferred right to life as a favor bestowed on us by those giants, or fight like dogs among ourselves when they toss us a few scraps. My melancholy and sorrow now come simply from realizing the difficulty human beings have in obtaining freedom and independence, because the ghosts of those historical giants have now been reincarnated in yet another group of people. The world under their rule is still one in which there is hunger, epidemics, war, and the death of innocents.

We must also acknowledge this fact: as individuals, we are separated and alone, but our spirits will meet somewhere between heaven and earth at the right time. Individuals move on their own; we needn't hypocritically embrace each other, but when the time comes for us to meet, we will realize that we love each other. Today, literature is our form of knowing and communicating. Tomorrow, all we shall need is the language of words flowing from the heart. Today, we rely on written symbols; tomorrow, we shall rely only on a natural tacit understanding. Remember: there was a day when human beings walked out of nature, and there will be a day when we return to nature; literature serves as a record of each stage of this journey.

* * *

I wasn't at all young when I began to write. I was twenty-four, but my sense of joy and curiosity was that of a malleable child. In addition to the eleven short stories published in the supplement of the *United Daily News* that first half year, I wrote prose about Black Eyes and me,[1] modeled after "Platero and I" by Juan Ramon Jimenez. Beyond that, I had two or three pieces published in *Crown Magazine*. After those joys of birth, the path of hardship unfolded. It has been fifteen years since then, and I am thirty-nine. I have written nearly a hundred pieces, long and short, and thirty-some poems. My whole life is reflected in these

---

[1]Black Eyes is a recurring name for a beloved young woman in Qideng Sheng's fiction, as in "I Love Black Eyes."

works. In them, I have covered both the external and internal worlds. In regard to the relationship between the self and the world, I go by my own natural inclinations, emotions, and rational ideas to record the things I've experienced in life. I even take myself as a subject in order to explore and search through philosophies of life. My innate love for and desire to possess aesthetic things led me to these techniques and styles of writing.

It is the individual's own sense of his smallness and insignificance that gives testimony to God's greatness, power, and omniscience. The fate of the individual undoubtedly is in the hands of the omnipotent. In my nebulous living and contemplation, I often find direction and inspiration in a sense of urgency and pressure. In reviewing my writings, there seems to emerge a spiritual form whose veins and outlines are vaguely traceable.

Thus, little pieces of life here and there become the raw materials of my writing. This material moves through my personality and thoughts and turns into particular images; practical matters acquire metaphysical implications. These themes of my emotions often expand from a mere point to a whole horizon, from the finite to the infinite. Often, by means of the smallest matters, my thoughts expand into the limitless space of the universe. I believe that human beings are born with a faculty for logical reasoning, imagination, and a sense of the beautiful.

Love makes me aware of the inconstancy of life, yet love is an expression of my will. As in the human pursuit of utopian ideals, consciousness of these two things intermingles and fills the pages of my work. I can never forget the way love becomes broken in this less-than-ideal world. The scenes in my work mostly linger at the margins of tragedy. Unavoidably perhaps, I shall come to enter into the center of this tragedy. The thought of this often makes me tremble with fear. Therefore, I look forward to the reappearance of the "White Horse," which represents the pure and unadorned paradise that is the typical way of life in the world of my mind. But it has passed by like a legend. The "I" that is born in the present unstintingly yearns for the "past" and longs for the "future."

Montaigne said: "A man must sequester and recover himself from himself. We should reserve a storehouse for ourselves . . . altogether ours . . . wherein we may hoard up and establish our true liberty." In fact, I did not hold to this profound truth in the early stages of my writing. I did not receive its sweet comfort until my moment of utmost loneliness, after a long period of searching and groping, and the tempering of many hardships in life. Montaigne also said: "The greatest thing in the world is for a man to know how to be his own."

This is in fact true for all human beings.

"Qing yu si: Xiao *Quanji* xu" (Feelings and thoughts: Short preface to the first edition of my collected works), July 10, 1977, in Qideng Sheng, *Baima* (White horse) (Taibei, 1977), pp. 9–14.

—Translated by Tien Rita Wang and Charles Belbin

Huang Chunming

HUANG CHUNMING (author prefers Hwang Chun-ming, b. 1939, in Ilan, Taiwan) has condensed his colorful adolescent experiences at all kinds of odd jobs into a humorous kaleidoscope of stories about poor Taiwanese in the countryside and, more rarely, in the cities. Apart from Wang Zhenhe, Huang is the only successful satirist among Taiwan's postwar writers.

Huang Chunming's stories "Shayonala, zaijian" (Sayonara, goodbye) and "Pingguo de ziwei" (The taste of apples), collected in *Sayonara, Goodbye* (1977), are burlesque treatments of average Taiwanese and their reservations about Americans and Japanese who might seek to "re-occupy" the island. Huang's oeuvre has remained comparatively small, but parts of it, compiled by the author himself in three volumes, have been successfully rendered into film versions under his own directorship. Inspired translations of his stories by Howard Goldblatt have won the author an international audience.

Father's Writings Have Been Republished

Or, The Sexuality of Women Students in a Taibei Bookstore

Huang Chunming

August 2, 1974, at the Grotesque Crag

THAT NIGHT, as I rode my motorcycle from Taibei back home to Grotesque Crag in Beitou, I sang loudly all the way.

When my wife opened the door, she stepped out and made a hushed gesture, reminding me, "Be quiet, it wasn't easy to coax Little Pigsy to sleep." Then she smiled, hesitatingly, and asked, "What happened to make you so happy? Did you pick up some money on the road?"

"*Sayonara, Goodbye* will be published in a second edition," I said excitedly.

"Sh-h-h, please be quiet!"

I entered the bedroom. Little Pigsy, holding his small fists tight, was already sound asleep. I leaned over, smelled his breath, and couldn't help but kiss him. Perhaps my mustache pricked him; he wrinkled up his face and stirred. I patted him lightly and whispered, "Daddy's book is going to be published again."

Several days later, I still laughed to think of how I'd behaved that night I got the good news. I never could have imagined that at my age such a thing could still excite me so—that it could make me dance like a child and sing all the way home. I'd even told my sleeping two-year-old baby. It was evident that I'd gone into ecstasy and got carried away. As I mulled it over, I became curious about the writers who had gone before me. How happy had they been when they learned that their books were to be republished? What about Qiong Yao? And so many others?

Since March, when my collections *The Gong* (*Luo*) and *Sayonara, Goodbye* were published, I'd become more eager than ever to visit bookstores. Even when I was away from Taibei, I would make a point of visiting bookstores in other cities, for I was constantly concerned about my books. For that reason, I could no longer feel at ease. I can't deny that my concern was a bit utilitarian, in the broad sense of the word. After all, I'm just one of the common folk. But this psychological experience of extraordinary concern about my own works was a first for me. I'd written things before, got them published, and been concerned about them afterward. But never like this—I would dash to the bookstores at every opportunity, with butterflies in my stomach. I knew that some of the salesgirls in the bookstores had already begun to notice me. Not that they knew me as Huang Chunming, or as the author of *The Gong* and *Sayonara, Goodbye*. They only knew "him again, the one who never buys a book." From the glances of the salesgirls, I could already discern that they no longer regarded me as a customer.

Once, in a Taibei bookstore, I saw a girl who looked like a college student pull *The Gong* off the shelf and start flipping through it. I suddenly became elated. My spirits soared, but I became apprehensive that she might put it back without reading it. I watched her at close range. Meanwhile, two salesgirls closed ranks at the other end of the room and began whispering and watching me. I could swear that they were talking about me, and not saying anything nice. All of a sudden, I felt so flustered that I picked out the first book at hand and gestured to the salesgirls that I intended to buy it. Only when one of them approached did I notice that the title of my book was *Sex and the College Girl*, but it was too late for me to put it back. The salesgirl picked up the book. She joked with the other girl as she wrapped it. My God! How could I keep them from getting funny ideas about me? I felt my face flush. As the salesgirl gave me the book and my change, I dropped my head and dared not look at her. I would have left, but it occurred to me that they would then laugh at me all the more. I pretended to be composed; I kept on browsing, throwing sidelong glances at the college girl as she turned the pages of *The Gong*. She was very much engrossed in one of my stories. I felt comforted. Before long, another thought arose: could it be that the girl liked my stories but found the book too expensive and intended to read it in the bookstore? Or that she came often, to read one story each time, until she could read them all? While indulging in such romantic fantasies, but for fear of causing further unbearable misunderstandings, I might well have walked over to her on an impulse and offered to send her my book as a gift. At the same time, I noticed that the salesgirls had not changed their unfavorable impression of me simply because I had bought a book from them. Just as I was about to condemn my crazy feelings and tear myself away, I saw the college girl shut the book, sigh, and ask the salesgirls to wrap it up. The same salesgirl walked over, took *The Gong*, and pulled out another book from the shelf. "This book, *Sayonara, Goodbye*, is by the same author. It's not bad. It sells very well, too," she said.

"I know," said the college girl, smiling, "I bought it the last time I was in."

Listening from the sidelines, I was deeply moved. As the salesgirl handed her the book, the student asked, out of curiosity, "Do you like Huang Chunming's stories, too?"

"I've just begun to read them. I like them very much."

I was so happy that I almost yelled out loud. Full of gratitude, I watched the buyer leave. Before I left the bookstore, I nodded and gave a terribly sincere smile to the salesgirl. Offended, she turned away and faced her coworker. As I exited the store, I heard myself cursed. "Crazy! Shameless!" Then I heard laughter from the other one. I would never dare to visit that bookstore again.

In the past three or four months, I've seen readers buy my books in many bookstores. In the small towns of central Taiwan, little bookstores sell my works and even hang posters advertising them. I hear discussions of my stories in the conversations of the younger generation. A number of veteran writers, too, have written newspaper and magazine articles to cheer me along. All of this has encouraged me. The events of these few months have evoked a great change deep in my heart. I've become confident, and suddenly my goals have become clear. I'm grateful for all the encouragement these people have given me, and wish shamelessly to trot out a cliché: "I regret that we met so late!"

Actually, most of the short stories collected in these books were written years ago. Why were there so few readers at the time? Not many people supported my approach to creative writing. I'd like first of all to set aside discussion of the test of time, and instead do some objective thinking about publication. Of course, pure creative individualists and anarchists are not concerned if they have forums or readers. They do not try to link up with third parties. They go so far as to regard creative writing as finished once the manuscript is completed. Writers with these kinds of ideas about creative writing may rise to very lofty realms in the mental world of creativity, but ordinary people cannot scale them.

I'm one of those ordinary people myself, without any particular views on creativity. I can only follow the insights of sagacious people before me, to save myself time and energy groping around and talking nonsense. Given the current impoverished state of Chinese literature, if I can contribute what little I have, I'll feel peace of mind. Therefore, I throw my full support to literature that concerns itself with man and society and is based on a sincere attitude toward life. This can be understood simply by looking at the things that make up literature and the process of its creation, quite apart from morals and conscience, and also apart from justice and responsibilities. If one were to remove the human element from literature and art, what would be left? On the other hand, if the human element were to be siphoned off from "livelihood" and "society," what kind of "life" would that be? And a literature that is concerned with man and his society has many other meanings besides that. Having said this much, I feel quite ashamed of myself. Here I am, shouting out for this kind of literature and also trying to write it, only to find myself hiding in one of society's little corners with like-minded friends, where we can shout, holler, and feel very pleased with ourselves. When you think about it, this is both pitiful and ridiculous. Unless there is another conception of literature, I ought to be sticking to literature that is concerned with man and society. Not only should the content be socially oriented, the medium should suit the masses. Therefore, I guess, no matter how much I throw the blame on myself, I have also by implication censured the literary magazine published by my colleagues. And yet the *Literature Quarterly* (*Wenxue jikan*) has been my cradle; many of my works are informed by the criticism of friends and veteran writers from that period of my life. Today I hold a different view of the "completion" of a literary work: I cannot regard a work as being complete simply because the manuscript is finished, or because the manuscript has been handed in to a magazine and published. I cannot call the work complete even when it is published as a book and distributed everywhere. I must know whether my work, once in the hands of readers, is cast aside or welcomed—that is, does society accept or reject it? Then, let that success or failure come home to me deep in my heart, there to give rise to new works. It is therefore natural that I'm concerned with the sales of my works. I will ceaselessly scout the bookstores, pricking up my ears to overhear what others are saying about my stories.

The night I was agog about the reprinting of *Sayonara, Goodbye*, without realizing it, I started rather seriously to discuss with my wife my writing plans in the days ahead. I don't know how much she understood; I seemed, in fact, to be talking to myself. Yet, at 2:00 A.M., she still hadn't slept a wink. Perhaps, in my conversation, I had revealed to her my attitude toward writing, or perhaps, for a short time, she had grown respectful toward my work. At that moment, she struck me as lacking sex appeal, even more than when we were mad at each other. I bade her go to sleep, as I remained in my study continuing to work on my plans. I couldn't sleep. However fully I might or might not realize my writing plan, I had never experienced such a night, a night when I could confidently draw up a plan as if it were real. Why, in the short space of one night, did I feel such a surge of elation, and yet also such a cloying and sinking feeling? The answer would seem to be simple. News that my collection would be republished naturally made me happy; yet the deeper significance of the "second edition" sent me crashing down from my elation. I was brought face-to-face with a chilling fact: frankly, my collection could not possibly have attracted an audience on its own merits. To some extent, it must have been due to recommendations and literary awards from many veteran writers, to distribution and advertisement by the publishers, and partly to luck—to chance encounters between book and reader, between the reader's pocketbook and the bookstore's cashbox, and so on. All these coalesced to produce the second edition and my opportunity to be read by thousands. At this, I seemed to see thousands of eyes staring at me. How can I not be grateful? But how can I not be afraid? These eyes of thousands may be filled with encouragement, trust, and expectations; or they may be filled with censure, demands, or, more likely, anger.

Here in my study, the ashtray is crammed with cigarette butts and the air is permeated with smoke, but in my mind, thousands of piercing eyes emerge. These two scenes are superimposed one on top of the other, as in a surrealistic nightmare from which there is no escape. But fear is only fear. Come to think of it, I really need to cogitate and work my pen with trepidation—under the glare of the multitude! I may draw the attention of still others, but that is what I yearn for.

"Hao ji qian ren de yanjing a! Zaiban xu" (*The eyes of thousands!* Preface to the second edition), August 2, 1974, in Huang Chunming, *Shayonala, zaijian* (Sayonara, goodbye) (Taibei, 1977), pp. 31–37.

—Translated by Raymond N. Tang

Wang Zhenhe

WANG ZHENHE (Wang Chen-ho, 1940–1990, from Hualian, Taiwan) enriched Taiwan's nativist *xiangtu* literature with his own peculiar style of burlesque humor. A staunch promoter of native Taiwanese culture in all forms, he turned down a chance to study abroad; it was not until the early 1970s that he ventured abroad to attend the International Writing Program at the University of Iowa, at the urging of Nie Hualing. After graduation from college, Wang Zhenhe taught English in a high school and worked at a variety of jobs for airlines. After 1969, he worked for a time as a censor for a local television network, being already a specialist on Western films. He began to write in 1960, at first under the Western modernist influence, but his plays, short stories, two novels, and volume of essays have since taken the *xiangtu* path. Wang Zhenhe's prose is mostly about ordinary people in his hometown of Hualian, on Taiwan's sparsely populated eastern shore.

In 1984, Wang Zhenhe produced a grotesque novel about a newly opened brothel in his hometown. Below he talks about this book to the writer and journalist Qiu Yanming. Wang Zhenhe died in 1990 of throat cancer, after many years of suffering.

Things Chinese and Foreign, Ancient and Modern

An Absurd Comedy

Wang Zhenhe

QIU YANMING: What motivated you to write this novel [*Rose, Rose, I Love You (Meigui Meigui wo ai ni)*]?

Wang Zhenhe: I had wanted to write this novel for ten, twenty years. I remember the first time American GIs came from Vietnam into Hualian by ship, for R & R. The whole town buzzed with activity. Some made preparations to welcome them, some were busy with schemes to make American dollars, and news of the GIs' arrival dominated newspaper headlines and gossip columns. The whole town was decked out and in a festive mood. The ultimate eye-opener for the Hualian locals was the appearance of a bar. A bar! Hualian folks had never even heard of one, let alone seen one. At that time I was still young, and I went there for a look with my mother. We lived on the street where the bar was; out of curiosity, I went there every night to "broaden my mind." The bar was built of bamboo. The bargirls plying their trade inside were so outrageously bold that we Hualian yokels were stunned. The "Look at me now!" kind of lascivious air they displayed, riding in pedicabs, and the swagger of the American GIs and MPs as they paraded about inside and outside the bar, left a very deep impression on me. From that time on, I wanted to write about this big event in a small town; I tried to do so several times, without much success until now. The American GIs in Vietnam did indeed go to Hualian for R & R, and Hualian did indeed set up a bar for their "urgent" needs. My novel is about how the bar was built. But the process of setting it up, the characters, and several episodes are all fictitious. I couldn't help but make them up, since I was not fortunate enough to join the "honored" ranks of bar-builders at the time.

Qiu: Although you had been conceptualizing the novel for a long time, you didn't start the actual writing until two years ago. During the process of writing, did you keep revising it? Is there a large gap between your original conception and the final product?

Wang: Yes, there is a very large gap. I feel that of all my novels, this is the one that has given me the most trouble; I had to rack my brains over how to write and develop each chapter. Originally, I planned to start with how prostitutes were trained to be bargirls, then go on to how the bargirls "serviced" the American GIs when they arrived, and how the bar owner "exploited" the bargirls. Once I put pen to paper, however, I made sweeping changes and ended up concentrating on the gestation of this bar that gave all the Hualian folks such a jolt of novelty. Also, at first I had planned to use only the point of view of the teacher, Dong Siwen. Then I found this viewpoint too restrictive; my pen was pinned down fast. I thought to myself, why be so "masochistic"? So I had an enlightenment: there is no bright mirror standing after all![1] That's why, in a few of the chapters, I totally ignored the point of view of the farting Dong Siwen. Instead, I used conversations between Big Nose Lion, the pimp, and Ahen, the prostitute, to advance the plot. Once I let go, I found my writing to be more animated and multifaceted. As to whether my attempt here works or not, I will have to ask the gentle reader to enlighten me. . . .

[Qiu expresses appreciation for Wang's approach.]

Wang: I hope the gentle reader agrees with you. One more thing: once I woke up and adopted a "free-for-all" kind of viewpoint, I felt very liberated. I was able to mix "Chinese and foreign, ancient and modern" (i.e., Japanese with Taiwanese, and archaic language with contemporary speech) for contrast; maybe this creates a comic effect of absurdity better than would a traditional approach.

Qiu: In your novel, we can see "natural development meticulously crafted"; this takes great technical control.

Wang: Your praise is too generous. Look, even this very thick-skinned face of mine is all red! When I worked on this novel, I ran into problems with every single chapter; the reason is that in every chapter I hoped to give the reader something new. For example, in the first chapter I wrote about the bargirl training class holding a solemn opening ceremony in a church; in the second, I wrote about a candidate for county assemblyman providing a striptease exhibition at a campaign meeting devoted to his political platform; in the third chapter, I wrote about the brothels and the selection of bargirls. In each, I strove to aim at "unprecedented novelty," to surprise the reader in various different ways. As a result, I spent a lot of time on each chapter. Sometimes I would keep tinkering

---

[1]Wang Zhenhe alludes to a well-known poem attributed to Huineng in Chan (Zen) Buddhist lore, on the mental, ephemeral nature of supposedly "real" obstacles to enlightenment: There never was a Bodhi Tree / nor bright mirror standing. / Fundamentally, not one thing exists / so where is the dust to cling? In *The Way of Zen*, trans. Alan W. Watts (London, 1965), p. 112.

away for a month, two months, just to try to get the opening of a chapter right. Whether the effect achieved is what I anticipated is not for me to say.

Qiu: In this novel, you made a kind of breakthrough in language, too. Your mixed diction, with its "Chinese and foreign, ancient and modern" elements, presents the novel's milieu, its time and place, very vividly and precisely.

Wang: I tried my best to represent the language of a particular age. During the period in which the story is set, the Japanese, Taiwanese, and Mandarin used in Taiwan were different from the Mandarin and Taiwanese used today, in 1983–84. I thought that a contrastive approach might delineate that period vividly.

Qiu: What makes this novel different from your previous works, which deal with the plight of the "little man," is that its protagonist is a "teacher"—an intellectual. Does this have any special significance?

Wang: When I represent characters, I don't make it a point to laud or condemn them. Each one is right in some ways, wrong in others. I think most of us modern men are "middle people," and I'm interested in writing about such "middle people" with their muddled mixture of right and wrong, wrong and right.

I've often heard that "scholars ruin a nation," and I've also heard the phrase "scholars save a nation." Which is true? My impression is that sometimes intellectuals do speak the unadulterated truth; in particular, their noble sense of mission to better the world is so touching that it can bring tears to one's eyes. But then, sometimes, their learning makes them cocksure. They're often unaware that what they say and what they do are wrong; their errors may in fact be egregious, misguiding society. Even more commonly, before the outcome of something becomes clear, what intellectuals say about it can appear right and wrong at the same time. What role intellectuals play in modern society is not an issue that my novel intends to discuss. What I'm interested in and attentive to is really their nature as "middle people."

Qiu: So, in your novel, things like brothels and bargirls are just a backdrop.

Wang: Yes, a backdrop for working out issues.

Qiu: Issues?

Wang: Only when there are issues is there material for a novel. From the time of the arrival of the American GIs and the setting up of the bar, many thought-provoking social issues are generated.

Qiu: For example?

Wang: The heartless rapacity that industrial, mercantile society fosters.

Qiu: Has your wife read this novel?

Wang: She can't get through it. Shufan, after reading it, said it had vision, but my wife still hasn't finished it; in fact, she refuses to finish it. She says, "What vision? The more I read it, the more I dislike it. What's the matter? How come you keep writing such off-color stuff?" Sometimes my little daughter, seeing me writing, will come by; she takes one look at my work, says "You old goat!" and runs off. I'm sure some others, especially women readers, must share this view, that novelists needn't always write about "that," that novel writing should after all be "respectable" and "edifying." But to a writer of fiction, all angles are important. If he is convinced that writing from a particular angle is the most effective way to make the characters credible and striking, he should have the courage to ignore all the berating and hold on to that. And the lady or gentleman reader should have the magnanimity to give the writer this freedom to express and create.

Qiu: From your first novel, *Ghost, North Wind, Man (Gui, beifeng, ren)*, to the current *Rose, Rose, I Love You*, what changes have you experienced in your feelings about writing?

Wang: Let me borrow a passage from Hemingway: Hemingway said something to the effect that for a real writer, every one of his books should be a brand-new beginning in his endless effort to develop his talent. He must try his best to do what he has never done before, or what other people have attempted but failed to attain. This is well said. I think every fiction writer should have such a frame of mind, hoping that every one of his works is different from the last, a breakthrough, a fresh beginning, a new challenge. Whether he succeeds is another matter, but every writer should have this aspiration and make this effort.

I, too, would like to do my utmost to make myself different from before. Have I accomplished it? This is for the reader to judge.

One more thing: I am drawn more and more to comic subject matter, to stories that make people laugh. For example, in the film script for "An Oxcart for Dowry" (*Jiazhuang yi niuche*), almost every scene is funny; the sadder it is, the more I reminded myself to put laughter in.

Qiu: Why are you partial to laughter?

Wang: Maybe it's because I experienced so much adversity in my life. Ozu Yasujiro, the Japanese director, was never married, and his life was filled with pain and misfortune, but all his films are paeans to the happiness and fulfillment of family life. I don't know how to put it; maybe because I have witnessed too many heartrending things, I keep hoping: Let there be a little more laughter on earth, if only a tiny ripple. Even a little would be good!

* * *

Laughing, we finished our hot lemon tea; laughing, we left the place where we had talked. Before we parted, he told me, his full face still showing a slightly toothy smile, "I am thinking of writing a novel about an old man who has absolutely nothing but is determined to go on living. Why does he go on living? Because he is alive. All his relatives and friends who have passed away are living on in his heart and so are still on earth with him. If he dies, these people will die with him. So he tries everything in his power to attain eternal life. This, too, is a tale of both laughter and pathos. I hope to be able to write it and share it with my readers."

Qiu Yanming, "Ba huanxiao saman renjian: Fang xiaoshuojia Wang Zhenhe" (Scattering laughter throughout the world: An interview with the novelist Wang Zhenhe), in Wang Zhenhe, *Meigui Meigui wo ai ni* (Rose, Rose, I love you) (Taibei, 1984), pp. 269–78.

—Translated by Sau-ling C. Wong

Chen Yingzhen

CHEN YINGZHEN (author prefers Chen Ying-Chen, b. 1937, in Taibei County) is one of very few local Taiwanese intellectuals to have spoken out publicly in favor of the reunification of Taiwan with the mainland on the grounds of a common cultural heritage. During the early phase of his creativity, Chen, having higher education and a Christian background, wrote a kind of romantic and existentialist prose about the fate of intellectuals. Like the early Bo Yang, he also exposed the complex relationship between Taiwan's mainlander establishment and the local Taiwanese population. From 1968 to 1975, he was incarcerated for his leftist convictions, which the KMT government viewed as an unpardonable threat at the time.

From 1977 on, he attacked "Westernization" and called for a "national style." In this later phase, Chen's fiction and essays concentrated on social problems, particularly in his "Washington Building" series, which satirizes U.S.-based multinational corporations and their Taiwan hangers-on. Many readers were disenchanted, having found better literary quality in his earlier writing. In the 1980s, Chen Yingzhen also launched the much admired journal *Renjian* (The world), a sort of Taiwanese *National Geographic* with glossy photo essays, but having a sharp social and environmentalist focus. The journal finally had to close down in 1989, due to declining interest on the part of Taiwan's newly affluent society.

In 1988, Chen Yingzhen published his collected works, in fifteen volumes. He lost much of his political support at home after the Peking massacre of June 4, 1989, when he made a high-profile trip to the mainland, where China's postmassacre leadership was only too eager to publicize his unreconstructedly rosy views about bringing Taiwan back under a mainland government.

Chen Yingzhen wrote the following article under the pen name Xu Nancun, the better to analyze critically his own earlier writing from a third-person perspective. The text seems to mirror his new literary credo.

Against Taiwan's "Orphan Mentality"

The Author as His Own Critic

Chen Yingzhen

September 26, 1975

IN ESSENCE, Chen Yingzhen is a writer of the small-town intelligentsia.

The small-town intellectual occupies a kind of middle status within today's social class structure. During times of economic prosperity and abundance of opportunity, these small intellectuals easily climb to the top and derive no small benefit from the higher social classes. When the economy is stagnant and opportunities are few, however, they inevitably sink to the bottom of the social ladder. When their rise to the top is smooth, they are high-spirited and glow with vitality; when they find themselves on the way down again, they often seem demoralized, depressed, and indecisive. Chen Yingzhen's early works express the profoundly sad state of mind of the small-town intellectual caught in this kind of situation. His father was born into a rural family that had fallen on hard times; by dint of hard work and self-cultivation, he became an intellectual and moved to town. In 1958, Chen Yingzhen's foster father passed away, and his family's financial situation abruptly deteriorated. The misery of this decline left deep scars on the impressionable youth. The pale-green tone of his early works can be attributed largely to these dark memories of the family's fall from grace, together with the hardships and feelings of failure and humiliation they engendered. When we read "My Younger Brother Kangxiong" (*Wo de didi Kangxiong*, 1960), "Hometown" (*Guxiang*, 1960), "The Dying" (*Sizhe*, 1960), and "Grandfathers and Umbrellas" (*Zufu he san*, 1960), we can feel how much these stories are steeped in the grief, the humiliation, and the bitterness of this kind of poverty. The author never did understand that, given the ebb and flow of capital accumulation in an industrial and commercial society, above all in a developing country, the decline of the small town and its petty tradesmen is a nearly inevitable law. He never understood how to look at the decline of his family and himself in light of the overall social situation. Nor did he ever learn to associate their decline with that of his country and his people. Instead, he only felt sorry for himself, all wrapped up with his own lonely and brittle little heart, a heart that bled green blood. And so he became a man who retreated, who ran away. He fled from everything that might puncture that sensitive heart of his, including the hometown that had given him birth and raised him. He sent himself into exile, into exile from the vitality of real life. . . .

Chen Yingzhen, stifled by the difficulties and humiliations of poverty, closed himself off, rejecting even the hometown that had been like a mother to him. His unhealthy suffering well exemplifies the weak, excessively self-centered pallor and unrealistic nature of the small-town intellectual.

But sometimes the small-town intellectual, stuck in this situation and frustrated by his decline and lack of opportunity, will have the consciousness and enthusiasm to reform the world.

Wu Jinxiang in "The Village Schoolteacher" (Xiangcun de jiaoshi, 1960), Kangxiong in "My Younger Brother Kangxiong," the elder brother in "Hometown," and Judas in "The Story of Judas Iscariot" (Jialüeren Youda de gushi, 1961) were all once enthusiastic about building a better and a happier world. However, the small-town intellectual, because of his in-between social status, is tied in hundreds of subtle ways to the upper classes who want to maintain the existing social order. He cannot completely identify with the lower classes who hope to reform the status quo. Therefore, his reformism cannot help but be incomplete and illusory. Kangxiong's idealism exemplifies this.

The incomplete and illusory character of small-town intellectuals' reformist talk becomes apparent also in the contradiction between what they know and what they do. Their thinking is often inconsistent with their actions—in fact, they may even cancel each other out. This contradiction marks their activities from the start with uncertainty, inertia, and despair.

Characters such as Kangxiong; the phony scholars in "The Comedy of Narcissa Tang" (Tang Qian de xiju, 1967); Wu Jinxiang; the elder brother in "Hometown"; and Zhao Ruzhou in "Migrant" (Yi lüse zhi houniao, 1964) show how the actions of the small-town intellectual are usually ineffectual. The gap between words and actions never ceases to prick their irresolute and sensitive consciences and burden them with pain and guilt; it causes them to stifle and mute themselves; and in the end, it turns them into the kind of person they had once completely rejected. They have fallen. Heaven crushes them, plunges them into the abyss where they turn into evil demons, until finally they are annihilated. The nihilist Kangxiong, who believes that he has rejected all existing value systems, is in fact tightly bound by the very rules of morality he has rejected. Because he cannot alleviate the pain arising from this contradiction, he poisons himself. Zhao Ruzhou, who once considered himself a Fabian socialist striving for social justice, in reality cruelly abandons both his wife, from an old-fashioned arranged marriage, and a Japanese woman named Setsuko. Afterward, he lives a life of callous venality, and finally, in old age, becomes senile and ends as a madman. The village school teacher, Wu Jinxiang, begins with disillusionment, proceeds to degeneracy, and ends up going mad and killing himself. The elder brother in "Hometown" who seeks truth in Christianity also ends up turning into a wretch, indulging himself in gambling and women and ruining his life.

During a period of historical transition, the in-between social status of small-town intellectuals often makes them the first to foresee the birth of the new from the ruins of the old. In early works by Chen Yingzhen like "Such Old and Feeble Tears" (*Neme shuailao de yanlei*, 1961), "The Dying," "The Sun Still Shines" (*Wuzi zhaoyaozhe de taiyang*, 1965), and "Migrant," we see a world that is disintegrating bit by bit. Yet once in a while Chen Yingzhen manages, with great difficulty, to build a tiny little fire that will bring a little light and warmth into this dark and despairing world. The mentally ill person in "Poor Poor Dumb Mouths" (*Qican de wuyan de zui*, 1964) has a dream about "a dark room" with "not a single ray of light, and a thick mold growing on everything," and yet the many lethal wounds on a woman's corpse change into the mouths of humankind that cry out, "Open up the windows, let the light shine in!" In the end, the darkness is broken, and "the light shot in like golden arrows."

In "A Clan of Generals" (*Jiangjun zu*, 1964), two low-life characters who have fully experienced failure and humiliation project a life of light and blessings onto a mysterious and unknowable future world—their next life. The world of "Migrant" is one in which "the fish live in a pool that is gradually drying up, and although they still energetically flap their gills and move their mouths, every second brings them closer to death and putrefaction." And yet Chen Yingzhen describes the son of the despairing and dry-as-ashes Ji Shucheng as follows: "The child started to play by himself in the courtyard. Sunlight flickered brilliantly upon his face, his hair, his hands, his feet." When one compares this with his description of the long, cold, rainy night, how feeble and ridiculously abrupt Chen Yingzhen's "sunlight" seems—it is as if a painter, taken aback at the mournfulness of his own tones, had forced himself to add a few strokes in a brighter color.

The small-town intellectuals in Chen Yingzhen's short stories all harbor this bitter grief of ineffectual atonement and self-annihilation; they gaze intently at the dawning of a new historical age. During periods of historical transition, the only salvation for a small-town intellectual is to get involved in concrete practice and work diligently toward his own reform, breaking once and for all with the old world of endless attachments, and plunging into a newer age. However, not a single small-town intellectual in Chen Yingzhen's world actually stands tall amid the stormy winds and surging waves of practice. It may be that objectively speaking, these kinds of characters do not exist; but this is also an expression of the demoralized character of the ordinary small-town intellectual and of Chen Yingzhen himself.

Anton Chekhov was one of the most skilled of all authors at depicting the weakness, despair, melancholy, self-abandonment, and ennui of unattached intellectuals during a period of social transition, as well as their feeling of ineffectuality toward the new things that press in closer and closer. The pallid and melancholy coloring of Chen Yingzhen's early short stories is very Chekhovian. When it comes to beauty and depth of expression, however, Chen Yingzhen is of course a long way from Chekhov.

In 1966, Chen Yingzhen began to submit manuscripts to the *Literature Quarterly*. After that, his style underwent a sudden change. Actually, if we read the works from the end of his first period very carefully, the ones he submitted to *Modern Literature* between 1961 and 1965, we can see traces of his turning toward a new style.

After 1966, the Chekhovian melancholy disappears. Satire and realism take the place of the sentimentality and dispirited self-pity that had characterized his work for so long. Rational scrutiny replaces emotional reaction; cold, realistic analysis takes the place of agitated, romantic expression. When Chen Yingzhen begins to use satire, when he begins to use reason to observe things carefully, he lets go of his melancholic and painfully frustrated denial of the world he lives in. He has now learned to adopt an even higher perspective—colder, more objective—and as a result, he begins to probe even deeper into the objects around him. His works of this period pretty much lack the dark and obscure style of his early works. His consciousness of problems also seems to be clearer, and he seems capable of greater breadth. This period, however, is still just a beginning for him; he is still in a stage of groping and experimentation. All we can say is that between 1959 and 1965, Chen Yingzhen broke out of a very long period of melancholy. I am afraid it would be premature to make any further judgment now.

Another special characteristic of Chen Yingzhen's stories regards his subject matter: he exhibits interest and concern in the life stories of the mainlanders who live in Taiwan and in relations between those who are not in Taiwan permanently and the Chinese who are native to the place.

Aggression against China over the past several hundred years by both old and new varieties of imperialism has had a far-reaching and complicated effect on the country. Taiwan Province, China's southeastern gateway, has experienced the evils of Eastern [Japanese] and Western colonialist rule even more acutely. The fact that it has suffered all sorts of colonial occupation—partial and complete, short-term and long-term—has resulted in its frequent separation, historically speaking, from China. The fifty-year colonial rule of the Japanese was the longest. During that lengthy occupation, Japan carried out the reforms necessary for Taiwan to be brought into the economic sphere of Japanese imperialism; hence, Taiwan was divorced from Chinese society, in both its traditional and modern aspects, very early on. Given this historical background, the 1945 retro-cession [to China] and the flight of the Kuomintang government to Taiwan in 1949 led to a wide-ranging contact in Taiwan between societies, economies, politics, and cultures from both sides of the Strait that were at very different stages of development. For the past thirty years, this contact has continued to push forward a process of perpetual mutual accommodation, reorganization, and joint development.

Chen Yingzhen, interested in how the process was mirrored in people's lives, was, to begin with, deeply interested in the past lives of the emigrant mainland-ers on Taiwan. Beginning with his story "Such Old and Feeble Tears," and continuing in others that portray both mainlanders and natives of the province, like "The Document" (*Wenshu*, 1963), "A Clan of Generals," "The Last Day of Summer" (*Zuihou de xiari*, 1966), and "My First Case" (*Diyi jian chaishi*, 1967), Chen Yingzhen captured tales of the mainlanders that he, who was born in Taiwan in 1937 and who led an uneventful life ever after, found fascinating. In Chen Yingzhen's world, the mainlanders have endless, unbroken memories. In their distant, faraway homeland, they once had wives, lovers, and old friends who still haunt their dreams. They have memories of the mountains and rivers of home; of the upheaval, exile, and suffering they have experienced; and of vast properties and towering mansions they once owned. They had glory in the past and suffer spiritual or material decline in the present. How the dramatic birth-pangs of twentieth-century China, crisscrossed with invasions and revolutions and moving into a more modern period of its history, have affected the main-landers living in exile in Taiwan—this is the interest Chen Yingzhen finds in these stories that transcends the oddity of the tales themselves.

When, before 1949, premodern China came into contact with Taiwan, a prov-ince that had been modernized and made capitalist by certain of the colonial policies of Japanese imperialism, problems arose between the mainlanders and the [Taiwan] natives. On the one hand, because the natives had so long been isolated by Eastern and Western and old and new imperialism, they could not really understand the China that was leaping from a premodern society to a modern one; they could not see the true face of China, which was hidden by the upheaval, underdevelopment, and misery that were inevitable in a country mov-ing into a modern era of history. And so their own pure small-town nationalism and patriotism were shattered and sent into reverse by the earth-rending upheav-als as China moved toward national independence and freedom for its people. This loss of their own place and direction in the torrent of modern Chinese history led some to feel that they [the people of Taiwan] were the "orphans," the "foundlings," and the wounded of Chinese history. That led them down the path of separatism [Taiwan Independence].

Some of the mainlanders, for their part, carried over from history the evils of continental Great Cathay chauvinism. This, too, contributed to the growth of separatism [among the Taiwan natives, in reaction].

To depict personal relationships between mainlanders and Taiwan natives, Chen Yingzhen places them in a social system that has never recognized a distinction between mainlanders and natives; letting his characters be social beings rather than regional types, he develops a complex drama of life. Three Corners and Little Skinny Maid in "A Clan of Generals" are completely wrapped up in each other because both of them are social rejects. We see this in the relationship between Mr. Kang and Ajin in "Such Old and Feeble Tears" (also between Hu Xinbao and Xuxiang in "My First Case"), and in the relationships between the Taiwan small-town petty propertied people who live within the heavy curtain and the multitude of laboring people outside of it in "The Sun Still Shines." The contrast between the weariness and prostration of the propertied people and the unimaginable vitality of the disinherited comes about because Chen Yingzhen's pen goes to the very roots of society, erasing regional differences.

As China emerges, dashing toward historical modernity, we deeply hope that the contemporary literature, music, and art that every Chinese in Taiwan loves and is concerned about will bring those Chinese who are estranged, or face the danger of mutual estrangement, back into the fold, so that we can work together for the renaissance and revival of China. We also deeply hope that the younger generation of up-and-coming reformist Chinese writers and artists who grew up on Taiwan—whether mainlander or native—will be able to overcome the harmful intellectual residue left by Great Cathay chauvinism and colonialism old and new, as well as the sense of being an "orphan" or "foundling." Thus will we be able to reestablish our major role within Chinese modern history and spiritedly move forward.

Every period of history finds people scouring all forms of artistic creation for answers to the most urgent and pressing questions in their lives; for principles to guide their lives; for people whom they can believe in and identify with in a changing world; for the hopes and heartthrob of the people themselves that are concentrated in all types of art. Therefore, writers and artists must have a consciousness that is self-conscious and self-critical, modest and circumspect; they must work together and move forward as one with all other artists who want to devote their energies to a better and more egalitarian tomorrow.

On this basis, we can offer a preliminary evaluation of Chen Yingzhen. Now in the 1970s, our up-and-coming reformist literature has clearly matured. In debates about modern poetry, social and national character were advocated for literature; stories appeared from authors such as Huang Chunming that embraced the vast ranks of the laboring people.[1] The magazine *Literature Quarterly* pointed the way to a literary path that was social, critical, and patriotic. These new literary events make it clear that a number of our outstanding reformist

---

[1] In 1975, words like "proletariat" and even "workers" were too sensitive to be freely used in print in Taiwan.

writers have enough life force and vital energy to transcend the melancholy and demoralization of the small-town intellectuals depicted in the early works of Chen Yingzhen. We hope that this criticism will not only be of value to Chen Yingzhen,[2] but also help the younger and better writers who are bound to surge forth.

Xu Nancun [Chen Yingzhen], "Shilun Chen Yingzhen" (Preliminary critique of Chen Yingzhen), September 26, 1975, in *Chen Yingzhen zuopin ji* (Works of Chen Yingzhen) (Taibei, 1988), 9:3–15.

—Translated by Beata Grant

---

[2]The unmentioned reason for the gap in Chen Yingzhen's literary career was his political imprisonment. He was released from his ten-year sentence in September 1975, the date of this writing, during a general amnesty following the death of Chiang Kai-shek.

Wang Tuo

WANG TUO (Wang T'o, b. 1944) comes from a family of fisherfolk who live near Taiwan's northern harbor city of Jilong (Keelung). He has taught high school and Chinese literature at the college level and, since 1970, penned two collections of short stories, as well as a volume of literary criticism. Strongly defending *xiangtu* literature as Taiwan's only legitimate tradition during the 1977 literary debate, Wang Tuo redefined it as a broad "realist literature" no longer strictly confined to writing about the island's impoverished peasants. His own writings often treat of Taiwan's petty intellectuals as well as rural life, and particularly the life of Taiwanese fishermen.

From 1979 to 1984, Wang Tuo was imprisoned by the KMT government in the wake of the Gaoxiong incident, which occurred just as he was attempting to run for office in a local election. During his prison term, he wrote two novels, including *Taibei, Taibei* (1981). In the local elections of 1989, Wang ran for office again, aspiring to become mayor of Jilong.

Wang Tuo delivered the autobiographical speech below during a visit to the United States. It reveals that literature was already only his second profession. The abandonment of literature for the socially "more relevant" role of political activist is a path chosen by Yang Qingchu, Chen Yingzhen, and others, all the more so now that Taiwan's government is democratizing and allowing the formation of opposition parties.

Native Literature as a Stimulus for Social Change
From a Writing Career to Political Activism

Wang Tuo

November 1986, San Jose, California

BEFORE the *Formosa* (*Meilidao*) magazine episode, many young people would come to see me about literary things. The question they particularly liked to ask at that time was: "Mr. Wang, why did you leave the privacy of your study to go out into the streets? Why are you the only writer who gets involved in political movements?" ...

When I speak of literature, I feel a little ridiculous. Only after I graduated from college did I realize that I would become a writer. I'd never imagined such a thing when I was small. In elementary school, I thought I'd be satisfied to become a worker for the electrical company. That sounds funny to you, but I was quite earnest. Do you know why? Because in our little village of Badouzi, we were all very poor.

My family was especially poor. When it rained outside, it rained inside, too. Often we had no rice in the winter. When we did, we just ate rice gruel with salt. Those times were trying.

For the electrical workers, though, the situation was different. Our Badouzi had a power plant left behind by the Japanese. The workers' dormitories were very comfortable. The Japanese dormitories not only didn't leak, they had beautiful gardens. The electrical workers all had guaranteed wages, so they didn't have to worry about going hungry in the winter. We all went to school barefoot and wore clothes made from flour sacks. The children of the electrical workers were better dressed. In winter, they had cloth shoes to wear. We were all very envious.

That's why my greatest ambition was to be an electrical worker. That a child from a family like mine would have the opportunity to study in a university seemed a miracle. My mother was the one who made that miracle. Even though her life was arduous, she was insistent that if ever I had the chance to attend school, she must let me go. . . .

In those days, everyone who got into college wanted to study science and engineering. If a good student went into the social sciences, people thought that ridiculous. At the Jilong Middle School, everyone was going to study science and engineering, so although I wasn't very good, I wouldn't give up on it. I, too, would study science and engineering. The result was that I passed the exams and was admitted into the technology education department of Taiwan Normal University. After the first year, I found it very hard. I studied physics, chemistry, and calculus, without understanding any of it. The teacher would be up front lecturing, and I would be at the back, dozing off.

When I studied philosophy or literature, I got very interested, so I resolved to change departments. I was set on becoming a philosopher, but the Normal University didn't have a philosophy department, and I didn't have the money to attend National Taiwan University. I could only transfer into the Chinese literature department at Normal.

The Chinese literature department did teach Chinese philosophy; among its so-called classics, history, prose, and individual collections, the prose works were the same as in a philosophy department, so I enrolled.

Unfortunately, it was a little like boarding the wrong ship. The literature department at the Normal University was very conservative, like a pickling vat; many creative people were inside, but it was as if they were stuck in glue and couldn't get out. All the teachers were very pedantic and full of talk about the greatness of Chinese history, what China's five thousand years of history were like, and so forth. If you could have read the old books themselves, Chinese culture might indeed have seemed great, but listening to their lectures, you would think it quite awful; the effect was the opposite of what they intended. Chinese culture during the Warring States period really was glorious and creative, but those old geezers made it sound terrible. So I started to slip out of class early. Then I started not going at all. My first urge to write really came out of personal considerations.

Many people think that Wang Tuo writes only on behalf of society. Later, I really did have such designs, but when I started, I honestly didn't. Why did I start writing? First, because I was disappointed in love; feelings can have a great impact on a person. I was going off to the Hualian Middle School to teach at the time, and I was very depressed. The second reason I started writing had to do with the fact that I had just been a student myself. I knew that student thought was subjected to a lot of control, and I didn't want the students to retrace my path. So in class, I told them about my experiences. But the school would not permit this. For example, I would go to used book stalls and buy lots of copies of the journal *Free China* and distribute them to my students. During class, I would introduce the thought of Professor Yin Haiguang and other ideas at odds with official views. I also encouraged the students to set up a literary association. Some students in this association, at the Hualian Middle School, wrote about dark, somber things. They wrote about the dark things they saw around them, and as a result, a conservative group of teachers began to think that this guy Wang was starting to spread Communist thought. Why Communist? Because dark things would destroy Chinese culture, just like the Communist party.

Therefore, the Bureau of Investigation began to put me under surveillance. If you have read my early stories, you know there's one entitled "A Young Middle School Chinese Teacher." Of course, it's not entirely about me, but one section describes how an older teacher and I were treated. People were being spied on.

Then I was young, and not as daring as I am now. Young people have less courage and have been tested less. If they haven't encountered that sort of thing before, they are afraid. The trees outside the Hualian Middle School were planted all in a row. When the wind swept through the trees, they made the scary sound of *sha, sha* [like "kill, kill"]. We all were constantly suspicious that someone was spying on us. . . .

Writing is very difficult for me. It is like giving birth to a child that just refuses to come out. But as soon as you're done, you really feel like you're the greatest in the world—also that you're the most fulfilled person in the world, and the most satisfied. I believe that anyone who has had the experience of writing will understand this. Writing gives a person great satisfaction. A person who has suffered a lot, a very depressed person, can free himself and gain much comfort through literature. So I started to write.

My writing has gone through many different stages. The greatest change occurred when, not long after I'd begun writing, the Diaoyutai movement took place. I don't know whether the Diaoyutai movement was a big affair over here, or whether most people here participated in it.[1] The movement in Taiwan had a great impact on me. It *was* the domestic movement, not the one among Chinese abroad, that influenced me. It was because of the movement that I really started to believe that literature and society ought to come together. A lot of people who were concerned about Diaoyutai became concerned about politics and society in Taiwan as a result. I distinctly felt that democratic ideas were spreading very fast in Taiwan at that time, particularly through the readers of our magazine, *The Intellectual* (*Daxue zazhi*). In addition to the spread of democratic ideals, social consciousness was becoming widespread among young people.

I was very concerned about the plight of farmers and workers, so I wrote a lot of reportage for *The Intellectual* about laborers and fisherfolk. Amid that climate of social change, my reportage literature began to get me in trouble. The greatest problem came in 1975, when I published two articles in the journal *Taiwan*

---

[1]On the Diaoyutai movement, see Chen Ruoxi's essay in this book.

Political Review (Taiwan zhenglun). I published two pieces in the first issue. The first was an essay on the novel *Water Margin*. I wrote on the theme of people being driven to revolt by tyranny, and I discussed Song Jiang's leadership. To put it simply, I regarded the theme of the whole novel to be oppression that provoked rebellion. In my critique of the merits and faults of the heroes of Liangshanbo, I argued that the most important factor in the eventual collapse of the group was the faulty leadership line of the hero Song Jiang, who made the mistake of capitulating.

After the article was published, the Taiwan authorities found it objectionable because they felt that it created a theoretical basis for the opposition movement led by Kang Ningxiang and Huang Xinjie, and that it hinted at the idea that the *Dangwai* ("Nonparty") opposition was running for office because government oppression had driven them to such drastic action. They also said that I had dropped hints about a certain person in the *Dangwai* opposition; some guessed that it was [the former mayor of Taibei] Gao Yushu, because at the time he [though a native Taiwanese] had been turned around by the Kuomintang, with the promise of a cabinet ministership or some such. This was very much like Song Jiang's leadership line.

The most unfortunate thing about this article arrived two weeks after publication, when people on the mainland also began to denounce Song Jiang, because Mao Zedong had launched a movement to criticize *Water Margin*. People came looking for me, asserting that I was taking my cue from the mainland. I said I wasn't chiming in with the mainland's tune at all; Mao must be taking his cue from me! It's something I can make light of now, but it was very serious then. You were planted by the Communists all along, they said. No, I kept insisting, my article preceded the Communists'. If my article had come later, *then* you could say I was a Communist mole. Besides, my own and my students' notes from my lectures one year earlier, when I was teaching at National Chengchi University, showed that I was already criticizing Song Jiang then. My article was based on those notes, so the formation of my ideas preceded the article by a year, proving even more conclusively that I had no connection with Mao Zedong. That's what saved me. . . .

From that time on, until the polemics over *xiangtu* literature, I enjoyed my most prolific period, both in criticism and fiction. The editor of the literary supplement to the *China Times* had changed; Gao Xinjiang had already left. Gao was a great friend of mine. When he had me write an article, we wouldn't use my name. If my name were used too often, the Taiwan Garrison Command would telephone and stir up a lot of trouble. "We want very much to publish your work, but we can't use your name," he would say. So we would use my students' names, or mix up my own name when we used it. For example, we would omit some strokes from the character "Tuo," or call me Wang something else. Later, when the *China Times* changed editors, the new person didn't know the situation, so my name would appear regularly. Not only did they print my fiction, they printed short essays of mine weekly. Every time the general manager saw them, he broke into a sweat.

Whenever I think about this, I think how different my articles now are from the ones I wrote then. They're nothing compared to what I write now—so low-key that no one in Taiwan would want to read them today. But ten years ago, they were enough to make people freeze in their tracks.

Our articles were really nothing special. We just wrote the truth. That's what led to the polemics about *xiangtu* literature, for I had a lot of proposals: that literature must be connected to the soil and to the people from which it springs, and that it must concern society and contribute to its reform. I felt that literature must have this mission. I also advocated that literary movements be integrated with social movements; only then could literature play its fullest role. Such advocacies aroused fear among KMT literary bureaucrats. So they started the *xiangtu* literature debate; or rather, they began to lay siege to *xiangtu* literature. Today we speak of the "debate," or "war of argument," but in reality there was no war and no argument. In a debate or a battle, you challenge me and I respond; you hit me, and I kick you back. We interact; that's a debate. But in the *xiangtu* literature debate, there was no interaction. They could hit us till we were down, but we couldn't respond because they tied our hands. During the debate, many articles maligning or criticizing us were published, but articles on our side, those truly refuting them, were few, particularly in the newspapers. Only the *United Daily* published one of my pieces, which was directed against Peng Ge's attacks. I also had a piece directed against the current president of Taiwan University, Sun Zhen. Sun Zhen said it must not be published, so, in the end, the *United Daily* echoed that they couldn't publish it. When two people have an argument and one side won't let the other respond, that's really unfair.

The *xiangtu* literature debate greatly affected my point of view. It was one of the primary factors in my movement from literature to politics. Because I was publishing articles in the journal *Taiwan Political Review*, [*Dangwai* leader] Kang Ningxiang came to see me. How he noticed me I don't know. At that time we had no political connection, and indeed had just met. But Kang Ningxiang and Huang Xinjie had some sort of misplaced faith in me. The two of them kept saying, "If this young man, Wang Tuo, would go into politics, he'd make quite a stir." It was the year 1975, and the election of members to the Legislative Yuan was pending, so Kang asked me to join his campaign staff. "Then, next year, you can return to Jilong to run for the provincial assembly," he said.[2] But I was very frightened. Having received the kind of education we have in Taiwan, I was just not prepared to engage in politics. Although I had written those articles, to really go into the streets and make speeches frightened me, so I didn't dare accept.

---

[2]Although the "Republic of China" and "Taiwan Province" are practically coterminous, except for Quemoy, Matsu, and so forth, Taiwan has both national and provincial legislative assemblies. The national assemblies represent mainland provinces and therefore were partly frozen, until reforms in 1991.

However, after the literary debate, I thought to myself, "If you don't engage in politics, politics will sooner or later engage you."

I also took into consideration the limited demand for literature. Everybody said my work *Aunt Jinshui* (*Jinshui shen*, 1976), for example, was quite good, but in one year it had only sold five to six thousand copies. Everyone thought that five or six thousand was all right, but it couldn't compare with Kang Ningxiang's speeches in Taibei, which drew twenty to thirty thousand people at a time. How long would it take for my book to reach that many people? I thought and thought, and finally I decided it wouldn't do. I decided to learn from Kang Ningxiang. . . . I already knew that you needed two things to run for election: connections and money. I had neither, so I decided to examine my own strengths and weaknesses.

Perhaps some of you have read my *Voices from the Dangwai Opposition* (*Dangwai de shengyin*). This book was the first step in my election strategy. I wrote it in order to raise money and make a name for myself. Going out on my own to establish a reputation would have been very difficult. It's faster when you borrow someone else's prestige to raise your own.

I thought of people who were famous—Kang Ningxiang, Huang Xinjie, and the like. When I interviewed them, I had another purpose, too. Because the *Dangwai* opposition was scattered, it didn't give people the impression that it was a unified opposition. I thought I had to give the common people of Taiwan a sense of the unity of the opposition. And how? By interviewing these persons and gathering their opinions into one volume, as *Voices from the Dangwai Opposition*. This voice was very consistent, from beginning to end. So off I went. . . .

The book had the effect I'd intended. Naturally, Wang Tuo's name became quite well known. Many people were very happy with the book. I recorded all that the local celebrities had to say. Not only that, sometimes I even improved on them as I wrote. Everybody was happy with the result.

People would buy one or two hundred books at a time, especially during the election. They were not as courageous as nowadays. People said they supported Wang Tuo, but who had the courage to support him openly with money? They didn't dare, so they did it through stealth. Some bought a single volume for ten thousand yuan, others for twenty thousand, even thirty thousand. Thus did we raise the funds to overcome my first weakness, which was money.

Second, everyone was familiar with my book, and everybody knew Yu Dengfa [who was in it], so everybody knew Wang Tuo, too. They also came to associate me with Huang Xinjie. Thus, I obtained my second objective, island-wide recognition. After these books were out, I considered how I would establish my connections in Jilong. . . .

I gained much valuable experience from the political movement. First, when you are under the rule of the KMT and engaged in political struggle with them, you absolutely must not be frightened by their laws. Their laws forbid you to do all kinds of things. My belief is that we have the right not to follow unreasonable laws; indeed, we have a right to oppose them. There were many unreasonable laws out. I didn't abide by them; I flouted them, and they couldn't do anything but let me go. This is how we should react to the current bans on newspapers and on new political parties. We are not advocating violence. We are promoting laws that are fair and just.

My second valuable experience was learning that to engage in politics, you must have courage. When the secret agents come to your home to look for you or something like that, as they are doing right now, it's as much as to say, "I'm coming for you, are you afraid?" The more you show fear, the more they'll come after you....

[The government] knows I always "draw a blank," that nothing I do has any effect. But whatever they say about me, I'll change only if they go straight. They'll never be able to influence me through dirty tricks—isn't that clear enough? So they don't dare to give me one of those telephone calls.

They telephoned me just once, at the end of last year, when I was lecturing all over the island. I was on parole. They called me at home and I wasn't there, so my wife answered. A man said: "Tell your husband to be a little more careful. Otherwise, we might have to incarcerate him again." When my wife heard this, she naturally became quite nervous, and, seeing her, I became nervous, too. But I knew that this was not likely. They were just trying to scare me.

They had no pretext to arrest me, because those lectures were really nothing. Nothing I'd said could be construed as unacceptable. Of course, they might not have liked what I said, but I had never advocated subversion....

"Wo de wenxue jingyan yu zhengzhi jingyan" (My literary and political experience), a talk given to the Taiwan Research Society of San Jose, California, November 1986, in *Taiwan wenhua* (Taiwanese culture) (February 1987): 81–87.

—Translated by Juliette Gregory

Song Zelai

SONG ZELAI (Sung Tse-lai, b. 1952), like Lin Shuangbu, is a native Taiwanese from Yunlin and a man of strong convictions. Since his university days, he has paid only one brief visit to the United States, to participate in the International Writing Program at the University of Iowa. In strong opposition to the ruling mainlander establishment, he has concentrated on the promotion of a new Taiwanese "cultural consciousness" for his fellow countrymen. To him, Taiwan's four decades of mainlander rule have been nothing more than forty years of repression. A somewhat eccentric partisan of *xiangtu* literature, Song Zelai lives in the countryside and claims to be content to write "little books for ordinary people." His writing career began with short stories about the countryside and the rapid, often destructive social change caused by capitalism. He has been strongly influenced by the Chinese translation of Spengler's *Decline of the West*.

During the 1980s, Song Zelai became strongly attracted to Zen Buddhism as a spiritual alternative to the prevailing Taiwanese alternatives, like left-wing ideologies, blind negation of Chinese tradition, and uncritical Westernization. Yet he had considerable success with an ecological and dystopian novel called *Feixu Taiwan* (Taiwan in ruins, 1985). The political and cultural commentary of Song Zelai and his friends in the volume of essays he edited entitled *Shui pa Song Zelai?* (Who's afraid of Song Zelai? 1986) had, on the other hand, considerable influence on local politics and the forces advocating Taiwan Independence.

Song's essay below is a reaction to the dominance over Taiwan's literature and literary criticism of mainlanders. He attacks émigré writers like Bai Xianyong and derides works by authors such as Wang Wenxing as mere copies of Western originals. Thus, Song Zelai challenges the position of the eminent literary historian C. T. Hsia (Xia Zhiqing), who tends, in Song's view, to think of China's literary tradition as inferior to the West's—as having producing mere works of "regionalism." Song Zelai evidently hopes, with all this bombast, to foster new pride among native Taiwanese intellectuals, countering their allegedly deep-seated inferiority complex.

231

Cold Ashes in the Heart
The Tragedy of Taiwanese Literature

Song Zelai

June 8–10, 1981

Literature from the West, China, and Taiwan (Diary Entry of June 8)

I CONSTANTLY feel driven to re-enter the discussions on the status of Taiwan literature. No outsider is capable of understanding how urgently the youth of Taiwan desire to articulate their views. Admittedly, I do not have a profound grasp of literature from the West, China, or Taiwan; nor have I read more than a smattering of books about literature. I'm simply basing my discussion on direct observations—which nevertheless have come from my own writing experience and acquaintance with life, not from literary critics with their inductive analyses. Nor are my observations founded on the ready-made phrases of others; they are neither authoritative nor derivative. In my desire to articulate them, I shall accept all reproofs and repent all my errors, that my learning may grow to be as distinguished as yours.

In my opinion, present-day views on Taiwan literature make for a confused lot. Almost every spokesman on the subject is off in his or her own corner. The confused views on Taiwan literature that result are particularly pronounced among critics. Perched high in their storied towers, critics of today play with their pen and ink, gathering about them jewels of literary theory taken from others to claim as their own and to use in any way they see fit. If they themselves dare not confirm whether the theories are true or false, how can they use them to judge others? If they encounter somebody who disagrees with them, they smoothly wag their tongues in meaningless debate; what was rash enough at the outset becomes wholly reckless! Therefore, to understand correctly current literature in Taiwan, you must simply become a Taiwanese. That is not difficult: as long as you love this land, understand it, and persistently act in its behalf, it will reveal itself to you in its every blade of grass. How much more so, then, in its native literature. By extension, if you intend to be Chinese, you must possess concern, love, and understanding for China as it is today, treasuring its every blade of grass, its every hill and stream; only then will China become a reality to you. You must do the same to become a Westerner.

There's a fad nowadays of neglecting the concrete matters of life to peddle a false image of oneself as a wandering prodigal. Such people basically end up resembling no one at all; when discussing the people of Taiwan, they disparage them from the Chinese point of view; when discussing the Chinese people, they disparage them from the Western point of view. When they try to become Westerners, after discovering certain intractable differences of skin color and personality and finding themselves neither one nor the other, they end up only as clowns. It's the same in literature. To be sure, there are still many worthy scholars. I cannot view the world as wholly benighted just because most people nowadays seem caught up in this muddle. Therefore, without concealing my lack of erudition, I shall venture the following classification of our literati, according to their greater or lesser merits:

1. *Those who care about Chinese literature, study Western literature, and benefit Taiwan literature.* I often think how unfortunate are those who are born into today's China. Those able to keep their bearings will be few indeed—only those of superior conscience who can fully harmonize theory and practice. Can such people be found nowadays? I searched for a long time indeed before realizing that they could only be found among veteran literary scholars the likes of Hu Qiuyuan and Xu Fuguan. "Literature" to them cannot be compared with the literature that my generation is busy dividing into categories. Their literature is a matter of conscience and nothing else. All literature that suits the conscience of mankind and benefits its existence stands equal under heaven. This conscience has been the same for all sages and worthies since time immemorial; how can any literary work that derives from conscience be excluded? The virtue of Hu, Xu, and their like made a deep imprint on my young mind; I hold them in deep respect. Several years ago, when literati holding absurd views were attacking *xiangtu* literature, you may have noticed that Hu and Xu put up with many an affront as they forcefully refuted those outrageous viewpoints, taking on friend and foe alike. I saw their hands soothe this wounded land. Thus, I find that only they fully recognize literature's true significance and possess a profound grasp of literature from the West, China, and Taiwan.

2. *Those who seek benefit from Western literature and contribute to Taiwan literature, without forgetting Chinese literature.* I feel that the majority of those who have inherited the tradition of Taiwan literature fall under this category. They have devoted themselves body and soul to Taiwan literature, never for a moment smug or haughty, and have turned to both China and the West for edification. They include, counting from the period of the Japanese occupation

up until today, Lai He, Lü Heruo, Yang Hua, Yang Kui, Zhu Dianren, Wu Zhuoliu, Zhong Lihe, Zhong Zhaozheng, Huang Chunming, Chen Yingzhen, Wang Zhenhe, Yang Qingchu, Wang Tuo, Li Shuangze, Ye Shitao, Li Qiao, Dongfang Bai, Shi Mingzheng, and even literati as young as Hong Xingfu, Zeng Xinyi, Wu Renzhen, Xu Daran, Gu Mengren, Wu Sheng, Zhang Dachun, and Zhong Yanhao—all have inherited this virtue. From the works of Huang Chunming and Chen Yingzhen we have seen the flawless blending of the literatures of the West, Japan, China, and Taiwan; yet they will not halt their stride, for their attention is still riveted upon China and the lessons it can provide. The China that these writers see is not the China conjured up by the wild conjectures that surround us, for these authors are critical, reflective, and skeptical.

3. *Those who draw on Western literary standards to disparage Chinese literature, and use Chinese literary standards to diminish Taiwan literature.* I believe that many Chinese literati overseas are of this type. I have always felt that once such literati leave their home soil to seek a living abroad, they ought to carry on the spirit of our émigré Chinese laborers and recall the sweat and blood of those forebears. As they work vigilantly at their new jobs, it is only proper that their thoughts turn to the elders of their native land, and that they treasure the soil from which they have departed more than ever. However, looking into how things really stand, I've discovered again and again that the overseas literati actually have no such virtue. It's not enough that they constantly slight Taiwan literature. They don't even give Chinese literature fair consideration.

I'll give an example here that I shouldn't, and which I find embarrassing, but which nevertheless will explain what I'm driving at: C. T. Hsia. I hesitate, because Hsia is one of my seniors on the literary scene; a latecomer like myself ought not to take on such a person. Nevertheless, I must.

In his *History of Modern Chinese Fiction*, C. T. Hsia discusses the good and bad points of Chinese fiction in comparison with Western fiction. This is a large topic; only one with a great deal of learning would dare pronounce upon it. Drawing upon his enormous breadth of knowledge, Hsia has judged Chinese fiction inferior to that of the West on account of the restrictiveness of Chinese moral norms. Many scholars at once came forward with refutations; I will not repeat them. I only wish to say that Hsia is excessively conversant with the concept of original sin and deficient in his understanding of the norms of morality in Chinese culture. I wish Hsia would select but one volume of the Chinese classics—the *Four Books*, the *Lao Zi*, the *Zhuang Zi*, the Song-Ming Neo-Confucianists, or the Buddhist sutras—and then try to put its contents into practice! Perhaps by fits and starts he could investigate the complex distinctions between appearance and reality in the Buddhist canon, the ethical concepts of sincerity and reverence in the Neo-Confucian philosophers, the morality of human relationships expounded by ancient Confucians, or perhaps the idea of nonaction and the illusory Butterfly Dream in the Daoist classics. Let Hsia compare all these with the Western idea of original sin and then judge which is better. Liang

Shuming, with a vast knowledge of Eastern philosophy, never dared to judge Chinese philosophy inferior to its Western counterpart, and the prominent modern Western philosopher Spranger held Chan (Zen) Buddhism in highest esteem. Hsia's understanding of China equals Liang's, and his understanding of Christianity matches Spranger's, yet neither Liang nor Spranger used the West to diminish China. Why, then, does Hsia consider China inferior to the West? Merely to cause others to think Chinese fiction inferior to Western fiction is not so serious. But to cause Westerners to feel Chinese culture is inferior to Western culture is to mislead the younger generation and invite derision from those who know better. How much less would anyone doggedly agree with him that the *Journey to the West, The Romance of the Three Kingdoms, Water Margin, The Golden Lotus,* and *The Dream of the Red Chamber* are inferior to the novels of Westerners. These claims are self-destructive. Although they reveal Hsia's infatuation with Western literature, how much difference is there between infatuation and recklessness?

As Hsia's junior, it is not my place to say what I've just said. I'm not qualified to force people to understand fully the distinctions between appearance and reality or the ethical concepts of sincerity and reverence, either—how can I take another to task? Yet I must speak out on this. I must take issue with Hsia's repeated references to "haughty" views on the flourishing development of Taiwan fiction, still more with his outlandish view that Taiwan fiction is a product of "regionalism." I pray only that you knowledgeable scholars bring an open and broad mind to the study of literature, from whatever clime. Only then will your interpretations serve the best interests of both yourself and others; only then will your learning have a soul at its core.

4. *Those who specialize in imitating Western literature, do not study Chinese literature, and in their ignorance defame Taiwan literature.* This type thrives in today's environment, particularly among my generation. More than once have I seen an intellectual of my generation shut himself deep within his own labyrinth and flounderingly try to attach himself to a Western author, as if everything in the present age had somehow conspired to reject him. Having chanced to hear about some Western writer in the bookstalls, or by word of mouth, he'd get some crazy idea that he'd penetrated the writer's soul, then look upon him as a kindred spirit and become his disciple. He'd swallow the author's words whole like a date, pit and all, without any critical or skeptical reflection. Then he'd publish an article brimming with high expectations and self-confidence, referring to himself as "Taiwan's Joyce" or "Taiwan's Lawrence," and patterning himself after the one or the other in every thought and gesture. How absurd! When it gets to the point of looking askance at all literature but that of their idol, these literati not only view Taiwan literature with disdain, they oppose the works of the ancient sages and philosophers in toto. In their insular and impoverished mental lives, there is no literary history and no writers, not even any living people; there is nothing at all but an exaggerated view of the "self."

There is another type of irresponsible writer who doesn't really understand or put into practice the essentials of Chinese culture, and who doesn't seek to understand China's present situation, either. His mind is totally wrapped up in the Tang-Song epoch. Ask him what it is in the Tang-Song epoch that so obsesses him, and he'll say something like "Along riverbanks of willow blow morning breezes under a waning moon." China is thus transformed into a fairy-tale princess for him to pursue. Perhaps he will boast that he is a rich young bravo, a footloose traveler who leaves a trail of flowers behind him. This sort of talk is sheer nonsense, first-class tommyrot.

Yet another irresponsible type is the fellow who is unwilling to attend to concrete business. He has never planted so much as a blade of grass on this land, and he holds no hope for its future. All he sees ahead is the debris of smoky conflagrations; the scene in front of what originally were beautiful eyes gradually forms into a battlefield layered with smoke stretching up to the heavens. In food and dress, he is as affluent as any man about town, yet he paints and composes poems in the Chinese style, proclaiming loudly that he is a descendant of the dragon, a son of China, and interminably shouting out its name in woe. Sometimes I wonder if he's still living in the same world we are.

I believe that literati like Hu Qiuyuan, Xu Fuguan, and Yang Kui have acted appropriately. They have calloused their hands and feet in order to irrigate this great land. They have suffered their share of damage in the battles of this era, and the lessons they have learned are measured in blood and sweat. But my generation has so far done nothing for this land, though it recklessly desires to mount to the sky. How can we face up to the likes of Hu, Xu, and Yang? My brothers, enough of your slogans; if your hearts are ill at ease, try going down to the fields with the peasants. If your spirit cannot tear itself away from the Tang-Song epoch, try going into business. If you are a captive of Joyce, please come out of the labyrinth and return to your parents' side. Then you will enjoy a fulfilling life and be able to see Taiwan, a beautiful island with a beautiful literature. Both you and your readers will be the beneficiaries.

As I have said repeatedly, I only hope that the people of this land will treasure instead of denigrate themselves. When we reach a happy medium between self-effacement and arrogance and are grateful for our happy lot, then may we count our blessings.

Taiwan's Writers Must Unite (Diary Entry of June 9)

"Split"—this is a word that everybody who is well acquainted with Taiwan's history can explain. It is a word of shame in the history of Taiwan, yet it has existed alongside that history from the beginning until today.

Generally speaking, immigration to Taiwan has gradually increased since Qing times. One group after another has come to settle this land, bringing with them pronounced clannishness, and therefore frequent internecine feuding. And because the people who lived in this land were always under the control of others, the Qing dynasty encouraged these feuds in order to divide the Taiwanese against themselves and thereby more easily rule them. There have been feuds between different surname groups, between villages, and between Fujianese and Hakkas: so many that the power of the Taiwanese has become diffused. This was also true during the Japanese occupation; the Japanese encouraged the people of Taiwan to split into factions, which the Taiwanese were bent on doing anyway. Cultural organizations and political parties alike constantly split into factions over the least difference in opinion.

I have seen this type of situation occur again recently and will draw an example from the current literary scene. I've heard repeated rumors that somebody had the rash idea of splitting Taiwan's literature into northern and southern schools, and into "relatively nativist" and "not so nativist" tendencies. I find this to be a mischievous viewpoint, ignorant in the extreme, and only able to lead Taiwan literature toward tragedy. It seems the product of appalling narrow-mindedness and lack of confidence in Taiwan's literature. I even hear that this opinion was concocted by a certain group of literary critics; they must really be off their rockers.

I believe that literary critics have their own faults. They constantly draw on Great Han chauvinism to malign the previous generation of literati. One critic has gone to the ridiculous length of conjuring up an imaginary "history of Taiwan" supposedly written three hundred years in the future, with only a few pages on Taiwan literature, as if that were all our literature deserved. Yet no one was willing to dispute him. I find his opinion, too, very mischievous, enough to lead the seventeen million people of Taiwan and their literature into the abyss. This is truly absurd! This sort of thing is precisely what I've always loathed about Taiwan's literary critics. They have trampled to death every stand of literature our forebears ever planted. I only hope that you literary critics will stop to think exactly for whom you are speaking. If you are not speaking for all people currently in Taiwan, but are just busy marking off territories, petty kingdoms, or labyrinths for yourselves, then I wish you all a rapid descent into hell! Taiwan is just a small island; suppose we give it all over to you to rule as emperor. Within a few decades, you will be dead, and what good will it do you then? Why not use your consciences to watch over the next generation? See to it that they all live as happily as kings.

I've noticed recently that most Taiwan young people have united around the same views. Some who operate "*Dangwai* (nonparty) journals" (most of these "nonparty youth" are actually members of the Kuomintang) all think the same; they constantly seek edification about Taiwan's history from their political elders. Their humility is touching, and their motives are pure and impartial. Only among Taiwan's literati do we see far-fetched dreams still holding sway, especially among those wicked, stubborn, and opinionated literary critics. If we allow them to continue unrestrained, the outcome will be truly awful. I pray that a new generation of standard-bearers can arise and sweep Taiwan clean of them. Then the new generation would have hope.

We must unite! You literary critics must not forget that many people are laughing at you, even spitting on you, behind your back!

Raise High the Banner of Taiwan Literature[1] (Diary Entry of June 10)

According to my plan, today was to be my tenth day of writing. Having now cudgeled my brains, I've said everything I ever had to say. I'm studious, so I really can't think of anything else. I'm truly ashamed, having lost even my former modesty.

To sum up, I still expect great things from Taiwan literature. Today, Taiwan literature has arrived at an important juncture. Our writers all more or less understand their importance. For example, Huang Chunming knows that his four books are important; why else would foreigners want to translate his fiction? Chen Yingzhen, too, certainly understands that his "Washington Building" series of novels is very important; if it weren't, why would people weep hot tears after reading his novella *Clouds* (*Yun*, 1980)? Li Qiao realizes what he has attained in his *Cold Nights* (*Hanye*, 1980) trilogy, and Wu Sheng knows that his novel *Earth* (*Nitu*, 1979) has thoroughly explained the pain and bitterness of a whole group of people. Otherwise, why would he be invited to the International Writing Program at the University of Iowa? Hong Xingfu, Zeng Xinyi—all of them are in this class. Yet, they don't actually know that they've been sucked into a huge river current. Without that grand sensation, their sense of their own importance begins to waver when they hear other people deny it. Moreover, the critics, with their inadequate knowledge and wicked minds, zero in on the writers' weaknesses to attack them. For instance, the critics labeled Huang Chunming nostalgic, then accused him of reducing his characters to the level of dogs. They said that Chen Yingzhen was utopian, that Wu Sheng's poetry was prose—a whole lot of incredible nonsense. When you get down to it, the critic wants to rub you out, negate you, force you into submission, and furthermore negate the literary tradition and all literature by the Taiwan people. But now we know that all of us describe the people of Taiwan, and that all of us belong to a common Taiwan literary tradition. Huang Chunming epitomizes the Taiwan people's struggles over the past twenty years. Chen Yingzhen symbolizes hope for Taiwan's economy. Wu Sheng stands for Taiwan's rustic and unpretentious people. You critics can't eliminate us, for behind us stand the people of Taiwan; if you negate us, then you negate the Taiwan people and their literary tradition. So literary critics and outsiders had better lay off.

If I may speak more emphatically still, the literature of Taiwan has everything

---

[1]This phrase satirically mimics PRC slogans such as "Raise High the Great Red Banner of Mao Zedong Thought."

going for it; it lacks only an east wind. This east wind is a mutual recognition of the literary tradition. As soon as it blows with full force, Taiwan literature will triumph. There is no use in saying more; I would like to ponder all that I have said over the past ten days, for I know that I have let many people down. I repent before God: I was forced to speak, and therefore I am now willing to be silent. I shall just leave you with this word of encouragement: "If you wish to write, you must tread on firm ground."

"Liu yue ba ri: Xiyang wenxue, Zhongguo wenxue, Taiwan wenxue" (June 8: Literature from the West, China, and Taiwan), June 8–10, 1981, in Song Zelai, *Shui pa Song Zelai?* (Taibei, 1986), pp. 279–93.

—Translated by Patricia Da-yi Pang and Philip Williams

Lin Shuangbu

LIN SHUANGBU (Lin Shuang-pu, pseud. of Huang Yande, b. 1950) is one of several rebellious local Taiwanese writers to have abandoned "mainlander-occupied" Taibei. Lin has opted for life as a schoolteacher in his hometown of Yunlin. Beginning to write during the early 1960s, he became a regular contributor to several newspapers. Yet his multivolume oeuvre has been largely ignored by the critics in Taiwan and the United States most active in promoting Taiwan literature's international reputation. The KMT-dominated literary scene of the 1970s and 1980s, including the influential *feuilletons* of major newspapers, likewise refused to recognize writers as radical as Lin Shuangbu and Song Zelai.

The redefinition of one's identity can be elegantly expressed in Chinese by a change of pen name, the subject of the piece below. Lin had already written two dozen books under his first pen name, Bizhu, before he switched to Lin Shuangbu in 1980. He had gone through a crisis, apparently coming to doubt his literary talent and despairing of the limits of literature. For a time, he considered becoming a social activist and politician like Wang Tuo. Finally he decided upon a more direct expression of "Taiwaneseness" in his future writing. He documented his symbolic rebirth by renaming himself.

When I [H. M.] visited Lin Shuangbu to talk about this anthology, Lin practically declined to be included in any selection representing "Chinese writers," insisting that he be considered instead a "Taiwanese writer." However, his many allusions to famous Chinese poets such as Tao Yuanming show this to be a rather shaky cultural dissociation. The militant Taiwanese views of such as Lin Shuangbu and Song Zelai are widespread in southern Taiwan, but they send a chill down the spine of many citizens of the island.

Concern about the Native Land
On the Taking of a Pseudonym

Lin Shuangbu

June 27, 1980

1. Bizhu

THIS is the last time I'll publish under the name of Bizhu.

At the end of 1975, I said nearly the same thing. At that time, I was still exceedingly reluctant to part with it; I felt as if a knife were twisting in my heart. I was troubled and perplexed, as if losing a close friend that had shared all my hardships. And I was unable to choose which road to take next.

But now, as I say it again, four and a half years later, the pain is gone, and the bewilderment and confusion have faded. Although a feeling of sadness still vaguely hovers about my heart, it is already as distant to me now as a winter star.

This distinct change came about because I determined that Bizhu, or that person called Bizhu, was gradually being reborn with the passage of time. I was gradually able to discern more clearly my future path, and I believed I would have the ability and patience to follow it. This firm belief has allowed me at last to affirm that in 1980, I will be able to, or at least ought to, wave farewell to Bizhu.

It was in early autumn 1963 that I first submitted a piece for publication. It was my first year of junior high, at Tiger Tail Middle School. The publication to which I submitted my piece was a journal for young people called *Youth of Yunlin (Yunlin qingnian)*, put out by the Youth Salvation League in my home-town of Yunlin. In the beginning, I wrote under my own name. After publishing a few things, it suddenly occurred to me that I should be using a pen name. And why should such a thought come up? I'm sure I wasn't 100 percent clear about it myself at the time. When I think back on it now, I suspect it was only out of vanity; I felt that if I didn't have a pen name, I couldn't be a "writer."

What pen name would be most appropriate? Above all, I thought it should come from my real name, Huang Yande. In Taiwanese, the character *de* (virtue) is pronounced the same as the character *zhu* (bamboo). So I determined that my pen name must include the character *zhu*. Bamboo is green in color, so why not *Bizhu* (Green Bamboo)? But a pen name of only two characters wasn't sufficiently impressive, and it didn't stand out enough. Even the hero in Ye Hongjia's cartoons, Zhuge Silang, had a name with more than two characters. I decided to add two more. *Yan* (swallow), the second character in my name, is a kind of bird, but birds in a flock do not stand out. So let it be *Guyan* (Solitary Swallow)! Thus was the project completed: my pen name was Bizhu Guyan (Solitary Swallow in Green Bamboo).

I put it to use right away, in a piece that was published in *Youth of Yunlin*. I don't know whether readers at the time were impressed with this awe-inspiring and outstanding pen name. When I think about it now, it seems an outpouring of youthful sentimentality at best.

I used this four-character pen name once again, when submitting a piece to a similar publication. When it appeared in print, the four characters had become two! The editor had waved his big brush and gotten rid of the second half. At the time, I couldn't imagine why the editor had to cut me in half. Perhaps I didn't give it much thought, for having one's work published was already enough to addle the brain of a kid in his first year of junior middle school. Considering the matter from all sides, however, I felt that the two characters were actually no less attractive than the four characters. Besides, the amount of money you got paid had nothing to do with the number of characters in your pen name. Thus, I might as well go ahead with Bizhu! And so I did, through all the years of my youth. Ah, how time passes.

Together, that unknown editor and I inadvertently created a pen name that I would use continuously for the next eighteen years. Today, on June 27, 1980, I still have no idea which gentleman had primary editorial responsibility for the magazine then, but I sincerely thank him.

At the end of 1975, twelve or thirteen years after I had begun using this pen name, concern for my native land, its social conditions, and the future of my people suddenly made me feel that it was not enough just to be involved in literary creation. If I truly yearned to do the utmost for my country and my people, perhaps I had better at least run for public office. That would not be easy, since I had neither money nor influence and belonged to no political party or faction. The first solution I thought of at the time was to have my fellow countrymen get to know the real me, Huang Yande, not Bizhu. And so I let it be known that I would no longer use my pen name; I would publish under my real name.

In 1976 and 1977, I did publish a collection of essays under my own name. Although ceasing to use my pen name caused me quite a bit of pain, I gritted my teeth and endured it, for the sake of my ideals.

Since seeking fame and fortune did not come naturally to me, however, this desire to throw myself into public life did not last very long. By May of 1978, when I had finished my military service, I was already completely clear about the direction I wanted my life to take. I knew with absolute certainty the work to which I would dedicate myself. Just then, those stubborn old yearnings for the past resurfaced. In September of that year, when the Yuanjing Publishing Company printed my collection of fiction, *Give Me a Telephone Call* (*Bo ge dianhua gei wo*), I again used the pen name Bizhu.

I proceeded to restore this pen name to several other works that were already written but not yet published.

In the next year or so, because of my inability to break through the limits of my creativity, the grimness of my work environment, and the increased burden of caring for my children, I let my fountain pen lie empty and my writing paper fallow. In this long period of silence and emptiness, I went through a painful and confusing but profound self-examination. The philosophical bent to my thinking and the will power forged by many ups and downs pulled me through. In the end, I arrived at a new understanding of my creative life. I knew I had just passed through a long, dark corridor and that I was moving toward the light again. Because of this enlightenment, I was certain that I could say farewell to Bizhu. It would no longer be like being stabbed with a knife. I would no longer feel troubled and perplexed at giving it up.

Thus, my Bizhu period—eighteen years from start to finish—came to an end. I had started as a novice and now was established; within those eighteen years, I completed twenty-two books, nineteen published and three about to be. Now, late at night in the last days of June, with the wave of my hand, I bid farewell to those twenty-two volumes. When the day comes that I reexamine my past, perhaps I shall further edit those works. Of course, it's also possible that I'll let them remain as they are, to continue to circulate among my readers. No matter what, the Bizhu period belongs to my past.

In March of this year, I began working hard on a piece of about 130,000 characters. Moreover, I started using a completely new pen name, to publish in the supplements of the *Central Daily News*, *Zhonghua*, *Xinsheng*, *Taiwan*, and other newspapers. What is this new pen name? For now I don't want to say. If my works are good enough, you readers will know very soon. If my works aren't any good, why should you waste your time feeling sentimental remembering Bizhu?

2. Lin Shuangbu

After I had used the pen name Lin Shuangbu to publish twelve pieces, by chance I ran into Liu Jingjuan. The following four lines contain the conversation Liu Jingjuan and I had on the subject of this pen name:

"What does Shuangbu (Neither, Nor) signify?"

"I neither accuse heaven nor lay the blame on men."[1]

"Are you really so accomplished?"

"Not yet, but I hope to be in the future."

Three days later I ran into Ji Xiaotai. Ji Xiaotai asked me the same question. I've recorded our conversation below:

"Why do you want to be called Shuangbu?"

"Because I have no shame and I'm not afraid of doing anything."

"That's the worst kind of person of all. Later on, will you change to Shuangyao (Wanting Both)?"

"Probably not, because I'd never get them."

Looking superficially at these two bits of dialogue using conventional wisdom, there would seem to be quite a discrepancy. The first is relatively serious; the second borders on cynicism. But getting rid of the moral standpoint and looking at them in light of the theory of knowledge, they are absolutely the same. The point of similarity is that neither touches on the real meaning of Lin Shuangbu.

At the beginning of 1979, I at long last was able to buy a house in Yuanlin. Finally, I had the space for a tiny study. Twenty-nine years had passed since my birth, twenty-two since I began attending school, and already three and a half since my marriage. During every moment and every second of that long, slow, stretch of time, I had longed for a quiet place where I could study and write undisturbed. But the "bare cupboard" nature of my household finances and the unsettledness of my single life had never let me fulfill this desire. After marriage, my life did become more settled, but there was never enough space, whether we rented a house or lived in government housing. So when at last I was allowed a study of my own, my joy knew no bounds.

Since moving into my own "real estate" at the end of March 1979, almost every day after returning from work, bathing, and eating, I go up to the third floor and close myself up in my study. To sit surrounded by books is one of the pleasures of life, and so is letting one's pen fly across the page—still more, cogitating there in silence. When tired from my reading and writing, I go out and pace back and forth on the balcony, looking at the gray-green trees on the hill to the east.

As the time I spend inside and outside this room of ease and tranquility flows along, lines of Tao Yuanming's poetry often float into my consciousness, particularly "In the midst of churning waves, neither happy nor afraid." With great changes taking place everywhere, I am a speck of dust seeking neither name nor profit. What joy or fear could I know? With so many intimate friends devoted to literature, history, and philosophy traveling the road of life with me, again, what joy or fear could I know? In the vast ocean of books and people from all the ages, I am but one infinitesimal visitor passing through. What am I to be joyful or fearful about?

---

[1]Confucius's words to Zigong, in the *Analects*, 14:37.

One day in June of that year, while in my study, I suddenly thought of Su Shi's exile to Huangzhou: after building himself a house on an eastern slope, he styled himself "Dweller of the Eastern Slope." Ouyang Xiu's exile to Chuzhou also came to mind: to pass the time he amused himself with poetry and wine, and so styled himself the "Drunken Old Man." In a flash of inspiration (I thought), since I was full of neither joy nor fear, why not put myself amidst other men of letters and style myself "Shuangbu"? Hence my decision to write under the name of Shuangbu ever after.

In the week following, as I turned this pen name over and over in my mind, I came to feel that despite its unexceptionable artistic beauty and ingeniousness, it had a flaw—the two syllables lacked cadence, as if a surname or something were needed for perfection. After pondering the matter for several days, I decided to put the character *lin* (forest) in front of Shuangbu. There were at least five reasons in favor of it:

1. The syllables went together perfectly.
2. I was living in Yuanlin.
3. My ancestral home was Yunlin.
4. My mother's maiden name was Lin.
5. To live surrounded by forest, spring, field, and garden had always been my greatest wish.

Those were my reasons at the time. It was only in time that I discovered the many other levels of meaning the name embodied. For example, "don't take bribes or break the law," "don't pick the flowers or step on the grass," "don't lead youth astray or write irresponsibly," and so on. There is no end to them. Of course, if you readers wish to give your imagination full rein, I guarantee to "neither oppose nor take offense," and "neither interfere nor lose heart."

As time goes on, I have to tell myself that all great things have multiple meanings. Since my pen name has many meanings, I have to spur myself on unstintingly and write works great enough to match it.

"Biming erti" (Pen names—two comments), June 27, 1980, in Lin Shuangbu, *Yi zhan mingdeng* (A bright lamp) (Taibei, 1983), pp. 200–9.

—Translated by Natasha Wild

Huang Fan

HUANG FAN (pseud. of Huang Xiaozhong, b. 1950, in Taibei) was one of the most prominent Taiwanese writers active at the time martial law was lifted, in 1986. Huang Fan's literary development shows a transition from *xiangtu* themes to portraits of city life. His attitude seems to represent that of a generation willing to abandon the deep rift between the Taiwanese and the mainlanders. He writes in a cultivated and urbane way for both audiences.

Huang Fan originally became famous for his dandified and rather cynical story "Lai Suo" (1979), about irresponsibility among the leaders of the opposition fighting for Taiwan Independence. Having worked several years for Taiwan's *United Daily News* trust, he exhibits in his essays and journalistic work a remarkable knowledge of the social and economic dynamism of the island, and indeed he has lately become a successful real estate broker. Readers overseas find the social references in his fiction complex, but the major newspapers of Taiwan have awarded him nearly every prize at their disposal.

From Taibei's Suburbs

Into the Hubbub of Taiwan's Economic Miracle

Huang Fan

I WAS born, a premature baby, at the end of the 1940s, in an alley in the [low-rent] Wanhua District of Taibei. My relatives all agreed that there wasn't much hope for this blue-skinned, red-faced baby. My mother, on the other hand, didn't pay any attention to all that. She found a piece of cotton cloth, soaked it in a solution of licorice root, and then wrapped it tightly around her baby. It's strange, but the baby lived after all, and in fact survived without further mishap until today.

My father was then a lowly clerk in the district offices of the municipal government public security bureau. In my memory, he was always fat and jolly. My mother said that he had served as a policeman during the Japanese occupation, but I could never find a picture of him in uniform. He must have looked very grand, all suited up. The oldest photograph that I have of him, now yellowed with age, is a group picture of him and his friends on the steps of the Zhinan Temple. I was in the picture, too—at the lower right-hand corner—a painfully shy little boy in black. His appointment paper from the district office, his diploma from the Amoy Middle School, and a Civil Service certificate approving his advancement to the next rank, were kept with it in a small metal box. He left behind a paltry sum besides, his share from the widows-and-orphans fund. Every year in July, a certified letter would arrive from somewhere, which my mother would open as if it were an unexpected present. Yet when she received it the first time, she broke down, sobbing and looking at us four young ones through her tears. "This is your father's."

My short story, "International Airport" (*Guoji jicheng*) was written in memory of my father. I set down his image at the very beginning.

> My favorite game as a child was to ride piggy-back on my father. Today, I can still remember how uncomfortable and awkward he looked on those unbearably hot summer nights: a roly-poly figure on his knees beneath the low

ceiling, clad in nothing but white muslin shorts, his head swathed in perspiration, and his knees chafed red on the tatami. I would grip his shoulders with both hands and chortle at those bulging rings of fat on the back of his neck. "Giddy-up horsy, giddy-up."

The scene of my father's death appeared in "Everyone Needs Qin Defu" (*Renren xuyao Qin Defu*):

> Maybe Qin Defu died quickly and felt nothing. That's really the best way. Just like going to sleep. Sometimes I also wonder how my last hours will be. Will I know that I am dying? Will I be sad? Afraid? Or will I feel indignant at this ultimate injustice? When Father passed away, I was still in college. That morning, he bent down to tie his shoes, and as his fingertips brushed against his ankle, the artery at the back of his neck burst wide open. He gave a loud cry and lay down on the floor, the blood rushing all at once to his head. His plump face became quite suffused with blood. We lifted him up and put him on the bed. Just then he burst out weeping. Did he know that he was about to die? Was he afraid? Sad? I don't know. A few hours later, he stopped breathing. He was still in the suit that he wore to work.

And yet, when he died, I wasn't really studying in college. I was only ten, ashamed to tell my schoolmates what had happened, for I knew full well that it would only bring jeers and laughter (though things may be different now). Sure enough, when word got out the next day, it all happened the way I expected. With this incident, I learned, at the tender age of ten, the baser side of human nature. After that, my homeless family drifted here and there in this metropolis of half a million people. Mother gritted her teeth, squared her shoulders, and did many things that she never wanted to do, while my relatives just stood by and watched, none of them lifting even a finger to help. We stayed at no fewer than twenty places, living among rickshaw-pullers, prostitutes, laborers, hawkers, and vagabonds. Once, we even moved into one of those housing projects for military dependents, where there lived not a single one of us native Taiwanese. The landlord was a retired army colonel, who, having nothing better to do, spent his waking hours reminiscing about the glorious past.

These childhood days are still vivid in my mind. I remember the tarred surface of the road that turned soft and yielding in the afternoon sun; the utility poles that blackened and smelled of rotten timber; the barefoot children who pranced about in the streets, playing cops and robbers, and kicking tin cans. I returned to these old haunts twenty years later, and despite the many changes, the skyscrapers, the traffic lights, the movie theaters, the modernized but vulgar Longshan Temple (I hear that the monk in charge of hospitality can speak fluent English), nostalgia welled up inside me until I became as sentimental as a little girl.

Some of these scenes and some of these little people who live and breathe in my memory have already appeared in my works. When I describe them, I can feel their sighs, their sorrows, their struggles, their anger and laughter. At times, they come right up to me and argue over petty things. Other times, some of them even get up from the manuscript paper to ask, resentfully, "Why are you making us live all over again?"

What should I say in reply?

It's a strange admission to make, but what shaped my personality was not so much the ethics taught in books, the moral instruction of my teachers, or what they call the influence of my environment, but those bits and pieces from my days in childhood. Thanks to those little people, I am now able to survive in two worlds with different values and, what's more, manage to get along very well in both.

Our present world is slowly taking shape, a mixture of New York, Tokyo, and Calcutta. Some of the old things will be totally abandoned. New communities springing up like forests present a frightening sameness (the era that exists in my memory has vanished beneath the wheels of bulldozers and tractors). Apartment dwellers materialize in droves on the streets. The newspaper takes up global crises, condenses them, and sticks them on page four. Human beings rush about beneath the signposts of modernization and development, cramming themselves full of all kinds of "counterwisdom" from television, radio, billboards and entertainment pages. Jarring sounds. Dust. An ever-increasing influx of people into the city. Political slogans. Commercial jingles. Always there are people telling you that no one is obliged to be good-tempered, that cheating at the polls is immoral, that you can learn English in seven days, that you'd intimidate the taxman himself, and, finally, that you can be a success before forty.

True, the times are changing. Yet while material culture is advancing by leaps and bounds, the soul is gradually withering. Nobody raises questions about it in the classroom anymore. Meanwhile, robberies take place on the streets without cease.

> *We are the hollow men*
> *We are the stuffed men*
> *leaning together*
> *headpiece filled with straw. Alas!*
> . . . .
> *Shape without form, shade without color,*
> *paralyzed force, gesture without motion;*
> . . . .
> . . . .*lost*
> *Violent souls, but only*
> *as the hollow men*
> *the stuffed men.*

This poem by T. S. Eliot is a fitting epitome of the Taibei man of the 1980s. In my controversial story, "Lai Suo," I attempted, through an individual lost in time, to criticize politics, society, culture, and human nature in Taiwan these past thirty years. The intent of this story was so ambitious that it shocked even me, but I went ahead with it anyway. As I wrote it, the people in my memory came alive again, one by one. I arranged for these characters, all of them content with petty goals, a more complicated environment—a political vortex, or an economic crisis. I imagined and noted down their reactions, their disorientation, and that precious bit of dignity that they try to maintain in times of adversity.

With the completion of "Lai Suo," I was fairly confident about my technique and my ability to express myself. I felt I had the competence and an obligation to present my views about what had been happening the last thirty years on the Communist side of the strait. Of course, I lacked the kind of understanding that comes from having actually lived under that kind of government, like Chen Ruoxi. Yet, if I could, from a relatively objective viewpoint, produce a criticism transcending time and space, then I would achieve my goal. Hence I wrote "Qingzhou Train Depot" (*Qingzhou chezhan*). Meanwhile, the so-called "Literature of the Wounded" and "Literature of Protest" appeared in succession on the scene. Victims of the Cultural Revolution had passionately unleashed their grief and anger in these stories. The reason for the inexplicable mass hysteria that held tens of millions of people in sway couldn't be simple or straightforward. In this age when civilization has reached its peak, totalitarianism is still in vogue. Just take, for example, China, with its five thousand years of autocratic history. The overwhelming majority of common people have long been accustomed to being controlled by authoritarian concepts created by upper-class intellectuals, who, with their innumerable abstract political terms and dogmatic slogans, tell them how they ought to live and how they ought to pursue their own individual values. Those scholars went so far as to inscribe their philosophies in books and set up schools of thought, that their every word and deed might be handed down as law for all eternity. Unfortunately, people like Lai Suo and Zhong Shida can be found everywhere, among your neighbors. In their naïveté, they believe that the humble goals of the individual must never come into conflict with the grand schemes of the community, while the masses, on the other hand, tacitly agree that sacrificing one or two such individuals for a noble cause is to be expected, not even worth mentioning.

The Cultural Revolution was, in fact, a warning signal. I personally feel that this tragic calamity could not have been the result of a few dreadful decisions made by a handful of individuals. The responsibility must be borne by every Chinese. In the past few centuries, human beings have become overdependent on their own achievements, on scientific knowledge, and on a small number of geniuses. As a result, they have finally lost what is most valuable: their spiritual strength. Think of the ridiculous revolution in Iran. The absurd administration of Uganda. The attempt at ruralization in Cambodia. The chaotic world situation. The energetic, wiser-than-ever leaders of various nations playing tag with each other in the air space above the Pacific. Philosophers and virtuous men, learned, visionary, and filled with a sense of mission, loudly exhorting us in the media. In spite of all these efforts, the situation has not improved. The Soviet Union has moved its army into Afghanistan. Japan has taken up the issue of arming itself once more. The Americans, for their part, engage in large-scale dumping of their weapons on the world market. Bigoted ethnocentrism is back in style. A constitutional government actually declared war on a neighboring country over a football game. Palestinian guerrillas, while noisily espousing brotherly love for people of the same ethnic background, open fire on innocent old people, women, and children. In this present age filled with violence, evil, and hatred, when our simple and kind citizens are already sick and tired of daily murders, our politicians continue to fabricate ideals, and our writers close their doors and spin beautiful tales.

And what about us? The past few years, our cultural activities, flourishing in the wake of a rising economy, have enjoyed a boom far more rapid than anyone could have imagined. Art galleries have sprung up in Taibei like bamboo shoots after a rain. Our painters vie to be first to rush from Surrealism to Impressionism; an art form that took centuries to mature in the West quickly comes into being in Taibei. Avant-gardists in dance and drama, intent on fusing East with West, work themselves into frenzied confusion. When the television series "Roots" took the country by storm, calls went out repeatedly for us to trace our ethnic identity and revitalize traditional culture, but soon, everything lapsed into silence again. After the severance of diplomatic relations between Taiwan and the United States, Chiang Kai-shek International Airport was suddenly bustling with activity. Scholars and professors from inside Taiwan and abroad passed through the airport coming and going, their suitcases stuffed with material, any material. When the Communist government began dispatching huge numbers of students overseas early this year, even more materials poured into those suitcases. A whole series of conferences on *The Dream of the Red Chamber*, on national construction, Sinology, and so forth were organized to facilitate communication and exchange. Berkeley, Princeton, Chicago, and Taibei were caught up in a tumultuous uproar.

As a result of this fervor, "Lai Suo" attracted the attention of certain people who proclaimed it "an unprecedented work, so humorous and yet sobering." Mr. Bai Xianyong even called it a "farce." Because of all this, however, I finally got to meet famous people in the cultural community and I attended several receptions. My general impression is that though the presence of celebrities adds luster to a gathering, it also adds to the sham. Amid the cordial toasts, beaming smiles, and the pervading air of culture, no one really knows what he is talking about.

Youth and bashfulness prompted me to try my best to avoid these occasions. Moreover, in June, I had the chance to work again (I'd been unemployed for four months), and a pattern emerged in my life once more. Every day, I buried my head among stacks of papers and files, trying to contribute to the noble goal of fulfilling my obligation to society. A month later, the first anthology of my short

252 TAIWAN: NEW GENERATIONS

stories came out. The critics thought it quite good, but my readers seemed to have all left town on vacation.

This anthology included the very first five short stories I ever wrote: "The Last Winter" (*Zuihou de dongtian*), "The Eagle in the Rain" (*Yu zhong zhi ying*), "Everyone Needs Qin Defu," "Qingzhou Train Depot," and "Lai Suo." "The Last Winter" and "Everyone Needs Qin Defu" were repeatedly rejected by publishers for two years, which made "Lai Suo" my first published work. It appeared when I was thirty, an age when many young writers have already achieved astounding success and international fame. Yet early fame is not necessarily a good thing. I have witnessed several writers of repute who, after chronicling their university days, threw down their pens in resignation.

In addition, at the request of the editor, I wrote a preface (which seems to be a must for every book) and said a whole lot of things that did absolutely nothing for the sales of the book—things like: Don't look for any pearls of wisdom or moral encouragement in this book. From me you'll only get sighs, sarcasm, and even a few insults.

I am fully aware that this does no good, that no one wants to spend money to buy "gloom" unless he or she has masochistic leanings. At a serious, bona-fide workshop, I stood up and made an inappropriate speech that embarrasses me to this day. The worst is that, up to now, I haven't taken this maxim to heart: "Treat your guests well. Don't spend money on them and then make them feel resentful."

My friend Ma Yigong is skilled in reading faces. Once she told me very soberly: "At thirty-nine, you will meet with calamity."

"Is it because someone will fabricate a sex scandal about me?"

"No," she said, her face turning pale. "You will be framed. Arrows will pierce your heart."

This reminds me of the highly-esteemed Spartan hero Leonidas of ancient Greece. At the battle of Thermopylae, when he heard that the enemy was shooting enough arrows to blot out the sun, he said, fearlessly, "How splendid! We will be in the shade when we fight!"

Of course, I am not so optimistic. If my literary life must come to an end some time, then I must prepare myself in advance. In these few remaining years, I must hurry up and say all that I want to say, and offend all those I want to offend. Then, bringing my young son to the steps of the Zhinan Temple, I will have a picture taken—a group picture that will turn yellow with time and be a worthy souvenir.

"Zunyan yu xinnian: Wo de wenxue lücheng" (Dignity and conviction—My literary odyssey), in Huang Fan, *Wo pipan* (My criticism) (Taibei, 1986), pp. 205–14.

—Translated by Ellen Lai-shan Yeung

Li Ang

LI ANG (pseud. of Shi Shuduan, b. 1952) has preserved in her writings much of the local flavor of her home, the old port of Lugang. Raised in a wealthy family, with the talented sisters Shi Shuqing, an author of short stories about Hong Kong, and Shi Shu, a literary critic, Li Ang was influenced by the modernist literature introduced to Taiwan in translation during the 1960s. In her impressive fictional oeuvre she has thematized sexuality, elaborating on the clash of values between modern Western and traditional Confucian ethics. Her openness brought her fame very early in Taiwan, and she has continued to bring feminist themes to the fore in her manifold journalistic activities. Her novel *Sha fu* (The butcher's wife, 1983) captured an audience for her overseas, although mainland publishers had problems with the openness, whereas younger generations on Taiwan have already begun to look back on parts of her work as "nostalgia," given the rapid pace of change on the island. By coincidence, Li Ang decided to "interview herself" in the same way as Zhang Xinxin from the PRC. Apparently both young women are weary of the stereotyped questions constantly put to them by the press.

Protest of a Woman Author against Reckless Accusations
Another Self-Interview, This Time from Taibei

Li Ang

December 1984

Q: Why do you want to "interview yourself"?

A: I've been interviewed many times in the past, and I have always been asked the same questions over and over again. I'm getting tired of repeating myself like a tape recorder. I finally decided to decline all interviews. Of course, it's impossible to turn all of them down, but I usually insist on not being interviewed. It took me a long time to learn this. I think it is necessary to learn how to say no in Taiwan, otherwise you will be always occupied by obligations. This time, they wanted me for a cover story, so I launched a preemptive strike.

Q: So how would you describe yourself?

A: I am very straightforward, and not small-minded (that's why I've been able to continue writing despite ten years of continuous ugly attacks on me). I'm not a schemer, either, for I've seen what truly wise people can be like. I might have been very complicated and difficult when I was younger; now, however, I've started to believe in certain values I once looked down on, such as simplicity, kindness, and love. . . .

Q: I am going to ask you a question you might be reluctant to answer. Where did you draw your inspiration to write about the sexual relations that are so vividly described in your stories, up to and including *The Butcher's Wife*? . . .

A: The longer I write, the more I believe that a writer cannot write only about his or her own experiences, simply because one's own experiences will be exhausted some day. Furthermore, personal experience is an unlikely source of great works. Your question is not important to my current stage of writing. I am very conscious of getting rid of my very personal feelings and sentiments in order to create works with a broader view and depth. Therefore, the next time someone asks me where I draw my inspiration to write about sex, I'm going to spare the niceties and call him an idiot.

Q: Since you say you're interviewing yourself to keep from repeating yourself, and not to avoid hard questions, I guess I can ask you the standard question: "How did you begin your career as a writer?"

A: There's no way around it. I am probably one of those "prodigies who failed to develop into a major talent." I have two older sisters who are prominent writers, Shi Shu and Shi Shuqing. Also, I grew up in Lugang, a unique town. I read many fairy tales and memorized lots of traditional poems when I was very young. I started my first novel when I was only in the second year of junior middle school. (Even my two stupid sisters could write, so it had to be easy.) The story was about fifty thousand characters long, and my sisters thought there were problems with its structure, so Shi Shu taught me how to cut out the excess. In my first year of senior middle school, I wrote "Flower Season" (*Hua ji*), which became my first published work. I've continued on my path of error ever since.

Q: Could you discuss the major stages your writing has gone through?

A: That is the territory of critics and readers.

Q: Let me ask another stupid question. How do you feel about being a woman?

A: I am very content being a woman, which includes the privileges of acting pettishly and being forgiven for small faults. I think I am a successful woman in the sense that I am completely independent and yet not threatening. Have you read some of my previous interviews, which said that I was sometimes like a kid?

Q: Does being a writer interfere with being a woman?

A: Yes. And I know that what you really want to ask is, "Do you write about sex in your novels because of the difficulties of being a woman?"

Q: Yes, that's what I want to know.

A: Naturally it has caused many difficulties. Most people think that female writers are weird. They think we can just go through the motions of writing about the wind, the clouds, and the moon, and thereby become "female writers," licensed to do strange things. Also, they think we must be very romantic, so they treat us differently. Did you know that for a while almost everybody who met me for the first time would tell me, with an equivocal smile, that I was different from what they'd imagined? I guess people expect me to be an avant-garde woman with a punk hairdo and backless dress. What gets me is that if I were a male writer, I wouldn't have these distasteful experiences. It goes without saying that men are allowed to do many things in our society. Also, I'm really disgusted by the many ignorant men who think they can read special messages in my stories, then go talk about me with a smirk on their face. I wish those male chauvinist pigs would look at themselves before acting so smug.

Q: Let's get back to literature.

A: Don't you think readers are interested in the peculiarities of the author? My answers show readers my personality, something they can hardly find in my stories.

Q: It seems I should be Li Ang, and you Shi Shuduan.

A: We can hardly go our separate ways. [As the song says,] "You've a part of me in you, and I've a part of you in me."

Q: Let's not be so mushy. Back to the subject. I'd like to know whether being a woman has any effect on your writing. In other words, do you consciously feel you are a "woman writer"?

A: I didn't when I first started. Gender simply wasn't so important at that stage. I had great ambitions then—I looked forward to winning a Nobel Prize in literature. I seldom thought about myself as a woman. And what did femaleness have to do with my writing? My works of that period were collected in *Mixed Chorus* (*Hun sheng he chang*, 1975). You couldn't tell whether the writer was male or female. Some people jokingly told me they had first thought Li Ang was a man of forty or fifty. Not until I went to college, in Taibei, did I consciously see myself as a woman. Owing to my youth, and my awakening to love, I began to write love stories. It was then that my style displayed what they call feminine "delicacy" and "sentimentalism." Representative is the series of stories in my collection *The Mundane World* (*Ren jian shi*, 1976). You can still see the experimental ambitions of my early works there, but the tone is very feminine. My life changed tremendously when I went to the United States to study. My "eyes were opened" for the first time, and I was able to rid myself of fatal female traits like small-mindedness, cattiness, back-stabbing, and sentimentalism. I began to feel that the only way I could broaden my range was to write like male writers. Unfortunately, I'm still entrapped in my own femaleness, so I've never been able to write like a man. I didn't realize this until I wrote *The Butcher's Wife*. I saw that however much I imitated male writers, I couldn't write like them, and I didn't need to. I was writing a column called "Women's Opinion" then, and I realized that historically, women have always been subordinate to men. Women have always lacked self-confidence and the courage to truly develop their own specifically female potential. Therefore, in history, the universally recognized "female characteristics" have been limited to virtues like tenderness, sensitivity, and consideration. I think women's potential is greater than that. As long as we are confident, I believe there should be a way to write something great as well as female. Women's literature will then no longer be considered the realm of proper ladies and their personal essays.

Q: What made you keep on writing for the past eighteen years?

A: Love. I did it for love. I started, when I was young, only because I was excited inside and felt I could express myself best in writing. Now, I do it because of the power of writing itself. Creative writing is a lover one can never conquer. You think you are in control, and then in a flash he appears in another guise that you have never seen before. All love fades in time, and all lovers become boring; only writing can be an eternal lover.

Q: In other words, you're willing to make many sacrifices for your writing? Is that why you're still single?

A: I don't think I have sacrificed anything for writing. I love this work, so how can I speak of sacrifice? The reason I'm still single may be that I can't find a husband who's as good as writing! I'm also very disappointed with most men's selfishness and chauvinism. . . .

Q: How do you evaluate your own work?

A: I hope I will write some really good stories some day. I am not there yet. I always believe and hope that my next work will be better, and I am working hard toward that goal. On the other hand, I know I can never be one of the world's great writers, like García Márquez, Hemingway, or Tolstoy, as I once dreamed. Given my limitations, I'll have to work very hard to be just a second- or third-class writer in world literature. . . .

Q: Do you mind other people's attacks on you?

A: I don't really care about them. Time will prove that they are just the clowns of our time. Those who attacked Flaubert and D. H. Lawrence only made themselves ridiculous in our eyes today.

Q: You just mentioned limitations that prevent you from becoming a great writer. What are they?

A: First of all, my talent. I don't think of myself as a genius, and to be a great writer you have to be one. My background is another limitation. Being the daughter of a successful self-made businessman, I grew up well-to-do and well protected. This caused me to like delicate and beautiful things, and also to be completely isolated from life at the lower end of the scale. If I hadn't worked at it, I would have found it hard to enter real life. I drive my own car, teach college, then return to my beautiful home. Most of my friends are intellectuals. Such a life naturally is very limiting. There was a time when I participated rather actively in social service work, to be in touch with real life and enlarge my own circle of experience, but I still found it difficult to enter into it completely. I started to write *The Butcher's Wife* at that time. When I begged my mother to take me to see pigs slaughtered at the Lugang slaughterhouse, so I could write about what went on there, she gladly accepted (though she thought it strange that I wanted to write about such a horrible thing). We stayed there over an hour. I thought my description of butchering in that novel was rather successful. That gave me a lot of confidence in writing, because I discovered and do believe that writing requires something more than just real life. I admit that I have limitations, but I want to overcome them. . . .

Q: Let's hear your writer's view of creative writing.

A: My fundamental belief about writing has always been that it expresses truth, especially in a society and culture full of white lies like ours. I think that telling the truth is the writer's most fundamental moral obligation. So, when I think something should be written about, I don't give much consideration to whether or not this violates custom (note that I say custom, not morality) or taboos. The result, of course, has been more than ten years of uninterrupted attacks on my character. Ask me if I still keep to my ideal, though, and I will affirm it absolutely. There are still many problems that, for one reason or another, I am not able to come to grips with or write about, but I must keep on struggling with them.

Q: About this truth you want to express—is it possible that it is not really "truth," but something that comes from each person's own opinions and biases?

A: I don't think so. We are now living in an information age. This is not a time when people debate whether the earth is round, or when theological disputes rage. It is very easy to obtain information from other countries or from different theories to correct our own views. I agree there is probably no absolute truth, but truth does exist, because it is concrete and can be verified with statistics and actual materials.

Q: Have you considered whether the truth you write about is so ugly and cruel, and so lacking in brighter long-term prospects, that it could be harmful to society?

A: I think you overestimate the power of a writer in the twentieth century. I only refer to serious works here, not literature for passing the time, like best-sellers and martial-arts novels. Tell me now, how many people read Tolstoy or Saul Bellow? The percentage is pitifully small. And who are these readers? Teenagers, smoking pot and listening to rock and roll? The lower classes that we're continually being told to care about? (I don't say this to put them down.) We have to admit that when art reaches a certain level of sophistication, it belongs only to a tiny minority that are able to appreciate it. It's sad, but it's true. It is every artist's ideal to be appreciated by all classes, but it rarely happens. Serious works can be accepted only by educated minorities. Need one worry about shocking *them* with squalor and cruelty? Ugly and distasteful truth will at least awaken their social conscience and perhaps cause them to do a little more for society. This, too, is what I consider the influence of art—not to influence the majority, but the minority (intellectuals, in the broad sense). Naturally, when I say this, some people think I don't care about poor people, that I look down on the proletariat. But I think an honest artist should admit that art belongs only to those who are able to appreciate it. . . .

Q: Do you agree, then, that society should promote appreciation of "high art"?

A: No. For one thing, I don't consider art to be the most important thing in life. Society ought first to provide more equal opportunity for education and participation. After the vast majority have their share of education, some people may like art and pursue it. Naturally, it would be good if one day they came to appreciate serious art. For those who aren't interested, there is no point encouraging them to use art as decoration or a means of climbing up the social ladder. I don't think that people who like only football or soap opera miss anything as long as they enjoy themselves. After all, art is not food. You won't starve without it. . . .

I believe that a society should be pluralistic, having different kinds of ideas, culture, and art, not all cast in one mold. So society can have both high art and soap operas. They serve different needs. . . .

Q: You've in effect been discussing the "popularization" of art among the masses. Could you also discuss "cosmopolitanism" and "nativism" in art?

A: Just as the spread of art among the populace creates the opportunity for appreciation, with art necessarily spreading upward from below, instead of high art being imposed from above, I think that art must be native before it takes on cosmopolitan characteristics. I have met many overseas Chinese scholars who like to criticize Taiwan as being a hermetic society, because its intellectuals seldom concern themselves with things from beyond Taiwan. What they say is true, but I don't regard it as a serious shortcoming. Take me, for example. I didn't even know that there were great Taiwanese writers during the Japanese occupation, such as Yang Kui and Zhang Wenhuan, until I went to study in the United States after college. That really stopped me cold. A few days before, I'd been talking with some foreign friends and been terribly embarrassed to learn, again for the first time, how Taiwan's economy was taken over by five big families after the retrocession [to China in 1945]. With me still so ignorant about Taiwan, I didn't feel I had to know what problems American writers of the 1980s were exploring. Now, of course, it's best if you do know about the things outside, but if my energy is limited, I'd first like to use it to understand Taiwan—to understand what my education left out, and what things the books don't cover. . . . I don't think a writer should completely ignore cosmopolitanism. A writer in our country should have the ideal to achieve world success—not because we write like Westerners, but because our works are so great that the West will look at us from a new perspective. It's idealistic, but not impossible—look at Kawabata and García Márquez. As for me, I constantly remind myself to avoid emotional arguments and dogmatic beliefs when giving rein to nativism, so that I don't stagnate.

Q: Have your beliefs made you strange?

A: Yes, I sometimes feel like a stranger in my native land. It seems that I'm always behind the current fashion. When, early on, I wrote a lot of "modern" fiction under the influence of existentialism and psychoanalysis, modernism was at its end. Then, when I started to write stories about my hometown of Lugang, the *xiangtu* literary tendency had not yet started; by the time I wrote what I considered to be a very "nativist" novel, *The Butcher's Wife*, the *xiangtu* trend was over. I am not really sorry that I was out of step, but sometimes I feel just a little helpless that for one reason or another, I seem always to be out of the mainstream. Another thing that makes me look strange is that I am always the target of some criticism. Twelve years ago, after I wrote *The Mundane World*, about the sexual problems of college students, I was called every bad name in the dictionary. Six years later, after I had come back from the United States, all the problems reflected in *The Mundane World* were openly discussed, and I became like a prophet. After the publication of *The Butcher's Wife* last year, I was called all sorts of dirty names again. Will *those* crimes still be crimes in another six years, I wonder? Sometimes I feel very lonely. It's the loneliness of being misunderstood. . . .

Q: What do you think about being called "the most controversial" writer [in Taiwan]?

A: I think I should be called the writer most often cursed at, not the most controversial writer. Being controversial means there are opposite opinions about you. All I ever got were detractions. No one ever defended me. (I think the only justice I can count on will be time.)

Q: Some people think *The Butcher's Wife* has a negative influence on society. It may encourage women to kill their husbands. What is your opinion of this?

A: Had I such influence, I would have run for office. Why knock myself out being an author? Ha! A major defect of Taiwan is that its intellectuals overestimate their influence. This is natural in a society where intellectuals want to do their utmost for their country and society, then discover that they're virtually impotent, and inflate their self-image out of feelings of impotence. *The Butcher's Wife*, for instance, is seventy thousand characters long and not easy to read to begin with. True, it appeared daily in a major newspaper with a circulation of one million, but only a thousand or so characters a day. Who will read a novel in pieces like that? —The minority who are really interested in literature. Talk about the influence of *The Butcher's Wife*! Compared to the daily news, filled with robberies, murders, rapes, and swindles, which is more influential? The news, of course—being short and easy to read, it has an immediate impact. If *The Butcher's Wife* has a bad influence on society, how about those news items? . . .

"Li Ang de zipou yu zixing: Shi Shuduan qinfang Li Ang (Li Ang's self-analysis and self-examination: An interview of Li Ang by Shi Shuduan), in *Xinshu yuekan* (New books monthly, Taibei) 12 (September 1984): 22–28.

—Translated by Pu-mei Leng

Wu Jinfa

WU JINFA (Wu Chin-fa, b. 1954), a journalist from Meinong in Gaoxiong County, southern Taiwan, has captured his audience through the passionate and unambiguous tone of his writings. In Wu Jinfa's prose, one finds the protracted identity crisis of local Taiwanese who are torn by affinities with Chinese culture from the mainland, a love-hate relationship with Japan, and strong arguments for local independence after decades of mainlander dominance. Wu Jinfa addresses his compatriots with mournful commiseration. He has published several volumes of short stories and essays; in 1989, he also edited Taiwan's first literary anthologies of essays and fiction by authors from Taiwan's aboriginal tribal peoples up in the mountains, based on materials that Wu had collected for several years. In 1984, Wu published the short novel *Chunqiu chashi* (Spring and autumn teahouse), a semi-autobiographical account of the elements depicted in the following essay.

Vanished Virility

Stories—My Last Remaining Castle

Wu Jinfa

1986

WHEN I was little, I was determined to do many things. At times, I wanted to become a scientist, at other times, a politician; after seeing a Japanese movie about the war in the Pacific, for a while I even secretly wanted to become a soldier—to rise to become an omnipotent military leader like Yamamoto Isoroku. All kinds of aspirations lingered in my tiny mind, but of all things I never thought that I would subsequently become a "writer." In fact, at the time, my writing was very poor; I often got a B or less. Moreover, in my childish notions I assumed that "writers" were people who could tell stories like the one about Snow White; they weren't so special. My grandfather and every other uneducated person his age could tell stories, and I'd never looked up to them, for among them were swineherds, pork butchers, undertakers, and so forth.

I don't know when this absurd idea of becoming a writer started to force its way into my mind. Probably it only arose because, as I grew older, I realized that my other childhood dreams were all becoming increasingly unobtainable.

Since I kept failing mathematics in high school, I naturally abandoned my dream of becoming a scientist. Similarly, I became completely disillusioned with my military aspirations. The year I passed the university entrance exam, I underwent military training in Chenggongling. In the six weeks I was there, I lost a rubber helmet, a uniform, two pairs of army shoes, and a set of underwear. Could a soldier who was constantly losing his equipment become a military leader? I thought about it briefly and felt scared. The squad leader's comment when I completed my training discouraged me even further: "If the Republic of China took one soldier like you, it would be tantamount to losing three." He meant that if I became a soldier it would only work if two other people took care of me.

And what about my dream of becoming a politician? I dismissed the idea only after I entered university. The reason was that I saw our officials constantly and brazenly lying on television, even those who were supposed to be profoundly learned scholars; without a blush or bated breath they, too, said ridiculous things in accordance with policy. I realized that they were covering up the facts with slogans that wouldn't convince a three-year-old. When they appeared on television it was more than I could bear. I particularly concentrated on their expressions as they talked. I was amazed at how vigorously they could perform a script they didn't even believe themselves.

So that was probably another reason why my dream of becoming a politician dissipated—I reckoned myself so scrupulous that I would flush crimson at the smallest lie. Such a performance was bound to fail in Chinese politics, and the penalty for that was jail.

Over the years, I relinquished my childhood fantasies one after the other; for a while, then, I was at a complete loss. I often asked myself what I *could* do in this world. I could not possibly be somebody whose existence was "tantamount to losing three others."

Luckily it was just then that I encountered literature. Within a very short time, I took up my pen and began writing fiction.

I was astonished that I immediately felt that I could keep on writing for a lifetime. It was truly a wonderful experience. Through fiction, I found the shattered ideals of my past being pieced together by my pen, one after another, as in a puzzle. Still more fascinating, the pen in my hand appeared to have the power to summon souls. It seized my soul, tightly, and I realized that it was moving in rhythm with the sway of the pen and the flux of the ink upon the paper. There it cried, laughed, raged indignantly, and sometimes also misbehaved. More important, sometimes it even banded friends together and bewailed their plight. One day I discovered, to my terror, not just the living, but the departed spirits of our predecessors on this island at my side, summoned one after another by my pen. They embraced my soul tightly, tearfully venting their resentment at past injustices.

Since then, this thing called "fiction" has been hanging on to me like a leech. I know that I'll never be able to escape its grip or, to put it another way, I'll never again want to leave its embrace. It has become my "eternal lover." More to the point, you could even say that since I have lost on the real "battlefield of my dreams," fiction has become my life's last redoubt. I withdrew from all the setbacks of reality into this fortification, this blockhouse, just as Kobo Abe describes it in *The Box Man*. I have made fiction into a thin paper box that protects me. Since I consider it the last fortress in my life, I deeply believe that if anyone were to besiege or attack the "redoubt of my dreams" with evil force of any kind, I would fight to the death. For I firmly believe that I have no territory to retreat to; therefore, I have no choice but to fight bravely.

Thus, it's quite right to say that literature is already the eternal, unchanging passion and dream of my life. This dream, however, is far removed from the "virility and the resolution" with which in my childhood years I meant to run the world and assist the people. Sometimes I cannot help feeling a little distressed to think of it.

"Zuihou de 'meng zhi diaobao': *Xiaoshi de nanxing* zixu" (The last "imaginary re-doubt": Author's preface to *The vanishing male*), in Wu Jinfa, *Xiaoshi de nanxing* (Taibei, 1986), pp. 1–4.

—Translated by Patricia Sieber

IV

The Republican Era Revisited

THIS final section provides a glimpse back into Republican times (1912–49), when China was in theory still united. These texts might at first seem peripheral to this anthology, which focuses on the 1980s, but in Taiwan these earlier writers have suddenly proved inspirational, after having been proscribed for almost four decades. The same is true, to a lesser degree, in the PRC, since most works from the Republican era other than Lu Xun's were as good as proscribed during the Cultural Revolution. Abroad, any reader must be reminded of these "big names" if he or she hopes to be able adequately to contextualize the new generations of writers on the mainland *and* on Taiwan.

Foreign invasion, an awakening modern consciousness, and the abrupt changes in the countryside and in the cities are the major themes in this limited review, particularly in the first subsection, entitled "Changing Times," most of whose authors exhibit a phenomenon that the literary critic and historian C. T. Hsia christened "obsession with China." Other writers remind us of the urbane cosmopolitanism of Shanghai and of sexual outspokenness among intellectuals in earlier days. These open phenomena completely faded away during long years of government-enforced prudishness on both sides of the Taiwan Strait. The more inspiring are these authors' "New Forms of Self-Consciousness" to Chinese writers today—forms that were new in the Republican era, and are new again today.

Lao She

LAO SHE (pseud. of Shu Qingchun, 1899–1966) was born in Peking into an impoverished Manchu family. He taught Chinese at the School of Oriental and African Studies in London for five years, beginning in 1924. Much influenced by Charles Dickens and Joseph Conrad, he began his writing career while still in England, going on to become one of China's favorite novelists.

Lao She's *Maocheng ji* (Cat country, 1933) is a bitterly satiric analysis of Chinese society in the form of a dystopic vision akin to science fiction. *Luotuo Xiangzi* (Rickshaw, 1938), which traces the degradation and ruin of a Peking rickshaw puller, came to be seen as a general study of China's social misery, and a twentieth-century classic. During the war, Lao She as patriotic propagandist wrote plays and ballads on wartime themes. His epic trilogy, *Sishi tongtang* (Four generations under one roof, 1947), depicts life in Peking during the Japanese occupation. After returning to China in 1949, following a three-year sojourn in the United States, Lao She wrote rather propagandistic plays under the people's government, among them, *Chaguan* (Teahouse, 1957). In 1966, he was murdered or driven to suicide by Red Guards in his native Peking. The text below gives insight into how Lao She conceived his art. On the occasion of writing a play about the Boxer uprising, he recalls the premature death of his father and protests against foreign aggression.

Suppressed Furor Against Foreign Troops

An Unwritten Novel and a Play about the Boxer Uprising

Lao She

1961

In 1960, on the sixtieth anniversary of the Boxer uprising, I wrote a four-act play about the Boxers called *Divine Fists (Shen juan)*.

I had had the idea of writing a novel about the Boxers for a long time. In fact, I had persistently been plying older people with questions about what they had seen and heard back then, and I had jotted down their stories. In the chaos and confusion of the war, however, these notes were all lost. Actually, even if they had not been lost, they would not have been enough to sustain a novel, since they were fragmentary, disorganized, and not without their own biases. Eventually, as there were fewer and fewer eyewitnesses around to question, I gave it up. So I have yet to realize my desire to write that novel.

In 1960, thanks to the sixtieth anniversary of the Boxer uprising, some anecdotes and historical material about the Boxer uprising were published, as well as essays reappraising it. This motivated me once again to write something. This play was the result.

Whether my script is good or bad is not for me to say. All I want to do here is talk a little about why I am so concerned with the Boxers.

I wasn't even two years old when the Boxer uprising occurred, so naturally I can't remember the madness and the violence, the sounds of killing that rent the air. However, from the time I began to remember things until my mother fell ill and passed away, I heard her emotion-filled tale about the atrocities committed by the armies of the eight allied powers many, many times. She did not have much to say about how Boxers from all over the country massed in Peking, since she, like most women in those days, hardly dared venture out into the street. But because she felt such deep hatred for the foreign soldiers who showed up on people's doorsteps to rape and to kill, she vividly remembered every one of the atrocities they committed. Mother's stories made a very deep impression on me, one that was difficult to erase.

During my childhood, I didn't need to hear stories about evil ogres eating children and so forth: the foreign devils my mother told me about were more barbaric and cruel than any fairy tale ogre with a huge mouth and great fangs. And fairy tales are only fairy tales, whereas my mother's stories were 100 percent factual, and they directly affected our whole family.

I don't remember what my father looked like—he perished that year in a street battle with the allied armies. He was a guard soldier drawing a salary of two ounces of silver a month, entrusted with guarding the Imperial City. When the allied powers fought their way through the Di'an Gate, my father died in a grain shop on Beichang Street.

Neither my mother nor my elder sister dared leave the house. My elder brother had just turned nine, and I spent most of the time sleeping on the *kang*. There was really no way of getting news of my father. How many Boxers, soldiers, and hapless civilians disappeared just like that!

Fortunately, Second Brother, my uncle on my mother's side, showed up with some news. Second Brother was a bannerman like my father. He ran errands inside the Imperial Palace. In the course of the losing battle, he happened to pass by the grain shop. He went in for a drink of water, for it was a hot day. The store employees were long gone; only my father lay there, his whole body feverish and swollen, already past the point of speech. Without a word, my father handed Second Brother the pair of cotton socks he'd taken off when his feet grew too swollen. How long he lay there in pain before he finally passed away, no one knows.

My father's gun was an old-fashioned two-man gingal, a ten-foot-long musket that had to be packed with gunpowder before every shot. When the long muzzles of several of those guns were mounted on their tripods side by side, a lot of gunpowder would spill out on the ground. Grenades tossed by the foreign soldiers set it off—and there was gunpowder on my father's body, and so—

In the great confusion, Second Brother could barely save himself; he had no way of carrying my half-dead father home on his back. He looked everywhere, but there was no carriage to be had, nor anyone to help. The emperor and empress dowager themselves were in flight.

When he walked in the door, Second Brother burst into loud sobs as he handed the pair of socks to my mother. Years later, Elder Brother still felt bad when anyone mentioned that day—he blamed himself for what had happened. But not one of us uttered a single word of blame. We hated the armies of the eight allied powers!

It isn't difficult to imagine the hardships and sorrows my mother suffered during those times. Flames lit up the sky all over the city, and the air resounded with the sound of gunfire. Those with money managed to escape, while the poor found themselves without water or grain. Father had been the major breadwinner; so long as he was alive, everyone in the family at least got a share of his "stale rice"[1] to eat. With him gone, we had to get by on our own. Mother gave her best, refusing to let grief get the better of her. By doing odd jobs day and night, she was able to scrape together just enough to keep her children alive. I was a rather depressed and unhappy child, for no sooner did I begin to understand life than I learned of its hardships and sorrows. Nor was mine a particularly unfortunate case. During those times, many children were sold off or died of hunger or cold.

It's true, nowadays every time I come across nursery school children walking in the street hand in hand, laughing, talking, and singing, lively as the birds that wake one up at dawn, I stop in my tracks and observe them closely. I count how many different ways their hair is braided, how many different kinds of shoes and socks they wear. I'm so happy, I want to take them home with me to play games all day long. Yes, in their healthy apple-cheeks, I see irrefutable evidence of our people's independence and freedom.

There's no telling how many people were killed, or how much was stolen, when the allied armies invaded Peking. It is a debt that can never be completely repaid. Talk of massacre, not even the chickens or dogs were spared. Every single family in Peking lost its chickens to the foreign soldiers. Any dog that dared to bark was immediately bayoneted to death, like the big brown dog that belonged to our family. Stealing chickens and killing dogs showed how courageous and heroic were the occupying troops. When it came to plunder, the soldiers were truly "civilized."[2] They weren't as rough and unsophisticated as outlaws of the greenwood, stealing and robbing with hoots of triumph. No! They had highly polished techniques of thievery. Very patiently, very thoroughly, they searched each house and home, taking it apart with all the care and attention of a young woman combing her hair.

The obscure alleyway in which we lived was too narrow even for a sedan chair. All the houses there belonged to destitute working folk, whose most valuable object might be Grannie Zhang's wedding ring (perhaps it was brass), or maybe Auntie Li's silver comb. And yet, like rats, the foreign soldiers cleverly ferreted out this small alleyway; first, just a few, and then a crowd—who knows how many contingents came in a single day! The door to our house must have been open all day long. The women hid shears in their blouses and silently sat along the wall, waiting for the arrival of the "civilized" plunderers and butchers

---

[1]Tribute rice shipped up to Peking from the south to feed government employees. It was brown from long-term storage.

[2]This word is even more facetious than it appears, for in early twentieth-century China, the word "civilized," or "enlightened," meant "Western," as opposed to "traditional Chinese."

who had no need for the cover of night. They went first for the chickens, then entered the rooms of the house, overturning and upsetting everything. Boldly they went, leaving no stone unturned and making off with everything of the slightest value. Anything missed by the first contingent would be patiently ferreted out by the second or third.

On top of our *kang* were two very old and dilapidated wooden chests. I was sleeping nearby when the civilized thieves came again—before the blood of our dog, killed by the previous group, was yet dry. They turned the chests upside down and emptied out their entire raggedy contents. After the vandals had left, mother came in. I was still concealed by the chests. I must have been sleeping very soundly; I'm sure the thieves, having failed to find anything worth stealing, would have killed me had they heard me cry. In those days, the life of a Chinese wasn't worth much. Besides, I was such a weak and disreputable-looking child.

These are but a few minor events from among many during that great massacre, that great plunder, that great humiliation. If I'd been old enough at the time to remember things, I could describe the allied armies' atrocities more vividly, better revealing their "grandeur" and "enlightenment." And of course, I would have even greater understanding and affection for the Boxers: no matter how many shortcomings they might have had, their patriotic, anti-imperialist zeal and courage are greatly to be admired.

However, 80 or 90 percent of all the accounts I've read of the Boxer uprising (all written by intellectuals of the day) censure the Boxers. Relatively little mention is made of the burning, killing, and looting carried out by the allied powers. It was the popular tales about the Boxers that were published last year, rather than the articles written by the intellectuals, that encouraged me to go ahead and write this play. Those stories gave me a true picture of the Boxers. Regardless of whether I've written a good play or not, at least I've managed to get off my chest something that's been weighing on me for several decades now.

I was so excited as I wrote this play! Thinking back on those terrible things my mother used to tell me, then seeing those big Three Red Flags before our very eyes—who can deny that we've escaped from Hell and caught a glimpse of Paradise?

The "civilized" thieves of today are still thieves, however, and they've even updated their techniques of looting and killing. Not only do they call themselves "civilized," they keep chanting "peace" and "freedom." To "peacefully" and "freely" kill and plunder, scheme and cheat—this new method is thoroughly evil—more horrendous even than the old one. Those who do not take heed now will pay heavily and suffer greatly when they discover it is too late!

"Tule yi kou qi: *Shenquan* houji" (I've finally got it off my chest: Postface to *Divine fists*), 1961, in *Lao She shenghuo yu chuangzuo zishu* (Lao She's own writings on his life and works) (Hong Kong, 1980), pp. 171–76.

—Translated by Beata Grant

Lu Xun

Lu Xun (pseud. of Zhou Shuren, 1881–1936, from Shaoxing, Zhejiang) was China's leading modern writer and social critic. He studied medicine in Japan before deciding to devote his energies to literature as a means of curing the Chinese soul—or, as he conceived it, the national character.

Beginning in 1918, he used vernacular Chinese to write short stories bearing devastating criticism of traditional culture. These were assembled in the collections, *Nahan* (Outcry, also translated as "Call to Arms" and "Cheering from the Sidelines," 1923), and *Panghuang* (Wondering, 1926). The text below, with its often cited metaphor of China as an iron prison house that suffocates those who live in it, was originally published as the preface to the first volume. Between 1918 and 1936, the author published many more volumes of essays and translations.

At the end of his life, Lu Xun turned increasingly to the left, playing an active role in the League of Left-Wing Writers after 1930. He was posthumously canonized by Mao Zedong, on the basis of his scathing criticism and sardonic *zawen* (miscellaneous) essays.

A Literary Outcry
Awakening from Unconsciousness

Lu Xun

December 3, 1922, in Peking

Preface to My First Collection of Short Stories, *Outcry*

When I was young I, too, had many dreams. Most of them came to be forgotten, but I see nothing in this to regret. For although recalling the past may make you happy, it may also make you lonely, and there is no point in clinging in spirit to lonely, bygone days. My trouble is that I cannot completely forget. These stories come from what I was unable to erase from my memory.

For more than four years, I used to go, almost daily, to a pawnbroker's, and to a medicine shop. I cannot remember how old I was then, but the counter in the medicine shop was the same height as I, and that in the pawnbroker's twice my height. I used to hand clothes and trinkets up to the counter twice my height, take the money so contemptuously given me, then go to the counter my own height to buy medicine for my father, who had long been ill. On my return home, I had other things to keep me busy, for since the physician who made out the prescriptions was very well known, he used unusual drugs: aloe root dug up in winter, sugar cane that had been three years exposed to frost, twin crickets, and ardisia— all of which were difficult to procure. But my father's illness went from bad to worse, until he died.

I believe that those who sink from prosperity to poverty will probably come, in the process, to understand what the world is really like. I wanted to go to the K___ school in N___,[1] perhaps because I was in search of a change of scene and faces. There was nothing for my mother to do but to raise eight yuan for my

---

[1] The Jiangnan (formerly Kiangnan) Naval Academy in Nanjing.

traveling expenses and say I might do as I pleased. That she cried was only natural, for at that time the proper thing was to study the classics and take the official examinations. Anyone who studied "foreign subjects" was looked down upon as a good-for-nothing fellow who'd sold his soul to the foreign devils out of desperation. Besides, she was sorry to part with me. Despite all that, I went to N___ and entered the K___ school; and it was there that I first heard the names of such subjects as "natural philosophy," arithmetic, geography, history, drawing, and physical training. They had no biology course, but we saw wood-block editions of such works as *A New Treatise on the Human Body* and *Treatise on Chemistry and Hygiene.* Recalling the talk and prescriptions of physicians I had known, and comparing them with what I now knew, I came to the conclusion that the Chinese doctors must be either unwitting or deliberate charlatans; and I began to sympathize with the invalids and families who suffered at their hands. From translated histories, I also learned that the Japanese reforms had originated, to a great extent, with the introduction of Western medical science to Japan.

These inklings took me to a provincial medical college in Japan. I dreamed a beautiful dream that on my return to China, I would cure patients like my father who had been wrongly treated, while if war broke out, I would serve as an army doctor, at the same time strengthening my countrymen's faith in reform.

I am no longer conversant with the pedagogy of microbiology, in which there have now been great advances, but in those days, lantern slides were used to show the microbes; and if the lecture ended early, the instructor might show slides of natural landscapes or current events to fill up the time. This was during the Russo-Japanese War, so there were many scenes from the war, and I had to join in the clapping and cheering in the lecture hall along with the other students. It was a long time since I had seen any fellow Chinese, but one day I saw a slide that had a lot of them in it. One of the fellows was bound, while a crowd of others stood around him. They all looked physically strong but completely apathetic in spirit. According to the commentary, the one with his hands bound was a spy working for the Russians. He was to have his head cut off by the Japanese military as a warning to others, while the Chinese beside him had come to enjoy the spectacle.

Before the term was over, I had left for Tokyo, for the incident had left me feeling that medical science was not so important after all. The people of a weak and backward country, however strong and healthy they might be, could only serve to be made examples of, or to witness such futile spectacles; it didn't really matter how many of them died of illness. The most important thing, therefore, was to change their spirit. Since, at that time, I felt literature to be the best means to this end, I determined to promote a literary movement. There were many Chinese students in Tokyo studying law and government, the natural sciences, even police work and engineering, but not one studying literature or art. Even in that uncongenial atmosphere, however, I was fortunate enough to find some kindred spirits. We gathered the few others we needed, and, after discussion, our first step, of course, was to publish a magazine, the title of which denoted that this was a new birth. As we were then rather classically inclined, we gave it a short title in classical Chinese: *New Life* (*Xin sheng*).

When the time for publication drew near, some of our contributors dropped out, and then our funds were withdrawn, until finally there were only three of us left, and we were penniless. Since we had started our magazine at an unlucky hour, there was naturally no one to whom we could complain when we failed; but later, even we three were destined to part, and our discussions of a dream future had to cease. So ended our *New Life*, before it was born.

Only later did I feel the futility of it all; at that time, I did not really understand anything. Later, I felt that if one's proposals met with approval, it should encourage one, whereas if they met with opposition, it should make one fight back. The real tragedy was to lift up one's voice among the living and meet with no response: no approval, and no opposition, as if one were left helpless in a boundless desert. So I began to feel lonely.

And this feeling of loneliness grew day by day, coiling about my soul like a huge poisonous snake. Yet in spite of my unaccountable sadness, I felt no indignation; for this experience had made me reflect and see that I was definitely not the heroic type who could rally multitudes at his call.

My loneliness had to be dispelled, however, for it was causing me agony. So I used various means to dull my senses, both by conforming to the spirit of the time and by turning to the past. Later, I experienced or witnessed even greater causes for loneliness and sadness, which I do not like to recall, preferring that they should perish with me. Still, my attempt to deaden my senses was not unsuccessful—I had lost the enthusiasm and fervor of my youth.

In S___ Hostel[2] there were three rooms where it was said a woman had lived who hanged herself on the locust tree in the courtyard. Although the tree had grown so tall that its branches could no longer be reached, the rooms remained deserted. For some years I stayed here, copying ancient inscriptions. I had few visitors, there were no contemporary "problems or isms" in those inscriptions,[3] and my only desire was that my life should slip quietly away like this. On summer nights, when there were too many mosquitoes, I would sit under the locust tree, waving my fan and looking at the specks of sky through the thick leaves, while the caterpillars that came out in the evening would fall, icy-cold, onto my neck.

The only visitor to come for an occasional talk was my old friend Jin Xinyi. He would put his big portfolio down on the shabby table, take off his long gown, and sit facing me, looking as if his heart was still beating fast after braving the dogs.

---

[2]Shaoxing. Fellow-townsmen from Shaoxing like Lu Xun could avail themselves of a Shaoxing-run inn whenever in Peking.

[3]A satiric reference to a 1919 polemic between Hu Shi and more radical intellectuals about whether China could be saved by sweeping ideologies.

"What is the use of copying these?" he demanded inquisitively one night, after looking through the inscriptions I had copied.

"No use at all."

"Then why copy them?"

"For no particular reason."

"I think you might write something—"

I understood. They were editing the magazine *New Youth*, but so far there seemed to be no response: no approval, and no opposition. I guessed that they must be feeling lonely. However, I said:

"Imagine an iron house without windows, absolutely indestructible, with many people fast asleep inside who will soon die of suffocation. But you know that since they will die in their sleep, they will not feel the pain of death. Now, if you cry aloud to wake a few of the lighter sleepers, making those unfortunate few suffer the agony of irrevocable death, do you think you are doing them a good turn?"

"But if a few awake, you can't say there is no hope of destroying the iron house."

True, in spite of my own conviction, I could not blot out hope, for hope lies in the future. I could not use my own evidence to refute his assertion that it might exist. So I agreed to write, and the result was my first story, "A Madman's Diary." From that time onward, I could not stop writing. I would compose some sort of short story from time to time at the request of friends, until I had more than a dozen of them.

I no longer feel any great urge to express myself. Yet, perhaps because I have not entirely forgotten the grief of my past loneliness, I sometimes call out, to comfort those fighters galloping on in loneliness, so that they will not lose heart. Whether my cry is brave or sad, repellent or ridiculous, I do not care. Since it is a cry from the sidelines, however, I must naturally obey orders from the commanders. This is why I often resort to euphemisms and unauthentic touches, as when I made a wreath appear from nowhere at the son's grave in "Medicine," while in "Tomorrow" I did not say that Fourth Shan's Wife really did not see her little boy in her dream. For our chiefs then were against pessimism. And I, for my part, did not want young people who were still dreaming the pleasant dreams I had when I was young to be infected with the loneliness I had found so bitter.

It is clear, then, that my short stories fall far short of being works of art; hence I count myself fortunate that they are still known as stories, and are even being collected in a book. Although such good fortune makes me uneasy, I am nevertheless pleased to think they have readers in this world, at least for the time being.

Since these short stories of mine are being reprinted in one collection, owing to the reasons given above, I have named it *Outcry*.

"Nahan zixu" (Preface to *Outcry*), Peking, December 3, 1922, revised from the translation in *Selected Stories of Lu Hsun* (Peking, 1963), in *Lu Xun lun chuangzuo* (Lu Xun on literary creation) (Shanghai, 1983), pp. 3–7.

—Translated by Yang Xianyi and Gladys Yang

Ba Jin

BA JIN (pseud. of Li Feigan, b. 1904, in Chengdu), who began life in an upper-class family in Sichuan, became one of China's most popular writers of the twentieth century. An anarchist in his youth, he was influenced in his writing by Gorky, Turgenev, and Tolstoy; he translated works by them and many others into Chinese. His pen name was chosen as an acronym from the Chinese transliterations of *Ba*kunin and Kropot*kin*.

In the memoirs in the form of essays that he has written since the late 1970s, Ba Jin looks back on the most creative years of his life, during the 1930s and 1940s; on the years when he was a submissive intellectual, in the early PRC; on the Cultural Revolution, when he was cruelly silenced; and finally, on the decade of Deng Xiaoping's reforms, when he was elected honorary chairman of the Chinese Writers' Association, following the death of Mao Dun (in 1981).

The essay below comments on what is still Ba Jin's most influential novel, *Jia* (Family, 1931), which he wrote after two formative years in France, 1927–29. The story portrays the clash between traditional and modern values within a wealthy family during the early 1930s. Each generation had to cope with the aftermath.

My *J'accuse* Against This Moribund System

Notes on a Crumbling Landlord Clan of Western Sichuan

Ba Jin

October 1956

MANY writers like to put everything they have to say into their works; others prefer to express their views outside of them. I mainly come into the latter category. Every one of my novels and collections of short stories is accompanied by my own foreword or afterword. Some of my overindulgent readers do not mind my longwindedness. There are even those who care so much about the fate of the characters in my fiction that they write me well-intentioned inquiries about what happens to them later. Take this novel, *Family,* which I wrote twenty-six years ago. I still get letters from readers who want me to put them in correspondence with characters in the book, and who can't rest easy until they know that the characters have lived to see the enlightened New China. For over twenty years, readers have been constantly writing to me to tell me that the character Gao Juehui [the young hero of the novel] is identical with me, the author. My repeated explanations make no difference: I received such a letter only yesterday. The main reason is because readers would like to have Juehui living among them and sharing today's happiness.

I find readers' kindness both moving and painful. I don't sigh over Juehui. I know how many Juehuis are alive today and working enthusiastically for New China's socialist construction. I find it extremely sad that Juexin [an elder brother of Juehui in the novel] could not have seen today's sunlight and let it bring some light and warmth out from his young life. Juexin was not only a character in a book; he was also my eldest brother. I received the news of his suicide in a telegram when I was writing *Family* in Shanghai twenty-six years ago and had just reached the sixth chapter. You can imagine what I felt as I finished the novel.

I made it public a long time ago that I'm not a cool, calm writer, and that I do not write fiction just to be an author. My past life forced me to take up the pen. I have also said, "I have loved or hated every character in my books, and I have seen or experienced many of the scenes in them." Truly, when writing *Family*, I felt I was suffering with some of them and struggling in the claws of the same monster. I laughed and wept with those dear young lives, and at every word I wrote it was as if I were digging up the graves of my memories and seeing again everything that had once stirred my heart. When I was a boy, I often saw dear young lives being ruined or even cruelly ended. Love made me suffer, but it also filled me with loathing and curses. I have experienced the emotions that Juehui felt in front of the coffin of his dead cousin Mei, and I have even said what Juehui said in front of his elder brother: "Let *them* be the sacrificial victims for once." It was only when I finished *Family*, at the end of 1931, that I had the chance to pour out my hatred of the feudal clan system. That is why in my 1937 piece, "In Lieu of a Foreword," I dared to write: "I want to shout out my *J'accuse* against this moribund system." I also said that it was my belief in the inevitable collapse of the feudal clan system that had spurred me to write this history of a feudal clan, this tale of the joys and sorrows, the partings and encounters of a crumbling, feudal landlord clan. I called the story *The Torrents Trilogy*, adding two sequels to *Family*: *Spring* and *Autumn*.

I can say that the reason I know so well the people and the life I wrote about is that I spent the first nineteen years of my life in just such a family. I had been with those people morning, noon, and night, loving them and hating them. But what I wrote was the story not of my own family, but of any family of land-owning officials. Chengdu, in the western Sichuan basin, was a city full of such households in those days. In such families, the senior generation had been officials of the Qing dynasty; the next lived a life of idle extravagance with the wealth their fathers or grandfathers had left them; and the young longed to break out of their gilded prisons. The area was carved up among warlords great and small who fought occasional minor wars among themselves. The elders wished for the restoration of the Qing dynasty, and their juniors either shut themselves in or went out drinking, whoring, and gambling. The young swore to create a new life with their own hands; some even wanted to redeem the crimes of their ancestors. Today, the elders are all dead and their immediate successors are no longer capable of supporting themselves. Of the young, some have given all their blood for the Chinese revolution and some are working to build the New China. But in 1920 and 1921, the time of *Family*, the whole Gao family is still under the rule of its grandfather even though the May Fourth movement has already happened and set the hearts of most young Chinese aflame. The old patriarch Gao is a feudal monarch with all the Confucian values as the theoretical basis of his rule. He is my grandfather, and the grandfather of some of my relations' families. He held the purse strings, and as the land rent he received every year was enough to support the whole extended family, they all had to obey him. The power of life and death over the young was in his hands. He thought that money could solve every problem. It never occurred to him that the young had souls. He lived on the land rent but had no idea how the peasants lived. Even when warlords ruthlessly extracted several years' advance land taxes from the peasants all at once, his income was still enough to keep the whole family in prosperity and comfort. He believed that the family would last forever. He thought that his sons would follow his example, and that his grandsons, too, would do as he had done. He had no idea that his money would only corrupt his sons' souls, and that his tyranny would force his grandsons into revolution. Even less was he aware that he was digging the family's grave with his own hands. He had built up the family fortune, and he destroyed it. His biggest dream was to have four generations under one roof. (Some big landlord families may have managed to hold on till the fifth generation.) It was not just my grandfather: all Grandfather Gaos had taken the same road. They wanted to see a harmonious family, but the peaceful surface concealed much jostling for position, much struggle and tragedy. So many young lives suffered, struggled, and ended up in inevitable destruction. But the naive and courageous rebels finally broke out, found a new world, and brought a breath of fresh air into a household where the atmosphere was almost fatally oppressive.

Although my grandfather was a diehard, he was no fool. Before his death, he realized that his dreams had been shattered. He died lonely and a failure. My second uncle tried, like a true gentleman, to hold the family property he had inherited from my grandfather together for a few years, but finally he departed this life with a sense of despair and desolation. Later, the house was sold and the family scattered, some to die and some to go away. When I was back in Chengdu in 1941, my fifth uncle died in prison a petty thief, destitute and in broken health. After he had spent everything left him by my grandfather and all that his wife had brought him, he could not face her or the children again, and so he became a homeless wanderer. There was another side to him that I did not put into the novel. He had a fine appearance and could write poetry and prose; in another age, he might have been able to make something of his talents. But the old-fashioned feudal family murdered his vitality, leaving him a menace to himself and to others. Because of him, I later wrote a novel called *Leisure Garden* (*Qi yuan*).

I said before that Juexin was my eldest brother. He was the person I loved best in all my life. I often think that if I had written *Family* earlier, he might have been able to see the abyss that was in front of him and avoid falling into it. But it was too late. Just when the Shanghai *Times* (*Shibao*) had started serializing the novel, he took poison and killed himself in Chengdu. Fourteen years later, another of my older brothers died of illness in Shanghai. Just like Juexin, Juemin, and Juehui, we three brothers had different characters and ended up differently. I have often said that these nearly twenty years of my early life weighed down on my heart like a nightmare. The nightmare cruelly destroyed the souls of many of my young contemporaries. I almost became one of the victims myself, but I was saved by "naïveté" and "boldness." In that, I was perhaps like Juehui. Trusting to my simple beliefs, I had a goal toward which I was striding: I wanted to be my own master and do what other people would not allow me to do. In the magazines I ran, I published some pieces that were superficial and open to suspicions of plagiarism. I could not claim to have mature ideas then. But I have always held to the memory of Danton's words: "*l'audace, encore de l'audace, toujours de l'audace.*" This triple boldness was in those circumstances unexpectedly effective, and it helped me win a preliminary liberation. Juehui, too, relied on his "boldness" to escape from that crumbling household and find a new world for himself. But devotion to courtesy and nonresistance killed Juexin.

Some readers are concerned about some of the leading female characters in the novel—Ruijue, Mei, Mingfeng, and Qin—and would like to know more about them. The four of them represent four different kinds of personal character, and they come to two kinds of end. Ruijue's personality is different from that of my sister-in-law. Although the latter was forced to move out of the city after my grandfather died and give birth in a thatched cottage, she did not meet the same cruel death there as Ruijue did. I had a maternal cousin the same age as Mei, and she was at first very close to my eldest brother. She often used to visit us, and everyone in my generation, both men and women, liked her. We were all hoping that she would become our sister-in-law, but later we heard that our paternal aunt was against marriage with a relative. (She had suffered enough herself because of such a marriage; the wife of my father's third brother was a girl from my aunt's husband's family.) The result was that the young lovers could never marry. Four or five years later, my cousin became the second wife of a rich man, and in the ensuing dozen or so years, she bore him a brood of children. By the time I saw her again, in Chengdu in 1942, she had become a ridiculous fat woman who lived only for money.

We had a maid in the family called Cuifeng. I can't remember anything about her, except that a distant relation of ours sent someone to ask for her as his concubine. When her uncle asked her whether she agreed, she turned it down flat. Although she was not in love with any of the young gentlemen [unlike Mingfeng, a maid in the novel], she did later choose to marry a poor peasant. In character, she was different from Mingfeng, and she was, besides, a self-supporting servant who earned her food and lodging through her labor and thus was still her own mistress. Her uncle was an old family retainer of ours, and he was not cruel to her. She was thus luckier than Mingfeng and did not have to end up in the waters of a lake.

When I wrote about Mei, Ruijue, and Mingfeng, my heart was full of sympathy, grief, and indignation. I am pleased that I was able to put my own feelings into the novel and cry out against injustice on behalf of all those young women who were needlessly sacrificed.

I really was extremely sad and angry. I remember that when I was a boy of five or six, I found an illustrated edition of the *Lives of Women Martyrs* (*Lie nü zhuan*) in my elder sister's room. There was a picture at the bottom of the page and text at the top. We had very few illustrated books in the house during my childhood, which is why I treasured that tattered book sewn in the traditional Chinese style. I lingered over every page. The book was full of beautiful ladies in old-fashioned clothes. Among them was one cutting off her own hand, one burning to death, one floating in the water, and one cutting her own throat with scissors. There was even a young woman hanging herself from the top of a high building. They were all horrifying stories. Why were such fates reserved for women alone? It made no sense to me. I asked my two elder sisters, and they told me these were the *Lives of Women Martyrs*. All young girls had to read books like that. It still made no sense to me. I asked my mother. She told me these were chaste heroines for all eras. One was a widow who, when a strange man took her by the hand, cut it off herself in front of him. Another was a royal consort. When there was a fire in the palace and her companions did not come for her, she preferred to burn to death in the palace rather than expose her face outside. Why did women, and especially young women, have to suffer or even lay down their lives for the sake of those ridiculous, old-fashioned notions, for that artificial Confucian ideology? Why was that blood-soaked *Lives of Women Martyrs* supposed to be an example for women to follow? Not even my mother's explanation could convince me. I could not believe in that gory and horrifying "morality." Even if other people supported it, I was against it. Soon afterward, that moral code was smashed by the Revolution of 1911, and after I had worn out that copy of the *Lives of Women Martyrs*, another copy could not be found, even in our house. But the atmosphere in our home still stank of blood. In the early years of the Republic, a cousin of mine "distinguished" herself by marrying the memorial tablet of her dead fiancé. She had been so carried away by reading the *Lives of Women Martyrs* that she wanted to remain faithful to the dead fiancé she had never even seen, dreaming that a memorial arch would be put up to her chastity. Even after the May Fourth movement, when Peking University had started taking women students, three women students who had bobbed their hair could no longer stay in Chengdu but had to flee to Shanghai or Peking. It goes without saying that none of my sisters enjoyed rights as human beings. In 1923, my third sister was carried off in a wedding sedan chair to be a second wife to a stranger. She was treated so badly by her parents-in-law that a year later she died alone in a hospital—the same end as Hui in *Spring*. Her husband left her coffin in a Buddhist nunnery, while he busied himself having the lanterns and decorations put out so that he could be a bridegroom for the third time. Finally, my eldest brother had to pay to have her buried.

I really cannot bear digging up the graves of my memories. I do not know how many unbearably painful stories are buried there.

Yet, in the dark night that was our family, "Qin" appeared. She is the image of a paternal cousin of mine, and I also put into her some blood from a few New Women I knew. In the two or three years before I left home, she might well have turned into a woman like Qin. She was an eager reader of books and magazines about the new thinking. My third elder brother used to spend a couple of hours reading and talking with her every evening, but later on, her mother and my stepmother quarreled. Soon after that, she and her mother moved out of our residence. Although we were still living on the same street, we never had another chance to meet. Third Brother and she continued writing to each other. The morning of the day my brother and I left Chengdu, we went to her house, so at least we caught sight of her. This was the last scene I wrote in the novel. Circumstances were cruel to that adorable young girl. Nobody helped her to escape from her cage, like Shuying. Her parents used their emotions like iron bars to keep her inside their house, which was like an ancient shrine. She could not see any strangers. It was said that after the mother's death, her father was too mean to pay for a wedding, keeping her at home and refusing to find her a husband. I saw her again when I went back to Chengdu in 1942. By then she was a frail old lady, though in fact she was only a year older than I. In the novel, I borrowed a couplet she wrote long ago and put it into Mei's mouth:

> *The past, as vague and unclear as a dream,*
> *comes into my mind with wind and rain.*

All the cutting edge of her talent was ground away by life in the prison of the family. She finished up as an eccentric old maid, confined to the house till the end of her days, and with nobody at all to sympathize with her. She left the thirty or forty mu [two or three hectares] of land that was her portion of her father's estate to two of her brothers.

If I say all this about the novel I wrote when I was twenty-seven and offer such repeated explanations, this may help today's readers to understand the author's frame of mind when he wrote it. When I reread *Family* recently, I was still very moved. I like this novel because it can tell me one thing at least: that youth is beautiful.

I will always remember that youth is beautiful. It has always been the source of my inspiration.

"Tan *Jia*" (About *Family*), October 1956, in Ba Jin, *Jia* (Family) (Changsha, 1981), pp. 16–23.

—Translated by W. J. F. Jenner

Mao Dun

MAO DUN (pseud. of Shen Yanbing, 1896–1981), a critic, novelist, and short-story writer noted for his commitment to the doctrine of realism, and as a realistic chronicler of the turbulent decades before the Communist victory, hailed from Tongxiang, Zhejiang. He worked for the Commercial Press in Shanghai and between 1921 and 1932 edited China's foremost literary journal, the *Xiaoshuo yuebao* (Short story monthly), while playing a leading role in the influential Literary Research Association. His novels, especially those in the trilogy *Shi* (Eclipse, 1930), portray the struggles of young intellectuals. His best-known novel continues to be *Ziye* (Midnight, 1933), which analyzes the industrial communities in Shanghai. The following essay explains his motivation for writing it.

Mao Dun served as minister of culture from 1949 to 1965. He mostly discontinued his creative writing.

Shanghai's Silk Industry
World Economic Crisis, Workers, and Civil War

Mao Dun

MY TOPIC can be divided into two parts: The first is my motivation for writing [*Midnight*]. It had not been very convenient for me to be in Shanghai in 1928, and I found it stifling living up on the third floor day after day. So I went to Japan, stayed about two years, and then returned to Shanghai in the spring of 1930. This was the time when Wang Jingwei was preparing to hold his Enlarged Party Conference in Peking; the battle between Northern and Southern forces had just been joined.[1] It was also the period when the workers' movement in Shanghai and the other large cities was at high tide. At the time, I was afflicted by a serious eye disease and my doctor had enjoined me from reading. If I did not give it up for eight months—perhaps a year—the illness would recur, even should it appear to get better temporarily. I respected the doctor's order to convalesce patiently, not only because of the eye disease, but also because I was suffering from neurasthenia. I devoted myself completely to recuperation. Having nothing to do, I wandered about the city and found that the time passed easily. My social relationships in Shanghai had been complex all along; my friends included both members of the revolutionary party engaged in political work and liberals. Among my older friends and fellow townspeople were entrepreneurs, public servants, merchants, and bankers. Since I was at leisure at the time, I had frequent contact with them, and they told me a good deal. I, who had theretofore had only the vaguest ideas about social phenomena, now saw things much more clearly. I planned to use this raw material to write a novel. Later,

---

[1]As northern warlords Yan Xishan and Feng Yuxiang battled the Nanjing government of Chiang Kai-shek in the South, Wang Jingwei and the northerners planned an enlarged Kuomintang conference to set up an anti-Chiang government in Peking in 1930.

when my eye disease was somewhat better and I could read again, I perused a number of essays on contemporary Chinese society and was able to contrast what I had observed personally with the theories presented in the essays. That increased my interest in writing a novel.

Political workers in Shanghai were busily engaged in a large-scale revolutionary movement and had begun a series of fierce struggles on every front. Although I was not then participating in political work, I had political experience from before 1927. And although 1930 was not 1927, I found that I could still comprehend the issues raised by the participants and the problems they had found in their work.

By the spring of 1930, the world economic panic had reached Shanghai. Under the pressure of foreign capital and the threat of the world economic panic, China's national capitalists tightened their exploitation of the working class, in order to pass their own crisis on to others. They increased the length of the workday, reduced wages, and fired large numbers of workers. This elicited strong resistance from the workers. So economic struggles broke out, many of which developed into political struggles; the objective conditions for popular struggle were very good then.

Recovery from my illness coincided with a new stage in the Chinese revolution and a time of acrimonious debates on the nature of Chinese society. I planned to use the genre of the novel to write on the following three issues: (1) how, under the pressure of imperialist economic aggression, the influence of world economic panic, and in an environment of agricultural bankruptcy, national industry had used still crueler methods to tighten its exploitation of the working class, to preserve itself; (2) how this, in turn, had provoked economic and political struggles on the part of the working class; and (3) how war between the Northern and Southern forces, economic bankruptcy in the countryside, and peasant insurrection had intensified the national industrial panic.

These three were all part of a chain of cause and effect. I planned to start from there and give it imagistic expression. Of course, this sort of novel would raise many questions, but I wished to answer only one. I wanted to reply to the Trotskyists, to show that China had not begun the course of capitalist development—that China, under the oppression of imperialism, was in fact becoming even more colonial. Although there were within the Chinese national bourgeoisie some who resembled the French bourgeoisie, the future of the Chinese national bourgeoisie was extremely bleak, for semicolonial China in 1930 was different from eighteenth-century France. It was this foundation that produced the wavering nature of the Chinese national bourgeoisie. At the time, they had two ways of escape: (1) to surrender to imperialism and become compradores, or (2) compromise with the feudal forces.[2] In the end, they took both routes.

In fact, I started writing this book before the summer vacation of 1931. In the

---

[2]China's traditional landlord class and the domestic warlords.

past, my habit had been not to write very much in the summer and winter; it was too hot in summer, and in the winter, keeping a stove burning inside was a bit stifling. In the winter of 1930 I assembled materials, wrote out a detailed outline, and made a list of the characters—male and female, capitalists, workers, and so forth. The character of each person, his or her upbringing and development, and so forth were all decided. The second step was to write a chapter-by-chapter outline, before beginning to write. At that point, I was very ambitious and planned to write about both country and city. For the several years previous, rural bankruptcy had given rise to waves of peasant insurrection, and this instability in the countryside had caused rural capital to concentrate in the cities. In theory, this should have furthered urban industrial development, but this was not in fact the case; the economic bankruptcy of the countryside had greatly diminished the purchasing power of the peasantry and shrunk the market for commodities. At the same time, the capital flowing into the cities not only failed to contribute to the development of production, it actually increased the instability of the marketplace. For the capital flowing into the cities was not invested in productive enterprises, but was used for speculation. The third chapter of *Midnight* describes the beginning of this process. I originally planned to develop the situation into a "symphony" of country and city, but summer arrived after I had written the first three or four chapters. The weather was particularly hot that year; for over a month, the temperature was over ninety degrees every day. My study, on the third floor, was especially hot, so I simply had to stop work for a while.

The novel was not finished until the outbreak of fighting with Japan in Shanghai, on January 28, 1932. Because I had stopped for a time in the midst of the work, my enthusiasm had diminished somewhat, along with my courage. More than that, the more I looked at what I had written, the poorer it seemed to me. I thus came to feel that my original plan was too grandiose, that I simply was not capable of it. The upshot was that I shrank my original project by half and decided to write only about the city and not about the country. In writing about the city, I sought to combine the depiction of three elements: (1) the speculative market; (2) the national bourgeoisie; and (3) the working class. Censorship was so strict at the time that if I overstressed or made too obvious the activities of the revolutionaries, the book would be unpublishable. So, to get it printed openly, there were many places where I had to use hints and indirection. The reader, however, could always read between the lines and perceive the activities of the revolutionaries. For instance, in describing the struggle against "yellow-dog unions" [pro-KMT unions], I could not use the phrase "yellow-dog union."

Why did I choose the owner of a silk factory to represent the national bourgeoisie? In this, I was bound by the nature of my material. For one thing, I was relatively familiar with the silk industry and, for another, silk knitted the country and the city together. In 1928–29, the price of silk dropped precipitously, which influenced the price of cocoons. So city and country alike were victims of the economic crisis.

The book's method of composition was as follows: I first thought through the characters and made a chart of them, in which I established the development of their personal qualities and their relationships with one another. I then drafted an outline of the story and divided it into chapters and sections, making sure they all linked up and worked in concert with each other. This method was not my invention but was copied from others. Balzac originally had no intention of being a novelist. He planned instead to run a bookshop that reprinted famous works in pocket editions. He made arrangements for it with a friend, and the two of them became partners. Later on, when they were losing money, Balzac had to take responsibility for his half. As he lacked money, he had to write novels; he entered into a contract with a publisher stipulating that he would deliver the goods within a fixed period of time. Since he was pressed for time, however, and could never meet his deadlines, he thought of an ingenious solution to his problem: he would first write a very simple outline, then make emendations and additions. In this way, he was able to get his manuscripts in on time and collect his fee. I was not as anxious as Balzac and so did not need to do exactly as he did. Sometimes I would write a one-or-two-thousand-word outline for a novel that ended up with only ten to twenty thousand words per chapter.

The first chapter of *Midnight* describes the senior Mr. Wu's journey from the country to the city, and his death from a brain hemorrhage. The senior Mr. Wu is like an "ancient corpse" that becomes desiccated as soon as it comes in contact with sunlight and air. There is a sort of double metaphor here: those of you who have read a certain masterpiece of economics will know what I am referring to. The second chapter consists of the bustling scene at the senior Mr. Wu's funeral, in which the main characters of *Midnight* all put in an appearance. A large number of the threads of the plot are thus all brought in at the same time, so that they can later be developed and intertwined. In terms of the technical structure, one wants at such a point to avoid flatness at all costs, but if it's too ingenious, it will seem unnatural.

"Ziye shi zenyang xiecheng de" (How *Midnight* was written), in *Changpian xiaoshuo chuangzuo jingyan tan* (Experiences in the creation of novels) (Changsha, 1981), pp. 11–15.

—Translated by Theodore Huters

Shen Congwen

SHEN CONGWEN (1902–1988), from Fenghuang, West Hunan, was born into a military family and joined a local army unit at the age of thirteen. West Hunan is a land of military tradition and non-Chinese cultures. In some of his works, Shen judged the larger Han culture from a regional or ethnic Miao perspective; he himself had a hushed-up Miao and Tujia ancestry. Shen Congwen was self-educated and never traveled abroad until he was an old man, in the post-Mao era. In 1922, he moved to Peking and began to write. Subsequently he taught modern Chinese literature courses and composition at the college level.

Shen Congwen's creativity was prolific and uneven. Short stories were his forte. Among his best-loved longer works are his autobiography (1934) and the novel *Bian cheng* (Border town, 1934). After the Communist victory in 1949, Shen Congwen was viciously attacked. He attempted suicide and stopped writing. Later, he occupied himself by publishing scholarly research on painting, lacquerware, bronze mirrors, textiles, costumes, and other relics in the ancient Peking palace. To the editors of this volume he expressed only contempt for the Communist government up until his dying days; the Nobel Prize in literature, for which he was nominated several times, would have been an embarrassing experience for the Chinese government had he been awarded it.

In the following essay from the early 1940s, Shen Congwen explores the meaning and functions of China's New Literature in light of the somewhat different role of traditional Chinese vernacular fiction.

Fiction and Society
Changes and Continuities in Mass Audiences

Shen Congwen

September 29, 1942, in Kunming

WE OFTEN hear people say, "I'm reading a novel for I've got nothing to do." Or, "How should I spend my vacation? Guess I'll read a novel." In spite of differences in their life-styles and social status, a variety of people—the shopkeeper sitting at leisure behind the counter, the civil servant having nothing to do in his office, even factory directors, commissioners, unlucky dentists, and hot-tempered nurses—use fiction to pass the time and derive pleasure and education from the lives of the characters. Observe the literate maidservant back home who's about fifty, or any elementary pupil over the age of ten; their infatuation with novels proves just how widespread is this phenomenon of "obtaining pleasure and education from fiction." Many parents who are dissatisfied with their children's grades will tell you, "This child simply won't buckle down—he's crazy about novels." But novels are books, so why should only children be crazy about them? . . .

The most interesting "sketchbook" account of the impact of fiction is found in Zou Tao's *Thrice Picking Up My Rustic Brush (San jie lu bi tan)*. It tells of a man named Jin from Suzhou who was obsessed with *The Dream of the Red Chamber*. This man set up a wooden memorial tablet in his home for the heroine Lin Daiyu and held a sacrificial ceremony for her every day. When he came to the passages where she refuses to eat and burns her papers, he so empathized with this sentimental and ill-fated girl-genius that he, too, would skip his meals and abandon himself to tears. Finally, of course, he went mad. Later, he secretly left home to visit the "Lady of the Bamboo Lodge" [Lin Daiyu]. This drove his family into a state of panic. Several months passed before they finally found him.

The Sketchbook from an Undistinguished and Idle Studio (Yong xian zhai bi ji), by Chen Qiyuan, tells the story of the beautiful young daughter of a Hangzhou merchant. She was a poetess, and her love for *The Dream of the Red Chamber* caused her to come down with consumption. As her death approached, her parents, grieved and angry, tossed the books she kept by her pillow into the fireplace, only to find themselves reproached tearfully by their daughter, "Why must you kill my Baoyu?" She died the moment the book caught fire. Such people and incidents may be common even today. There are many who idolize Baoyu as their "true love." Many others, having a little flair for composition and frequently suffering from mild ailments, imagine themselves to be Daiyu. The difference between then and now is only that, while the man Jin from Suzhou was in love with the novel's heroine and the Hangzhou poetess its hero, young ladies and gentlemen today take themselves to be the heroes. They've fallen in love with themselves. . . .

Moving from fiction's "effect" to its "value," we see that whether a literary work is good or bad depends on the reader. Take *The Dream of the Red Chamber* or *Water Margin*. To an ardent defender of traditional morality, these novels can only propagate sex and violence; but our own teenagers, and our servants, too, may take these novels to be personal treasures; and if the sociologist Fei Xiaotong should come along, he might say, after a careful reading, "These novels are simply the most authentic and useful materials on social history to come out of China in the past five hundred years!" . . .

When we try to judge a novel's value on the basis of its usefulness, we seldom get a unanimous opinion. To see how fiction and society influence each other, let us look at the development of Chinese fiction these past thirty years. Understanding the past may give us hope for the future.

The relation between fiction and society in the early Republican years had three aspects: the popularity of traditional novels, the rise of the *new* chapter-driven (*zhanghui*) novels, and the reassessment of the value and social significance of fiction by the reform faction. . . .

The older traditional novels were and are mostly read by ordinary folk. Some people are familiar with the stories from listening to opera or traditional story-tellers. Reading *The Romance of the Three Kingdoms* and *Water Margin* satisfies their hankering for hero-worship; reading *Journey to the West* and *Flowers in the Mirror*, they enjoy a combination of fantasy and humor; and, after reading *Investiture of the Gods*, they feel compelled to wash their hands in compliance with the old superstitious beliefs in ghosts and spirits. The later traditional novels are mostly read by scholars and denizens of the women's quarters. Some readers discover lovers or bosom-friends in novels. The continuing popularity of *Strange Tales from a Chinese Studio* comes from its simple, moving quality and because its beautiful fox-fairies and ghost-heroines fulfill the love needs of many a poor and lonely scholar who imagines himself a great lover. Stories from *Wonders New and Old*, such as "Bondmaid Golden Jade Beats up Her Fickle Lover" or "The Oil Hawker Boy Wins the Renowned Singing Girl," arouse many tears and also many fantasies when read to prostitutes and shopkeepers.

The new chapter-driven novel arose along with newspapers and magazines. Novels like *The Nine-tailed Turtle, Exposure of the Official World, Magnificent Dreams in Shanghai, A Flower in a Sea of Evil, An Unofficial History of Student Life in Japan*, and *Jade Pear Spirit* gained wide readership because they were serialized in newspapers. In those days, Shanghai's *Shenbao* and *Xinwenbao* had subscribers in every province of the nation. The new chapter-driven novels were characterized by an increasingly consistent social orientation. The stories were topical, mainly describing people and events. They mocked Peking officialdom, portrayed the Westernized Shanghai Bund, told of late Qing celebrity scholars and beauties, and recorded the revolutionary activities and love lives of Chinese students in Japan. Others, like Su Manshu and Xu Zhenya, continued to use traditional tear-jerking scholar-beauty (*caizi jiaren*) plots. Their works became known as boudoir novels (*xiang yan xiaoshuo*). Although these novels were not as widely known as the traditional ones, owing to their brief and geographically limited circulation, they had a substantial impact. They gave readers an unforgettable introduction to the degeneracy of Peking, the chic of Shanghai, the fashionable life-styles of the urbane, and the love lives of pasty-faced scholars. By exposing society's weaknesses, these novels naturally contributed to the progress of the revolution. But as some writers began using fiction to blackmail the rich and to fawn on prostitutes and actors, the social image of the novelist continued to be that of "rogue genius," and the value of fiction declined accordingly. This eventually helped stimulate the rise of the New Literature. It led directly to the demise of the chapter-driven novel.

The reformers who reevaluated the social significance of fiction did so in accordance with their modernization platform. To promote scientific education, Mr. Wu Zhihui wrote *A Comprehensive Discussion of Past and Present*. Mr. Lin Shu, who translated large numbers of European novels into Chinese, always discussed the relation between fiction and moral education in his prefaces. Mr. Liang Qichao thought fiction even more important and useful to a people, and he urged that it be assessed anew within literary studies and properly cultivated. A new concept that was all the easier for readers to accept, given the universal popularity of the novels translated by Lin Shu, was that "one is educated about life through literature." This new concept did not necessarily improve people's ability to choose novels, for *The Adventures of Sherlock Holmes* was as popular as Lin's better translations. But a newer literary movement was already taking shape among these new readers, a movement that finally got the chance to develop in 1919. It was by revising this new concept, and securing the benefits of free use of the vernacular, that New Literature has arrived at its present achievements.

When we discuss the relation between fiction and society today, we notice that many conditions have changed. First, except for a few important ones that are read due to reprinting, most traditional novels have lost their former impact, either because their readership keeps declining or because they are irrelevant to contemporary life. This includes not only the "sex and violence" novels feared by the old moralists, but the "superstitious" and "scandalous" novels that worried the reformists. While we may still generally think of it as entertainment, fiction and its writers already have a definite effect and influence on young people who have more than a primary education. In the universities, fiction is already a research topic that can be approached from multiple perspectives. "Fiction" is even more a fixture in our libraries, which hold many volumes of it. The national academic awards even lend fiction the same academic weight as mathematics, history, and so forth. The government spends a good deal of money every year besides, to support and cultivate fiction. The investments made by the publishing industry are even more considerable. An accomplished writer today can attract a degree of reader respect and sympathy that is unprecedented in our history. Even among those who are professionally successful in today's society, the writer has no equal.

And yet many promising writers have been sacrificed in times of political instability because the New Literature movement of the past decade has been too closely involved with politics. Other writers have been suppressed because of their "dissident ideology" and so been unable to go on with their writing. Still others, who cannot bring themselves to write even under relatively liberal conditions, have decided to give up their writing to go into politics. This is a real loss to our country. Thoughtful people ought to be concerned.

Meanwhile, relations between the literary movement and the commercial world have been poor and copyrights have not been honored. Therefore, though their novels have been printed by the millions, making the new presses rich, our famous authors generally receive nothing for themselves. Even now, there are probably not more than three or four writers who can live on royalties from their books. Even these—say, Bing Xin, Mao Dun, Lao She, and Ba Jin—are not paid much. So, even though a writer may have worked hard for ten years and made great contributions to his country, our society doesn't give him any real support. He still needs to take another job to raise his family. It's not surprising, then, that some have given up and become teachers, businessmen, bureaucrats, or politicians—it's much easier. Others, being honest, stubborn, and reluctant to change, persist in the dream of fighting with their pen, only to end up dying from a minor illness in their poverty. What a loss this is to our country. For this to change, publishers must improve their ethics and copyrights must become legally binding; none of the measures before us now is enough! If it is difficult to enforce such restrictions by abstract law, then we ought to have a national publishing bureau to do it. From the point of view of businessmen, a good book is simply a means of profit, nothing more. Standards generated that way cannot be high. But from the point of view of the nation, a good book deserves official publication and distribution. As things stand in China right now, 100,000 to 500,000 copies of a good book can surely be disposed of. If the nation were to do this, it would be investing in the good minds and noble sentiments of all China, to honor those minds and spread their lofty sentiments. An investment of thirty to fifty million yuan would not be wasted. True, such a program might take a bit of trouble, but it would be much simpler and more practicable than other proposals. Once writers can receive their royalties by this legitimate means, our country can stop worrying about and spending money on this problem.

Of course, these reasonable proposals can't be implemented at this point. But a writer who has self-respect and self-confidence need not lose hope. Even if the writer is not gaining materially from his work, he is in spiritual communication with a half-million to a million readers throughout the country. Though many of these readers are, as I mentioned above, the kind who read for entertainment because they have nothing else to do, it usually doesn't take long for a good book to captivate them when it falls into their hands. How much more so the younger generation that has been to secondary school during the past twenty years. They seem quite willing to accept the healthy and enthusiastic world view that an author offers through his work of fiction. The valuable effect of good literature could not be clearer. Our country must have a deeper understanding of the effect of literature, and it needs for our writers to better understand and respect themselves. Once a writer realizes the permanent historical significance that his work can embody, by transmitting truth and passion, he will believe in progress and see what a bright future may lie ahead. However difficult his circumstances, they won't matter any more.

"Xiaoshuo yu shehui" (Fiction and society), Kunming, September 29, 1942, in *Lianhe wenxue* 27 (January 1987): 100-17.

—Translated by Rey Chow and Ming-bao Yue

Zhang Ailing

AFTER attending the University of Hong Kong, Zhang Ailing (b. 1921, in Shanghai) gained early recognition in the cosmopolitan atmosphere of Shanghai, until the Japanese occupation intervened. Her short stories are known for their skeptical portraits of Europeans, Eurasians, and upper-class Chinese, as is her famous early novella, *Jinsuo ji* (The golden cangue, 1943). Zhang Ailing excels in psychological studies of human relationships, unmasking petty passions and the inconsistency of the human heart. Critics have particularly admired the complexity of her women characters.

Zhang Ailing lived as a recluse after leaving Shanghai in 1952. She emigrated to Hong Kong and finally settled in the United States, where she married a friend of Bertold Brecht. She managed to publish three novels under her English name, Eileen Chang, including the vivid anti-Communist novel *Yang ge* (The rice-sprout song, 1955), and *Chidi zhi lian* (Naked earth, 1956), about Chinese cadres as prisoners of war in Korea. Zhang Ailing continued to have a strong influence in Taiwan, particularly since so many of China's other major authors were proscribed for having remained on the mainland, but her influence in the PRC has been nil.

The essay below provides a glimpse of the Europeanized Shanghai life-styles that Zhang Ailing so well portrayed.

International Shanghai, 1941

Coffee House Chat about Sexual Intimacy and the Childlike Charm of the Japanese

Zhang Ailing

1941, in unoccupied Shanghai

MUMENG and Zhang Ailing go shopping for shoes together. No matter what they set out to do, once they're together, they always end up eating.

"What'll we have to eat?" Mumeng asks as usual.

Zhang Ailing always thinks it over, until she ends up with the same answer as the time before: "Something soft, easy to digest, creamy."

In the coffee shop, an extra portion of cream comes with each person's cream cake, and an extra portion of cream accompanies each cup of hot chocolate. Although it's Dutch treat, they still ply each other, taking turns playing host and guest: "Won't you have something more? Sure you can't eat another bite?"

Zhang Ailing says, "Since we've just finished eating, if we go outside we'll freeze with the first gust of wind. Why don't we sit here a bit longer?" So they launch into long conversations, until the topics start to turn serious, and she says, "You know, we're beginning to sound a lot like we're holding a meeting."

At first, Mumeng starts talking about a Christmas ball: "They play a game. It's called 'Bow to the wisest, kneel to the loveliest, then kiss the dearest.'"

"Oh, so did you get a lot of kneelers?"

Mumeng smiles in the faint red lamplight: "I wore black to the party. I made a collar out of an old-fashioned Chinese child's bib—you've seen it—the one with a string of pink-colored flat peaches hung with gold thread. I actually did look pretty that day."

"And was there anyone who said that you were the dearest?"

"There was. Everyone was madly kissing all around, not necessarily even knowing whom. It was really stupid. That game is disgusting, but if you stand there all by yourself and don't join in, that looks even stupider. I'm the type who tries to go along with things. That's what a friend of mine said: 'You may be anti-Communist now, but if by any chance you ever do join them, you'll be a party activist supreme, just because you can't stand to be left out of things.' . . .

"I guess I'm too old fashioned, but I don't approve at all. Not only when other people are around, but even in private. If a man truly likes you, he'll think you like him as much. That's unfair to him, gives him the wrong impression. And then there are times when he doesn't take you seriously, so to let him take all sorts of liberties makes you look even cheaper."

"Really it's not good. Dorothy Dix—it seems ridiculously shallow to cite 'The Proper Thing,' her advice column on love, as some sort of authority, but she does say some things that make sense—she said that American young people are too casual when it comes to 'necking.' They get so used to it that it seems nothing special. When they finally find someone they really love, physical contact should give them enormous pleasure, but their feelings have already been blunted. So what should be pleasure only amounts to—"

Mu: "I suppose they can't wait—they'd rather have whatever pleasures they can beforehand. Here's how I feel about it: If they like it, then there's nothing wrong with it. But if the girl herself doesn't actually have the urge and just goes along with it because she's afraid people will laugh at her and think she's backward or frigid, then I believe that's wrong.

Zhang: But then if she does feel the urge and acts provocatively, that can be dangerous, too, since it can get out of hand and there can be more serious consequences. Don't you think so? Kissing isn't the issue.

Mu: True.

Zhang: If she doesn't feel the urge, then of course it's dangerous for her to force herself—it could leave her disgusted and affect her sexual psychology later on.

Mu: I would make an exception for Russian women. A Russian girl should be forgiven if she's a bit loose. They age so quickly they turn fat as cows as soon as they're married. So by then, whether they have the urge or not, romance is over for them. Really, in just a few years, Russian women are unbearable to look at. There's an old saying: "Look at your mother-in-law before you marry" (because the mother-in-law is the future image of your wife). If men actually did that, no Russian woman would ever stand a chance of getting married! At the banquet that night, some young Russian men put on a skit, pretty entertaining, called "The Eternal Triangle." It was very simple: A man and a woman enter from opposite directions and embrace, saying in unison, "My love!" A figure darts past the window and the woman, all upset, cries, "My husband!" And the man quickly starts to sneak out, saying, "My hat!" The end.

Zhang: Great!—I don't know why, but so many young White Russians are so bright. Then, later on, you never hear anything about them. They never amount to anything. Eurasians are the same, too, so bright, so gifted, capable—(suddenly, she starts to feel frightened for Mumeng).

Mu: True. Probably because they lack encouragement. There's some social prejudice against them.

Zhang: No, I think Shanghai is pretty liberal on that score. There's free competition in everything. I think it's because they don't have any background, don't belong anywhere. They can't absorb the essence of what their environment has to offer them.

Mu: Perhaps. Oh, I never finished their skit. Next, there was "The Eternal Triangle in England." The wife and her lover are embracing when her husband returns and sees them. So he mumbles some excuse, picks up his umbrella, and goes out again. Then, "The Eternal Triangle in Russia": The wife and the lover are embracing when the husband comes back and sees them. He's so angry he pulls out a pistol and shoots them both right in the temple, and then himself, wham, right in the temple.

Zhang: Really ridiculous. That's just the way they are!

Mu: Jealousy is beyond reason. For example, if I had a husband, as your friend, I'd only say good things about you. Then he'd know only your good side and like you very much. So I wouldn't do it. What if it were you?

Zhang: I'd be jealous.

Mu: And it's too hard to explain, so you bottle up your unhappiness inside. You get a bit spiteful with a friend about some other matter—maybe very spiteful. It's terrible to let a long-standing friendship gradually be destroyed by such feelings, when really there's nothing you can't talk about. Promise me that if that day comes you'll tell me, "Mumeng, I'm jealous. Watch yourself, keep your distance."

Zhang: (*smiling*) I will, for sure.

Mu: I can hardly imagine how I'd react if one day I discovered my husband kissing you, whether I'd storm around foaming at the mouth, or just quietly slip out with embarrassment like that Englishman. And something else is odd—if I discovered my husband kissing you, I'd be jealous of you, not him.

Zhang: (*laughing*) Of course, that's the way you're supposed to feel. What's so odd about that? Really, sometimes you are hopelessly confused.

Mu: (*continuing her own train of thought*) I think I'd throw a fit, and after that, a few days later, I'd have another. Probably I'd call you on the phone and say, "Zhang Ai, when are you coming to see me!"

Zhang: I wouldn't throw a fit on the spot. I'd probably act as if I hadn't seen a thing, until the visitor left. Then, with my back turned to you, I'd ask just what was going on. Really, the question would be superfluous. I've always felt that any man has plenty of reason to kiss you. But as for forgiving, in the end I couldn't.

Mu: Of course. Just walk right in and say it straight out: "Hey, you can't do this."

Zhang: Between the two of us, that would work, but not if it were a different woman. To throw a fit, then make up and be friends? Everyone would say that's crazy. What's so painful is that it's not just your friend that you can feel jealous of. If he says the slightest good thing about any woman, it's hard to bear. And you can't throw a fit every time he does that. What's more, if you make a habit of blowing up, he won't talk to you at all. Even if you do talk about something completely irrelevant, he'll always feel on guard, until it gets to the point that you can't talk about anything. I think patience is the best course. The more you give in to your temper, the more temperamental you get. It's better to be patient.

Mu: But that's so unbearable. Always to be suspicious—of course, you figure everyone likes him, since he's the very best—otherwise you wouldn't have married him. Life is really vicious!

Zhang: As for polygamy—

Mu: In theory I approve, but not in practice.

Zhang: Me too. What if the two women are sisters or sworn sisters, the way it is in the old-fashioned novels?

Mu: That would only make it worse.

Zhang: True. But then, what if the other woman were someone you had absolutely no respect for? You couldn't accept that either, out of self-respect. So the result would likely be that you'd have to try to find something positive in her, to force yourself to like her. That's the psychology of this situation. Of course, after you'd gotten to like her, you'd only hate her all the more.

Mu: Fortunately, our turn hasn't come yet. So many men have died in Europe that they're about to adopt polygamy there. You'd think they could come up with a better solution.

Zhang: (abruptly, sadly) Mumeng, when you grow old, what sort of clothes will you wear?

Mu: I'll wear an Indian cotton sari—I think that's the most flattering. No matter whether I marry an Indian or a Chinese, I'll wear an Indian sari. It's statuesque, so it doesn't matter whether you're a bit fat or a bit thin. Or, then again, perhaps old-fashioned Chinese quilted pants.

Zhang: (spirits reviving) Perfect, yes, I can wear quilted pants, too. They cover up everything and still look presentable; green, black, ocher, and so many great old-fashioned colors.

Mu: Oh, relax! You're not afraid of old age, are you? I've never seen Zhang Ai act that way before! She even wants me to tell her what clothes she ought to wear when she gets old! Do you want me to spell it all out in my will? Hereafter, Zhang Ai may wear such-and-such.

Zhang: (smiling) No—you know how I absolutely despise today's old-lady types. They all wear such drab clothes, so timid. If they have any individuality at all, they dress like Christian missionaries. But old ladies in other countries are so uninhibited they'll wear any color or pattern—great big backs all covered with bunches of tiny white flowers, it's enough to make your head spin. But nothing's uglier than some shapeless body bundled up in blue silk print or red cotton print.

Mu: Oh, do you remember last time, when I was talking with a friend about Eastern and Western cultures? I just remembered something I wanted to tell him: In Western fashion, each age rejects the previous one, so the more things change the more they stay the same, while the different trends multiply. By contrast, the Indian sari is eternal. It was adopted very, very slowly, until it finally became the established fashion. When beauty is that universal, that forgiving, you can't change it, even one little bit. Then, there's Japanese culture—but I'm no longer infatuated with Japanese culture.

Zhang: Me neither. It was three years ago that I first saw their wood-block prints, their clothes, their porcelain, and those naive fresh-faced little soldiers. And then there was this old Japanese sailor on the boat we took back to Shanghai [from Hong Kong] who showed us photos of his three daughters. When we stopped off in Taiwan, the mountains there floated above the sea like the blue-green mountains in a Chinese landscape painting. I never imagined there really were mountains like that! I've heard that Japanese scenery is like that too. I looked out a porthole at night, when the sea was blue-gray. So calm and still, a single small fishing boat with a red lantern—I really felt intoxicated with joy!

Mu: Yes, they have a kind of childlike charm that's very endearing.

Zhang: But for me, it wasn't so much because they're childlike, but because I'm Chinese, and I like that old-fashioned Chinese modesty and reserve. They have this air of reserve about them.

Mu: It's just that air that I like. It's like a mountain covered in silvery mist. The mist is beautiful, yes, but then, still there's a mountain behind it. The mountain is reality. There's no mountain behind their mist.

Zhang: Right. So many of their feelings are superficial. They have no feelings for things they aren't already familiar with. And they have a prescribed way of feeling about things they *are* familiar with: "This is the way you should think."

Mu: Whenever I used to look at their paintings, I always thought there must still be more meaning within all that perfected beauty, to make people bide their time in such humility. But now I know that what you see at first glance is all there is.

[*Note:* twelve lines of dialogue at this point were excised from the original text by the censor, evidently so as not to offend the Japanese.]

Mu: Do you think we're being too harsh in our criticisms? We're insatiable critics, never satisfied.

Zhang: I don't think we're being too harsh. But, compared to modern Western or Chinese civilization, I'm partial to Japanese civilization.

Mu: So am I.

Zhang: There's not much to say for contemporary China and India. And as for foreign countries, because of the Anglo-American atmosphere we've grown up in, we've had plenty of opportunity to see their flaws. I used to like [Aldous] Huxley, but now I'm gradually getting so that I don't even like even him any more.

Mu: Yes, he really isn't as great as we thought he was.

Zhang: He's so profound when you first read him, but actually he's rather simple-minded.

Mu: Even Egyptian art, with all its immense stillness—I'm a little dubious about it. There isn't much to it after all, except the meaning we've brought to it ourselves.

Zhang: Ah, but isn't all art like that? That's a little unfair of you.

Mu: (smiling) I am myself afraid, lacking any constant, and rejecting everything I once liked. It can shatter all your illusions.

Zhang: I think that's the way it should be. Only then can you have comparison and progress. There are people who don't even get beyond Wilde—imagine that!

Mu: Wilde's beauty really is elementary. It also worries me that, well, talking with you now, I know that *you* understand, while other people may not, even if they nod their heads. My family would think me crazy. So don't leave me!

Zhang: No, I won't. Probably I'll always be in Shanghai.

Mu: There's a sort of thoroughness in the Japanese character—a thoroughness that is simply discouraging. A Japanese woman married to a foreigner may spend half her life living like a foreigner and seem completely acculturated. But once her husband dies, she takes her children and goes back to Japan. Right away, she turns back into a thoroughgoing Japanese: bowing, smiling, reciting polite phrases, fervently patriotic, and at the same time more or less desolate.

Zhang: Ah, I don't know why, but you just can't take the homeland out of the Japanese. It can't be done. Take the Japanese-Americans, born and raised in America. They're lively and attractive, completely unlike Japanese. But there's hardly a good soul among them. I don't like them. It's not that way with Chinese. There can be Europeanized Chinese who are still Chinese down inside, and there are good ones and bad ones. The Japanese can't be part this and part that.

Mu: Do you remember telling me about the ethnologist who discovered that whites think in a straight line, and Chinese in a wavy line? Whites are strictly logical, but Chinese logic is usually very convoluted, comparatively flexible. The Japanese style of thinking is even stranger: It's two parallel dotted lines, the left one with a little break here and the right one with a little break there, then another break in the left one and another in the right one, and so on and on. Like a person's footprints, you see? There's a gap between each footprint, but even if you raise one foot, step down with the other, or skip over a step, it doesn't matter. It still doesn't break, the way a piece of thread does, so that you can't splice it back together.

Zhang: That's good, comparing parallel dotted lines to footprints.

They leave the coffee shop.

"Shuangsheng" (Alliteration), in Zhang Ailing, *Yuyin* (Lingering sound) (Taibei, 1987), pp. 53–68.

—Translated by Edward Gunn

Ding Ling

DING LING (pseud. of Jiang Bingzhi, 1904-1986), from Linli, Hunan, began her career (1927–30) by writing stories in which young women characters stand up against the world with unprecedented audacity and acute sensitivity. Ding Ling won a wide readership through her bold descriptions of youthful love and her psychological portraits of tortured conflicts between body and mind—especially in "Shafei nüshi de riji" (Miss Sophie's diary, 1928), which contains passionate descriptions of Sophie's sexuality and provocative exploration of the limits of subjectivism in literature.

In 1930, Ding Ling joined the League of Left-Wing Writers, and in 1932, the Communist party. After 1933, she was in the custody of the KMT, until she escaped in 1936 to join Communist literary circles in Yan'an. She changed from writing sketches to a kind of reportage style. After further halting attempts to create a Chinese socialist realism, she wrote *Taiyang zhao zai Sanggan He shang* (The sun shines over the Sanggan River, 1949), a novel about the land reform in 1946 and 1947. It won a Stalin Prize.

Beset by campaigns in the 1950s and purged once and for all as a rightist in 1957, partly on account of her earlier critical essays and writings, including "Miss Sophie's Diary," Ding Ling did not reemerge until 1979, after many more years of imprisonment. At that point, she became vice-president of the Chinese Writers' Association but squandered most of the good will she had earned by backing official attacks on younger writers in subsequent ideological campaigns. Ding Ling's life is a tragic story of a talented writer's gradual decline into a mere propagandist. Loyal to the Communist party to the end of her days, she was disinclined to question its wisdom.

The following essay appeared in a 1935 collection of the *chuangzuotan* auto-biographical genre.

Foolish Dreams
Like a Blind Person Going Fishing

Ding Ling

April 1933

I'VE WRITTEN a little fiction, but nothing I was ever satisfied with. I've never read the books about how to write, nor dictionaries of adjectives and descriptions. I often fear that younger friends who love literature will come to ask me how to write fiction. Opportunities for embarrassing situations abound. Once, a young people's literary society asked me to give a talk on my experience in writing. I managed to say a few simple things, expecting them to be disappointed at the naïve nature of my remarks. Now, I'm honored by those who still insist that I write something on the subject, and, after repeated declinations, I can no longer refuse. Therefore, I am again writing a few simple things.

Although I am now close to being recognized as a fiction writer, and do plan to write a little more, I often find myself rejecting the road I have taken. I keep thinking that if I had done something else, I might have accomplished something. I never liked my own works, and I'm often amazed by some other writers' self-confidence and pride. Why, then, do I write fiction? I think this has a lot to do with my environment.

I remember getting sick several times when I was a child. My younger brother was a sickly child, too. Whenever we couldn't play outdoors, my mother's stories became our sole comfort. Under the lamp light, I lay next to mother, cuddled up around her with my cousins. We all watched her with our wide-open and innocent eyes. She tirelessly related the stories of the cave with waterfalls, the prince who could hold up a pagoda, and on and on. She imprinted those stories so deeply on our minds that even today, scenes from them appear right before my eyes. My mother was more than a storyteller to me. Her own life and her brave attitude greatly inspired me, even though I was very young. When I grew a little older, I no longer wanted my mother's stories. I liked to sit in the rear garden and observe the world at my leisure. Between the ages of ten and fourteen, I saw my family only during the winter and summer vacations. I was the youngest boarder in my school. When I was not at school, I lived in my uncle's rear garden, with only an amah and a young maid to keep me company. During the day, I joined a pack of mischievous school kids, seeking amusement by pestering the teachers. But as soon as school was over, I would be left alone again. In the slowly darkening garden at home, or on the big playground at school, I would stare at the crows flying home and count the first stars to come out in the evening. I always spent the quiet afternoons and evenings with a book. In this period, I almost finished reading all the old paperback novels I found in my uncle's home. I also read a lot in the *Collection of Fiction* (*Shuo bu congshu*) published by the Commercial Press, namely, the foreign novels translated by Lin Shu. I also often read the *Short Story Monthly* (*Xiaoshuo yuebao*) (with the beautiful ladies on the cover) and the *Grand Magazine* (*Xiaoshuo daguan*), edited by Bao Tianxiao. My mother was not happy about this, because I gave up on other things. But when I entered middle school, a new, completely communal life began for me. On top of it, the waves of the May Fourth movement also surged into that small town of ours. I became an activist at school and found myself in the limelight. I transferred several times to different schools. Although I had a vernacular poem printed in a newspaper supplement and was encouraged by my Chinese teacher, I never mustered real enthusiasm for literature. I thought it more useful to skim through the "Awakening" (*Juewu*) supplement of the *Republic Daily* (*Minguo ribao*) than to read from our textbook, [Hu Shi's] *Collection of Experiments* (*Changshi ji*). So, despite the sensation at middle school caused by [Guo Moruo's] "The Goddesses," I never did pay it much attention.

I ran away to Shanghai to learn the most practical knowledge. At least that's what I planned at the time. Later, after many twists and turns and running up against several stone walls, I began to feel like a blind person trying to catch fish. A youth with muddled dreams, I looked for a way out, but in vain. I can't say that I lost heart, but when I lived in Peking I was in low spirits. I lived there for two years. Shen Congwen and Hu Yepin were among my friends. Only shortly before leaving Peking did I begin to write "Mengke" and "Miss Sophie's Diary." In the five years since then, I've done little else but write.

I think it was solitude that drove me to write fiction. Dissatisfied with society, and lacking a direction in my own life, I needed to speak out about so many things, but I couldn't find an audience. I wanted very much to do something, but again I couldn't find the opportunity. Since it was easier, I let my pen analyze society instead of doing it myself. I was good at complaining in those days, so unconsciously I smothered my story collection, *In the Darkness* (*Zai heian zhong*, 1928), in a layer of sentimentality. Since I had intended simply to do some analysis, the reality of society was depicted all right, but the stories lacked any vision of the appropriate solutions. Mr. He Danren sternly criticized my writings of that period. I was not convinced when I first read it, but after much soul-searching, I have accepted his criticism. As a result, although I wrote *In the Darkness* with care, and much pleasure, I have to admit that it takes off in a very bad direction.

I wrote *Wei Hu* (1930) with the same attitude as I had *In the Darkness*. In view of its date of publication, many people mistakenly criticized it as a contribution to proletarian literature. I really felt an injustice had been done to me. Because my attitude was different, as were my expectations of literature, I intended neither to depict Wei Hu as a hero nor to write about revolution. I only wanted to write about a few characters on the eve of the May Thirtieth incident. Therefore, I wrote five thousand characters a day for several days, feeling extremely excited and happy. Only upon a rereading, when it was printed by the *Short Story Monthly*, did I experience intense regret. I discovered that it was simply a mediocre story that relied on the hackneyed conventions of writers like Jiang Guangci, who played on conflicts between romance and revolution.

Later on, the reader could see that my attitude toward writing gradually changed, as in my *Shanghai, Spring 1930 (Yijiusanlingnian chun Shanghai,* 1930), *Tian Family Village (Tianjiachong,* 1931), and so forth. *Tian Family Village* was criticized by many people. The material itself was real enough. The problem lay in my failing to depict just how Third Mistress was transformed from a landowner's daughter into a daughter of the revolution. Although that kind of transformation was possible, the effect was to overromanticize the story. I also idealized the countryside. I am fond of writing about the countryside because I love it. But what I love is the stable countryside of the past; my emotional ties with it merely reflect a middle-peasant consciousness. This kind of consciousness still partially remains with me today, but I believe I can overcome it.

Before writing *Flood (Shui,* 1931), I went for a long time without completing anything, and I felt quite depressed. A lot of people and events troubled and irked me, but I could not recreate them on paper. I could not grasp the pen that would free my imagination. I detested my "style" (let me borrow this word here, since no suitable word can be found) and felt that it restricted my thinking. I worked out many stories in my mind; many beginnings have been left unfinished to this day, each of them three to five thousand words long. But I put them all aside, because they failed to satisfy me. Only when the first issue of the *Big Dipper (Beidou)* was about to go to press did I hurriedly write the first installment of *Flood* [for publication there], all in one night. The later installments were all written in haste on the night before they were due. The ending of *Flood* may therefore be called unpolished. Originally it was to be a work of eighty thousand words. Later, though, I was too busy reading manuscripts for the *Big Dipper* to have time to plan out the story. Moreover, I did not think that such a long piece would be appropriate for the *Big Dipper*, so I finished it off in haste. I thought several times of revising it or adding another section, but time constraints left these plans unfulfilled. This was followed by the failure of my grand project, *The Eventful Autumn* (*Duo shi zhi qiu*, 1932). Of the hundred thousand words in my original plan, I've written little more than twenty thousand to date.

The idea of writing my third novel, *Mother* (*Muqin*, 1932), goes back to 1931. Last summer, a newspaper, through friends of friends, sent me a very earnest letter asking that I write a novel for them. I wanted to seize the opportunity to get to work on it. Shortly after, however, the newspaper [*Continental News* (*Dalu xinwen*)] unexpectedly ceased publishing, so I put down my pen. Later, the Literature Series of the Liangyou Press asked me for the novel, so I resumed writing. Nevertheless, owing to sickness and various other problems, I worked only sporadically, writing one day and then resting for ten, so that I had no idea when I might finish. I do not intend to write any more long novels. Slipshod work and aborted projects make me feel sad.

In the past year or so, I've written several stories, but I didn't have much to say.

On rereading the above, I realize that there is a slight discrepancy between it and what the editor asked me to write. I still have not described my writing "experience." But I have to turn my effort in, even though the title, "My Writing Career," is not apt. If I have the time and the opportunity in the future, I may write more about what I've gained from creative writing.

"Wo de chuangzuo shenghuo" (My writing career), April 1933, in *Chuangzuo de jingyan* (Experiences in creative writing) (Shanghai, 1935), pp. 19-28.

—Translated by Zha Jianying

Yu Dafu

YU DAFU (1896–1945), from Fuyang, Zhejiang, was one of China's most controversial authors of the 1920s and 1930s. He wrote in a very subjective mode,
bringing to light the secrets and innermost feelings of his characters. The style
was much influenced by the modern Japanese *watakushi shōsetsu* (I novel), a
prose form that Yu Dafu read while living and studying in Tokyo between 1912
and 1922. Well-read in Chinese classical literature and Western novels from the
time of his formative years, Yu Dafu also became fluent in Japanese, English,
and German. His major short story, "Chenlun" (Sinking, 1921), is a partly autobiographical account of the loneliness and sexual temptation experienced by its
neurotic hero, a young Chinese student in Japan. With Guo Moruo, Yu Dafu was
a founder of the Creation Society (1921); like Lu Xun, he also joined the League
of Left-Wing Writers in 1930, although he left it one year later. In 1938, Yu
Dafu fled to Singapore and worked as a journalist. When the city fell to the
Japanese in 1942, he went underground in Sumatra, working ostensibly as a
part-time interpreter for the Japanese military police, who killed him in 1945.
Ten volumes of his collected works were published in Hong Kong in 1982.

In the text below, Yu Dafu views China against the background of modernized Japan, which despised China for its backwardness. Yu Dafu's melancholic
mixture of sexual remorse and feelings of national shame is to be found in
several of his stories.

Early Autobiographical Fragments:
A Young Sojourner in a Foreign Land

Yu Dafu

The last day of January, 1936

ALTHOUGH Japanese culture lacks creativity, its capacity to imitate is itself highly creative. In its ethical teachings it follows China, in its political, legal, military, and educational systems it follows Germany, and in economic production it generally imitates Europe and America. But this is all propped up by a native, self-sacrificing patriotism and an ability to endure. So, although its roots do not run deep, its leaves and branches luxuriate; and although invention, discovery, and other such creative acts are wholly lacking, progress has come quickly. When I was there as a student, the Meiji era had already completed its reformist work; young branches had been grafted onto an old tree and new wine had been poured into an old skin. It had been done with complete proficiency, so that there were virtually no detectable flaws. The atmosphere of a burgeoning new country was imposing enough, and the bearing of its burgeoning new people was magnanimous and liberal. But to people from ancient oriental nations at their last gasp, particularly we Chinese who cannot help betraying the cultural backwardness of our nation, all this was a huge threat. To call it a humiliation is of course not incorrect, but since we have only ourselves to blame, it is better to be somewhat more reserved and simply call it a threat.

To teach the concept of the nation-state to the descendants of the Yellow Emperor, who live in such befuddled complacency, vying for power and profit within their small confines, it would be best to send them to live for two or three years in any foreign country at all. The reason Indians have become anti-British and the Koreans anti-Japanese is that their homelands have become the foreigners'. Educated Japanese from the middle and upper classes were always condescending in their blandishments toward Chinese students. Daggers were hidden in their smiles, and we oversensitive youths who profoundly felt that it was "better to misunderstand" could not even bear to be as candid as our present political leaders. As for the uneducated in the middle and lower strata-- the vast majority, of course—the people of Yamato were frank in their derision. Their attitudes, their language, and their actions all seemed to shout out to us: "You inferior breed, you despicable spawn from an extinct country, what are you doing in our Japanese empire, which rules you anyway?" They are quite simply the most effective professors of the concept of nationalism a Chinese could have.

It was only in Japan that I began to recognize the position of China in the competitive world. It was there that I began to understand the greatness and profundity of modern science (whether physical or metaphysical). And it was in Japan that I immediately perceived China's current and future fate, and the course of purgatory that my 450 million countrymen would have to undergo. I felt the inferiority of our international position, and the insults and humiliations due the denizen of a weak country, most sharply and unbearably in relationships between the sexes. It happened the moment I was hit by one of Cupid's poison arrows.

Japanese women are as a rule lovely and gentle; since the time their country began, right up until the present day, they have been educated to be submissive to men. Moreover, because the Japanese population is not so dense and the style of life has always been rather crude, Japanese women have never been as prudish as our Chinese women. Add to this the fact that customs like footbinding and female seclusion never existed in Japan, and that labor, access to public places, and moving about were the same for women as for men. Japanese women, therefore, tend to be full-bodied and sturdy, without the defects of willowy fragility or lilyish delicacy. Also, the archipelago has a unique endowment of volcanoes and springs, causing the water to be full of minerals. As a result, the skin of women from near the mountains in both the east and west of the country is creamy and translucent, as finely white as china. And even in Japan, the beauties from the snowy regions of the northeastern interior are called "snowy lovelies"; their rich fairness and tender beauty hardly require comment. So, after I became familiar with Japanese language and customs, secured my own economic footing, respectfully took leave of my blood relatives, and took up residence all by myself in Tokyo, what most vexed my spirit were the many attractions of the opposite sex and my grief at China's lagging international position. These afflictions were with me both at home, under the cold light of my hotel room, and when I was out, roaming the streets.

The new age of liberation of the sexes had long since arrived at the upper reaches of Tokyo society, especially among intellectuals and students. Bewitching photographs of famous actresses such as Kujaku Kinugawa and Ritsuko Morikawa—seminaked and without makeup—stories about prominent young debutantes in ladies' picture magazines, colorful news about the mistresses of

prominent Tokyo personalities, and all sorts of potential love objects and affairs
sufficient to turn a young man's heart came thick and fast in the *fin de siècle*
atmosphere of that transitional period. The problem plays of Ibsen and the loves
and marriage of Ellen Key, the theories of exposing evil held by the literary
naturalists, the highly stimulating ideas on the two sexes held by the socialists--
all these issues swept over Tokyo simultaneously, like a tide. A young sojourner
from a foreign land like me, with his spotless soul, his aloof nature, his frail
emotions, and his indecisiveness, could merely join the foam at the top. Again
and again, I was pummeled by that tide, sucked into its vortex, and inundated,
until I went under.

In the Tokyo of that time, besides the several famous large parks and the
amusement park near Asakusa, the pure and secluded places one could visit
included the botanical garden in Koishikawa-ku and Inokashira Park at
Musashino, outside the city. These places had flowers and plants in all seasons,
rows of trees dripping with verdure, clear brooks that trickled through them, and
endearing tame animals and rare birds. If, on a spring day of soft breezes and
warm sun, or on a fall evening with its bracing air and lofty sky, you went there
for a stroll, you would always meet some young ladies of good families who
were about your age; they would be picking flowers, singing, wading in the
streams, and climbing hills. If you went up to chat with them, they would
respond; everyone would talk and laugh, lie on the grass, and eat the sweets that
had been brought along. It was all like a dream, or an intoxication. Without ever
being aware of it, a whole day's time would fly by like an arrow. But after this
sort of occasion, or sometimes even during it, you would fall suddenly from the
very height of pleasure into the pit of despair. These innocent young women,
these beauties who obeyed men without question, had, it turned out, all been
tutored by their fathers and brothers to abandon their customary behavior and
their normally favorable dispositions at the first mention of the word "China" or
"Chinaman." Whenever those words were uttered by our eastern neighbors, but
particularly by these young women in their most wonderful years, those on the
receiving end felt a mingled wave of insult, despair, and indignation rise in their
minds and hearts, a feeling that fellow Chinese who have never been to Japan
simply cannot imagine.

By the time I had been in the preparatory course at the First Higher School in
Tokyo for a year, I had experienced such irritations countless times. In the
autumn of 1915, I left Tokyo for the western commercial center of Nagoya.
When I entered the Eighth Higher School there, my heart was full of both
discouragement and curses. As for the capital of this foreign country, to which I
had earlier rushed, so full of hope and enthusiasm—I never wanted to see her
again.

The Higher School in Nagoya was situated in the country, some two or three
miles from the heart of the city. Because there were not very many Chinese
students in this rural district, the maltreatment and disrespect I received from the

Japanese citizenry decreased somewhat, but as I had now reached twenty and the physical development attendant upon that, my sexual frustration was entering an uncontrollable stage. It was in the winter of the year I finished my exams that it snowed steadily for two days on the Kansai plain. I lived by myself in an area that had been completely snowed in, and I felt that I couldn't take it any more. So, on an afternoon when the snow was still flying, I boarded a Tokyo-bound train on the main Tokaido line. In the cold and lonely carriage, I drank several bottles of warm sake; determining that none of the passengers was an acquaintance, I had a sudden rush of courage. Like a man possessed, I tottered off the train at the next small station, though it was the middle of the night. Brothels are ubiquitous in Japan, but because I feared being seen by someone I knew, as well as the complications of disease, I had until then only imagined myself entering one—I had never actually dared to see what one was like. But this time was different: both the place and the people were unknown to me, and it was the middle of the night; several blasts of the cold wind and the day-long snow further stimulated my blood, which the hot sake had already warmed. I trudged up to a rickshaw stand and jumped into a waiting vehicle. Wrapping my face in a scarf, I shouted to the puller to take me to a bordello.

After receiving the welcome of the madam, I chose a fair and well-built whore; we sat up late and, after some wild singing and prodigious drinking, I gave up my virginity. Awakening the next day at noon, I reached under the quilt and touched warm, soft flesh. I hazily recalled the crazy wildness of the night before; I felt like one who, in the dog days of summer, suddenly has ice-water splashed all over his body. The ignorant young girl was still lying there with her body completely exposed, sleeping soundly on her back. The snowstorm outside had cleared up; reflected light poured into the large, eight-mat room with extraordinary brilliance and clarity. I looked at the corner of blue sky visible through the window and then at the pink tissue-paper scattered all around the pillow as two streams of tears suddenly and uncontrollably flowed from my eyes.

"This is such a waste, such a waste! My ideals, my aspirations, my love for my country, what's left of all that now? What's left?"

Remorse welled up in my heart and another wave of hot tears came to my eyes; I draped the brothel's lounging kimono over me and leaned back against the wall. I sat there blankly and regretfully, crying silently and interminably, until the girl woke up and accompanied me to the bath. When we returned, it was only after a few more glasses of warm sake that I returned to my normal state of mind. Three hours later, scowling and seated near the window of a train traveling toward the snowy high plains of Gotemba, my mind was rippling with things that had simply never been there before; it was as if, in the short space of one evening, someone had come along and changed my whole body.

"If I'm going to sink, I might as well sink to the bottom. If you don't enter hell, how can you see the Buddha-nature? Human life has been a complicated mystery palace all along."

This is a rough translation of the mass of confused thoughts going through my head at the time.

"Xueye, Riben guoqing de jishu: Zizhuan zhi yi zhang" (Snowy night--notes on the Japanese condition: A chapter of my autobiography), January 31, 1936, in *Yuzhou feng* (Winds of the cosmos, Shanghai) 11 (February 2, 1936).

—Translated by Theodore Huters

Glossary

Ah Q
The most famous fictional character ever created by Lu Xun, a pathetic bachelor who claimed illusory moral victories and bolstered his self-esteem by lording it over characters still more wretched than he.

April 5th movement
See entry on Tiananmen incident of 1976.

Bad elements
PRC term for nonpolitical criminals.

The Ballad of Li Youcai (*Li Youcai banhua*)
A "village storyteller's" tale (1943) of the Chinese revolution, by Zhao Shuli.

Bao Tianxiao
(1876–1973) Editor and writer of entertainment fiction, active in the 1920s and 1930s. See Perry Link, *Mandarin Ducks and Butterflies: Popular Fiction in Early Twentieth-Century Chinese Cities* (Berkeley, 1981).

Bei Dao
Pseudonym of Zhao Zhenkai, b. 1949. Leader of the school of "misty" or "obscure" poetry, and an accomplished fiction writer.

Big Dipper (*Bei dou*)
A literary journal sponsored by the League of Left-Wing Writers and edited by Ding Ling. Its debut was in September 1931.

Bing Xin
(b. 1900) China's first great woman writer of modern vernacular prose, a sensation of the 1920s.

Bo Juyi
(772–846) Great Tang poet known, among other things, for his social consciousness. See Arthur Waley, *Life and Times of Po Chü-i* (London, 1945), and Howard S. Levy, *Translations from Po Chü-i's Collected Works* (New York, 1971–75), 4 vols.

Bo Yang
(b. 1920) Author of *Choulou de Zhongguoren* (The ugly Chinaman) (Taibei, 1985), a book of essays criti-

cal of the Chinese national character that was roundly denounced by old-line patriots on both sides of the Taiwan Strait, but much appreciated by Chinese overseas for its satiric irreverence. See Jürgen Ritter, *Kulturkritik in Taiwan: Bo Yang* (Bochum, 1987), and Lin Ziyao, *One Author Is Rankling Two Chinas* (Taipei, 1989).

The Book of Odes (Shijing)

A canonical ancient Chinese classic, whose elegant poetry had its origins in folk songs. Also called *The Book of Songs*, trans. Arthur Waley (New York, 1957), and *The Confucian Odes*, trans. Ezra Pound (New York, 1954).

Cao Xueqin

(1715?–1763) See entry on *The Dream of the Red Chamber*.

Cao Yu

Pseudonym of Wan Jiabao, b. 1910. A leading modern playwright, famous for his *Leiyu* (Thunderstorm, 1934) and other well-made, socially conscious plays in the style of O'Neill and Ibsen, written before 1949. Joined the Communist party in 1957.

Cement

A Soviet novel (1925) of socialist realism by Fyodor Vasilievich Gladkov.

Central Daily News (Zhongyang ribao)

Official organ of the KMT on Taiwan.

Chapter-driven (*zhanghui*) novels

China's traditional full-length works of fiction, influenced by the art of traditional storytellers. See C. T. Hsia, *The Classic Chinese Novel* (New York, 1968).

Characters in the middle

In the relatively relaxed climate of 1962, Shao Quanlin wanted to ameliorate the lifelessness of Maoist literature by letting writers write not only of good and bad characters, but of characters in the middle— "flawed," yet "reformable." Culture bureaucrats had beat down this advocacy and impugned its motives before the end of 1964. See Donald A. Gibbs, "Shao Ch'üan-lin (1905?–) and the 'Middle Character' Controversy," in *Literature of the People's Republic of China*, ed. Kai-yu Hsu (Bloomington, IN, 1980), pp. 642–52.

Chen Huangmei

(b. 1913) Author of short stories prior to 1949, later an influential critic and culture bureaucrat in the

PRC; has served as vice-president of the Chinese Writers' Association and vice-minister of culture.

Chen Jiangong

(b. 1949) Prose writer who lives in Peking, having been rusticated for ten years as a miner. A representative of the Literature of the Wounded, Chen uses traditional literary devices.

Chen Qiyuan

(1812–?) His *Yong xian zhai bi ji* (Sketchbook from an undistinguished and idle studio) is a collection of odd and supernatural anecdotes and tales, in classical Chinese.

China Times (Shibao)

Taiwan's most influential liberal daily.

Chuangzuotan

Chinese genre of autobiographical essays, literally, "writing about writing," or "casual remarks on the creative process." See Jeffrey Kinkley's Overview in this volume.

Collection of Experiments (Changshi ji)

China's first collection of experimental new poetry in the vernacular (1920), by the famous New Intellectual Hu Shi. See Jerome Grieder, *Hu Shih and the Chinese Renaissance* (Cambridge, MA, 1970).

Collection of Fiction (Shuo bu congshu)

A compendium of popular adventure novels in classical Chinese from the Commercial Press of Shanghai, featuring works by authors such as H. Rider Haggard and Arthur Conan Doyle.

Common Words to Warn the World (Jingshi tongyan)

A collection of short stories (1620s) by the Ming writer Feng Menglong (1574–1646).

Communist Youth League (Qingniantuan)

The youth organization of China's Communist party.

Cong Su

(b. 1939) Writer, editor, and critic from Taiwan, she is now affiliated with Rockefeller University, New York City.

Crown Magazine (Huangguan zazhi)

A high-circulation Taibei fiction journal featuring both serious authors and popular authors like Qiong Yao.

Dagongbao (L'Impartial)

A fiercely independent proreform daily newspaper, founded in the Tianjin French concession in 1902 by Ying Lianzhi. Reorganized in 1926 by Wu Ding-chang, Hu Lin, and Zhang Jiluan, it became North China's major liberal nonpartisan daily, a "Chinese *Manchester Guardian*." A Hong Kong branch office, founded during the Sino-Japanese War, survived the Communist revolution, but since 1949 it has been run from the PRC by the Communist party.

Dai Mingshi

(1653–1713) A victim of the Qing literary inquisition for purported disdain of the dynasty.

Dangwai (nonparty) opposition

An organizational surrogate for a new (non-KMT) political party that formed islandwide prior to provincial assembly elections in 1977, at a time when opposition political organizations were strictly banned. *Dangwai* adherents were mostly native Taiwanese professionals, businessmen, and intellectuals. The whole leadership of the movement was arrested in 1979 (see the entry on *Formosa* magazine), but they survived to become the nucleus of Taiwan's first declared opposition party, the Democratic Progressive party (Minjindang), founded in September 1986, when new political parties began to be tolerated.

"Delving into life" (*ganyu shenghuo*)

A Communist slogan describing the work of writers. In the 1980s, Liu Binyan and others gave it a more dissident connotation, of writing for social exposure.

Deng Youmei

(b. 1931, in Tianjin, of Shandong ancestry) An ex-rightist short story writer best known for his 1980s fictional "studies of local folkways," notably those of the common people of Peking, as in *Snuff-Bottles*, trans. Gladys Yang, *Chinese Literature* (Autumn 1985): 3–79. Deng was secretary of the Chinese Writers' Association until he was forced out in 1989.

Diaoyutai movement

Ownership of the tiny Senkaku Islands (Diaoyutai in Chinese), disputed between Japan, the People's Republic of China, and Taiwan, became a bone of contention when successful exploration began there for offshore oil. The islands are northeast of Jilong, Taiwan, and southwest of Okinawa. Protests in the United States by students from Taiwan were at their height in 1971.

Dongfang Bai

(b. 1938) Engineer and writer from Taiwan resident in Canada, author of novels with philosophical and social themes.

The Dream of the Red Chamber (Honglou meng)	China's greatest classic novel (ca. 1760), by Cao Xueqin (1715?–1763). Translated by David Hawkes and John Minford as *The Story of the Stone* (Bloomington, IN, 1973–86), 5 vols.
Du Fu	(712–770) World-famous Tang dynasty poet. See William Hung, *Tu Fu: China's Greatest Poet* (Cambridge, MA, 1952).
Du Nanfa	Noted Singapore journalist.
Du Pengcheng	(b. 1921) Communist party journalist and writer, author of the heroic *Baowei Yan'an* (In defense of Yan'an).
Duoduo	(b. 1951) Pseudonym of Li Shizheng, post–Cultural Revolution poet of the "misty" or "obscure" group. His work is anthologized in *Looking Out from Death*, trans. Gregory Lee and John Cayley (London, 1989).
Encounter Monthly (Wenhui yuekan)	Leading Shanghai literary and current affairs journal of the 1980s, closed in 1990.
Exploratory *(tansuo)* literature	Mid-1980s' term for experimental works in the style of international modernism. Approbatory when used by avant-garde young people; not so when used by conservatives and even middle-aged reformers such as Bai Hua and Liu Binyan.
The Explorers (Tanqiuzhe)	Literary society founded by Gao Xiaosheng, Lu Wenfu, and others. It came under heavy attack by the Communist leadership in 1957.
Exposure of the Official World (Guanchang xianxingji)	Epic satirical late-Qing novel by Li Baojia (1867–1906). *Das Haus zum gemeinsamen Glück*, trans. M. Liebermann and W. Bettin (E. Berlin, 1964).
Fang Bao	(1668–1749) Scholar-official, literary theorist, and celebrated essayist of the Tongcheng school.
Fei Xiaotong	(b. 1910) China's most famous sociologist. He was educated abroad and did fieldwork in China during the 1930s but conformed with the party line under communism. See R. David Arkush, *Fei Xiaotong and Sociology in Revolutionary China* (Cambridge, MA, 1981).

"Finding Our Roots" (*xungen*, lit. "searching for roots")

A 1985–86 literary "school" (*xungen pai*), and topic of friendly polemics concerning China's heritage, associated with young PRC writers such as Han Shaogong, Li Hangyu, Zheng Wanlong, and Zheng Yi. Roots writers wanted to be influenced by the literature and culture of their own country's past rather than simply copy foreign trends—although the term "roots" originated from the book of the same name by Alex Haley. The tendency took on a traditionalist flavor in works by Zhong Acheng but could express antitraditionalism in the hands of Han Shaogong.

The Flower Drum Song

Popular 1957 novel by the Chinese-American writer Chin Y. Lee (Li Jinyang, b. 1917), about generational conflicts in San Francisco's Chinatown; best known from the 1958 Rodgers and Hammerstein musical of the same name.

A Flower in a Sea of Evil (*Niehai hua*)

Novel (1904–7) by Zeng Pu (1872–1935). Translated by Isabelle Bijon as *Fleur sur l'océan des péchés* (Paris, 1983).

Flowers in the Mirror (*Jinghua yuan*)

Satirical Qing novel by Li Ruzhen (1763–1830). Abridged edition: Li Ju-chen, *Flowers in the Mirror*, trans. Lin Tai-yi (Berkeley, 1966).

Folk Literature (*Minjian wenxue*)

A popular, nonscholarly PRC monthly of collected folk songs and tales.

Formosa magazine episode

In the late 1970s, the editors of *Meilidao* (Formosa), including Shi Mingde, Huang Xinjie, Yao Jiawen, Xu Xinliang, and the writers Wang Tuo and Yang Qingchu, used their magazine to organize an extra-legal (*Dangwai*) opposition to the Kuomintang, since opposition political parties were strictly banned. After violence broke out at a December 10, 1979, human rights rally in Gaoxiong (the "Gaoxiong incident"), the government in April 1980 sentenced all the above to harsh prison terms (fifteen years for Shi Mingde), charging them with sedition and using *Formosa* to plot the overthrow of the government. Dozens of other *Dangwai* leaders were arrested, decapitating the movement. Wang Tuo, master of ceremonies at the rally, had urged nonviolence, but he was given six years.

Four Books	The heart of the classical Confucian canon: *The Analects* of Confucius, the *Mencius*, the *Great Learning*, and the *Doctrine of the Mean*.
Four Clean-ups campaign	A movement of left-wing criticism, typically of cadres in the countryside, in 1963–65. Also called the Socialist Education movement; the movement was one of several preludes to the Cultural Revolution.
Fourth National Congress of Writers and Artists	A 1979 meeting at which several noted Chinese authors spoke up on behalf of literary freedom and asked that authors be politically daring. See Howard Goldblatt, ed., *Chinese Literature for the 1980s: The Fourth Congress of Writers and Artists* (Armonk, NY, 1982).
Free China (*Ziyou Zhongguo*)	A leading 1950s' forum for dissent by liberal intellectuals, typically cosmopolitan mainlanders on Taiwan rather than Taiwanese nativists like the later *Formosa* and other *Dangwai* groups. Its death knell sounded when its editor, Lei Zhen, attempted in 1960 to organize an opposition party and was imprisoned. An eminent magazine contributor was Yin Haiguang (1919–1969), a liberal-minded mainlander philosopher at National Taiwan University.
Fu Lei	(1908–1966) A leading translator of French literature into Chinese; was forced to commit suicide during the Cultural Revolution.
Gang of Four (*Si ren bang*)	The radical, ultraleftist (Maoist right-or-wrong) faction in the Politburo during the years of the Cultural Revolution; removed from power in October 1976, after the death of Mao Zedong.
Gao Xingjian	(b. 1940, in Zhejiang) Avant-garde PRC playwright and painter now living in Paris. See Monica Basting, Yeren—*Tradition und Avantgarde in Gao Xingjians Theaterstück "Die Wilden"* (1985) (Bochum, 1988), and Gao Xingjian, *Die Busstation: Eine lyrische Komödie aus der VR China* (Bochum, 1988).
Gao Xinjiang	Noted journalist, editor, and critic of Taiwan.
Genzi	Pseudonym of Yue Zhong. Young 1980s' PRC poet and singer, now living in the United States.

The Golden Lotus (*Jin ping mei*)	Classic Ming dynasty erotic novel by an unknown author. Translated into English by Clement Egerton and Lao She (London, 1939).
The Grand Magazine (*Xiaoshuo daguan*)	Late Qing journal of light entertainment fiction in classical Chinese, edited by Bao Tianxiao.
Gu Long	(b. 1941) Prolific Taiwan author of martial-arts novels.
Gu Mengren	(b. 1951) Taiwan journalist noted for reportage literature (*baodao wenxue*).
Guangming Daily (*Guangming ribao*)	Peking newspaper aimed at intellectuals and often reporting on their fate.
Gui Youguang	(1507–1571) Famous *guwen* (ancient-style) essayist.
Guo Moruo	(1892–1978) An iconoclastic young romantic poet and favorite of student radicals in the 1920s. Guo ended up a canonized Communist statesman and, in the eyes of many, a classic yes-man of Mao Zedong, who made him president of the Academy of Sciences. Communist officials' continued deference to Guo as a great man of letters was cause for derision among young people of the 1980s. See David Tod Roy, *Kuo Mo-jo: The Early Years* (Cambridge, MA, 1971).
He Liwei	(b. 1954, in Changsha, Hunan) PRC writer of lyric short stories with Hunanese local color.
The Heroes of Lüliang (*Lüliang yingxiong zhuan*)	Novel (1945) by Xi Rong and Ma Feng, about Communist battles against the Japanese.
Historical Chronicles Made Simple (*Gangjian yizhilu*)	A multivolume, annotated popular history of China (preface 1711) from the mythological founders through the Ming dynasty, compiled and adapted by Wu Chengquan (fl. 1695–1711).
Historical Records (*Shi ji*)	Master work by China's most eminent historian, Sima Qian (ca. 145–ca. 85 B.C.), and a model of prose style. Portions translated by Burton Watson in *Ssu-ma Ch'ien: Grand Historian of China* (New York, 1958).
Hong Xingfu	(1949–1982) Talented Taiwanese *xiangtu*-style writer of social protest from Zhanghua County, Taiwan; known for writing about rural poverty during the Japanese occupation and postwar years.

Hou Baolin

China's most famous performer of *xiangsheng* comic dialogues. See Perry Link, "Hou Baolin: An Appreciation," *Chinese Literature* (February 1980): 84–94. See also the entry on *xiangsheng*.

How the Steel Was Tempered

Soviet novel (1923) of socialist realism by Nikolai A. Ostrovsky.

Hsia, C. T. (Xia Zhiqing)

(b. 1921) Mainland-born professor of Chinese literature at Columbia University, author of the standard *History of Modern Chinese Fiction* (New Haven, 1961, 1971) and many works on traditional literature; also a respected critic and promoter of new Taiwan authors of the 1950s and 1960s. See Helmut Martin's postscript to C. T. Hsia, *Der klassische chinesische Roman* (Frankfurt, 1989), pp. 361–80.

Hsia, Helen (Xia Yun)

Pseudonym Wang Yu, b. 1939. Ex-Taiwan cultural and political critic who became a major force in 1980s Chinese cultural circles as editor of the cultural page of the New York-based pro-PRC *Meizhou Huaqiao ribao* (China daily news). The PRC terminated the paper in 1989, over displeasure with its pro-democracy line. In 1991, Hsia became the research director of Human Rights in China, Inc., New York.

Hu Qiuyuan

(b. 1901) Literary critic, political commentator, and philosopher on Taiwan, of mainland origins. Originally a Shanghai Marxist, Hu in 1932 won notoriety by calling himself a "free intellectual" opposed to the degradation of literature by politics; this touched off polemics against him by the Communists. In his second career on Taiwan, Hu became popular among local intellectuals for defending *xiangtu* literature during a 1977 polemic.

Hu Yaobang

(1915–April 15, 1989). Secretary-general of the Chinese Communist party until he was purged in January 1987, for being too soft on the student demonstrators of December 1986. News of his death inspired the initial 1989 protests in Peking, Changsha, and other cities.

Hu Yepin

(1903–1931) Romantic poet and writer; Ding Ling's first husband. One of the "Five Martyrs," young leftist writers who were executed near Shanghai on February 7, 1931, in a demonstration of Chiang Kai-shek's "White Terror."

Huang Xinjie

(b. 1928) Legislator from Taibei and long-time *Dangwai* opposition politician on Taiwan. In prison, 1979–87. Was elected chairman of the Democratic Progressive party in 1988.

Huang Yongyu

(b. 1924, in Fenghuang, Hunan) Famous painter, woodblock artist, poet, and essayist from the PRC, resident in Hong Kong since the 1980s. His experiences on returning to China in 1949 from a prior stay in Hong Kong partly inspired the plot of Bai Hua's filmscript, *Unrequited Love.* Huang is a cousin of Shen Congwen.

"Hundred Flowers"

A brief period during 1956–57, when Mao Zedong encouraged intellectuals to "let a hundred flowers bloom and a hundred schools of thought contend," that is, speak out freely and criticize from all points of view. Those who did speak went to prison in the Antirightist movement afterward. See Hualing Nieh, *Literature of the Hundred Flowers* (New York, 1981).

Huo Qubing

A brave Former Han dynasty general known for his victories over the Xiongnu barbarians.

The Intellectual
(*Daxue zazhi*)

Influential journal centering on the National Taiwan University community.

International Writing Program

A program of the University of Iowa, Iowa City, that granted several months' residence and seminars for poets and writers from all nations. Funded with help from the U.S. Information Agency, the program provided neutral ground where writers from the PRC and Taiwan could meet, informally and without fear of political repercussions, for the first time since 1949. The late American poet Paul Engle and his wife, Nie Hualing, a writer formerly resident on Taiwan, launched the program in 1967 and directed it until their retirement in 1987.

Investiture of the Gods
(*Fengshen yanyi*)

A historical fantasy novel of the Ming dynasty. Trans. W. Grube, Fengshen yen-yi: *Die Metamorphosen der Götter* (Leiden, 1912; Taipei, 1970).

Iron Flood	Soviet novel (1923) of socialist realism by Aleksandr Serafimovich.
Jade Pear Spirit (*Yulihun*)	An old-fashioned romantic novel (1912) by Xu Zhenya (b. 1876, d. after 1924), written for middle-brow taste, in classical Chinese.
Japanese occupation of Taiwan	The period 1895–1945, when Taiwan belonged to the Japanese empire.
Jiang He	(b. 1952, in Hebei) PRC poet belonging to the school of "misty" or "obscure" poetry.
Jiang Jingguo (Chiang Ching-kuo)	(1909–1988) Eldest son of Jiang Jieshi (Chiang Kai-shek), and president of the Republic of China government on Taiwan from 1978 until his death. Jiang Jingguo ruled virtually as a dictator, like his father before him, until the last two years of his life, when he allowed martial law to end and began tacit toleration of parties opposing the ruling KMT. This unexpected turn of events initiated a rapid liberalization and democratization of Taiwan, particularly after his death, when a native Taiwanese president, Li Denghui, acceded to power.
Jiang Qing	(1914–1991) Fourth and last wife of Mao Zedong, who acted as her husband's secretary in the 1950s and took up the cause of ultraleftist opera reform in the 1960s. Allowed to police China's performing arts during the Cultural Revolution, she dictated that artistic creation and performance be limited to a handful of "model" works that she and her collaborators considered politically correct.
Jinshan, Shanghai	Site of an international conference on contemporary Chinese literature. Initiated by Wang Meng and convened by the Chinese Writers' Association, November 4–6, 1986, this was to be China's last 1980s' literary meeting held in a liberal and internationalist climate.
Journey to the West (*Xiyouji*)	Novel typically attributed to Wu Cheng'en (ca. 1506–1582), also known under Arthur Waley's title, *Monkey*. Complete translation by Anthony Yu, *The Journey to the West* (Chicago, 1976–83), 4 vols.
Kang Ningxiang	(b. 1938) Legislator from the Wanhua slums of Taibei

and a long-time leader of Taiwan's *Dangwai* opposition. Kang was one of the few prominent dissidents not arrested after the *Formosa* magazine episode of 1979–80, although his own magazine, *Bashi niandai* (The eighties), was closed down for a year. Kang is now a centrist leader in the Democratic Progressive party.

Ke Qingshi	(1902–1965) The ranking Communist party secretary in Shanghai, from 1955 until his death.
Keep the Red Flag Flying (Hongqi pu)	Novel (1957) by Liang Bin celebrating revolutionary resistance to landlords and the KMT. Translated by Gladys Yang (Peking, 1961).
KMT	The Kuomintang (Guomindang) or Nationalist party, ruling party of the Republic of China (ROC) from the time of its refounding in Nanjing by Chiang Kai-shek in 1928, to the present day, when the government remains confined to Taiwan.
Kong Jiesheng	(b. 1953) Cantonese writer known for fiction about the rusticated youth generation; in exile in the United States since 1990.
Kong Luosun	(b. 1912) Party critic in the PRC and past editor-in-chief of the *Literature and Arts Gazette (Wenyibao)*, an authoritative official journal, now a newspaper, published in Peking.
Kui Gate	The Qutang Gorge, one of the three major gorges on the Yangzi River.
Lai He	(1894–1943) A founder of a new Taiwanese literature, who directed a hospital for the poor.
Lao Zi	China's Daoist classic, attributed to an ancient sage by that name. Lao Tzu, *Tao Te Ching*, trans. D. C. Lau (Baltimore, 1963).
Learn from Dazhai	A campaign to emulate a Shanxi model production brigade in agriculture during the radical period of the Cultural Revolution. The Dazhai model emphasized political and ideological incentives in production and egalitarianism in pay.
Li Bo	(701–762) World-famous Tang poet. See Arthur Waley, *The Poetry and Career of Li Po* (London, 1950).

Li He	(791–817) Brilliant Tang dynasty poet. See J. D. Frodsham, trans., *The Poems of Li Ho* (Oxford, 1970).
Li Liweng (Li Yu)	(1611–1680) Leading story writer of the early Qing, best known for his collection, *Jueshi mingyan* (Famous words to awaken the world), retold by Nathan Mao in *Li Yü's Twelve Towers* (Hong Kong, 1975), and his erotic novel, *Rou putuan* (The carnal prayer mat), trans. Patrick D. Hanan (New York, 1990). See also Hanan's *The Invention of Li Yu* (Cambridge, MA, 1988) and Helmut Martin, *Li Liweng über das Theater* (Heidelberg, 1966).
Li Qiao	(b. 1934) Taiwanese teacher and author from Miaoli who writes in opposition to the ruling KMT, typically about life in the Taiwan countryside.
Li Shangyin	(813?–858) Famous allegorical Tang poet. See James J. Y. Liu, *The Poetry of Li Shang-yin* (Chicago, 1969).
Li Xifan	(b. 1927) Leftist critic from Peking acknowledged by Mao Zedong after he attacked the scholar Yu Pingbo in a 1954 campaign. Past editor of *People's Daily* and *Guangming Daily*.
Liang Qichao	(1873–1929) Major political and intellectual figure of the late Qing and early Republican era; with Kang Youwei, instigated the 1898 Hundred Days of Reform. See Hao Chang, *Liang Ch'i-ch'ao and Intellectual Transition in China* (Cambridge, MA, 1971).
Liang Shuming	(1893–1988). Advocate of Confucianism active in philosophical debates and rural construction during the Republican era, silenced by Mao Zedong after 1949; author of *Dong Xi wenhua ji qi zhexue* (Eastern and Western cultures and their philosophies) (Shanghai, 1922). See Guy S. Alitto, *The Last Confucian* (Berkeley, 1979).
Liberation	Long-standing PRC usage referring to the founding of the Communist regime in 1949 (or earlier, in North China).
The Life of Ji Gong (*Ji Gong quanzhuan*)	Old-style vernacular novel about the supernatural and martial-arts adventures of a Song dynasty monk.

The Life of Yue Fei (*Shuo Yue quanzhuan*)	Eighteenth-century novel by Qian Zai. See Jochen Degwitz, *Yue Fei und sein Mythos* (Bochum, 1983).
Lin Biao and Confucius, movement to repudiate	Promulgated in 1974, after Lin's death.
Lin Jinlan	(b. 1923, in Wenzhou, Zhejiang) Minor short-story writer known for describing socialism in Chinese countryside, active in 1950s and 1980s. Also wrote dramas, which may explain Wang Zengqi's affinity for him.
Lin Shu	(1852–1924) China's preeminent turn-of-the-century translator of Western fiction, some of which appeared in the *Shuo bu congshu* (Collection of fiction). Lin Shu translated into classical Chinese. See Leo Ou-fan Lee, *The Romantic Generation of Modern Chinese Writers* (Cambridge, MA, 1973).
Literature of Reflection (*Fanxing wenxue*)	An unofficial term, popular among young readers in the PRC, for works of the 1979–82 era that were more forthright in exposing flaws of post–Cultural Revolution China than the initial 1977–79 Literature of the Wounded that began the turn toward exposure. Roughly the same as "the new realism" in PRC literature identified by Lee Yee, editor of the Hong Kong magazine *The Nineties*, Literature of Reflection was no longer obligated to blame China's problems on "Lin Biao and the Gang of Four."
Literature of the New Era (*Xin shiqi wenxue*)	The official Chinese term for China's new literature since 1976. Originally an abbreviation of the phrase "Literature of the New Socialist Era."
Literature of the Wounded (*Shanghen wenxue*)	Works of PRC fiction, 1977–79, that helped initiate the post-Mao thaw by exposing problems in contemporary society. The problems were typically traced back no further than the Cultural Revolution, but at the time, such a reversal of attitude toward a once sacred movement had profound shock value.
Literature Quarterly (*Wenxue jikan*)	Taiwan literary journal.
Liu Daren	(b. 1939) Novelist and admired political commentator in overseas Chinese publications, employed as a translator at the United Nations in New York.

Liu, Henry	Pseudonym Jiang Nan, or "South China." Journalist from Taiwan and author of a reputedly "tell-all" biography of Jiang Jingguo. Liu was murdered on October 15, 1984, outside his home in Daly City, California, on the order of Taiwan's Defense Intelligence Bureau or higher organs. This created an international scandal for the KMT government at a time when it remained under scrutiny for human rights abuses and was increasingly linked with the Zhu Lian Bang (United Bamboo Gang), the Taiwan-based international criminal group that carried out the murder.
Liu Qing	(1916–1978) Peasant writer and cadre, known for *Gangqiang tiebi* (Walls of brass and iron, 1951), a novel about the war, and *Chuangye shi* (The builders, 1960, translated into English under that title [Peking, 1964]).
Liu Xiaobo	(b. 1955, in the Northeast) Outspoken iconoclastic cultural and literary critic who gained notoriety for proclaiming a "crisis in Chinese literature" in the mid-1980s, and then for his unremitting castigation of Chinese intellectuals, ancient and modern, liberal and conservative. Imprisoned in June 1989 for having joined the Tiananmen protests, Liu was singled out by the PRC authorities for denunciation as a "Black Hand" of the "turmoil," then unexpectedly released for alleged "contrition" and "good behavior" after being pronounced guilty at his trial in early 1991.
Liu Zaifu	(b. 1941, in Fujian) Noted literary critic, and, until the 1989 Peking massacre, one of the few elected directors of the Institute of Literature, Chinese Academy of Social Sciences. Resident in the United States since 1989.
Liu Zongyuan	(773–819) Famous Tang dynasty prose writer and poet. See William H. Nienhauser, *Liu Tsung-yuan* (New York, 1973).
Liulichang	Old Peking neighborhood, literally, "Colored Glaze Kiln," after a porcelain works that was located there; now known for narrow streets crowded with art and antique shops that have outlasted urban renewal.

Lives of Women Martyrs (Lienü zhuan)	Traditional book about exemplary self-sacrificing Chinese women of the past, today generally considered to have been a tool for the indoctrination of Chinese women for lives of suppression. Trans. Albert Richard O'Hara, *The Position of Women in Early China* (Hong Kong, 1946). See also T. C. Martin-Liao, *Frauenerziehung im Alten China: Eine Analyse der Frauenbücher* (Bochum, 1984).
Lü Heruo	(1914–1947) Literary critic during Taiwan's years as a Japanese colony, from Taizhong County. Lü wrote on rural and family life.
Ma Ji	Contemporary Chinese comedian and *xiangsheng* comic dialogue performer. See the entry on *xiangsheng*.
Ma Sen	(b. 1930s) Cosmopolitan Taiwan novelist from Shandong; past editor of the Taiwan literary journal *Lianhe wenxue* (Unitas).
Magnificent Dreams in Shanghai (Haishang fanhua meng)	Romantic late-Qing novel by Sun Jiazhen, set in the pleasure quarter.
Mao Zedong, Yan'an Talks	The "Talks at the Yan'an Forum on Literature and Art"; the major source of Mao's views on literature, used to bring about intellectual uniformity at Yan'an in the 1942 Rectification movement, and instrumental in the control and suppression of writers since. See Bonnie S. McDougall, *Mao Zedong's "Talks at the Yan'an Conference on Literature and Art"* (Ann Arbor, 1980).
May Fourth movement	A broad-based, nationalistic movement of China's modern intellectuals and students for revolutionizing Chinese culture, making it more rational, progressive, scientific, democratic, and in touch with international trends. Although named after protest activities of May 4, 1919, historians trace the larger movement to 1915, when *New Youth* magazine dedicated itself to revolutionary culture. See Chow Tse-tsung, *The May Fourth Movement* (Cambridge, MA, 1960), and Vera Schwarcz, *The Chinese Enlightenment* (Berkeley, 1986).
May Thirtieth incident	A nationalistic wave of student demonstrations, worker strikes, and Chinese merchant boycotts in

1925 that arose chiefly in Shanghai, Guangzhou, and Hong Kong, following the May 30 killing of eleven Chinese demonstrators on Nanking Road, Shanghai, by Chinese and Sikh policemen officered by a British inspector.

Mingbao

Politically moderate Hong Kong daily published by Zha Liangyong (Louis Cha, who appears in this anthology under his novelist's pseudonym, "Jin Yong").

"Misty" or "obscure" poetry (*menglong shi*)

New poetry of the post-Mao era by Bei Dao, Gu Cheng, Jiang He, Mang Ke, Shu Ting, and many others, attacked during the 1980s by Communist party hacks and conservatives (and also the veteran poet Ai Qing) for alleged incomprehensibility and lack of social usefulness.

Model operas

See the entry on Jiang Qing.

Modern Literature (*Xiandai wenxue*)

Leading Taiwan journal.

Most Incredible Marvels among the Swordsmen (*Jiaxia qizhongqi*)

Traditional adventure novel.

My Two Hosts (*Wo de liangjia fangdong*)

Short story collection (1950) by Kang Zhuo (b. 1920), a Communist propagandist and literary cadre. The title story features problems of women and the family system.

New Era

An official term for the period of reforms since the ascension to power of Deng Xiaoping. See the entry on Literature of the New Era.

New Literature

Refers to modern vernacular literary works produced after and in the spirit of the May Fourth movement, which was also called the New Culture movement.

New Wave

Catchall term for the newest wave of young avant-garde writers, including Ge Fei, Liu Heng, Ma Yuan, Ye Zhaoyan, and Yu Hua—writers typically younger than the ex–Red Guard generation, who came to prominence after 1987, often after being discovered by *Beijing wenxue* (Peking literature), edited by Li Tuo. New Wave works were notably "difficult," even as they restored traditional elements of plot and action to China's new experimental tradition of short-story writing.

New Youth
(Xin qingnian)

Magazine promoting cultural and literary revolution after Chen Duxiu assumed its editorship in 1915; the New Culture movement's most influential journal.

Nexø, Martin Andersen

(1869–1954) Marxist novelist and story writer of Denmark. His fiction exalts the poor and oppressed class, into which he was born. Known for his works *Pelle the Conqueror* (1906–10) and *Ditte, Child of Man* (1917–21).

Ni Kuang

Extremely successful Hong Kong popular novelist (now banned in the PRC), specializing in science fiction, Gothic, and erotic novels; also an author of *zawen* essays, and a Hong Kong television personality.

Nie Hualing (Hua-ling Nieh Engle)

(b. 1926) Born in Hubei on the mainland, she moved to Taiwan in 1949 and became an editor of the opposition journal *Ziyou Zhongguo* (Free China) under Lei Zhen. She left for the United States with American poet Paul Engle in 1964. See the entry on the International Writing Program.

The Nine-Tailed Turtle
(Jiuwei gui)

Wu dialect novel (1906–10) written by Zhang Chunfang (d. 1935). See Jean Duval, "The Nine-Tailed Turtle," in *The Chinese Novel at the Turn of the Century*, ed. Milena Doleželová-Velingerová (Toronto, 1980), pp. 177–88.

The Nineties
(Jiushi niandai)

Influential Hong Kong monthly magazine of current affairs like *Newsweek*, edited by Lee Yee (Li Yi), sold also in Taiwan since 1990, but long banned in the PRC. Called *Qishi niandai* (The seventies) until the 1980s.

Outcry (Nahan)

Also translated as *Call to Arms* and *Cheering from the Sidelines*; the title of Lu Xun's first collection of short stories (1923), the preface of which is translated in this anthology.

Ouyang Shan

(b. 1908, in Hubei). Communist party culture bureaucrat and writer about city life in Guangdong. His novel *Gao ganda* (Uncle Gao) describes the early phase of collectivization after the 1942 Yan'an rectification.

Ouyang Xiu

(1007–1072) Song dynasty writer and statesman. See Ronald C. Egan, *The Literary Works of Ou-yang Hsiu* (Cambridge, 1984).

Ouyang Zi

(b. 1939) Taiwanese writer from Nantou County, resident in the United States since 1962, who emulates Western literary models. Since 1969, she has specialized in translations and criticism.

Peking Spring

The liberal period of 1979, known for Democracy Wall and the publication of nonofficial journals in China.

Peng Ge

(b. 1926, in Hebei) Mainlander writer of Taiwan and influential journalist close to the KMT; author of more than seventy books.

People's Daily (Renmin ribao)

Official organ of the Chinese Communist party.

People's Literature Publishing House (Renmin wenxue chubanshe)

Major official publisher of literature and literary studies.

Popular History of the Tang Dynasty (Shuo Tang)

Old vernacular novel (latest extant edition has a 1736 preface) whose editing is commonly attributed to Luo Guanzhong.

Qiong Yao

(b. 1938, in Hunan) Very successful Taiwan author of more than forty pulp novels; Taiwan's Jacqueline Susann. Her works have generated many Taiwan television soap operas and were all the rage in the PRC during the 1980s, particularly among young female readers. See Leo Ou-fan Lee, " 'Modernism' and 'Romanticism' in Modern Taiwan Literature," in *Chinese Fiction from Taiwan*, ed. Jeannette L. Faurot (Bloomington, IN, 1980), pp. 21–27.

Qu Yuan

(329–299 B.C.). Poet and loyal official betrayed by his king; author of *Encountering Sorrow* and perhaps other books of the *Chu ci*, one of China's greatest ancient poetry anthologies: David Hawkes, trans., Ch'u Tz'u: *The Songs of the South* (London, 1959).

On the legend and political use of Qu Yuan's name, see Laurence A. Schneider, *A Madman of Ch'u: The Chinese Myth of Loyalty and Dissent* (Berkeley, 1980).

Red Crag (Hongyan)

Reportage novel (1961) by Luo Guangbin and Yang Yiyan, known in China as a "textbook of the revolution." It describes Chongqing in the 1940s, with concentration camps run by the KMT secret service and its American military allies, the urban student movement, and the underground work of the Communist party. After the 1989 massacre, the novel was officially reissued, although ironically the story ends with a mass prison breakout. There is an English translation in *Chinese Literature*, 1962, nos. 5–7.

Republic Daily (Minguo ribao)

Organ of the Kuomintang, 1915–31. Shao Lizi edited its supplement *Juewu* (Awakening) in the early 1920s.

Republican era

The period of Chinese history from 1912 to 1949.

Research Materials on Contemporary Chinese Literature (Zhongguo dangdai wenxue yanjiu ziliao)

Important biographical series of the 1980s, on contemporary authors.

The Romance of the Three Kingdoms (San guo yanyi)

Popular old historical novel, compiled in final form by Luo Guanzhong (ca. 1330–1400). Trans. C. H. Brewitt-Taylor, *Romance of the Three Kingdoms* (Shanghai, 1925).

Romance of the Western Chamber (Xixiangji)

Famous romantic drama by thirteenth-century playwright Wang Shifu, translated by Stephen H. West and Wilt Idema as *The Moon and the Zither* (Berkeley, 1991).

Rou Shi

(1901–1931) One of the "Five Martyrs," young leftist writers who were executed near Shanghai on February 7, 1931, in a demonstration of Chiang Kai-shek's "White Terror."

Scholar-beauty plots *(caizi jiaren)*

A group of fifty popular narratives centered on the relationship between a male scholar and a female beauty, written between 1650 and 1730. The stories speak of love, courtship, knight-errantry, and military romance, filtered through a very didactic Confucian moralism. See Richard C. Hessney, "Beautiful, Talented, and Brave: Seventeenth-Century Chinese Scholar-Beauty Romances," Ph.D. dissertation, Columbia University, 1979.

The Scholars
(Rulin waishi)

Great satiric novel of the eighteenth century: Wu Ching-tzu, *The Scholars*, trans. Yang Hsien-yi and Gladys Yang (New York, 1972). In a famous chapter satirizing the examination system, Fan Jin, who has become an old man after many fruitless tries at the exam, finally passes—no thanks to his own competence.

Seven Knights-Errant
and Five Gallants
(Qi xia wu yi)

Quasi-historical novel (1889) of adventure, crime detection, and political intrigue revolving around the legendary figure of Judge Bao. Edited by the scholar Yu Yue and based on the earlier nineteenth-century novel, *Three Knights-Errant and Five Gallants*. See Susan Blader, "A Critical Study of *San-hsia wu-yi*," Ph.D. dissertation, University of Pennsylvania, 1977, and Bernd Schmoller, *Bao Zheng (999–1062) als Beamter und Staatsmann* (Bochum, 1982).

Shenbao (Shun pao)

High-circulation daily newspaper of Shanghai, established in 1872; a news staple throughout China during the Republican era, and a printer of popular fiction.

Shi Shu

Taiwan scholar, professor of Chinese at Tamkang University, and critic, sister of Li Ang. Author of *Lixiangzhuyizhe de jianying* (Silhouettes of idealists) (Taibei, 1990), on leftist writers of the 1930s.

Shi Shuqing

(b. 1945) Writer and critic from Taiwan, sister of Li Ang; sometime resident of the United States and Hong Kong. Shi Shuqing is known for her literary portraits of Hong Kong people and has published a volume of interviews with mainland writers.

Short Story Monthly
(Xiaoshuo yuebao)

Late-Qing publisher of light amusement and adventure novels in classical Chinese, owned by the Commercial Press of Shanghai. In 1921, it switched to vernacular fiction, becoming a leading purveyor of the "New Literature" under the editorship of Mao Dun of the Literary Research Association.

Shui Jing

(b. 1935). Taiwan writer now living in the United States; has written a study of Zhang Ailing (1973).

Sima Qian

(ca. 145–ca. 85 B.C.) China's most famous historian. See Burton Watson, *Ssu-ma Ch'ien, Grand Historian of China* (New York, 1958).

Slapping the Table in Amazement (Paian jingqi)

Collection of stories (1628) by the Ming writer Ling Mengchu (1580–1644). See Patrick Hanan, *The Chinese Vernacular Story* (Cambridge, MA, 1981).

Song Jiang

Hero of the classic novel *Shuihu zhuan* (Water margin). Ultraleftists in the PRC leadership launched a campaign against old cadres and Deng Xiaoping during September 1975 by attacking the "capitulationism" of Song Jiang, a character in the novel who leads its bandit heroes.

The Song of Youth (Qingchun zhi ge)

Yang Mo's stirring revolutionary novel (1958) of student romance and political commitment in Peking during the period of Japanese encroachment in the early 1930s. Available in English (Peking, 1964).

Songs of the South (Chu ci)

See the entry on Qu Yuan.

The Story of an Iron Bucket (Yangtietong de gushi)

Modern novel (1944) with a traditional chapter-driven structure by the Communist writer Ke Lan (b. 1920, in Changsha), about Communist battles against the Japanese.

Strange Tales from a Chinese Studio (Liao zhai zhi yi)

Collection of tales (1679) in classical Chinese by Pu Songling (1640–1715). Herbert A. Giles, trans., *Strange Stories from a Chinese Studio* (London, 1880, 1926).

Su Manshu

(1884–1918) Anti-Manchu revolutionary and romantic poet-novelist raised in Yokohama. Noted for his autobiographical novel, *Duanhong lingyan ji* (The lone swan, 1912). See Liu Wu-chi, *Su Man-shu* (New York, 1972).

Su Shi

(1037–1101) Famous Song dynasty poet, prose writer, scholar, and statesman. See Burton Watson, *Su Tung-p'o: Selections from a Sung Dynasty Poet* (New York, 1965) and Lin Yutang, *The Gay Genius* (New York, 1947).

Sun Li

(b. 1913, in Hebei) Author of novels about war resistance to the Japanese, such as *Luhuatang* (The marshes), translated in *Chinese Literature*, September 1962. After Liberation, he concentrated on stories about the countryside and on lyric essays. Sun Li remained popular in the 1980s; see his *The Blacksmith and the Carpenter* (Beijing, 1982).

Sun Zhen

U.S.-trained economist born on the mainland, president of National Taiwan University, Taibei.

Taiwan Garrison
Command

Taiwan's secret service, a military organ known for opening mail, banning publications, intimidating dissidents, and putting down "rebellions."

Taiwan Independence

Uncompromising political opposition movement demanding that the government of Taiwan renounce any claim to the mainland, which would delegitimate the Republic of China government of the KMT and close the door on reunification with the mainland. The movement originally grew out of clashes between Taiwan natives and the new mainlander government, particularly the incident of February 28, 1947, in which KMT armies executed ten to twenty thousand natives. After years of exile in Japan and the United States, the movement began to gain converts again on Taiwan in the late 1980s.

*Taiwan Political
Review (Taiwan
zhenglun)*

Opposition journal published in Taibei by *Dangwai* legislators Huang Xinjie and Kang Ningxiang. The magazine was the only one of its kind when it appeared in 1975, following the repression of the last years of Chiang Kai-shek; it was banned after five issues.

*Tale of Heroic Young
Lovers (Ernü yingxiong
zhuan)*

Popular traditional-style Qing dynasty novel by the Sinicized Manchu Wen Kang. Translated by Franz Kuhn as *Die Schwarze Reiterin* (Zürich, 1954).

Tao Yuanming

(365–427) World-famous bucolic poet. See A. R. Davis, *Tao Yuan-ming* (Cambridge, 1984).

The Ten-Year Calamity

The negative buzzword used since the ascendancy of Deng Xiaoping to speak of the Cultural Revolution years, which in retrospect have been lengthened to include the entire period of 1966–76.

Third Plenum of the Eleventh Central Committee of the Communist Party

The meeting at which Deng Xiaoping's reform program became Communist party policy, in December 1978.

Three Knights-Errant and Five Gallants (*Sanxia wuyi*)

See the entry on *Seven Knights-Errant*.

Three Prominences

Jiang Qing's tri-partite Cultural Revolution injunction to stress undiluted heroism in socialist literature. "Lofty perfection" was another goal trumpeted at the time.

Three Red Flags

Mao's great communistic policies of 1958: the General Line for Socialist Construction, the Great Leap Forward, and the People's Communes.

The Three Years of Adjustment (*san nian tiaozheng zhengce*)

Euphemism for the three years that brought starvation to China (1959–61), during and after the disastrous Great Leap Forward.

Tiananmen incident of 1976

An April 5 commemoration in the great square, through the laying of wreaths and recitations of poetry, of the recently deceased Zhou Enlai. It took on the character of a mass protest against China's ultra-leftist policies and was brutally suppressed. Newly rehabilitated Deng Xiaoping was held responsible for the disturbance and purged again.

Tie Ning

(b. 1957, in Peking, of Hebei ancestry) A writer known for stories of China's young people, including both the sent-down generation and peasants coping with a modernizing world.

Tongcheng school

Talented writers of several generations from Tongcheng County, Anhui, notably Fang Bao (1668–1747) and Yao Nai (1730–1814), who revived an ancient, pre-Han classical style. Their own accomplishments in this less ornate and purified style continued to inspire some Chinese writers in the twentieth century. See David E. Pollard, *A Chinese Look at Literature* (Berkeley, 1973).

United Daily News (*Lianhebao*)

A major Taibei newspaper, regarded as conservative and close to the KMT.

An Unofficial History of Student Life in Japan (*Liudong waishi*)	Old-style popular novel (1916) by Xiang Kairan.
Wang Ruoshui	(b. 1926, in Hunan) Ideologist and journalist criticized in the 1980s for his concepts of "humanism" and "alienation," and deprived of his position as deputy editor (since 1977) of the *People's Daily*. See David A. Kelly, "The Emergence of Humanism: Wang Ruoshui and the Critique of Socialist Alienation," in *China's Intellectuals and the State*, ed. Merle Goldman et al. (Cambridge, MA, 1987), pp. 159–82.
Warring States	The era 403–221 B.C., when China was divided into independent kingdoms at war with each other, and great philosophers holding opposite opinions were in their heyday.
Water Margin (*Shuihu zhuan*)	Classic Ming dynasty novel beloved of Mao Zedong and millions of others, known for characters that are Robin Hood bandits. Translated by Pearl S. Buck as *All Men Are Brothers* (New York, 1933).
Wei Jingshen	(b. 1950) Outspoken Democracy Wall activist who won Deng Xiaoping's enmity by calling for "The Fifth Modernization—Democracy." When he was imprisoned in 1979 and sentenced to fifteen years, the injustice made Wei a cause célèbre to human rights activists, first in the West, and then in China. Demands for his release by Fang Lizhi and others helped fuel and focus the democracy movement of spring 1989.
Wei Junyi	(b. 1917) Communist party editor and writer, past vice-president of the People's Literature Publishing House. During the decade of reforms, she began to publish short stories containing portraits of older cadres.
Wen Tingyun	(ca. 812–870) Tang poet. See I. Lu, *Wen Fei-ch'ing und seine literarische Umwelt* (Würzburg, 1939).
Wen Yiduo	(1899–1946) Poet, scholar, and critic, who studied in the United States and taught Western and Chinese literature upon his return to China. Assassinated by

the KMT because of his activism in the opposition political party alliance, the Democratic League. See Kai-yu Hsu, *Wen I-to* (Boston, 1980).

The White-haired Girl (*Baimao nü*)

A legend transformed into an opera (1945) by the Shandong poet He Jingzhi (b. 1924; acting minister of culture after the 1989 Peking massacre) and the army dramatist Ding Yi (b. 1921). See *He Jingzhi zhuanji* (Nanjing, 1982).

The Woman Warrior

Critically acclaimed 1976 bestselling novel by the Chinese-American author Maxine Hong Kingston.

Wonders New and Old (*Jin gu qiguan*)

Ming dynasty digest of tales by Feng Menglong and Ling Mengchu still read by Chinese youngsters today. See E. Jean Kern, "The Individual and Society in the Chinese Colloquial Short Story: The *Chin-ku ch'i-kuan*," Ph.D. dissertation, Indiana University, 1973.

Wu Cheng'en

(ca. 1500–1582) Author of the classic novel *Journey to the West*.

Wu Han

(1909–1969) Famous for his 1961 Peking opera, *Hai Rui baguan* (Hai Rui dismissed from office), official 1965 criticism of which helped launch the Cultural Revolution. Though the play is set in the Ming dynasty, Mao Zedong's faction saw in it allegorical criticism of the chairman.

Wu Sheng

(b. 1944) Nativist poet from Taiwan. Wu participated in the International Writing Program at the University of Iowa in 1980.

Wu Zhihui

(1864–1953) Reformer and veteran KMT revolutionary, scholar, and educator interested in language reform.

Wu Zhuoliu

(1900–1976) A teacher from Xinzhu County, Taiwan; one of the major Taiwanese writers of the Lai He and Yang Kui generation, active during the Japanese occupation and during the 1950s; founded the journal *Taiwan wenyi* (Taiwanese literature) in 1964.

Xiangsheng

Comedians' dialogues, literally "face and voice" acts, originally delivered by amateur and professional stand-up joke tellers in northern China, today spread nationwide by radio and television. They often have a satiric purpose. Examples are translated in Perry Link, ed., *Stubborn Weeds* (Bloomington, IN, 1983), pp. 252–75, and in Lang Defang and others, *Comic Sketches*, trans. Simon Johnstone (Beijing, 1990).

Xiangtu

Literally means "of the countryside and the soil," or "local." As used in Taiwan, it means "nativist" or "native-soil"—that is, "of the *Taiwanese* locality" rather than of mainlander or foreign extraction in Taiwan's modern cosmopolitan culture. Taiwan *xiangtu* literature, which flourished in the late 1960s and 1970s, was typically about the countryside and employed local dialect, but also included local nonbureaucratic Taiwanese urban life by extension. On the mainland, Lu Xun in the 1930s had used the term without sectionalist connotations, to refer to any "rural" literature. The word *xiangtu* nevertheless mostly dropped out of PRC literary critical vocabulary, to be revived only in the 1980s by Liu Shaotang, Sun Li, and others who claimed to have written fiction that had a unique, evidently un-Maoist rural quality.

Xinhua (New China) Bookstore

The major nationwide chain of government-owned bookstores in China. It had a near monopoly of over-the-counter book sales in China during the Mao era, which it retains in most small communities and some cities even today. Xinhua also prints books under its imprint and others'.

Xinwenbao (*Sin wan pao*)

High-circulation Shanghai newspaper of the Republican era, whose literary page printed popular fiction by writers such as Zhang Henshui.

Xu Daran

(b. 1940) Poet and essayist from Taiwan, now living in the United States.

Xu Fuguan

(1904–1982) Conservative, Hubei-born teacher of traditional Chinese literary criticism at Taiwan's Donghai University, 1950–69, and subsequently at the Chinese University of Hong Kong. Also a KMT legislator and combatively disputatious critic of literature, art, and politics. Xu Fuguan's many books on literary history and four volumes of *zawen* essays (Taibei, 1980) made him an intellectual force in Taiwan until his death. His late 1970s' attack on the poet Yu

	Guangzhong won kudos from Taiwan's *xiangtu* writers.
Xu Zhenya	See the entry on *Jade Pear Spirit*.
Yan Huo	Pseudonym of Poon Yiu Ming (Pan Yaoming), a Hong Kong writer and critic and, in the 1980s, deputy editor-in-chief of the PRC's Joint Publishing Company (Sanlian Shudian) in Hong Kong. Now editor-in-chief of *Mingbao Monthly*.
Yan Wenjing	(b. 1915) Author of children's literature, critic, and president of the People's Literature Publishing House.
Yang Hua	(1906–1936) Poet and fiction writer from Taiwan who lived in great poverty.
Yang Kui	(1905–1985) One of the best-known modern Taiwanese authors active before 1945; edited the journal *Taiwan xinwenxue* (New Taiwanese literature). Ten years in KMT prisons after 1949 left him a broken man.
Yang Qingchu	(b. 1949) Taiwanese writer who has described the lives of and identified with workers; also a publisher and opposition politician. Incarcerated by the KMT, 1979–84. See Ingrid Schuh, *Die Erzählungen des taiwanesischen Schriftstellers Yang Qingchu bis 1975* (Bochum, 1989). A bilingual edition of five of his stories is *Selected Stories of Yang Ch'ing-ch'u*, trans. Thomas B. Gold (Gaoxiong, 1978).
Yao Nai	(1732–1815) Prose stylist and classicist, essayist of the *guwen* (ancient prose) style and member of the Tongcheng school.
Yao Wenyuan	(b. 1931) Prominent member of the Cultural Revolution ultraleftist faction around Jiang Qing ("Gang of Four") responsible for ideology and propaganda. See Lars Ragvald, *Yao Wen-yuan as a Literary Critic and Theorist: The Emergence of Chinese Zhdanovism* (Stockholm, 1978).
Ye Shitao	(b. 1925) Teacher from Tainan, southern Taiwan, and a respected critic and author; wrote the first outline of Taiwanese literature (*Taiwan wenxue shigang*, 1987).

The Yellow Emperor and the Yan Emperor	Legendary sovereigns of China's revered antiquity, traditionally considered the progenitors of the Chinese race.
Yin Fu	(1909–1931) One of the "Five Martyrs," young leftist writers who were executed near Shanghai on February 7, 1931, in a demonstration of Chiang Kai-shek's "White Terror."
Yin Haiguang	See the entry on *Free China*.
Yu Dengfa	(1901–1990) Wealthy, established local politician who was arrested, with his son, on January 21, 1979, allegedly for consorting with a "Communist agent." The dissident magazine *Xia chao* (China tide) was also banned. A past magistrate of Gaoxiong County, Yu was on the verge of chairing a meeting to form an islandwide opposition to the KMT. The government had postponed elections after Washington announced a rapprochement with the PRC.
Yu Lihua	(b. 1931, in Shanghai) Graduated from National Taiwan University in 1953 and then went to the United States for graduate study. One of the earliest writers from Taiwan to be internationally known, she wrote novels typically concerning students and other Chinese living overseas.
Yuefu	Ancient Chinese verse form dating back to the Han dynasty and probably beyond that, to folk ballads; literally, "Bureau of Music ballads," after the poems collected by an official bureau founded in 120 B.C. Imitated in the Tang by Bo Juyi, Li He, and others, the form retains the mystique of its folk origins.
Zeng Xinyi	(b. 1948, in Taiwan) Author of short stories active in the 1970s.
Zha Liangyong (Louis Cha)	Represented in this anthology under his pseudonym, Jin Yong.
Zhang Chengzhi	(b. 1948, in Peking, of the Hui nationality) Creative young author of the 1980s who once worked in the archeology division of Peking's Museum of History and as a researcher of the National Institute of Minorities.

Zhang Chunqiao

(b. 1917) Member of the ultraleftist faction during the Cultural Revolution (the "Gang of Four") and vice-premier until his removal in 1976.

Zhang Dachun

(b. 1957) Versatile writer and journalist from Taiwan, very much in touch with the latest fads of the American literary scene.

Zhang Henshui

(1895–1967) Prolific writer of popular novels in the 1930s and 1940s, too sentimental and lowbrow to be accepted by the "May Fourth writers" as one of their own. See Hsiao-Wei Rupprecht, *Departure and Return: Chang Hen-shui and the Chinese Narrative Tradition* (Hong Kong, 1987), and Eva Wagner, *Zhang Henshui's 'Einundachtzig Träume,' Gesellschaftskritik zwischen Tradition und Utopie* (Bochum, 1990).

Zhang Wenhuan

(1909–1978) Noted Taiwanese author of the Japanese colonial period, who wrote in Japanese.

Zhang Xiguo

(b. 1944, in Chongqing) Fiction writer formerly of Taiwan, who now works as a computer specialist at the University of Illinois Chicago Circle campus. Also noted as an author of science fiction in Chinese.

Zhao Shuli

(1906–1970) Peasant writer, killed during the Cultural Revolution.

Zhao Ziyang

(b. 1919) Took over from Hu Yaobang in 1987 as secretary-general of the Communist party and head of the progressive faction. Party hard-liners dismissed him in June 1989 and made him the scapegoat for the spring "turmoil."

Zhong Dianfei

(1919–1987) Film critic from Sichuan, father of Zhong Acheng; was declared a rightist in 1957 for his essay "Dianying de luogu" (Gongs and drums in the film industry). Rehabilitated in 1978, he became president of the Chinese society of film criticism.

Zhong Lihe

(1915–1960) *Xiangtu* author from rural Taiwan who began to write during the Japanese occupation. Between 1938 and 1942, he lived in the Japanese-occupied cities of Shenyang and Peking. His works were published in 1976, in ten volumes.

Zhong Zhaozheng

(b. 1925) Author and editor of Taiwan's *xiangtu* literature; served as a teacher in the countryside and as editor of the journal *Taiwan wenyi* (Taiwanese literature).

Zhou Libo

(1908–1979) Hunan peasant writer and literary cadre who won a 1951 Stalin prize in literature. *Baofeng zouyu* (The hurricane) is his famous novel about the land reform, published in English in 1955.

Zhu Dianren

(1903–1947) Taiwanese writer and collector of folklore from Taibei; worked during the Japanese colonial period.

Zhu Ziqing

(1898–1948) May Fourth essayist and poet, one of the few not banned on Taiwan. See Julia C. Lin, *Modern Chinese Poetry* (Seattle, 1972).

Zhuang Zi

Great third-century B.C. work of Daoist philosophy and imaginative literary prose, attributed to a man of the same name of the fourth century B.C. Trans. Burton Watson, *The Complete Works of Chuang Tzu* (New York, 1968).

Translators and Writers Translated

Backstrom, Marty: Jin Yong

Besio, Kim: Chen Ruoxi

Campbell, Catherine Pease: Wang Meng

Chow, Rey, and Ming-bao Yue: Shen Congwen

Ding Naifei: Bai Xianyong

Duke, Michael S.: Wu Zuguang

Fung Mei-cheong: Gao Xiaosheng

Goldblatt, Howard: Liu Xinwu

Grant, Beata: Chen Yingzhen, Lao She, Liu Xinwu, Lu Wenfu

Gregory, Juliette: Wang Tuo

Gunn, Edward: Zhang Ailing

Huters, Theodore: Mao Dun, Yu Dafu

Jenner, W. J. F.: Ba Jin, Chen Rong, Zhang Xianliang

Kinkley, Jeffrey: Wang Zengqi, Zhang Xinxin (second text)

LaFleur, Frances: Dai Houying

Lee, Linette: Zhong Acheng

Leng, Pu-mei: Li Ang

Li, Peter: Jia Pingwa

Martin, Helmut: Wang Wenxing

Pang, Patricia Da-yi, and Philip Williams: Song Zelai

Pruyn, Carolyn S.: Liu Binyan

Rudolph, Deborah: Wang Ruowang

Sieber, Patricia: Wu Jinfa

Tang, Raymond N.: Huang Chunming

Wagner, Marsha, and Tang Yiming: Bai Hua

Wakefield, David: Han Shaogong
Wang, Linda Greenhouse: Gu Hua
Wang, Tien Rita, and Charles Belbin: Qideng Sheng
Wild, Natasha: Lin Shuangbu
Williams, Philip: Feng Jicai, Song Zelai
Wong, Sau-ling C.: Wang Zhenhe
Yang Xianyi and Gladys Yang: Lu Xun
Yeung, Ellen Lai-shan: Huang Fan, Wang Anyi, Zhang Xinxin (first text)
Yu Fanqin: Zhang Jie
Zha Jianying: Ding Ling
Zhang Yingjin: Cong Weixi

Bibliographies

The Select General Bibliography emphasizes fiction translations and criticism of 1980s' Chinese works in English—and in German and other Western languages when no English item is available. A few Chinese titles are provided for underrepresented authors. Translations in *Chinese Literature* and *The Chinese P.E.N.*, as well as many works by and about Republican-era authors and their literary movements, are not listed below. The headings are as follows:

1. Reference
2. Topical Studies and Symposium Volumes
3. Anthologies of Translations
4. Individual Authors (listed alphabetically, by the pinyin spelling)
5. Notable Works by 1980s' Authors Not Represented in This Anthology
6. Select Items on China's Late 1980s Democracy Movement and the June 4 Massacre

The Source Bibliography, A Survey of *Chuangzuotan* (Writers on Writing), is for specialists who seek further, untranslated materials of the sort anthologized in this book.

Select General Bibliography

1. Reference

Bibliography of Asian Studies. Ann Arbor, MI: Association for Asian Studies. Quarterly.
Catalog of Chinese Underground Literatures. Compiled by T. C. Chang, C. F. Chen, and Y. T. Lin. Taipei: Institute of Current China Studies, 1982. 2 vols.
Chinese Literature. Beijing: Foreign Languages Bureau. Quarterly (formerly monthly) magazine translating contemporary and traditional Chinese literary selections. Indexed annually in the winter issue.
Chinese Literature: Essays, Articles, Reviews. Bloomington: Indiana University. Biannual journal of research and book reviews on traditional and modern Chinese literature.
The Chinese P.E.N. Taipei: Taipei Chinese Center, International P.E.N. Quarterly magazine translating contemporary literary selections from Taiwan.
Gibbs, Donald A., and Yun-chen Li. *A Bibliography of Studies and Translations of*

Modern Chinese Literature, 1918–1942. Cambridge: East Asian Research Center, Harvard University, 1975.

Hsia, C. T. *A History of Modern Chinese Fiction*. Rev. ed. New Haven: Yale University Press, 1971.

Human Rights Tribune. New York: Human Rights in China. Provides articles and timely updates on the imprisonment of writers and other intellectuals.

Klein, Leonard S., ed. *Far Eastern Literatures in the 20th Century*. New York: Ungar, 1986.

Malmqvist, N. G. D., ed. *A Selective Guide to Chinese Literature: 1900–1949*. Leiden: E. J. Brill, 1988–1990. Vol. 1, *The Novel*. Ed. Milena Dolezelová-Velingerová. Vol. 2, *The Short Story*. Ed. Zbigniew Slupski. Vol. 3, *The Poem*. Ed. Lloyd Haft. Vol. 4, *The Drama*. Ed. Bernd Eberstein.

Modern Chinese Literature. Boulder. Biannual academic journal of articles on literature from the Chinese mainland and Taiwan.

Nienhauser, William H., ed. *The Indiana Companion to Traditional Chinese Literature*. Bloomington: Indiana University Press, 1986.

Prušek, Jaroslav, ed. *Dictionary of Oriental Literatures*. Vol. 1, *East Asia*. Ed. Zbigniew Slupski. London: George Allen & Unwin, 1974.

Renditions. Hong Kong: Research Centre for Translation, Chinese University of Hong Kong. Annual journal that often translates contemporary Chinese literature.

Tamkang Review. Tamsui, Taipei County: Tamkang University. A quarterly of comparative studies between Chinese and foreign literatures.

Tsai, Meishi. *Contemporary Chinese Novels and Short Stories, 1949–1974: An Annotated Bibliography*. Cambridge: Council on East Asian Studies, Harvard University, 1979.

World Literature Today. Norman: University of Oklahoma. Quarterly with timely reviews of contemporary Chinese literature, chiefly in translation.

2. Topical Studies and Symposium Volumes

Anderson, Marston. *The Limits of Realism: Chinese Fiction in the Revolutionary Period*. Berkeley: University of California Press, 1990.

Bady, Paul. "The Modern Chinese Writer: Literary Incomes and Best Sellers." *China Quarterly* 88 (December 1988): 645–657.

Benton, Gregor, ed. *Wild Lilies, Poisonous Weeds: Dissident Voices from People's China*. London: Pluto Press, 1982.

Bucher, Ida. *Chinesische Gegenwartsliteratur: Eine Perspektive gesellschaftlichen Wandels der achtziger Jahre*. Bochum: Brockmeyer (Chinathemen), 1986.

China's Literary Image. China issue of *Review of National Literatures* 6,1 (Spring 1975).

Chow, Rey. *Woman and Chinese Modernity: The Politics of Reading between West and East*. Minneapolis: University of Minnesota Press, 1991.

Contemporary Chinese Literature. *World Literature Today* 65, 3 (Summer 1991).

Dillard, Annie. *Encounters with Chinese Writers*. Middletown, CT: Wesleyan University Press, 1984.

Duke, Michael S. *Blooming and Contending: Chinese Literature in the Post-Mao Era*. Bloomington: Indiana University Press, 1985.

———, ed. *Modern Chinese Women Writers: Critical Appraisals*. Armonk, NY: M. E. Sharpe, 1989.

Faurot, Jeannette L., ed. *Chinese Fiction from Taiwan: Critical Perspectives*. Bloomington: Indiana University Press, 1980.

Free China Review 41, 4 (April 1991): 1–47, "Special Section: Contemporary Literature in Taiwan."

Gálik, Marián. *Interliterary and Intraliterary Aspects of the May Fourth Movement 1919 in China*. Bratislava: Veda, 1990.

————. *Milestones in Sino-Western Literary Confrontation (1898–1979)*. Wiesbaden: Otto Harrassowitz, 1986.

Goldblatt, Howard, ed. *Chinese Literature for the 1980s: The Fourth Congress of Writers and Artists*. Armonk, NY: M. E. Sharpe, 1982.

————, ed. *Worlds Apart: Recent Chinese Writing and Its Audiences*. Armonk, NY: M. E. Sharpe, 1990. (Selected papers of the 1986 international conference "The Commonwealth of Chinese Literature," Schloss Reisenburg, organized by Helmut Martin and Joseph S. M. Lau.)

Goldman, Merle. *China's Intellectuals: Advise and Dissent*. Cambridge: Harvard University Press, 1981.

————. *Literary Dissent in Communist China*. Cambridge: Harvard University Press, 1967.

————, ed. *Modern Chinese Literature in the May Fourth Era*. Cambridge: Harvard University Press, 1977.

Goodman, David S. G. *Beijing Street Voices: The Poetry and Politics of China's Democracy Movement*. London: Marion Boyers, 1981.

Gunn, Edward. *Rewriting Chinese: Style and Innovation in Twentieth-Century Chinese Prose*. Stanford: Stanford University Press, 1991.

————. *Unwelcome Muse: Chinese Literature in Shanghai and Peking, 1937–1945*. New York: Columbia University Press, 1980.

Harnisch, Thomas. *Chinas neue Literatur: Schriftsteller und ihre Kurzgeschichten in den Jahren 1978–1979*. Bochum: Brockmeyer (Chinathemen), 1985.

Hsia, Tsi-an. *The Gate of Darkness: Studies on the Leftist Literary Movement in China*. Seattle: University of Washington Press, 1968.

Hsu, Kai-yu. *The Chinese Literary Scene*. New York: Random House, 1975.

Huang, Joe C. *Heroes and Villains in Communist China: The Contemporary Chinese Novel as a Reflection of Life*. New York: Pica Press, 1973.

Huters, Theodore, ed. *Reading the Modern Chinese Short Story*. Armonk, NY: M. E. Sharpe, 1990.

Jenner, W. J. F. "1979: A New Start for Literature in China?" *China Quarterly* 86 (June 1981): 274–303.

Kinkley, Jeffrey C. "New Realism in Contemporary Chinese Literature" (review article). *Journal of the Chinese Language Teachers Association* 17, 1 (February 1982): 77–100.

————, ed. *After Mao: Chinese Literature and Society, 1978–1981*. Cambridge: Council on East Asian Studies, Harvard University, 1985, 1990.

Kubin, Wolfgang. *Die Jagd nach dem Tiger: Sechs Versuche zur modernen chinesischen Literatur*. Bochum: Brockmeyer, 1984.

————, and Rudolf G. Wagner, eds. *Essays in Modern Chinese Literature and Literary Criticism*. Bochum: Brockmeyer (Chinathemen), 1982.

Lau, Joseph S. M. "How Much Truth Can a Blade of Grass Carry?" *Journal of Asian Studies* 32, 4 (1973).

Lee, Gregory. *Dai Wangshu: The Life and Poetry of a Chinese Modernist*. Hong Kong: Chinese University Press, 1989.

Lee, Leo Ou-fan. *The Romantic Generation of Modern Chinese Writers*. Cambridge: Harvard University Press, 1973.

Leung, Laifong. *Morning Sun: Interviews with Post-Mao Writers*. Armonk, NY: M. E. Sharpe, forthcoming.

Liang Heng and Judith Shapiro. *Intellectual Freedom in China After Mao: With a Focus on 1983*. New York: Fund for Free Expression, 1984.

————. *Intellectual Freedom in China: An Update.* New York: Fund for Free Expression, 1985.

Lin, Julia C. *Essays on Contemporary Chinese Poetry.* Athens: Ohio University Press, 1985.

————. *Modern Chinese Poetry: An Introduction.* Seattle: University of Washington Press, 1972.

Link, Perry. *Mandarin Ducks and Butterflies: Popular Fiction in Early Twentieth-Century Chinese Cities.* Berkeley: University of California Press, 1981.

————, Richard Madsen, and Paul G. Pickowicz, eds. *Unofficial China: Popular Culture and Thought in the People's Republic.* Boulder: Westview Press, 1989.

Liu Ts'un-yan, ed. *Chinese Middlebrow Fiction from the Ch'ing and Early Republican Eras.* Hong Kong: Renditions, 1984.

Louie, Kam. *Between Fact and Fiction: Essays on Post-Mao Chinese Literature and Society.* Broadway, New South Wales: Wild Peony, 1989.

Malmqvist, N. G. D., ed. *Modern Chinese Literature and Its Social Context.* Stockholm: Institutionen för orientaliska språk, Stockholms Universitet, 1977.

Martin, Helmut, ed. *Cologne-Workshop 1984 on Contemporary Chinese Literature: Chinesische Gegenwartsliteratur.* Köln: Deutsche Welle, 1986.

————, and Karl-Heinz Pohl, eds. *Chinesische Schriftsteller der 80er Jahre.* Special issue of *Akzente* (München) 2 (April 1985).

McDougall, Bonnie S. *Mao Zedong's "Talks at the Yan'an Conference on Literature and Art": A Translation of the 1943 Text with Commentary.* Ann Arbor: Center for Chinese Studies, University of Michigan, 1980.

————. "Problems and Possibilities in Translating Contemporary Chinese Literature." *Australian Journal of Chinese Affairs* 25 (January 1991): 37–67.

————, ed. *Popular Chinese Literature and Performing Arts in the People's Republic of China, 1949–1979.* Berkeley: University of California Press, 1984.

Ng, Mau-sang. *The Russian Hero in Modern Chinese Fiction.* Hong Kong: The Chinese University Press, 1988.

Owen, Stephen. "What Is World Poetry?" *The New Republic*, November 19, 1990, pp. 28–32.

Robinson, Lewis Stewart. *Double-Edged Sword: Christianity and 20th Century Chinese Fiction.* Hong Kong: Tao Fong Shan Ecumenical Center, 1986.

Schwartz, Benjamin I., ed. *Reflections on the May Fourth Movement: A Symposium.* Cambridge: East Asian Research Center, 1972.

Seymour, James D. *The Fifth Modernization: China's Human Rights Movement, 1978–1979.* Stanfordville, NY: Human Rights Publishing Group, 1980.

Spence, Jonathan D. *The Gate of Heavenly Peace.* New York: Viking, 1981.

Ting, Lee-hsia Hsu. *Government Control of the Press in Modern China: 1900–1949.* Cambridge: East Asian Research Center, Harvard University, 1974.

Tung, Constantine, and Colin Mackerras, eds. *Drama in the People's Republic of China.* Albany: State University of New York Press, 1987.

Wagner, Rudolf G. "The Chinese Writer in His Own Mirror: Writer, State, and Society— the Literary Evidence." In *China's Intellectuals and the State: In Search of a New Relationship.* Ed. Merle Goldman, Timothy Cheek, and Carol Lee Hamrin. Cambridge: Council on East Asian Studies, Harvard University, 1987, pp. 183–231.

————. *The Contemporary Chinese Historical Drama: Four Studies.* Berkeley: University of California Press, 1990.

Wang, Jing. "Taiwan *Hsiang-t'u* Literature." In *Chinese Fiction from Taiwan: Critical Perspectives.* Ed. Jeannette L. Faurot. Bloomington: Indiana University Press, 1980, pp. 43–70.

Wang, Mason Y. H., ed. *Perspectives in Contemporary Chinese Literature*. University Center, MI: Green River Press, 1983.

Widmer, Ellen, and David Wang, eds. *From May Fourth to June Fourth: Fiction and Film in Twentieth-Century China*. Cambridge: Harvard University Press, forthcoming.

Wong, Wang-chi. *Politics and Literature in Shanghai: The Chinese League of Left-Wing Writers, 1930-36*. Manchester: Manchester University Press, 1991.

Yan Jiayan, gen. ed. Chen Pingyuan and Xiao Xiaohong, vol. eds. *Ershi shiji Zhongguo xiaoshuo shi* (A history of Chinese fiction in the twentieth century). Vol. 1. Beijing, 1990.

Yang, Jane Parish. "The Evolution of the Taiwanese New Literature Movement from 1920 to 1937." Ph.D. dissertation, University of Wisconsin, Madison, 1981.

Yang, Winston L. K., and Nathan K. Mao, eds. *Modern Chinese Fiction*. Boston: G. K. Hall, 1981.

Yeh, Michelle. *Modern Chinese Poetry: Theory and Practice since 1917*. New Haven: Yale University Press, 1991.

Yue Daiyun. *Intellectuals in Chinese Fiction*. Trans. Deborah Rudolf and Yeh Wen-hsing. Berkeley: Institute of East Asian Studies, University of California, 1988.

——— and Carolyn Wakeman. "Women in Recent Chinese Fiction—A Review Article." *Journal of Asian Studies* 42 (August 1983): 884-87.

3. Anthologies of Translations

Barmé, Geremie, and John Minford, eds. *Seeds of Fire: Chinese Voices of Conscience*. 2d ed. New York: Farrar, Straus and Giroux, 1986, 1989.

———, and Bennett Lee, trans. *The Wounded: New Stories of the Cultural Revolution, 77-78*. Hong Kong: Joint Publishing Company, 1979.

Barnstone, Tony, Howard Goldblatt, and Wang Fang-yu, eds. *China Today*. China issue of *Nimrod* 29, 2 (Spring/Summer 1986).

Berninghausen, John, and Ted Huters, eds. *Revolutionary Literature in China: An Anthology*. White Plains, NY: M. E. Sharpe, 1976.

Best Chinese Stories, 1949-1989. Beijing: Panda Books, 1989.

Carver, Ann C., and Sung-sheng Yvonne Chang, eds. *Bamboo Shoots after the Rain: Contemporary Stories by Women Writers of Taiwan*. New York: Feminist Press, 1990.

Cheung, Dominic, ed. and trans. *The Isle Full of Noises: Modern Chinese Poetry from Taiwan*. New York: Columbia University Press, 1987.

Ch'i Pang-yuan et al., eds. *An Anthology of Contemporary Chinese Literature—Taiwan: 1949-1974*. Taipei: National Institute for Compilation and Translation, 1975. 3 vols.

Chin Ann-ping. *Children of China: Voices of Recent Years*. New York: Knopf, 1988.

Duke, Michael S., ed. *Contemporary Chinese Literature: An Anthology of Post-Mao Fiction and Poetry*. Armonk, NY: M. E. Sharpe, 1985.

———, ed. *Worlds of Modern Chinese Fiction: Short Stories and Novellas from the People's Republic, Taiwan, and Hong Kong*. Armonk, NY: M. E. Sharpe, 1991.

Finkel, Donald, trans. *A Splintered Mirror: Chinese Poetry from the Democracy Movement*. San Francisco: North Point Press, 1991.

Fragrant Weeds: Chinese Short Stories Once Labelled as "Poisonous Weeds." Hong Kong: Joint Publishing Company, 1983.

Gunn, Edward M., ed. *Twentieth-Century Chinese Drama: An Anthology*. Bloomington: Indiana University Press, 1983.

Die Horen, Zeitschrift für Literatur, Kunst und Kritik (Hannover) 138 (1985) and 155, 156 (1989).

Hsia, C. T., ed., with the assistance of Joseph S. M. Lau. *Twentieth-Century Chinese Stories*. New York: Columbia University Press, 1971.

Hsu, Kai-yu, ed. *Literature of the People's Republic of China*. Bloomington: Indiana University Press, 1980.

——, trans. and ed. *Twentieth Century Chinese Poetry: An Anthology*. Ithaca: Cornell University Press, 1963.

Hsu, Vivian Ling, ed. *Born of the Same Roots: Stories of Modern Chinese Women*. Bloomington: Indiana University Press, 1981.

Hung, Eva, ed. *Contemporary Women Writers: Hong Kong and Taiwan*. Hong Kong: Renditions, 1990.

Ing, Nancy Chang, ed. *New Voices: Stories and Poems by Young Chinese Writers [of Taiwan]*. Taipei: Heritage Press, 1961.

——, ed. *Winter Plum: Contemporary Chinese Fiction [from Taiwan]*. Taipei: Chinese Materials Center, 1982.

Isaacs, Harold R., ed. *Straw Sandals*. Cambridge: M.I.T. Press, 1974.

Jenner, W. J. F. *Modern Chinese Stories*. Oxford: Oxford University Press, 1970.

Kinkley, Jeffrey C., ed. *Fiction* (special Chinese edition) 8, 2/3 (1987).

Lane, Stephen, curator, and Ginny MacKenzie, ed. *Beijing—New York: Chinese Artists, Chinese Poets*. New York: Sister City Program of the City of New York and Coyote Press, 1988.

Lau, Joseph S. M., ed. *The Unbroken Chain: An Anthology of Taiwan Fiction since 1926*. Bloomington: Indiana University Press, 1983.

Lau, Joseph S. M., and Howard Goldblatt, eds. *Chinese Literature: The Modern Tradition, an Anthology*. New York: Columbia University Press, forthcoming.

Lau, Joseph S. M., and Timothy A. Ross, eds. *Chinese Stories from Taiwan: 1960–70*. New York: Columbia University Press, 1976.

Lau, Joseph S. M., C. T. Hsia, and Leo Ou-fan Lee, eds. *Modern Chinese Stories and Novellas, 1919–1949*. New York: Columbia University Press, 1981.

Lee, Gregory, and Duoduo, eds. *Four Contemporary Chinese Poets*. Harmondsworth: Penguin, forthcoming.

Lee Yee, ed. *The New Realism: Writings from China after the Cultural Revolution*. New York: Hippocrene, 1983.

Link, Perry, ed. *Roses and Thorns: The Second Blooming of the Hundred Flowers in Chinese Fiction, 1979–80*. Berkeley: University of California Press, 1984.

——, ed. *Stubborn Weeds: Popular and Controversial Chinese Literature after the Cultural Revolution*. Bloomington: Indiana University Press, 1983.

Liu, Nienling, et al., trans. *The Rose Coloured Dinner: New Works by Contemporary Chinese Women Writers*. Hong Kong: Joint Publishing Company, 1988.

Liu, Wu-chi, and Irving Lo. *Sunflower Splendor: Three Thousand Years of Chinese Poetry*. Bloomington: Indiana University Press, 1975.

Martin, Helmut, Charlotte Dunsing, and Wolf Baus, eds. *Blick übers Meer: Chinesische Erzählungen aus Taiwan*. Frankfurt, Suhrkamp, 1982.

Morin, Edward, ed. Trans. Fang Dai, Dennis Ding, and Edward Morin. *The Red Azalea: Chinese Poetry since the Cultural Revolution*. Honolulu: University of Hawaii Press, 1990.

Munro, Stanley R. *Genesis of a Revolution: An Anthology of Modern Chinese Short Stories*. Singapore: Heinemann, 1979.

Nieh, Hualing, ed. *Literature of the Hundred Flowers*. New York: Columbia University Press, 1981. 2 vols.

Palandri, Angela, ed. and trans. *Modern Verse from Taiwan*. Berkeley: University of California Press, 1972.

Pang Bingjun and John Minford, with Séan Golden, eds. *100 Modern Chinese Poems.* Hong Kong: Commercial Press, 1987.
Prize-Winning Stories from China, 1978–1979. Beijing: Foreign Languages Press, 1981.
Prize-Winning Stories from China, 1980–1981. Beijing: Foreign Languages Press, 1985.
Renditions Special Issue on Contemporary Taiwan Literature. *Renditions* 35/36 (Spring/Autumn 1991).
Roberts, R. A., and Angela Knox, trans. *One Half of the Sky: Stories from Contemporary Women Writers of China.* New York: Dodd, Mead, 1987.
Seven Contemporary Chinese Women Writers. Beijing: Panda Books, 1982.
Siu, Helen F., ed. *Furrows: Peasants, Intellectuals, and the State: Stories and Histories from Modern China.* Stanford: Stanford University Press, 1990.
———, and Zelda Stern, eds. *Mao's Harvest: Voices from China's New Generation.* New York: Oxford University Press, 1983.
Soong, Stephen C., and John Minford, eds. *Trees on the Mountain: An Anthology of New Chinese Writing.* Hong Kong: Chinese University Press, 1984.
Tai, Jeanne, trans. and ed. *Spring Bamboo: A Collection of Contemporary Chinese Short Stories.* New York: Random House, 1989.
Vidor, Claude, ed. *Documents on the Chinese Democratic Movement, 1978–80.* Hong Kong: The Observer Publishers, 1981.
Wagner, Rudolf G., ed. *Literatur und Politik in der Volksrepublik China.* Frankfurt: Suhrkamp, 1983.
Wu, Lucian, ed. *New Chinese Writing [from Taiwan].* Taipei: Heritage Press, 1962.
Yang, Winston L. Y., and Nathan K. Mao, eds. *Stories of Contemporary China.* New York: Paragon, 1979. (Reprints of stories from *Chinese Literature*)
Ying Bian, ed. *The Time Is Not Yet Ripe.* San Francisco: China Books, 1991.
Zhu Hong, ed. *The Chinese Western: Short Fiction from Today's China.* New York: Ballantine, 1988.

4. Individual Authors

Ba Jin

Ba Jin [Pa Chin]. *Cold Nights.* Trans. Nathan K. Mao. Hong Kong: Chinese University Press, 1978.
——— [Pa Chin]. *The Family.* Trans. Sidney Shapiro. Peking: Foreign Languages Press, 1958, 1978.
———. *Gedanken unter der Zeit.* Trans. Sabine Peschel. Ed. Helmut Martin. Köln, 1985. (Partial translation of *Suixianglu*)
———. *Random Thoughts.* Trans. Geremie Barmé. Hong Kong: Joint Publishing Company, 1984. (Partial translation of *Suixianglu*)
———. *Selected Works of Ba Jin.* Trans. Jock Hoe. Beijing: Foreign Languages Press, 1988. 2 vols.
Lang, Olga. *Pa Chin and His Writings: Chinese Youth Between Two Revolutions.* Cambridge: Harvard University Press, 1967.
Mao, Nathan K. *Pa Chin.* Boston: Twayne, 1978.

Bai Hua

Bai Hua. "A Bundle of Letters." Trans. Ellen Yeung. In *Stubborn Weeds.* Ed. Perry Link. Bloomington: Indiana University Press, 1983, pp. 114–42.
———. "Oh! Ancient Channels." Trans. Adrienne Tien and Richard Altwarg. *The World*

354   BIBLIOGRAPHIES

& *I* 4, 10 (October 1989): 418–59. With three interpretive essays, by Jerry Dennerline, Jeffrey C. Kinkley, and Michael S. Duke, pp. 460–93.

——— [Pai Hua]. *Pai Hua's Cinematic Script UNREQUITED LOVE, with Related Introductory Materials.* Ed. T. C. Chang, S. Y. Chen, and Y. T. Lin. Taipei: Institute of Current China Studies, 1981.

Doležalová, Anna. "Two Waves of Criticism of the Film Script *Bitter Love* and of the Writer Bai Hua in 1981." *Asian and African Studies* 19 (1983): 27–54.

Martin, Helmut. "The Drama *Tragic Song of Our Time* (*Shidai de beige*): Functions of Literature in the Eighties and Their Socio-political Limitations." In *Drama in the People's Republic of China.* Ed. Constantine Tung and Colin Mackerras. Albany: State University of New York Press, 1987, pp. 254–81.

Bai Xianyong

Bai Xianyong [Pai Hsien-yung]. *Crystal Boys.* Trans. Howard Goldblatt. San Francisco: Gay Sunshine Press, 1990.

——— [Pai Hsien-yung]. "A Day in Pleasantville." Trans. Julia Fitzgerald and Vivian Hsu. In *Born of the Same Roots.* Ed. Vivian Ling Hsu. Bloomington: Indiana University Press, 1981, pp. 183–192.

———. *Einsam mit Siebzehn.* Ed. Helmut Martin. Köln: Diedrichs, 1986. (Selected stories from *Taibeiren*)

——— [Pai Hsien-yung]. "Li T'ung: A Chinese Girl in New York." Trans. by the author and C. T. Hsia. In *Twentieth-Century Chinese Stories.* Ed. C. T. Hsia and Joseph S. M. Lau New York: Columbia University Press, 1971, pp. 218–39.

——— [Pai Hsien-yung]. *Wandering in the Garden, Waking from a Dream: Tales of Taipei Characters.* Trans. Pai Hsien-yung and Patia Yasin. Ed. George Kao. Bloomington: Indiana University Press, 1982. (*Taibeiren*)

——— [Pai Hsien-yung]. "Winter Nights." Trans. John Kwan-Terry and Stephen Lacey. In *Chinese Stories from Taiwan.* Ed. Joseph S. M. Lau and Timothy A. Ross. New York: Columbia University Press, 1976, pp. 336–54.

Ou-yang Tzu. "The Fictional World of Pai Hsien-yung." In *Chinese Fiction from Taiwan.* Ed. Jeannette L. Faurot. Bloomington: Indiana University Press, 1980, pp. 166–78.

Chen Rong

Chen Rong [Shen Rong]. *At Middle Age.* Beijing: Panda Books, 1987.

———. "At Middle Age." Trans. Margaret Decker. In *Roses and Thorns.* Ed. Perry Link. Berkeley: University of California Press, 1984, pp. 261–338.

——— [Shen Rong]. "Not Your Average Girl." Trans. Geremie Barmé. *Renditions* 27/28 (Spring/Autumn 1987): 158–62.

———. "Regarding the Problem of Newborn Piglets in Winter." Trans. Chun-Ye Shih. In *The Rose Coloured Dinner.* Hong Kong: Joint Publishing Company, 1988, pp. 80–94.

———. "The Rose Coloured Dinner." Trans. Ruth Yu Hsiao. In *The Rose Coloured Dinner.* Hong Kong: Joint Publishing Company, 1988, pp. 19–37.

Larson, Wendy. "Women, Writers, Social Reform: Three Issues in Shen Rong's Fiction." In *Modern Chinese Women Writers.* Ed. Michael S. Duke. Armonk, NY: M. E. Sharpe, 1989, pp. 174–95.

Chen Ruoxi

Chen Ruoxi [Chen Jo-hsi]. *The Execution of Mayor Yin and Other Stories from the Great Proletarian Cultural Revolution.* Trans. Nancy Ing and Howard Goldblatt. Bloomington: Indiana University Press, 1978.

—— [Chen Jo-hsi]. "The Last Performance." Trans. Timothy A. Ross and Joseph S. M. Lau. In *Chinese Stories from Taiwan.* Ed. Joseph S. M. Lau and Timothy A. Ross. New York: Columbia University Press, 1976, pp. 2–14.

—— [Chen Jo-hsi]. "My Friend Ai Fen." Trans. Richard Kent and Vivian Hsu. In *Born of the Same Roots.* Ed. Vivian Ling Hsu. Bloomington: Indiana University Press, 1981, pp. 276–302.

——. *The Old Man and Other Stories.* Hong Kong: Renditions, 1986.

—— [Lucy H. M. Chen]. *Spirit Calling: Five Stories of Taiwan.* Taipei: Heritage Press, 1962.

Duke, Michael S. "Personae: Individual and Society in Three Novels by Chen Ruoxi." In *Modern Chinese Women Writers.* Ed. Michael S. Duke. Armonk, NY: M. E. Sharpe, 1989, pp. 53–77.

Hsu, Kai-yu. "A Sense of History: Reading Chen Jo-hsi's Stories." In *Chinese Fiction from Taiwan.* Ed. Jeannette L. Faurot. Bloomington: Indiana University Press, 1980, pp. 206–33.

Kao, George, ed. *Two Writers and the Cultural Revolution: Lao She and Chen Jo-hsi.* Hong Kong: Chinese University Press, 1980.

Chen Yingzhen

Chen Yingzhen [Ch'en Ying-chen]. *Exiles at Home: Stories by Ch'en Ying-chen.* Trans. Lucien Miller. Ann Arbor: Center for Chinese Studies, University of Michigan, 1986.

——. "Mountain Road." Trans. Rosemary Haddon. In *Worlds of Modern Chinese Fiction.* Ed. Michael S. Duke, Armonk, NY: M. E. Sharpe, 1991, pp. 99–119.

—— [Ch'en Ying-chen]. "My First Case." Trans. Cheung Chi-yiu and Dennis T. Hu. In *Chinese Stories from Taiwan.* Ed. Joseph S. M. Lau and Timothy A. Ross. New York: Columbia University Press, 1976, pp. 28–61.

—— [Ch'en Ying-chen]. "Night Freight." Trans. James C. T. Shu. In *The Unbroken Chain.* Ed. Joseph S. M. Lau. Bloomington: Indiana University Press, 1983, pp. 102–32.

Kinkley, Jeffrey C. "From Oppression to Dependency: Two Stages in the Fiction of Chen Yingzhen." *Modern China* 16, 3 (July 1990): 243–68.

Lau, Joseph S. M. "Death in the Void: Three Tales of Spiritual Atrophy in Ch'en Ying-chen's Post-Incarceration Fiction." *Modern Chinese Literature* 2, 1 (Spring 1986): 21–27.

Miller, Lucien. "A Break in the Chain." In *Chinese Fiction from Taiwan.* Ed. Jeannette L. Faurot. Bloomington: Indiana University Press, 1980, pp. 86–109.

Pieper, Anke. *Der taiwanesische Autor Chen Yingzhen—mit einer Übersetzung der Erzählung 'Wolken.'* Bochum: Brockmeyer (Chinathemen), 1987.

Cong Weixi

Cong Weixi. "The Blood-Stained Magnolia." *Chinese Literature* 1980, 4 (April 1980): 3–56.

——. *Cong Weixi ji* (Novellas of Cong Weixi). Fuzhou: Haixia wenyi chubanshe, 1986.

Liu Shaotang. "A Profile of Cong Weixi." *Chinese Literature* 1980, 4 (April 1980): 57–60.

Dai Houying

Dai Houying. *Stones of the Wall.* Trans. Frances Wood. London: Michael Joseph, 1985. (*Ren a, ren!*)

Pruyn, Carolyn S. *Humanism in Modern Chinese Literature: The Case of Dai Houying.* Bochum: Brockmeyer (Chinathemen), 1988.

Ding Ling

Barlow, Tani E. "Gender and Identity in Ding Ling's *Mother.*" *Modern Chinese Literature* 2, 2 (Fall 1986): 123–42.
Ding Ling [Ting Ling]. "The Diary of Miss Sophie." Trans. A. L. Chin. In *Straw Sandals.* Ed. Harold R. Isaacs. Cambridge: M.I.T. Press, 1974, pp. 129–69.
———. *I Myself Am a Woman: Selected Writings of Ding Ling.* Ed. Tani E. Barlow, with Gary J. Bjorge. Boston: Beacon, 1989.
———. *Miss Sophie's Diary and Other Stories.* Trans. W. J. F. Jenner. Beijing: Panda Books, 1985.
——— [Ting Ling]. *The Sun Shines Over the Sanggan River.* Trans. Yang Hsien-yi and Gladys Yang. Peking: Foreign Languages Press, 1954.
Feuerwerker, Yi-tsi Mei. *Ding Ling's Fiction: Ideology and Narrative in Modern Chinese Literature.* Cambridge: Harvard University Press, 1982.

Feng Jicai

Feng Jicai. *Chrysanthemums and Other Stories.* Trans. Susan Wilf Chen. San Diego: Harcourt Brace Jovanovich, 1985.
———. *The Miraculous Pigtail.* Beijing: Panda Books, 1987.
———. *Voices from the Whirlwind: An Oral History of the Cultural Revolution.* Trans. Denny Chu, Cao Hong, Cathy Silber, and Lawrence Tedesco. New York: Pantheon, 1991.
Martin, Helmut. "What If History Has Merely Played a Trick on Us? Feng Chi-ts'ai's Writing, 1979–1984." In *Reform and Revolution in Twentieth Century China.* Taipei: Institute of International Relations, 1987, pp. 277–90.

Gao Xiaosheng

Feuerwerker, Yi-tsi Mei. "An Interview with Gao Xiaosheng." *Modern Chinese Literature* 3, 1/2 (Spring/Fall 1987): 113–36.
Gao Xiaosheng. *The Broken Betrothal.* Beijing: Panda Books, 1987.
———. *Geschichten von Chen Huansheng.* Trans. Eike Zschacke. Göttingen: Lamuv, 1988.
———. "Li Shunda Builds a House." In *The New Realism.* Ed. Lee Yee. New York: Hippocrene, 1983, pp. 31–55.
Kuiper, P. N. "A Critical Writer Feasted by his 'Characters': Gao Xiaosheng's Novelette *Hutu* (Foolishness)." In *Cologne-Workshop 1984 on Contemporary Chinese Literature: Chinesische Gegenwartsliteratur.* Ed. Helmut Martin. Köln: Deutsche Welle, 1986.

Gu Hua

Gu Hua. *Chaste Women.* Trans. Howard Goldblatt. Forthcoming. (*Zhen nü*)
———. *Pagoda Ridge and Other Stories.* Trans. Gladys Yang. Beijing: Panda Books, 1985.
———. *The Scholars' Garden.* Trans. Richard King. Forthcoming. (*Rulin yuan*)
———. *A Small Town Called Hibiscus.* Trans. Gladys Yang. Beijing: Panda Books, 1983. (*Furongzhen*)

Han Shaogong

Han Shaogong. "Blue Bottlecap." Trans. Michael S. Duke. In *Worlds of Modern Chinese*

Fiction. Ed. Michael S. Duke. Armonk, NY: M. E. Sharpe, 1991, pp. 3–12.
———. "The Homecoming." In *Spring Bamboo.* Trans. Jeanne Tai. New York: Random House, 1989, pp. 19–40.
———. *Pa pa pa.* Trans. Noël Dutrait and Hu Sishe. Aix-en-Provence: Alinéa, 1990.
———. *Séduction.* Trans. Annie Curien. Paris: Philippe Picquier, 1990. (Selected stories from *Youhuo*)

Huang Chunming

Goldblatt, Howard. "The Rural Stories of Hwang Chun-ming." In *Chinese Fiction from Taiwan.* Ed. Jeannette L. Faurot. Bloomington: Indiana University Press, 1980, pp. 110–33.
Grueber, Isa. *Moderne Zeiten—Chinesische Literatur aus Taiwan: Huang Chunmings Erzählungen 1967–1977.* Bochum: Brockmeyer (Chinathemen), 1987.
Huang Chunming [Hwang Chun-ming]. *The Drowning of an Old Cat and Other Stories.* Trans. Howard Goldblatt. Bloomington: Indiana University Press, 1980.
——— [Huang Ch'un-ming]. "A Flower in the Rainy Night." Trans. Earl Wieman. In *Chinese Stories from Taiwan.* Ed. Joseph S. M. Lau and Timothy A. Ross. New York: Columbia University Press, 1976, pp. 194–241.
——— [Huang Ch'un-ming]. "I Love Mary." Trans. Howard Goldblatt. In *The Unbroken Chain.* Ed. Joseph S. M. Lau. Bloomington: Indiana University Press, 1983, pp. 133–74.

Huang Fan

Huang Fan. *Dushi shenghuo* (City life). Taibei: Lianjing chubanshiye youxian gongsi, 1987.
———. *Fanduizhe* (The opponent). Taibei: Zili wanbaoshe, 1985.
———. "Lai Suo." Trans. Eric B. Cohen. In *Worlds of Modern Chinese Fiction.* Ed. Michael S. Duke. Armonk, NY: M. E. Sharpe, 1991, pp. 76–98.
———. *Manna wudao jiaoshi* (Manna's dance studio). Taibei: Lianhe wenxue chubanshe, 1987.

Jia Pingwa

Jia Pingwa. *The Heavenly Hound.* Beijing: Panda Books, 1991.
———. "How Much Can a Man Bear?" and "Family Chronicle of a Wooden Bowl Maker." In *The Chinese Western.* Trans. Zhu Hong. New York: Ballantine, 1988, pp. 1–52, 100–16.
———. *Turbulence.* Trans. Howard Goldblatt. Baton Rouge: Louisiana State University Press, 1991.
Louie, Kam. "The Macho Eunuch: The Politics of Masculinity in Jia Pingwa's 'Human Extremities.' " *Modern China* 17, 2 (April 1991): 163–87.

Jin Yong

Jin Yong. *Jin Yong zuopin ji* (The works of Jin Yong). Hong Kong: Mingbao youxian gongsi, 1959, rev. ed. 1985. Multivolume.
Shen Dengen et al., eds. *Zhuzi baijia kan Jin Yong: Jinxue yanjiu congshu* ("Philosophers and writers of all schools" look at Jin Yong: A collection of "Jin-ology" research). Taibei: Yuanjing chubanshe, 1985.

Lao She

Bady, Paul. *Lao She, Lao niu po che: Essai autocritique sur le roman et l'humor.* Paris: Presses universitaires de France, 1974.

Chan, Stephen Ching-Kiu. "Split Consciousness: The Dialectic of Desire in *Camel Xiangzi.*" *Modern Chinese Literature* 2, 2 (Spring 1986): 171–95.

Grossholtforth, Petra. *Chinesen in London: Lao She's Roman* Er Ma. Bochum: Brockmeyer (Chinathemen), 1985.

Jameson, Fredric. "Literary Innovation and Modes of Production: A Commentary." *Modern Chinese Literature* 1, 1 (September 1984): 67–77.

Lao She. *Beneath the Red Banner.* Beijing: Panda Books, 1982.

———. *Cat Country.* Trans. William A. Lyell, Jr. Columbus: Ohio State University Press, 1970.

———. *Crescent Moon and Other Stories.* Beijing: Panda Books, 1985.

——— [Lau Shaw]. *The Drum Singers.* Trans. Helena Kuo. New York: Harcourt, Brace, 1952.

———. *Heavensent.* Trans. Xiong Deni. Hong Kong: Joint Publishing Company, 1986. (*Niu tianci zhuan*)

———. *Rickshaw.* Trans. Jean M. James. Honolulu: University of Hawaii Press, 1979.

———. *Teahouse.* Trans. John Howard-Gibbon. Beijing: Foreign Languages Press, 1980.

———. *The Two Mas.* Trans. Kenny K. Huang and David Finkelstein. Hong Kong: Joint Publishing Co., 1984.

Slupski, Zbigniew. *The Evolution of a Modern Chinese Writer: An Analysis of Lao She's Fiction.* Prague: Czechoslovak Academy of Science, 1966.

Vohra, Ranbir. *Lao She and the Chinese Revolution.* Cambridge: East Asian Research Center, Harvard University, 1974.

Wang, David D. W. "Radical Laughter in Lao She and His Taiwan Successors." In *Worlds Apart.* Ed. Howard Goldblatt. Armonk, NY: M. E. Sharpe, 1990, pp. 44–63.

Li Ang

Dell, Sylvia. *Chinesische Gegenwartsliteratur aus Taiwan: Die Autorin Li Ang: Erzählprosa und Rezeption bis 1984.* Bochum: Brockmeyer (Chinathemen), 1988.

Goldblatt, Howard. "Sex and Society: The Fiction of Li Ang." In *Worlds Apart.* Ed. Howard Goldblatt. Armonk, NY: M. E. Sharpe, 1990, pp. 150–65.

Li Ang. *The Butcher's Wife.* Trans. Howard Goldblatt and Ellen Yeung. Berkeley: North Point Press, 1986. (*Shafu*)

———. "Curvaceous Dolls." Trans. Howard Goldblatt. *Renditions* 27/28 (Spring/Autumn 1987): 49–60.

———. "A Love Letter Never Sent." Trans. Howard Goldblatt. In *Worlds of Modern Chinese Fiction.* Ed. Michael S. Duke. Armonk, NY: M. E. Sharpe, 1991, pp. 145–62.

Martin, Helmut. "From Sexual Protest to Feminist Social Criticism: Li Ang's Works 1967–1987." In *Chinese Literature in Southeast Asia.* Ed. Wong Yoon Wah. Singapore: Goethe-Institut, 1989, pp. 127–51.

Ng, Sheung-Yuen Daisy. "Li Ang's *The Butcher's Wife.*" *Modern Chinese Literature* 4, 1/2 (Spring/Fall 1988): 177–200.

Yeh, Michelle. "Shapes of Darkness: Symbols in Li Ang's *Dark Night.*" In *Modern Chinese Women Writers.* Ed. Michael S. Duke. Armonk, NY: M. E. Sharpe, 1989, pp. 78–95.

Lin Shuangbu

Lin Shuangbu. *Taiwan zhongtianren* (Tiller of the Taiwan soil). Taibei: Shuifurong chubanshe, 1983.

———. *Xiao labashou* (The little trumpeter). Taibei: Qianwei chubanshe, 1986. (Contains author's bibliography)

Liu Binyan

Béjà, Jean-Philippe, ed. *Liu Binyan: Le cauchemar des mandarins rouges.* Paris: Gallimard, 1989.

Blank, Carolin, and Christa Gescher. *Gesellschaftskritik in der Volksrepublik China: Der Journalist und Schriftsteller Liu Binyan.* Bochum: Brockmeyer (Chinathemen), 1991.

Liu Binyan. *China's Crisis, China's Hope: Essays from an Intellectual in Exile.* Trans. Howard Goldblatt. Cambridge: Harvard University Press, 1990.

———. *A Higher Kind of Loyalty: A Memoir by China's Foremost Journalist.* Trans. Zhu Hong. New York: Pantheon, 1990.

———. *People or Monsters? And Other Stories and Reportage from China after Mao.* Ed. Perry Link. Bloomington: Indiana University Press, 1983.

———, with Ruan Ming and Xu Gang. *Tell the World: What Happened in China and Why.* New York: Pantheon, 1989.

Wagner, Rudolf G. "Liu Binyan and the *Texie.*" *Modern Chinese Literature* 2, 1 (Spring 1986): 63–98.

Liu Xinwu

Liu Xinwu. *Black Walls.* Ed. Don J. Cohn. Hong Kong: Renditions, 1990.

———. "Bus Aria." Trans. Stephen Fleming. *Chinese Literature* 1986, 4 (Winter 1986): 81–115.

———. "Overpass." Trans. Michael Crook. In *Mao's Harvest.* Ed. Helen F. Siu and Zelda Stern. New York: Oxford University Press, 1983, pp. 29–89. ("Litijiaochaqiao," abridged)

———. "Ruyi." Trans. Richard Rigby. *Renditions* 25 (Spring 1986): 53–85.

Lu Xinhua, Liu Xinwu, and Others. *The Wounded: New Stories of the Cultural Revolution.* Hong Kong: Joint Publishing Company, 1979. ("Class Counsellor" and "Awake, My Brother!")

Lu Wenfu

Lu Wenfu. *The Gourmet and Other Stories of Modern China.* Trans. Judith Burrows. London: Readers International, 1987.

———. "The Wealthy Farmer." Trans. Jeffrey C. Kinkley. *Fiction* 8, 2/3 (1987): 115–41. ("Wanyuanhu")

———. *A World of Dreams.* Beijing: Panda Books, 1986.

Lu Xun

Alber, Charles J. "*Wild Grass,* Symmetry and Parallelism in Lu Hsun's Prose Poems." In *Critical Essays on Chinese Literature.* Ed. William H. Nienhauser, Jr. Hong Kong: Chinese University of Hong Kong Press, 1976, pp. 1–29.

Hanan, Patrick D. "The Technique of Lu Hsun's Fiction." *Harvard Journal of Asiatic Studies* 34 (1974): 53 96.

Hsu, Raymond S. W. *The Style of Lu Hsun: Vocabulary and Usage.* Hong Kong: University of Hong Kong, 1979.

Huang Sung-k'ang. *Lu Hsun and the New Cultural Movement of Modern China.* Amsterdam: Djambatan, 1957.

Kubin, Wolfgang. *Lu Xun: Die Methode wilde Tiere abzurichten.* Berlin: Oberbaum, 1979.

Last, Jef. *Lu Hsun—Dichter und Idol.* Frankfurt, 1959.

Lee, Leo Ou-fan. *Voices from the Iron House: A Study of Lu Xun.* Bloomington: University of Indiana Press, 1987.

————, ed. *Lu Xun and His Legacy.* Berkeley: University of California Press, 1985.
Lu Xun [Lu Hsun]. *A Brief History of Chinese Fiction.* Trans. Yang Hsien-yi and Gladys Yang. Peking: Foreign Languages Press, 1959, 1964.
———— [Lu Hsun]. *Dawn Blossoms Plucked at Dusk.* Trans. Yang Hsien-yi and Gladys Yang. Peking: Foreign Languages Press, 1976.
————. *Diary of a Madman and Other Stories.* Trans. William A. Lyell. Honolulu: University of Hawaii Press, 1990.
———— [Lu Hsun]. *Old Tales Retold.* Peking: Foreign Languages Press, 1972.
————. *Selected Works of Lu Xun.* Trans. Yang Xianyi and Gladys Yang. Beijing: Foreign Languages Press, 1956, 1980. 4 vols.
———— [Lu Hsun]. *Wild Grass.* Peking: Foreign Languages Press, 1974.
————. *"Zawen."* Trans. D. E. Pollard. *Renditions* 31 (Spring 1989): 140–47.
Lyell, William A., Jr. *Lu Hsun's Vision of Reality.* Berkeley: University of California Press, 1976.
Renditions 26 (Autumn 1986): 108–64. ("Special Section on Lu Xun")
Semanov, V. I. *Lu Xun and His Predecessors.* Trans. Charles J. Alber. White Plains, NY: M. E. Sharpe, 1980.

Mao Dun

Chen, Yu-shih. *Realism and Allegory in the Early Fiction of Mao Tun.* Bloomington: Indiana University Press, 1986.
Gálik, Marián. *Mao Tun and Modern Literary Criticism.* Wiesbaden: Franz Steiner, 1969.
Gruner, Fritz. "Der literarische-künstlerische Beitrag Mao Duns zur Entwicklung des Realismus in der neuen chinesischen Literatur." Leipzig, Habilitationsschrift, 1967.
Mao Dun [Mao Tun]. *Midnight.* Trans. Hsu Meng-hsiung and A. C. Barnes. Peking: Foreign Languages Press, 1957. Hong Kong: C & W Co., 1976.
———— [Mao Tun]. *Spring Silkworms and Other Stories.* Trans. Sidney Shapiro. Peking: Foreign Languages Press, 1956, 1979.

Qideng Sheng

Qideng Sheng [Ch'i-teng Sheng]. "I Love Black Eyes." Trans. Timothy A. Ross and Dennis T. Hu. In *Chinese Stories from Taiwan.* Ed. Joseph S. M. Lau and Timothy A. Ross. New York: Columbia University Press, 1976, pp. 62–73.
Wang, C. H. "Fancy and Reality in Ch'i-teng Sheng's Fiction." In *Chinese Fiction from Taiwan.* Ed. Jeannette L. Faurot. Bloomington: Indiana University Press, 1980, pp. 194–205.

Shen Congwen

Kinkley, Jeffrey C. *The Odyssey of Shen Congwen.* Stanford: Stanford University Press, 1987.
Nieh, Hua-ling. *Shen Ts'ung-wen.* New York: Twayne, 1972.
Shen Congwen. *The Border Town and Other Stories.* Trans. Gladys Yang. Beijing: Panda Books, 1981.
———— [Shen Tseng-wen, or Shen Tsung-wen, in the reprint edition]. *The Chinese Earth.* Trans. Ching Ti and Robert Payne. London: George Allen & Unwin, 1947. New York: Columbia University Press, 1982.
————. *Recollections of West Hunan.* Trans. Gladys Yang. Beijing: Panda Books, 1982.

Song Zelai

Martin, Helmut. "The Future of China, Taiwan and Hongkong: Perspectives Explored by Contemporary Chinese Writers." In *Ideology and Politics in Twentieth Century China*. Ed. King-yuh Chang. Taipei: Institute of International Relations, National Chengchi University, 1988, pp. 174–95.

Song Zelai. *Penglai zhiyi* (Strange tales from fairyland). Taibei: Dexinshi, 1980.

———. *Ruoxiao minzu* (A weak race). Taibei: Qianwei chubanshe, 1987.

———. *Shui pa Song Zelai?* (Who's afraid of Song Zelai?). Taibei: Qianwei chubanshe, 1986.

———. *Taiwanren de ziwo zhuixin* (Taiwanese searching for their self). Taibei: Qianwei chubanshe, 1988.

Wang Anyi

Wang Anyi. *Baotown*. Trans. Martha Avery. New York: Viking, 1989.

———. "Friends." Trans. Nancy Lee. In *The Rose Coloured Dinner*. Hong Kong: Joint Publishing Company, 1988, pp. 123–33.

———. *Kleine Lieben*. Trans. Karin Hasselblatt. München: Hanser, 1988. (*Huangshan zhi lian* and *Jinxingu zhi lian*)

———. "Lao Kang Come Back." In *Spring Bamboo*. Trans. Jeanne Tai. New York: Random House, 1989, pp. 41–55.

———. *Lapse of Time*. San Francisco: China Books, 1988.

———. *Love in a Small Town*. Trans. Eva Hung. Hong Kong: Renditions, 1988. (*Xiao cheng zhi lian*)

———. *Love on a Barren Mountain*. Trans. Eva Hung. Hong Kong: Renditions, 1991.

———. "The Mouth of a Famous Female Impersonator." Trans. Zhu Zhiyu, with Janice Wickeri. *Renditions* 27/28 (Spring/Autumn 1987): 174–83. ("Ming dan zhi kou")

Wang Zheng. "Three Interviews: Wang Anyi, Zhu Lin, Dai Qing." *Modern Chinese Literature* 4, 1/2 (Spring/Fall 1988): 99–148.

Wang Meng

Cornelssen, Inse, and Sun Junhua, eds. *Wang Meng, lauter Fursprecher und andere Geschichten*. Bochum: Brockmeyer (Chinathemen), 1986.

Martin, Helmut. "Painful Encounter: Wang Meng's Novel *Hsiang chien shih nan* and the 'Foreign Theme' in Contemporary Chinese Literature." In *China and Europe in the Twentieth Century*. Ed. Yu-ming Shaw. Taipei: Institute of International Relations, National Chengchi University, 1986, pp. 32–42.

Tay, William. "Wang Meng, Stream-of-consciousness, and the Controversy over Modernism." *Modern Chinese Literature* 1, 1 (September 1984): 7–24.

Wang Meng. "Anecdotes of Chairman Maimaiti." In *The Chinese Western*. Trans. Zhu Hong. New York: Ballantine, 1988, pp. 152–63.

———. *Bolshevik Salute: A Modernist Chinese Novel*. Trans. Wendy Larson. Seattle: University of Washington Press, 1989.

———. *The Butterfly and Other Stories*. Beijing: Panda Books, 1983.

———. "Eye of the Night." Trans. Donald A. Gibbs. In *Roses and Thorns*. Ed. Perry Link. Berkeley: University of California Press, 1984, pp. 43–55.

———. *Figure Intercambiabili*. Trans. Vilma Costantini. Milano, 1989 (*Huodong bianrenxing*)

———. *Selected Works of Wang Meng*. Vol. 1, *The Strain of Meeting*. Trans. Denis Mair. Vol. 2, *Snowball*. Trans. Cathy Silber and Deirdre Huang. Beijing: Foreign Languages Press, 1989.

————. "The Young Man Who Has Just Arrived at the Organization Department." Trans. Gary Bjorge. In *Literature of the People's Republic of China*. Ed. Kai-yu Hsu. Bloomington: Indiana University Press, 229–41.

Williams, Philip. "Stylistic Variety in a PRC Writer: Wang Meng's Fiction of the 1979–1980 Cultural Thaw." In *Australian Journal of Chinese Affairs* 11 (January 1984): 59–80.

Wang Ruowang

Mahoney, Alysoun. "The Story of Wang Ruowang." *Human Rights Tribune* 2, 6 (February 1991): 16–17.

Rubin, Kyna. "Keeper of the Flame: Wang Ruowang as Moral Critic of the State." In *China's Intellectuals and the State: In Search of a New Relationship*. Ed. Merle Goldman, Timothy Cheek, and Carol Lee Hamrin. Cambridge: Council on East Asian Studies, Harvard University, 1987, pp. 233–50.

Schell, Orville. *Discos and Democracy*. New York: Pantheon, 1988, pp. 162–76.

Wang Ruowang. *Hunger Trilogy*. Trans. Kyna Rubin, with Ira Kasoff. Armonk, NY: M. E. Sharpe, 1991. (*Ji'e sanbuqu*)

————. *Wang Ruowang zizhuan* (Autobiography). Hong Kong, 1991.

Wang Tuo

Wang Tuo. *Jie xiang gu sheng* (Drumbeats in the streets and alleyways). Taibei: Yuanjing chubanshe, 1977.

———— [Wang T'o]. "May He Return Soon." Trans. Vivian Hsu and David Wank. In *Born of the Same Roots*. Ed. Vivian Ling Hsu. Bloomington: Indiana University Press, 1981, pp. 237–75.

————. *Wang jun zao gui* (I hope you'll return soon). Taibei: Yuanjing chubanshe, 1977.

Wang Wenxing

Chang, Sung-sheng. "Language, Narrator, and Stream-of-consciousness: The Two Novels of Wang Wen-hsing." *Modern Chinese Literature* 1, 1 (September 1984): 43–65.

Gunn, Edward. "The Process of Wang Wen-hsing's Art." *Modern Chinese Literature* 1, 1 (September 1984): 29–41.

Lachner, Anton. *Sprachinkonvention und Sprachmanipulation: Linguistische und stilistische Untersuchungen zu Wang Wenxings Roman JIABIAN*. Zürich: Peter Lang, 1989.

Shan Te-hsing. "Wang Wen-hsing on Wang Wen-hsing." *Modern Chinese Literature* 1,1 (September 1984): 57–65.

Shu, James C. T. "Iconoclasm in Wang Wen-hsing's *Chia-pien*." In *Chinese Fiction from Taiwan*. Ed. Jeannette L. Faurot. Bloomington: Indiana University Press, 1980, pp. 179–93.

Wang Wenxing [Wang Wen-hsing]. "Flaw." Trans. Ch'en Chu-yun. In *Chinese Stories from Taiwan*. Ed. Joseph S. M. Lau and Timothy A. Ross. New York: Columbia University Press, 1976, pp. 14–27.

Wang Zengqi

Wang Zengqi. "The Love Story of a Young Monk" and "Story After Supper." Trans. Hu Zhihui and Shen Zhen. *Chinese Literature* 1982, 1 (January 1982): 58–96. ("Shoujie" and "Wanfan hou de gushi")

————. "Small-Hands Chen." Trans. Howard Goldblatt. *Fiction* 8, 2/3 (1987): 142–45.

————. "A Tale of Big Nur." Trans. Xu Qiaoqi. In *Prize-winning Stories from China,*

1980–1981. Beijing: Foreign Languages Press, 1985, pp. 240–61.

————. *Les trois amis de l'hiver*. Trans. Annie Curien. Arles: Philippe Picquier, 1989. ("Sui han san you," "Da Nao ji shi," "Shoujie")

Wang Zhenhe

Huang I-min. "A Postmodern Reading of *Rose, Rose I Love You*." *Tamkang Review* 17, 1 (Autumn 1986): 27–45.

Wang Zhenhe [Wang Chen-ho]. "An Oxcart for Dowry." Trans. Wang Zhenhe and Jon Jackson. In *Chinese Stories from Taiwan*. Ed. Joseph S. M. Lau and Timothy A. Ross. New York: Columbia University Press, 1976, pp. 74–99.

————. "Shangri-La." Trans. Michael S. Duke. In *Worlds of Modern Chinese Fiction*. Ed. Michael S. Duke. Armonk, NY: M. E. Sharpe, 1991, pp. 246–67.

———— [Wang Chen-ho]. "The Story of Three Springs." Trans. Jane Parish Yang. In *The Unbroken Chain*. Ed. Joseph S. M. Lau. Bloomington: Indiana University Press, 1983, pp. 195–217.

Yang, Robert Yi. "Form and Tone in Wang Chen-ho's Satires." In *Chinese Fiction from Taiwan*. Ed. Jeannette L. Faurot. Bloomington: Indiana University Press, 1980, pp. 134–47.

Wu Jinfa

Wu Jinfa. *Chenmo de hechuan* (Silent river). Taibei: Lanting shudian, 1982.

————. *Taiwan wuyongren* (Superfluous Taiwanese). Taibei: Chenxing, 1991.

————. *Xiaoshi de nanxing* (The vanishing male). Taibei: Chenxing chubanshe, 1986. (Contains chronology of the author's writings)

Wu Zuguang

Wu Zuguang. *Wu Zuguang juzuo xuan* (Selected plays by Wu Zuguang). Beijing: Zhongguo xiju chubanshe, 1981.

————. *Wu Zuguang wenxuan* (Selected works of Wu Zuguang). Hong Kong: Mingbao, 1989.

Yu Dafu

Dolezalová, Anna. *Yü Ta-fu—Specific Traits of His Literary Creation*. New York, Paragon, 1971.

Egan, Michael. "Yu Dafu and the Transition to Modern Chinese Literature." In *Modern Chinese Literature in the May Fourth Era*. Ed. Merle Goldman. Cambridge: Harvard University Press, 1977, pp. 309–24.

Lee, Leo Ou-fan. *The Romantic Generation of Modern Chinese Writers*. Cambridge: Harvard University Press, 1973, pp. 81–123.

Wong Yoon Wah. "Yu Dafu in Exile: His Last Days in Sumatra." *Renditions* 23 (Spring 1985): 71–83.

Yu Dafu. *Nights of Spring Fever and Other Stories*. Beijing: Panda Books, 1984.

———— [Yü Ta-fu]. "Sinking." Trans. Joseph S. M. Lau and C. T. Hsia. In *Modern Chinese Stories and Novellas, 1919–1949*. Ed. Joseph S. M. Lau, C. T. Hsia, and Leo Ou-fan Lee. New York: Columbia University Press, 1981, pp. 123–41.

Zhang Ailing

Chang, Sung-sheng Yvonne. "Yuan Qiongqiong and the Rage for Eileen Zhang." *Modern Chinese Literature* 4, 1/2 (Spring/Fall 1988): 201–23.

Cheng, Stephen. "Theme and Technique in Eileen Chang's Stories." *Tamkang Review* 8, 2 (1977).

Hsia, C. T. "Eileen Chang." In his *A History of Modern Chinese Fiction*. Rev. ed. New Haven: Yale University Press, 1971, pp. 389–431.

Miller, Lucien, and Hui-chuan Chang. "Fiction and Autobiography: Spatial Form in "The Golden Cangue" and *The Woman Warrior*. In *Modern Chinese Women Writers*. Ed. Michael S. Duke. Armonk, NY: M. E. Sharpe, 1989, pp. 25–43.

Zhang Ailing [Eileen Chang]. "The Golden Cangue." Trans. Eileen Chang. In *Modern Chinese Stories and Novellas, 1919–1949*. Ed. Joseph S. M. Lau, C. T. Hsia, and Leo Ou-fan Lee. New York: Columbia University Press, 1981, pp. 528–59. *(Jinsuo ji)*

——— [Eileen Chang]. *Naked Earth*. Hong Kong: Union Press, 1956. *(Chidi zhi lian)*

——— [Eileen Chang]. *The Rice Sprout Song*. New York: Charles Scribner, 1955. (Composed in English)

——— [Eileen Chang]. *The Rouge of the North*. London: Cassell, 1967. (Composed in English)

——— [Eileen Chang]. "Stale Mates." *Renditions* 27/28 (Spring/Autumn 1987): 10–16. (Composed in English, 1956)

Zhang Jie

Bailey, Alison. " Travelling Together: Narrative Technique in Zhang Jie's *The Ark*." In *Modern Chinese Women Writers*. Ed. Michael S. Duke. Armonk, NY: M. E. Sharpe, 1989, pp. 96–111.

Zhang Jie. Fangzhou: *Die Arche, Roman*. Trans. Nelly Ma. München: Frauenoffensive, 1985.

———. *Heavy Wings*. Trans. Howard Goldblatt. New York: Grove Weidenfeld, 1989. (Chenzhong de chibang.)

———. *As Long as Nothing Happens, Nothing Will*. Trans. Gladys Yang, Deborah J. Leonard, and Zhang Andong. London: Virago, 1988.

———. *Love Must Not Be Forgotten*. San Francisco: China Books, 1986.

———. "Love Must Not Be Forgotten." Trans. William Crawford. In *Roses and Thorns*. Ed. Perry Link. Berkeley: University of California Press, 1984, pp. 244–60.

———. Schwere Flügel, *Roman*. Trans. Michael Kahn-Ackermann. München: Hanser, 1985.

———. "An Unrecorded Life." Trans. Nienling Liu. In *The Rose Coloured Dinner*. Hong Kong: Joint Publishing Company, 1988, pp. 38–50.

Zhang Xianliang

Kinkley, Jeffrey C. "A Bettelheimian Interpretation of Chang Hsien-liang's Concentration Camp Novels." *Asia Major* 3d ser. 4, 1 (1991).

Williams, Philip F. " 'Remolding' and the Chinese Labor Camp Novel." *Asia Major* 3d ser. 4, 1 (1991).

Wu, Yenna. "Women as Sources of Redemption in Chang Hsien-liang's Labor Camp Fiction." *Asia Major* 3d ser. 4, 1 (1991).

Zhang Xianliang. *Getting Used to Dying*. Trans. Martha Avery. New York: Harper-Collins, 1991.

———. "Good Morning, Friends." Trans. Mark Kruger. *Renditions* 31 (Spring 1989): 7–30. (Zaoan pengyou, excerpts)

———. *Half of Man Is Woman*. Trans. Martha Avery. New York: W. W. Norton, 1988.

———. *Mimosa and Other Stories*. Beijing: Panda Books, 1985.

———. "The Story of an Old Man and a Dog" and "Shorblac: A Driver's Story." In *The*

Chinese Western. Trans. Zhu Hong. New York: Ballantine Books, 1988, pp. 75–99, 117–51.

Zhang Xinxin

Kinkley, Jeffrey C. "The Cultural Choices of Zhang Xinxin, a Young Writer of the 1980s." In *Ideas Across Cultures: Essays on Chinese Thought in Honor of Benjamin I. Schwartz.* Ed. Paul A. Cohen and Merle Goldman. Cambridge: Council on East Asian Studies, Harvard University, 1990.

Martin, Helmut. "Social Criticism in Contemporary Chinese Literature: New Forms of *Pao-kao*-Reportage by Zhang Xinxin." *Proceedings on the Second International Conference on Sinology.* Taipei: Academia Sinica, 1989.

Torgeson, Kristina. "Returning Home." B. A. honors thesis, Wesleyan University, Middletown, CT, 1987. (Translation of "Hui lao jia")

Wakeman, Carolyn, and Yue Daiyun. "Fiction's End: Zhang Xinxin's New Approaches to Creativity." In *Modern Chinese Women Writers.* Ed. Michael S. Duke. Armonk, NY: M. E. Sharpe, 1989, pp. 196–216.

Zhang Xinxin. "Dust." Trans. W. J. F. Jenner. *Renditions* 27/28 (Spring/Autumn 1987): 163–73.

———. *Une folie d'orchidés.* Trans. Cheng Yingxiang. Paris: Actes Sud, 1988. ("Fengkuang de junzilan")

———. *Am gleichen Horizont.* Trans. Marie-Luise Beppler-Lie. Bonn: Engelhard-Ng, 1986. ("Zai tongyi diping xianshang")

———. "How Did I Miss You?" Trans. Nienling Liu. In *The Rose Coloured Dinner.* Hong Kong: Joint Publishing Company, 1988, pp. 134–66.

———. *Sur la même ligne d'horizon.* Trans. Emmanuelle Péchenart. Paris: Actes Sud, 1987. ("Zai tongyi diping xianshang")

———. "Theatrical Effects." Trans. Jeffrey C. Kinkley. *Fiction* 8, 2/3 (1987): 146–66. ("Juchang xiaoguo")

Zhang Xinxin and Sang Ye. *Chinese Lives.* Ed. W. J. F. Jenner and Delia Davin. New York: Pantheon, 1987. (*Beijingren*, abridged)

———. *Chinese Profiles.* Beijing: Panda Books, 1986. (*Beijingren*, abridged)

———. *Pekingmenschen.* Ed. Helmut Martin. Köln: Diederichs, 1986. (*Beijingren*, abridged)

Zhong Acheng

Zhong Acheng [Ahcheng]. "The Chess Master." Trans. W. J. F. Jenner. *Chinese Literature* 1985, 2 (Summer 1985): 84–132.

——— [Ah Cheng]. "King of Trees." Trans. Gladys Yang. *Chinese Literature* 1986, 4 (Winter 1986): 44–80.

——— [Ah Cheng]. *Three Kings.* Trans. Bonnie S. McDougall. London: Collins Harvill, 1990.

——— [A Cheng]. "The Tree Stump." In *Spring Bamboo.* Trans. Jeanne Tai. New York: Random House, 1989, pp. 229–43.

——— [A Cheng]. *Les trois rois.* Trans. Noël Dutrait. Aix-en-Provence: Alinéa, 1988.

Huters, Theodore. "Speaking of Many Things: Food, Kings, and the National Tradition in Ah Cheng's 'The Chess King.' " *Modern China* 14, 4 (October 1988): 388–418.

5. Notable Works by 1980s Authors Not Represented in This Anthology

Ai Bei. *Red Ivy, and Green Earth Mother.* Trans. Howard Goldblatt. Salt Lake City: Peregrine Smith Books, 1990.

Bei Dao [pseud. of Zhao Zhenkai]. *The August Sleepwalker*. Trans. Bonnie S. McDougall. New York: New Directions, 1990.

———. *Waves*. Trans. Bonnie S. McDougall and Susette Ternent Cooke. New York: New Directions, 1990.

Can Xue. *Dialogues in Paradise*. Trans. Ronald R. Janssen and Jian Zhang. Evanston, IL: Northwestern University Press, 1989.

Cheng Naishan. *The Blue House*. Beijing: Panda Books, 1990.

———. *The Piano Tuner*. San Francisco: China Books, 1989.

Duoduo [pseud. of Li Shizheng]. *Looking Out from Death: The New Chinese Poetry of Duoduo*. Trans. Gregory Lee and John Cayley. London: Bloomsbury, 1989.

Gao Yang. *Stories by Gao Yang: "Rekindled Love" and "Purple Jade Hairpin."* Trans. Chan Sin-wai. Hong Kong: Chinese University Press, 1989. (Stories by a Taiwan writer)

Lao Gui [pseud. of Ma Bo]. *Blood-Red Sunset*. Trans. Howard Goldblatt. New York: Viking, forthcoming.

Liu Heng. *The Obsessed*. Trans. David Kwan. Beijing: Panda Books, 1990.

Mo Yan. *La mélopé d l'aïl paradisiaque*. Trans. Chantal Chen-Andro. Paris: Sociales-Messidor, 1990. (*Tiantang suantai zhi ge*)

———. *Red Sorghum: A Family Saga*. Trans. Howard Goldblatt, forthcoming.

Nie Hualing [Hualing Nieh]. *Mulberry and Peach*. London: The Women's Press, 1986. (*Sangqing yu Taohong*)

Ru Zhijuan. *Lilies and Other Stories*. Beijing: Panda Books, 1985.

Tie Ning. *Haystacks*. Beijing: Panda Books, 1990.

Xi Xi. *A Girl Like Me and Other Stories*. Hong Kong: Renditions, 1986. (By a Hong Kong writer)

Yang Lian. *The Dead in Exile*. Trans. Mabel Lee. Kingston: Tiananmen Publications, 1990.

———. *Masks and Crocodile*. Trans. Mabel Lee. Broadway, New South Wales: Wild Peony, 1990.

Yu Luojin. *A Chinese Winter's Tale*. Hong Kong: Renditions, 1986.

Zhang Chengzhi. *The Black Steed*. Beijing: Panda Books, 1990.

Zhang Xiguo [Chang Shi-kuo]. *Chess King*. Trans. Ivan David Zimmerman. Singapore: Asiapac, 1986. (By an ex-Taiwan writer)

6. Selected Items on China's Late 1980s Democracy Movement and the June 4 Massacre

Baum, Richard, ed. *Reform and Reaction in Post-Mao China: The Road to Tiananmen*. New York: Routledge, 1991.

Cheng, Chu-yuan. *Behind the Tiananmen Massacre: Social, Political, and Economic Ferment in China*. Boulder: Westview Press, 1990.

Duke, Michael S. *The Iron House: A Memoir of the Chinese Democracy Movement and the Tiananmen Massacre*. Layton, Utah: Gibbs Smith, 1990.

Fang Lizhi. *Bringing Down the Great Wall: Writings on Science, Culture, and Democracy in China*. Ed. James H. Williams. New York: Knopf, 1991.

Fathers, Michael, and Andrew Higgins. *Tiananmen: The Rape of Peking*. New York: Doubleday, 1990.

Feigon, Lee. *China Rising: The Meaning of Tiananmen*. Chicago: I. R. Dee, 1990.

Han Minzhu [pseud.] and Hua Sheng [pseud.]. *Cries for Democracy: Writings and Speeches from the 1989 Chinese Democracy Movement*. Princeton: Princeton University Press, 1990.

Hicks, George, ed. *The Broken Mirror: China after Tiananmen*. Chicago: St. James Press, 1990.

Kane, Anthony J., ed. *China Briefing, 1990*. Boulder: Westview Press, 1990. Books in this annual series often contain an essay on cultural developments, like the essay by Leo Ou-fan Lee in the 1990 volume.

Kwan, Michael David. *Broken Portraits: Encounters with Chinese Students*. San Francisco: China Books, 1990.

Li, Peter, Steven Mark, and Marjorie H. Li, eds. *Culture and Politics in China: An Anatomy of Tiananmen Square*. New Brunswick, NJ: Transaction Publishers, 1991.

Link, Perry. *Evening Chats in Beijing: Probing China's Predicament*. New York: W. W. Norton, 1992.

Martin, Helmut. *China's Democracy Movement 1989: A Selected Bibliography of Chinese Source Materials*. Köln: Bundesinstitut für ostwissenschaftliche und internationale Studien, 1990.

———. *Origins and Consequences of China's Democracy Movement 1989: Social and Cultural Criticism in the PRC*. Köln: Bundesinstitut für ostwissenschaftliche und internationale Studien, 1990.

Nathan, Andrew J. *China's Crisis: Dilemmas of Reform and Prospects for Democracy*. New York: Columbia University Press, 1990.

Oksenberg, Michel, Lawrence R. Sullivan, and Marc Lambert, eds. *Beijing Spring, 1989: Confrontation and Conflict: The Basic Documents*. Armonk, NY: M. E. Sharpe, 1990.

Saich, Tony, ed. *The Chinese People's Movement: Perspectives on Spring 1989*. Armonk, NY: M. E. Sharpe, 1990.

Schell, Orville. *Discos and Democracy: China in the Throes of Reform*. New York: Pantheon, 1988.

Shen Tong, with Marianne Yen. *Almost a Revolution*. Boston: Houghton-Mifflin, 1990.

Simmie, Scott, and Bob Nixon. *Tiananmen Square*. Seattle: University of Washington Press, 1989.

Wasserstrom, Jeffrey N., and Elizabeth Perry, eds. *Popular Protest and Political Culture in Modern China: Learning from 1989*. Boulder: Westview Press, 1991.

Yang, Winston L. Y., and Marsha L. Wagner, eds. *Tiananmen: China's Struggle for Democracy*. Baltimore: School of Law, University of Maryland, 1990.

Yi Mu and Mark V. Thompson. *Crisis at Tiananmen*. San Francisco: China Books, 1989.

Source Bibliography
A Survey of Chuangzuotan (Writers on Writing)

This survey is an expanded version of:

Martin, Helmut, and Bangtai Xu, eds. "Zhongguo dangdai zuojia chuangzuotan shumu wenzhang suoyin" (A list of short autobiographies by contemporary Chinese writers). Berkeley: Center for Chinese Studies, University of California, July 1987. Manuscript.

1. General

Beijing zuojia tan chuangzuo (Peking authors talk about literary creation). Beijing: Beijing Shiyue wenyi chubanshe, 1985. Print run 10,400.

Changpian xiaoshuo chuangzuo jingyan tan (Experiences in the creation of novels). Changsha: Hunan renmin chubanshe, 1981. Print run 21,300.

Chuangzuo huiyi lu (Reminiscences about creative writing). Hong Kong: Wanyuan tushu gongsi, 1979.

Chuangzuo xunzong (Tracking the creative process). Beijing: Beijing Shiyue wenyi chubanshe, 1984. Print run 21,000.

Dangdai Zhongguo zuojia bairen zhuan ([Auto]biographies of one hundred contemporary Chinese writers). Ed. [Xu] Jiemin. Beijing: Qiushi chubanshe, 1989. Contains short essays by the authors as well as autobiographies.

Dangdai zuojia tan chuangzuo (Contemporary authors talk about creative writing). Beijing: Zhongyang Guangbo Dianshi Daxue, 1984.

Huojiang duanpian xiaoshuo chuangzuo tan, 1978–1980 (On the creation of prizewinning short stories). Beijing: Wenhua yishu chubanshe, 1982. Print run 26,000.

Lun duanpian xiaoshuo chuangzuo (On the creation of short stories). Beijing: Renmin wenxue chubanshe, 1979. Prepared by the editorial board of the journal *Renmin wenxue*.

Sulian zuojia zishu (Accounts by Soviet writers). Beijing: Zhongguo wenyi lianhe chuban gongsi, 1984. 3 vols. A translation of *Sovjetskie pisateli* (covering 270 writers, from 1917 to the 1950s). Print run 11,800.

Wentan fansi yu qianzhan: Shi Shuqing yu dalu zuojia duihua (Writers rethinking the situation and future prospects: Conversations between Shi Shuqing and mainland Chinese writers). Hong Kong: Mingbao chubanshe, 1989.

Wenxue chengcai zhi lu (The path to literary maturity). Hefei: Anhui renmin chubanshe, 1984.

Wenxue zhi lu (The path of literature). Xinxiang: Henan renmin chubanshe, 1983. Print run 21,970.

Wo de yipian xiaoshuo (A short story of mine). Beijing: Zhongguo wenlian chubanshe, 1986. Edited by the journal *Shanxi wenxue*. Print run 6,300.

Wo shi zenmeyang zoushang wenxue daolu de (How I came to take the path of literature). Beijing: Zhongguo wenyi lianhe chuban gongsi, 1984. Edited by the journal *Feitian* of the Gansu Federation of Literature and Art Circles. Print run 32,000.

Xiandai zuojia chuangzuo lun (Modern authors on literary creation) (Shanghai, 1933); 4th ed. (Shanghai, 1935). Print run 9,000.

Xiaoshuo chuangzuo ershi jiang (Twenty lectures on fiction creation). Beijing: Zhongguo wenlian chubanshe, 1985. Edited by the journal *Beijing wenxue*. Print run 10,000.

Xiaoshuo chuangzuo jingyan tan (Talking about experiences in fiction creation). Nanjing: Jiangsu renmin chubanshe, 1981. Print run 13,000.

Xin shiqi huojiang xiaoshuo chuangzuo jingyan tan (Talking about experiences in the creation of prize-winning fiction of the new era). Changsha: Hunan renmin chubanshe, 1985.

Xin shiqi zuojia tan chuangzuo (Writers of the new era talk about creative writing). Beijing: Renmin wenxue chubanshe, 1983. Print run 13,600.

Yan Huo (pseud. of Poon Yiu Ming, or Pan Yaoming). *Dangdai Zhongguo zuojia fengmao* (The contemporary Chinese writers' scene). 2 vols. Hong Kong: Zhaoming chubanshe, 1980.

Zenmeyang tashang zuojia zhi lu (How to get started on the path of being a writer). Beijing: Zhongguo wenlian chubanshe, 1986. Print run 4,920.

Zhongguo xiandai zuojia tan chuangzuo jingyan (Modern Chinese writers talk about their experiences in writing). Jinan: Shandong renmin chubanshe, 1980. 2 vols. Ed. Chinese Department of Shandong Normal College.

Zhongqingnian zuojia chuangzuo jingyan tan (Younger and middle-aged writers talk about their experiences in creative writing). Hangzhou: Zhejiang wenyi chubanshe, 1983. Print run 14,000.

Zhongqingnian zuojia tan chuangzuo (Younger and middle-aged writers talk about literary creation). Jinan: Shandong wenyi chubanshe, 1984. 2 vols. Print run 15,000.

Zou xiang wenxue zhi lu (Taking the path of literature). Changsha: Hunan renmin chubanshe, 1983.

Zuojia tan chuangzuo (Writers talk about literary creation). Guangzhou: Huacheng chubanshe, 1981. 2 vols.
Zuojia yu zuopin lun (On writers and their works). Beijing: Wushi niandai chubanshe, 1952. Prepared by a group from Peking Normal University. Print run 5,000.

2. Republican Period

Chuangzuo huiyi lu (Reminiscences of literary creation). Hong Kong: Senyuan tushu gongsi, 1979.
Wenxue huiyi lu (Literary memoirs). Chongqing: Sichuan renmin chubanshe, 1983. Print run 22,500.
Wenxue: huiyi yu sikao (Literature: Reminiscences and reflections). Beijing: Renmin wenxue chubanshe, 1980. Edited by the journal *Wenyibao.*

3. Individual Writers on Writing

Ba Jin. *Chuangzuo huiyilu* (Reminiscences of literary creation). Hong Kong: Sanlian shudian, 1981.
Bai Xianyong. *Mingxing kafeiguan: Bai Xianyong lunwen zawen ji* (Celebrity coffeehouse: A collection of essays by Bai Xianyong). Taibei: Huangguan chubanshe, 1984.
Gao Xiaosheng. *Chuangzuotan* (On writing). Guangzhou: Huacheng chubanshe, 1981.
Jia Pingwa. *Pingwa wenlunji* (Collected essays of Jia Pingwa). Xining: Qinghai renmin chubanshe, 1985.
Lao She. *Lao She shenghuo yu chuangzuo zishu* (Lao She's own writings on his life and works). Hong Kong: Sanlian shudian, 1980.
Liu Xinwu. *Tong wenxue qingnian duihua* (Conversations with literary young people). Beijing: Wenhua yishu chubanshe, 1983. Print run 75,000.
Lu Wenfu. *Xiaoshuo menwai tan* (A layman talks about fiction). Guangzhou: Huacheng chubanshe, 1982.
Lu Xun. *Lu Xun lun chuangzuo* (Lu Xun on literary creation). Shanghai: Shanghai wenyi chubanshe, 1983.
Shen Dengen et al., eds. *Zhuzi baijia kan Jin Yong: Jinxue yanjiu congshu* ("Philosophers and writers of all schools" look at Jin Yong: A collection of "Jin-ology" research). Taibei: Yuanjing chubanshe, 1985. Multivolume work.
Wang Meng. *Chuangzuo shi yizhong ranshao* (Literary creation is a kind of incandescence). Beijing: Renmin wenxue chubanshe, 1985.
————. *Wang Meng tan chuangzuo* (Wang Meng on creative writing). Beijing: Zhongguo wenyi lianhe chuban gongsi, 1983.
Ye Shengtao. *Ye Shengtao lun chuangzuo* (Ye Shengtao on literary creation). Shanghai: Shanghai wenyi chubanshe, 1982.

4. On Taiwan Writers

Dangdai zuojia duihua lu (Conversations with contemporary authors). Taibei: Zhuanji wenxue chubanshe, 1986. From the journal *Zhuanji wenxue* (Biographical literature).
Xiang Yang, ed. *Rensheng zhuan: Zuojia riji san liu wu* (Lives: Scattered entries from writers' diaries). Taibei: Erya chubanshe, 1985.
Xie Bingying, ed. *Nüzuojia xiezuo shenghuo yu shijian* (The literary lives and practices of women writers). Taibei: Cihui chubanshe, 1973.

Ye Weilian, ed. *Zhongguo xiandai zuojia lun* (On modern Chinese writers). Taibei: Lian jing chubanshe, 1976.

Ying Fenghuang, ed. *Bigeng de ren: Nanzuojia qunxiang* (Plowers with the pen: Portrait of the male writers). Taibei: Jiuge chubanshe, 1987.

Index

Cha, Louis. *See* Jin Yong
Chai Ling, xxiii
Character, national and regional, xxviii,
    xxix, 103–5, 150, 155, 173, 176,
    186, 221, 240, 272, 297–301
Chekhov, Anton, 87, 143, 148, 149, 159,
    219
Chen Huangmei, 13, 314–15
Chen Jiangong, 150, 315
Chen Qiyuan, 291, 315
Chen Rong, xv, xvi, xvii, 61–72, 354
Chen Ruoxi, xv, xxv, 182, 184–85,
    186–92, 250, 354–55
Chen Yi, 8
Chen Yingzhen, xvi, xvii, 186, 215–22,
    223, 234, 238, 355
Chen Yizi, xxvi
Chengdu, 47, 63, 277, 279–83
Chernyshevsky, Nikolai, 119, 148
Chiang Kai-shek, 5, 36, 55, 181, 222, 285
Childhood, 84, 85, 92–93, 125, 143, 197,
    210, 241, 247–49, 262–64, 268–71,
    273–74, 279, 281, 303–4
Chinese Academy of Social Sciences, ix,
    xxiii; Institute of Literature, xxiv, 109
Chinese-American literature, 188
Chinese Writers' Association. *See*
    Writers' Association
Christianity, 215, 217–18, 234, 299
Chu (Hunan-Hubei), 150, 151, 152–53
Chuangzuotan, xiii–xiv, 302
Class struggle, 10, 26, 28, 97
Comic skits (*xiangsheng*), 59, 338–39
Comic strips, 85, 242
Commercial success, xiii, 169, 173, 176,
    194, 204–5, 207–8, 258, 277, 293
Communist party, xxi, xxii, xxiii, xxvi,
    xxix, xxxi, 5, 6–8, 13, 27, 28, 34, 35,
    37, 57, 66–71, 83, 87, 88, 97, 102,
    109, 128, 130–32, 136, 147, 226,
    302; major meetings, 23, 71, 97, 336
Communist revolution, 285–87
Communist Youth League, 54, 55, 315
Conscience, 18, 28, 42, 51, 56, 121, 128,
    138, 166, 186, 190, 206, 217, 233,
    237, 258
Confucius and Confucianism, 66, 67, 88,
    151, 152, 154, 156, 193, 234, 244,
    253, 279, 282
Cong Su, 183, 315
Cong Weixi, ix, x, xv, 20-25, 355

Conrad, Joseph, 267
Constitution, 39
Copyright, 293
Creation Society, 307
Criticism and theory, literary, xvi, 14, 25,
    30–32, 80, 109, 123, 143, 144, 145,
    159, 175, 176, 194, 223, 231, 232,
    237–38, 240, 252, 253, 255, 265,
    284, 295
Cultural Revolution ("the Ten-Year
    Calamity"), xvi, xxii, xxiv, xxv,
    xxix, xxx, 5, 14–19, 22, 25, 26, 28,
    32, 40, 45, 55, 64, 73, 74, 76, 77, 88,
    95, 106, 109, 110, 124, 126, 129,
    133, 134, 136, 140, 143, 149, 154,
    162, 166, 184–86, 250, 277
Culture bureaucracy of China, xxi–xxiv,
    xxx
Cultures of nations, xxviii, 150, 151–54

Dagongbao, 177–78, 315–16
Dai Houying, xv, xvi, xxv, 26–33, 355–56
Dai Qing, xxiii, xxviii–xxix
Dangwai opposition, 227, 229, 237, 316
Danton, Georges-Jacques, 281
Daoism, 94, 101, 106, 150–52, 196, 234
Daudet, Alphonse, 87
Daxue zazhi, 226, 322
Dazhai, 68, 69, 71, 324
Delving into life, 59, 132, 316
Democracy. *See* Freedom; Tiananmen
    democracy movement
Democracy Wall, 113
Democratic Progressive Party, 316
Deng Xiaoping, xxii, 3, 69, 73, 99, 118,
    136, 189, 277
Deng Youmei, 162, 316
Denmark, xxv
Diaoyutai, 183–84, 226, 316
Dickens, Charles, 267
Dictionary, 88
Ding Cong, ix
Ding Ling, xv, xvi, 55, 87, 143, 184–85,
    302–6, 356
Dissent, xv, xvi, 20, 22–23, 128, 180, 293
Divorce, 7
Dix, Dorothy, 297
Documentary and reportage literature
    (*baogao wenxue*), xx, xxv,
    xxviii–xxix, 3, 128-35, 145, 186,
    226, 302